MODERN INDIA

MODERN INDIA

WILLIAM ELEROY CURTIS

GYAN

Published by

GYAN

Gyan Publishing House
5, Ansari Road
Daryaganj, New Delhi-110002
Phone: 011-47034999, 9811692060
E-mail: books@gyanbooks.com

Distribution Network
gyanbooks.com
India, USA, Canada, UK, Australia, France

ISBN : 978-81-212-9492-8 (PB)
First Published, 1905

2nd Impression 2023

Printed at: Gyan Press, Delhi.

MODERN INDIA
Author: WILLIAM ELEROY CURTIS

MODERN INDIA

BY

WILLIAM ELEROY CURTIS

Author of "The Turk and His Lost Provinces," "To-day in Syria and Palestine," "Egypt, Burma and British Malaysia," etk.

MCMV

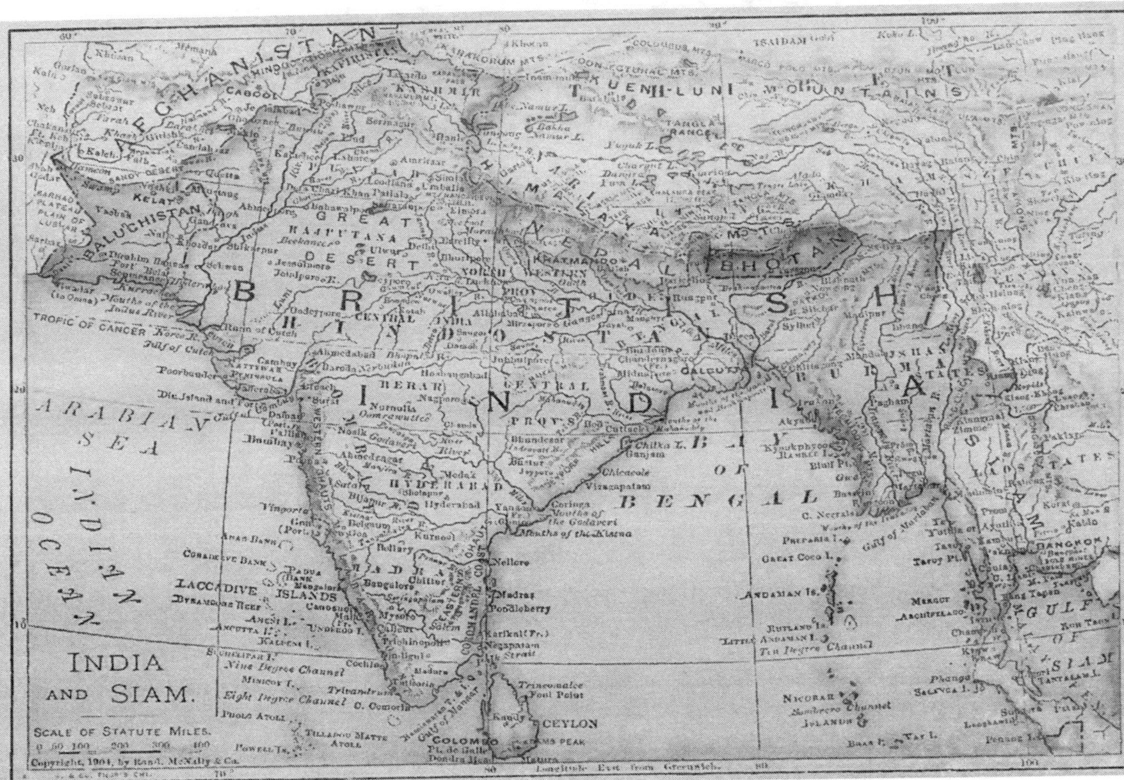

INDIA
AND SIAM.
SCALE OF STATUTE MILES.
0 50 100 200 300 400
Copyright, 1904, by Rand, McNally & Co.
AFGHANISTAN
BALUCHISTAN
BRITISH INDIA
HINDOSTAN
GREAT DESERT
RAJPUTANA
CENTRAL INDIA
CENTRAL PROVS
BERAR
HYDERABAD
NEPAL
BHOTAN
KUEN-LUN MOUNTAINS
HIMALAYA
BURMA
SIAM
LAOS STATES
SHAN STATES
ARABIAN SEA
INDIAN OCEAN
BAY OF BENGAL
GULF OF SIAM
LACCADIVE ISLANDS
CEYLON
COLOMBO
CALCUTTA
BANGKOK
Madras
Bombay
Hyderabad
Nellore
Bangalore
TROPIC OF CANCER
Gulf of Cutch
Andaman Is.
Nicobar Islands
Ten Degree Channel
Nine Degree Channel
Eight Degree Channel
Longitude East from Greenwich

To

LADY CURZON

An Ideal American Woman

This volume contains a series of letters written for *The Chicago Record-Herald* during the winter of 1903-04, and are published in permanent form through the courtesy of Mr. Frank B. Noyes, Editor and publisher of that paper.

TABLE OF CONTENTS

LIST OF ILLUSTRATIONS

MODERN INDIA

MODERN INDIA

I

THE EYE OF INDIA

A voyage to India nowadays is a continuous social event. The passengers compose a house party, being guests of the Steamship company for the time. The decks of the steamer are like broad verandas and are covered with comfortable chairs, in which the owners lounge about all day. Some of the more industrious women knit and embroider, and I saw one good mother with a basket full of mending, at which she was busily engaged at least three mornings. Others play cards upon folding tables or write letters with portfolios on their laps, and we had several artists who sketched the sky and sea, but the majority read novels and guide books, and gossiped. As birds of a feather flock together on the sea as well as on land, previous acquaintances and congenial new ones form little circles and cliques and entertain themselves and each other, and, after a day or two, move their chairs around so that they can be together. Americans and English do not mix as readily as you might expect, although there is nothing like coolness between them. It is only a natural restraint. They are accustomed to their ways, and we to ours, and it is natural for us to drift toward our own fellow countrymen.

In the afternoon nettings are hung around one of the broad decks and games of cricket are played. One day it is the army against the navy; another day the united service against a civilian team, and then the cricketers in the second-class salon are invited to come forward and try their skill against a team made up of first-classers. In the evening there is dancing, a piano being placed upon the deck for that purpose, and for two hours it is very gay. The ladies are all in white, and several English women insisted upon coming out on the deck in low-cut and short-sleeved gowns. It is said to be the latest fashion, and is not half as bad as their cirgarette smoking or the ostentatious display of jewelry that is made on the deck every morning. Several women, and some of them with titles, sprawl around in steamer chairs, wearing necklaces of pearls, diamonds, emeralds and other precious stones, fit for only a banquet or a ball, with their fingers blazing with jewels and their wrists covered with bracelets. There seemed to be a rivalry among the aristocracy on our steamer as to which could make the most vulgar display of gold, silver and precious stones, and it occurs to me that these Englishwomen had lived in India so long that they must have acquired the Hindu barbaric love of jewelry.

My attention was called not long ago to a cartoon in a British illustrated paper comparing the traveling outfits of American and English girls. The American girl had a car load of trunks and bags and bundles, a big bunch of umbrellas and parasols, golf sticks, tennis racquets and all sorts of queer things, and was dressed in a most conspicuous and elaborate manner. She was represented as striding up and down a railway platform covered with diamonds, boa, flashy hat and fancy finery, while the

English girl, in a close fitting ulster and an Alpine hat, leaned quietly upon her umbrella near a small "box," as they call a trunk, and a modest traveling bag. But that picture isn't accurate. According to my observation it ought to be reversed. I have never known the most vulgar or the commonest American woman to make such a display of herself in a public place as we witnessed daily among the titled women upon the P. and O. steamer Mongolia, bound for Bombay. Nor is it exceptional. Whenever you see an overdressed woman loaded with jewelry in a public place in the East, you may take it for granted that she belongs to the British nobility. Germans, French, Italians and other women of continental Europe are never guilty of similar vulgarity, and among Americans it is absolutely unknown.

It is customary for everybody to dress for dinner, and, while the practice has serious objections in stormy weather it is entirely permissible and comfortable during the long, warm nights on the Indian Ocean. The weather, however, was not nearly as warm as we expected to find it. We were four days on the Red Sea and six days on the Indian Ocean, and were entirely comfortable except for two days when the wind was so strong and kicked up so much water that the port-holes had to be closed, and it was very close and stuffy in the cabin. While the sun was hot there was always a cool breeze from one direction or another, and the captain told me it was customary during the winter season.

The passengers on our steamer were mostly English, with a few East Indians, and Americans. You cannot board a steamer in any part of the world nowadays without finding some of your fellow countrymen. They are becoming the greatest travelers of any nation and are penetrating to uttermost parts of the earth. Many of the English passengers were army officers returning to India from furloughs or going out for service, and officers' families who had been spending the hot months in England. We had lots of lords and sirs and lady dowagers; generals, colonels and officers of lesser rank, and the usual number of brides and bridegrooms, on their wedding tours; others were officials of the government in India, who had been home to be married. And we had several young women who were going out to be married. Their lovers were not able to leave their business to make the long voyage, and were waiting for them in Bombay, Calcutta or in some of the other cities. But perhaps the largest contingent were "civil servants," as employes of the government are called, who had been home on leave. The climate of India is very trying to white people, and, recognizing that fact, the government gives its officials six months' leave with full pay or twelve months' leave with half pay every five years. In that way an official who has served five consecutive years in India can spend the sixth year in England or anywhere else he likes.

We had several notable natives, including Judge Nayar, a judicial magistrate at Madras who has gained eminence at the Indian bar and was received with honors in England. He is a Parsee, a member of that remarkable race which is descended from the Persian fire worshipers. He dresses and talks and acts exactly like an ordinary English barrister. There were three brothers in the attractive native dress, Mohammedans, sons of Adamjee Peerbhoy, one of the largest cotton manufacturers and wealthiest men in India, who employs more than 15,000 operatives in his mills and furnished the canvas for the tents and the khaki for the uniforms of the British soldiers during the South African war. These young gentlemen had been making a tour of Europe, combining business with pleasure, and had inspected nearly all the great cotton mills in England and on the continent, picking up points for their own improvement. They are intelligent and enterprising men and their reputation for integrity, ability and loyalty to the British government has frequently been recognized in a conspicuous manner.

Our most notable shipmate was the Right Honorable Lord Lamington, recently governor of one of the Australian provinces, on his way to assume similar responsibility at Bombay, which is considered a more responsible post. He is a youngish looking, handsome man, and might easily be mistaken for Governor Myron T. Herrick of Ohio. One night at dinner his lordship was toasted by an Indian prince we had on board, and made a pleasant reply, although it was plain to see that he was not an orator. Captain Preston, the commander of the ship, who was afterward called upon, made a much more brilliant speech.

The prince was Ranjitsinhji, a famous cricket player, whom some consider the champion in that line of sport. He went over to the United States with an English team and will be pleasantly remembered at all the places he visited. He is a handsome fellow, 25 years old, about the color of a mulatto, with a slender athletic figure, graceful manners, a pleasant smile, and a romantic history. His father was ruler of one of the native states, and dying, left his throne, title and estates to his eldest son. The latter, being many years older than Ranjitsiṇhji, adopted him as his heir and sent him to England to be educated for the important duty he was destined to perform. He went through the school at Harrow and Cambridge University and took honors in scholarship as well as athletics, and was about to return to assume his hereditary responsibility in Indian when, to the astonishment of all concerned, a boy baby was born in his brother's harem, the first and only child of a rajah 78 years of age. The mother was a Mohammedan woman, and, according to a strict construction of the laws governing such things among the Hindus, the child was not entitled to any consideration whatever. Without going into details, it is sufficient for the story to say that the public at large did not believe that the old rajah was the father of the child, or that the infant was entitled to succeed him even if he had been. But the old man was so pleased at the birth of the baby that he immediately proclaimed him his heir, the act was confirmed by Lord Elgin, the viceroy, and the honors and estates which Ranjitsinhji expected to inherit vanished like a dream. The old man gave him an allowance of $10,000 a year and he has since lived in London consoling himself with cricket.

Another distinguished passenger was Sir Cowasji Jehangir Readymoney, an Indian baronet, who inherited immense wealth from a long line of Parsee bankers. They have adopted as a sort of trademark, a nickname given by some wag to the founder of the family, in the last century because of his immense fortune and success in trade. Mr. Readymoney, or Sir Jehangir, as he is commonly known, the present head of the house, was accompanied by his wife, two daughters, their governess, and his son, who had been spending several months in London, where he had been the object of much gratifying attention. His father received his title as an acknowledgment of his generosity in presenting $250,000 to the Indian Institute in London, and for other public benefactions, estimated at

A BOMBAY STREET

$1,300,000. He built colleges, hospitals, insane asylums and other institutions. He founded a Strangers' Home at Bombay for the refuge of people of respectability who find themselves destitute or friendless or become ill in that city. He erected drinking fountains of artistic architecture at several convenient places in Bombay, and gave enormous sums to various charities in London and elsewhere without respect to race or creed. Both the Roman Catholic and the Presbyterian missions in India have been the recipients of large gifts, and the university at Bombay owes him for its finest building.

Several of the most prominent native families in India have followed the example of Mr. Readymoney by adopting the nicknames that were given their ancestors. Indian names are difficult to pronounce. What, for example, would you call Mr. Jamshijdji or Mr. Jijibhai, and those are comparatively simple? Hence, in early times it was the habit of foreigners to call the natives with whom they came in contact by names that were appropriate to their character or their business. For example, "Mr. Reporter," one of the editors of the Times of India, as his father was before him, is known honorably by a name given by people who were unable to pronounce his father's Indian name.

Sir Jamsetjed Jeejeebhoy, one of the most prominent and wealthy Parsees, who is known all over India for his integrity and enterprise, and has given millions of dollars to colleges, schools, hospitals, asylums and other charities, is commonly known as Mr. Bottlewaller. "Waller" is the native word for trader, and his grandfather was engaged in selling and manufacturing bottles. He began by picking up empty soda and brandy bottles about the saloons, clubs and hotels, and in that humble way laid the foundation of an immense fortune and a reputation that any man might envy. The family have always signed their letters and checks "Bottlewaller," and have been known by that name in business and society. But when Queen Victoria made the grandfather a baronet because of distinguished services, the title was conferred upon Jamsetjed Jeejeebhoy, which was his lawful name.

Another similar case is that of the Petit family, one of the richest in India and the owners and occupants of the finest palaces in Bombay. Their ancestor, or the first of the family who distinguished himself, was a man of very small stature, almost a dwarf, who was known as Le Petit. He accepted the christening and bore the name honorably, as his sons and grandsons have since done. They are now baronets, but have never dropped it, and the present head of the house is Sir Manockji Petit.

The Eye of India, as Bombay is called, sits on an island facing the Arabian Sea on one side and a large bay on the other, but the water is quite shallow, except where channels have been dredged to the docks. The scenery is not attractive. Low hills rise in a semicircle from the horizon, half concealed by a curtain of mist, and a few green islands scattered about promiscuously are occupied by hospitals, military barracks, villas and plantations. Nor is the harbor impressive. It is not worth description, but the pile of buildings which rises on the city side as the steamer approaches its dock is imposing, being a picturesque mingling of oriental and European architecture. Indeed, I do not know of any city that presents a braver front to those who arrive by sea. At the upper end, which you see first, is a group of five-story apartment houses, with oriental balconies and colonnades. Then comes a monstrous new hotel, built by a stock company under the direction of the late J. N. Tata, a Parsee merchant who visited the United States several times and obtained his inspirations and many of his ideas there. Beside the hotel rise the buildings of the yacht club, a hospitable association of Englishmen, to which natives, no matter how great and good they may be, are never admitted. Connected with the club is an apartment house for gentlemen, and so hospitable are the members that a traveler can secure quarters there without difficulty if he brings a letter of introduction.

Next toward the docks is an old castle whose gray and lichen-covered walls are a striking contrast to the new modern buildings that surround it. These walls inclose a considerable area, which by courtesy is called a fort. It was a formidable defense at one time, and has been the scene of much exciting history, but is obsolete now. The walls are of heavy masonry, but a shot from a modern gun would shatter them. They inclose the military headquarters of the Bombay province, or Presidency, as it is called in the Indian gazetteer, the cathedral of this diocese, quarters and barracks for the garrison, an arsenal, magazines and other military buildings and a palatial sailors' home, one of the finest and largest institution of the kind in the world, which is supported by contributions from the various shipping companies that patronize this place. There are also several machine shops, factories and warehouses which contain vast stores of war material of every sort sufficient to equip an army at a fortnight's notice. About twelve hundred men are constantly employed in the arsenal and shops making and repairing military arms and equipments. There is a museum of ancient weapons, and many which were captured from the natives in the early days of India's occupation are quite curious; and there the visitor will have his first view of one of the greatest wonders of nature, a banyan tree, which drops its branches to take root in the soil beneath its overspreading boughs. But you must wait until you get to Calcutta before you can see the best specimens.

Bombay is not fortified, except by a few guns behind some earthworks at the entrance of the harbor, but it must be if the Russians secure a port upon the Arabian Sea; not only Bombay, but the entire west coast of India. The only protection for the city now is a small fleet of battle ships, monitors and gunboats that lie in the harbor, and there are usually several visiting men of war at the anchorage.

Bombay is the second city in population in India, Calcutta standing first on the list with 1,350,000 people, and, if you will take your map for a moment, you will see that the two cities lie in almost the same latitude, one on each side of the monstrous peninsula—Bombay at the top of the Arabian Sea and Calcutta at the top of the Bay of Bengal. By the census of 1891 Bombay had 821,764 population. By the census of 1901 the total was 776,006, the decrease of 45,758 being attributed to the frightful mortality by the plague in 1900 and 1901. It is the most enterprising, the most modern, the most active, the richest and the most prosperous city in India. More than 90 per cent of the travelers who enter and leave the country pass over the docks, and more than half the foreign commerce of the country goes through its custom-house. It is by all odds the finest city between modern Cairo and San Francisco, and its commercial and industrial interests exceed that of any other.

The arrangements for landing passengers are admirable. On the ship all our baggage was marked with numbers corresponding to that of our declaration to the collector of customs. The steamer anchored out about a quarter of a mile from a fine covered pier. We were detained on board until the baggage, even our small pieces, was taken ashore on one launch and after a while we followed it on another. Upon reaching the dock we passed up a long aisle to where several deputy collectors were seated behind desks. As we gave our names they looked through the bundles of declarations which had been arranged alphabetically, and, finding the proper one, told us that we would have to pay a duty of 5 per cent upon our typewriter and kodaks, and that a receipt and certificate would be furnished by which we could recover the money at any port by which we left India. Nothing else was taxed, although I noticed that nearly every passenger had to pay on something else. There is only one rate of duty—5 per cent ad valorem upon everything—jewelry, furniture, machinery—all pay the same, which simplified the transaction. But the importation of arms and ammunition is strictly prohibited and every gun, pistol and cartridge is confiscated in the custom-house unless the owner can present evidence that he is an officer of the army or navy and that they are the tools of his trade, or has a permit issued by the proper authority. This precaution is intended to anticipate any conspiracy similar to that which led to the great mutiny of 1857. The natives are not allowed to carry guns or even to own them, and every gun or other weapon found in the hands of a Hindu is confiscated unless he has a permit. And as an additional precaution the rifles issued to the native regiments in the army have a range of only twelve hundred yards, while those issued to the white regiments will kill at sixteen hundred yards; thus giving the latter an important advantage in case of an insurrection.

After having interviewed the deputy collector, we were admitted to a great pen or corral in the middle of the pier, which is inclosed by a high fence, and there found all our luggage piled up together on a bench. And all the trunks and bags and baskets from the ship were similarly assorted, according to the numbers they bore. We were not asked to open anything, none of our packages were examined, the declarations of passengers usually being accepted as truthful and final unless the inspectors have reason to believe or suspect deception. Gangs of coolies in livery, each wearing a brass tag with his number, stood by ready to seize the baggage and carry it to the hotel wagons, which stood outside, where we followed it and directed by a polite Sikh policeman, took the first carriage in line. Everything was conducted in a most orderly manner. There was no confusion, no jostling and no excitement, which indicates that the Bombay officials have correct notions of what is proper and carry them into practice.

The docks of Bombay are the finest in Asia, and when the extensions now in progress are carried out few cities in Europe can surpass them. They are planned for a century in advance. The people of Bombay are not boastful, but they are confident of the growth of their city and its commerce. Attached to the docks is a story of integrity and fidelity worth telling. In 1735 the municipal authorities of the young city, anticipating commercial prosperity, decided to improve their harbor and build piers for the accommodation of vessels, but nobody around the place had experience in such matters and a commission was sent off to other cities of India to find a man to take

CLOCK TOWER AND UNIVERSITY BUILDINGS—BOMBAY

charge. The commission was very much pleased with the appearance and ability of Lowji Naushirwanji, the Parsee foreman of the harbor at the neighboring town of Surat, and tried to coax him away by making a very lucrative offer, much in advance of the pay he was then receiving. He was too loyal and honest to accept it, and read the commission a lecture on business integrity which greatly impressed them. When they returned to Bombay and related their experience, the municipal authorities communicated with those of Surat and inclosed an invitation to Naushirwanji to come down and build a dock for Bombay. The offer was so advantageous that his employers advised him to accept it. He did so, and from that day to this a man of his name, and one of his descendants, has been superintendent of the docks of this city. The office has practically become hereditary in the family.

A decided sensation awaits the traveler when he passes out from the pier into the street, particularly if it is his first visit to the East. He already has had a glimpse of the gorgeous costumes of the Hindu gentleman and the priestly looking Parsees, and the long, cool white robes of the common people, for several of each class were gathered at the end of the pier to welcome friends who arrived by the steamer, but the moment that he emerges from the dock he enters a new and a strange world filled with vivid colors and fantastic costumes. He sees his first "gherry," a queer-looking vehicle made of bamboo, painted in odd patterns and bright tints, and drawn by a cow or a bullock that will trot almost as fast as a horse. All vehicles, however, are now called "gherrys" in India, no matter where they come from nor how they are built—

the chariot of the viceroy as well as the little donkey cart of the native fruit peddler.

The extent of bare flesh visible—masculine and feminine—startles you at first, and the scanty apparel worn by the common people of both sexes. Working women walk by with their legs bare from the thighs down, wearing nothing but a single garment wrapped in graceful folds around their slender bodies. They look very small, compared with the men, and the first question every stranger asks is the reason. You are told that they are married in infancy, that they begin to bear children by the time they are 12 and 14 years old, and consequently do not have time to grow; and perhaps that is the correct explanation for the diminutive stature of the women of India. There are exceptions. You see a few stalwart amazons, but ninety per cent or more of the sex are under size. Perhaps there is another reason, which does not apply to the upper classes, and that is the manual labor the coolies women perform, the loads they carry on their heads and the heavy lifting that is required of them. If you approach a building in course of erection you will find that the stone, brick, mortar and other material is carried up the ladders and across the scaffolding on the heads of women and girls, and some of these "hod carriers" are not more than 10 or 12 years old. They carry everything on their heads, and usually it requires two other women or girls to hoist the heavy burden to the head of the third. All the weight comes on the spine, and must necessarily prevent or retard growth, although it gives them an erect and stately carriage, which women in America might imitate with profit. At the same time, perhaps, our women might prefer to acquire their carriage in some other way than "toting" a hodful of bricks to the top of a four-story building.

The second thing that impresses you is the amount of glistening silver the working women wear upon their naked limbs. To drop into poetry, like Silas Wegg, they wear rings in their noses and rings on their toeses, and bands of silver wherever they can fasten them on their arms and legs and neck. They have bracelets, anklets, armlets, necklaces, and their noses as well as their ears are pierced for pendants. You wonder how a woman can eat, drink or sleep with a great big ornament hanging over her lips, and some of the earrings must weigh several ounces, for they fall almost to the shoulders. You will meet a dozen coolie women every block with two or three pounds of silver ornaments distributed over their persons, which represent their savings bank, for every spare rupee is invested in a ring, bracelet or a necklace, which, of course, does not pay interest, but can be disposed of for full value in case of an emergency. The workmanship is rude, but the designs are often pretty, and a collection of the silver ornaments worn by Hindu women would make an interesting exhibit for a museum. They are often a burden to them, particularly in hot weather, when they chafe and burn the flesh, and our Bombay friends tell us that in the summer the fountain basins, the hydrants and every other place where water can be found will be surrounded by women bathing the spots where the silver ornaments have seared the skin and cooling the metal, which is often so hot as to burn the fingers.

Another feature of Bombay life which immediately seizes the attention is the gay colors worn by everybody, which makes the streets look like animated rainbows or the kaleidoscopes that you can buy at the 10-cent stores. Orange and scarlet predominate, but yellow, pink, purple, green, blue and every other tint that was ever invented appears in the robes of the Hindus you meet upon the street. A dignified old gentleman will cross your path with a pink turban on his head and a green scarf wound around his shoulders. The next man you meet may have a pair of scarlet stockings, a purple robe and a tunic of wine-colored velvet embroidered in gold. There seems to be no rule or regulation about the use of colors and no set fashion for raiment. The only uniformity in the costume worn by the men of India is that everybody's legs are bare. Most men wear sandals; some wear shoes, but trousers are as rare as stovepipe hats. The native merchant goes to his counting-room, the banker to his desk, the clergyman discourses from a pulpit, the lawyer addresses the court, the professor expounds to his students and the coolie carries his load, all with limbs naked from the ankles to the thighs, and never more than half-concealed by a muslin divided skirt.

The race, the caste and often the province of a resident of India may be determined by his headgear. The Parsees wear tall fly-trap hats made of horse hair, with a top like a cow's foot; the Mohammedans wear the fez, and the Hindus the turban, and there are infinite varieties of turbans, both in the material used and in the manner in which they are put up. An old resident of India can usually tell where a man comes from by looking at his turban.

II

THE CITY OF BOMBAY

There are two cities in Bombay, the native city and the foreign city. The foreign city spreads out over a large area, and, although the population is only a small per cent of that of the native city, it occupies a much larger space, which is devoted to groves, gardens, lawns, and other breathing places and pleasure grounds, while, as is the custom in the Orient, the natives are packed away several hundred to the acre in tall houses, which, with overhanging balconies and tile roofs, line the crooked and narrow streets on both sides. Behind some of these tall and narrow fronts, however, are dwellings that cover a good deal of ground, being much larger than the houses we are accustomed to, because the Hindus have larger families and they all live together. When a young man marries he brings his bride home to his father's house, unless his mother-in-law happens to be a widow, when they often take up their abode with her. But it is not common for young couples to have their own homes; hence the dwellings in the native quarters are packed with several generations of the same family, and that makes the occupants easy prey to plagues, famine and other agents of human destruction.

The Parsees love air and light, and many rich Hindus have followed the foreign colony out into the suburbs, where you find a succession of handsome villas or bungalows, as they are called, half-hidden by high walls that inclose charming gardens. Some of these bungalows are very attractive, some are even sumptuous in their appointments—veritable palaces, filled with costly furniture and ornaments—but the climate forbids the use of many of the creature comforts which American and European taste demands. The floors must be of tiles or cement and the curtains of bamboo, because hangings, carpets, rugs and upholstery furnish shelter for destructive and disagreeable insects, and the aim of everybody is to secure as much air as possible without admitting the heat.

Bombay is justly proud of her public buildings. Few cities have such a splendid array. None that I have ever visited except Vienna can show an assemblage so imposing, with such harmony and artistic uniformity combined with convenience of location, taste of arrangement and general architectural effect. There is nothing, of course, in Bombay that will compare with our Capitol or Library at Washington, and its state and municipal buildings cannot compete individually with the Parliament House in London, the Hotel de Ville de Paris or the Palace of Justice in Brussels, or many others I might name. But neither Washington nor London nor Paris nor any other European or American city possesses such a broad, shaded boulevard as Bombay, with the Indian Ocean upon one side and on the other, stretching for a mile or more, a succession of stately edifices. Vienna has the boulevard and the buildings, but lacks the water effect. It is as if all the buildings of the University of Chicago were scattered along the lake front in Chicago from the river to Twelfth street.

The Bombay buildings are a mixture of Hindu, Gothic and Saracenic architecture, blended with taste and success, and in the center, to crown the group, rises a stately clock tower of beautiful proportions. All of these buildings have been erected during the last thirty years, the most of them with public money, many by private munificence. The material is chiefly green and gray stone. Each has ample approaches from all directions, which contribute to the general effect, and is surrounded by large grounds, so that it can be seen to advantage from any point of view. Groves of full-grown trees furnish a noble background, and wide lawns stretch before and between. There is parking along the shore of the bay, then a broad drive, with two sidewalks, a track for bicycles and a soft path for equestrians, all overhung with far-stretching boughs of immense and ancient trees, which furnish a grateful shade against the sun and add to the beauty of the landscape. I do not know of any such driveway elsewhere, and it extends for several miles, starting from an extensive common or parade ground, which is given up to games and sports. Poor people are allowed to camp there in tents in hot weather, for there, if anywhere, they can keep cool, because the peninsula upon which Bombay stands is narrow at that point, and if a breeze is blowing from any direction they get it. At intervals the boulevard is intersected by small, well-kept parks with band stands, and is broken by walks, drives, beds of flowers, foliage, plants and other landscape decorations; and this in the midst of a great city.

On the inside of the boulevard, following the contour of the shore of the bay, is first, Elphinstone College, then the Secretariat, which is the headquarters of the government and contains several state apartments of noble proportions and costly decorations. The building is 443 feet long, with a tower 170 feet high. Next it are the buildings of the University of Bombay, a library with a tower 260 feet high, a convocation hall of beautiful design and perfect proportions and other buildings. Then comes the Courts of Justice; an immense structure nearly 600 feet long, with a tower 175 feet high, which resembles the Law Courts of London, and is as appropriate as it is imposing. The department of public works has the next building; then the postoffice department, the telegraph department, the state archives building and patent office in order. The town hall contains several fine rooms and important historic pictures. The mint is close to the town hall, and next beyond it are the offices of the Port Trust, which would correspond to our harbor commissioners. Then follow in order the Holy Trinity Church, the High School, St. Xavier's College, the Momey Institute, Wilson College, long rows of barracks, officers' quarters and clubs, the Sailors' Home, several hospitals, a school of art and Elphinstone High School, which is 452 by 370 feet in size and one of the most palatial educational institutions I have ever seen, the splendid group culminating in the Victoria Railway station, which is the finest in the world and almost as large as any we have in the United States.

It is a vast building of Italian Gothic, with oriental towers and pinnacles, elaborately decorated with sculpture and carving, and a large central dome surmounted by a huge bronze figure of Progress. The architect was Mr. F. W. Stevens, a Bombay engineer; it was finished in 1888 at a cost of $2,500,000, and the wood carving, the tiles, the ornamental iron and brass railings, the grills for the ticket offices, the restaurant and refreshment rooms, the balustrades for the grand staircases, are all the work of the students of the Bombay School of Art, which gives

VICTORIA RAILWAY STATION — BOMBAY

it additional interest, although critics have contended that the architecture and decorations are too ornate for the purpose for which it is used.

Wilson College, one of the most imposing of the long line of buildings, is a memorial to a great Scotch missionary who lived a strenuous and useful life and impressed his principles and his character upon the people of India in a remarkable manner. He was famous for his common sense and accurate judgment; and till the end of his days retained the respect and confidence of every class of the community, from the viceroy and the council of state down to the coolies that sweep the streets. All of them knew and loved Dr. Wilson, and although he never ceased to preach the gospel of Christ, his Master, with the energy, zeal and plain speaking that is characteristic of Scotchmen, the Hindus, Mohammedans, Parsees, Jains, Jews and every other sect admired and encouraged him as much as those of his own faith.

One-fourth of all these buildings were presented to the city by rich and patriotic residents, most of them Parsees and Hindus. The Sailors' Home was the gift of the Maharajah of Baroda; University Hall was founded by Sir Cowasjee Jehangir Readymoney, who also built Elphinstone College. He placed the great fountain in front of the cathedral, and, although a Parsee, built the spire on the Church of St. John the Evangelist.

Mr. Dharmsala, another Parsee, built the Ophthalmic Hospital and the European Strangers' Home and put drinking fountains about the town. David Sassoon, a Persian Jew, founded the Mechanics' Institute, and his brother, Sir Albert Sassoon, built the tower of the Elphinstone High School. Mr. Premchand Raichand built the university library and clock tower in memory of his mother. Sir Jamsetji Jijibhal gave the school of art and the Parsee Benevolent Institute; the sons of Jarahji Parak erected the almshouse. Mr. Rustam Jamshidji founded the Hospital for Women, the East India Company built the Town Hall and other men gave other buildings with the greatest degree of public spirit and patriotism I have ever seen displayed in any town. The guide-book says that during the last quarter of a century patriotic residents of Bombay, mostly natives, have given more than $5,000,000 for public edifices. It is a new form for the expression of patriotism that might be encouraged in the United States.

Several statues were also gifts to the city; that of Queen Victoria, which is one of the finest I have ever seen, having been erected by the Maharajah of Baroda, and that of the Prince of Wales by Sir Edward Beohm. These are the best, but there are several others. Queen Victoria's monument, which stands in the most prominent plaza, where the busiest thoroughfares meet, represents that good woman sitting upon her throne under a lofty Gothic canopy of marble. The carving is elaborate and exquisite. In the center of the canopy appears the Star of India, and above it the Rose of England, united with the Lotus of India, with the mottoes of both countries intertwined—"God and My Right" and "Heaven's Light Our Guide."

Queen Victoria was no stranger to the people of India. They felt a personal relationship with their empress, and many touching incidents are told that have occurred from time to time to illustrate the affection of the Hindus for her. They were taught to call her "The Good Lady of England," and almost every mail, while she was living, carried letters from India to London bearing that address.

They came mostly from Hindu women who had learned of her goodness, sympathy and benevolence and hired public scribes at the market places to tell her of their sufferings and wrongs.

In the center of another plaza facing a street called Rampart row, which is lined by lofty buildings containing the best retail shops in town, is a figure of Edward VII. in bronze, on horseback, presented by a local merchant. Near the cathedral is a statute to Lord Cornwallis, who was governor general of India in 1786, and, as the inscription informs us, died at Ghazipur, Oct. 5, 1805. This was erected by the merchants of Bombay, who paid a similar honor to the Marquis of Wellesley, younger brother of the Duke of Wellington, who was also governor general during the days of the East India Company, and did a great deal for the country. He was given a purse of $100,000, and his statue was erected in Bombay, but he died unhappy because the king refused to create him Duke of Hindustan, the only honor that would have satisfied his soul. There are several fine libraries in Bombay, and the Asiatic Society, which has existed since the beginning of the nineteenth century, has one of the largest and most valuable collections of oriental literature in existence.

For three miles and a half the boulevard, and its several branches are bounded by charming residences, which overlook the bay and the roofs of the city. Malabar Point at the end of the drive, the extreme end of the island upon which Bombay is built, is the government house, the residence of the Lord Lamington, who represents King Edward VII. in this beautiful city. It is a series of bungalows, with large, cool rooms and deep verandas, shaded by immense trees and luxurious vines, and has accommodations altogether for about 100 people. The staff of the governor is quite large. He has all kinds of aides-de-camp, secretaries and attaches, and maintains quite a little court. Indeed, his quarters, his staff and his style of living are much more pretentious than those of the President of the United States, and his salary is quite as large. Everywhere he goes he is escorted by a bodyguard of splendid looking native soldiers in scarlet uniforms, big turbans and long spears. They are Sikhs, from the north of India, the greatest fighters in the empire, men of large stature, military bearing and unswerving loyalty to the British crown, and when the Governor of Bombay drives in to his office in the morning or drives back again to his lovely home at night, his carriage is surrounded by a squad of those tawny warriors, who ride as well as they look.

About half-way on the road to the government house is the Gymkhana, and I venture to say that nobody who has not been in India can guess what that means. And if you want another conundrum, what is a chotohazree? It is customary for smart people to have their chotohazree at the Gymkhana, and I think that you would be pleased to join them after taking the beautiful drive which leads to the place. Nobody knows what the word was derived from, but it is used to describe a country club—a bungalow hidden under a beautiful grove on the brow of a cliff that overhangs the bay—with all of the appurtenances, golf links, tennis courts, cricket grounds, racquet courts and indoor gymnasium, and everybody stops there on their afternoon drive to have chotohazree, which is the local term for afternoon tea and for early morning coffee.

There are peculiar customs in Bombay. The proper time for making visits everywhere in India is between 11

a. m. and 1:30 p. m., and fashionable ladies are always at home between those hours and seldom at any other. It seems unnatural, because they are the hottest of the day. One would think that common sense as well as comfort would induce people to stay at home at noon and make themselves as cool as possible. In other tropical countries these are the hours of the siesta, the noonday nap, which is as common and as necessary as breakfast or dinner, and none but a lunatic would think of calling upon a friend after 11 in the morning or before 3 in the afternoon. It would be as ridiculous as to return a social visit at 3 or 4 o'clock in the morning, and the same reasons which govern that custom ought to apply in India as well as in Egypt, Cuba or Brazil. But here ladies put on their best gowns, order their carriages, take their card cases, and start out in the burning noontide glare to return visits and make formal dinner and party calls. Strangers are expected to do the same, and if you have letters of introduction you are expected to present them during those hours, and not at any other time. In the cool of the day, after 5 o'clock, everybody who owns or can hire a carriage goes out to drive, and usually stops at the Gymkhana in the country or at the Yacht Club in the city for chotohazree. It is a good custom to admit women to clubs as they do here. The wives and daughters of members have every privilege, and can give tea parties and luncheons in the clubhouses, while on certain evenings of the week a band is brought from the military barracks and everybody of any account in European society is expected to be present. Tables are spread over the lawn, and are engaged in advance by ladies, who sit behind them, receive visits and pour tea just as they would do in their own houses. It is a very pleasant custom.

All visitors who intend to remain in Bombay for any length of time are expected to call upon the governor and his wife, but it is not necessary for them to drive out to Malabar Point for such a purpose. On a table in the reception room of the government building down-town are two books in which you write your name and address, and that is considered equivalent to a formal visit. One book is intended exclusively for those who have been "presented" and by signing it they are reminding his excellency and her excellency of their continued existence and notifying them where invitations to dinners and balls can reach them. The other book is designed for strangers and travelers, who inscribe their names and professions, where they live when they are at home, how long they expect to be in Bombay and where they are stopping. Anybody who desires can sign this book and the act is considered equivalent to a call upon the governor. If the caller has a letter of introduction to His Excellency he can leave it, with a card, in charge of the clerk who looks after the visitors' book, and if he desires to see the governor personally for business or social reasons he can express that desire upon a sheet of note paper, which will be attached to the letter of introduction and delivered some time during the day. The latter, if he is so disposed will then give the necessary instructions and an aide-de-camp will send a "chit," as they call a note over here, inviting the traveler to call at an hour named. There is a great deal of formality in official and social life. The ceremonies and etiquette are modeled upon those of the royal palaces in England, and the governor of each province, as well as the viceroy of India in Calcutta, has his little court.

A different code of etiquette must be followed in social

relations with natives, because they do not usually open their houses to strangers. Letters of introduction should be sent with cards by messengers or through the mails. Then, if the gentleman to whom they are addressed desires, he will call at your hotel. Many of the wealthier natives, and especially the Parsees, are adopting European customs, but the more conservative Hindus still adhere to their traditional exclusive habits, their families are invisible and never mentioned, and strangers are never admitted to their homes.

Natives are not admitted to the European clubs. There is no mingling of the races in society, except in a few isolated cases of wealthy families, who have been educated in Europe and have adopted European customs. While the same prejudice does not exist theoretically, there is actually a social gulf as wide and as deep as that which lies between white and black families in Savannah or New Orleans. Occasionally there is a marriage between a European and a native, but the social consequences have not encouraged others to imitate the example. Such unions are not approved by public sentiment in either race, and are not usually attended with happiness. Some of the Parsees, who are always excepted, and are treated as a distinct race and community, mingle with Europeans to a certain degree, but even in their case the line is sharply drawn.

The native district of Bombay is not so dirty nor so densely populated as in most other Indian cities. The streets are wider and some of them will admit of a carriage, although the cross-streets are nearly all too narrow. The houses are from three to five stories in height, built of brick or stone, with overhanging balconies and broad eaves. Sometimes the entire front and rear are of lattice work, the side walls being solid. Few of them are plastered, ceilings are unknown and partitions, for the sake of promoting circulation, seldom go more than half way to the top of a room. No glass is used, but every window has heavy blinds as a protection from the hot air and the rays of the sun. While our taste does not approve the arrangements in many cases, experience has taught the people of India how to live through the hot summers with the greatest degree of comfort, and anyone who attempts to introduce innovations is apt to make mistakes. The fronts of many of the houses are handsomely carved and decorated, the columns and pillars and brackets which support the balconies, the railings, the door frames, the eaves and architraves, are often beautiful examples of the carvers' skill, and the exterior walls are usually painted in gay colors and fanciful designs. Within doors the houses look very bare to us, and contain few comforts.

The lower floor of the house is commonly used for a shop, and different lines of business are classified and gathered in the same neighborhood. The food market, the grocery and provision dealers, the dealers in cotton goods and other fabrics, the silk merchants, the shoe and leather men, the workers in copper and brass, the goldsmiths, jewelers and dealers in precious stones each have their street or quarter, which is a great convenience to purchasers, and scattered among them are frequent cook-shops and eating places, which do not resemble our restaurants in any way, but have a large patronage. A considerable portion of the population of Bombay, and the same is true of all other Indian cities, depends upon these cook-shops for food as a measure of economy and convenience. People can send out for dinner, lunch, or breakfast at any hour, and have it served by their own servants without being troubled to keep up a kitchen or buy fuel.

There are said to be 6,000 dealers in jewelry and precious stones in the city of Bombay, and they all seem to be doing a flourishing business, chiefly with the natives, who are very fond of display and invest their money in precious stones and personal adornments of gold and silver, which are safer and give more satisfaction than banks.

You can see specimens of every race and nation in the native city, nearly always in their own distinctive costumes, and they are the source of never-ending interest—Arabs, Persians, Afghans, Rajputs, Parsees, Chinese, Japanese, Malays, Lascars, Negroes from Zanzibar, Madagascar and the Congo, Abyssinians. Nubians, Sikhs, Thibetans, Burmese, Singalese, Siamese and Bengalis mingle with Jews, Greeks and Europeans on common terms, and, unlike the population of most eastern cities, the people of Bombay always seem to be busy.

Many enterprises usually left for the municipal authorities of a city to carry on cannot be undertaken by the government of India because of the laws of caste, religious customs and fanatical prejudices of the people. The Hindu allows no man to enter his home; the women of a Mohammedan household are kept in seclusion, the teachings of the priests are contrary to modern sanitary regulations, and if the municipal authorities should condemn a block of buildings and tear it down, or discover a nuisance and attempt to remove it, they might easily provoke a riot and perhaps a revolution. This has happened frequently. During the last plague a public tumult had to be quelled by soldiers at a large cost of life because of the efforts of the government to isolate and quarantine infected persons and houses. These peculiar conditions suggested in Bombay the advantage of a semi-public body called "The Improvement Trust," which was organized a few years ago by Lord Sandhurst, then governor. The original object was to clear out the slums and infected places after the last plague, to tear down blocks of rotten and filthy tenement-houses and erect new buildings on the ground; to widen the streets, to let air and light into moldering, festering sink holes of poverty, vice and wretchedness; to lay sewers and furnish a water supply, and to redeem and regenerate certain portions of the city that were a menace to the public health and morals. This work was intrusted to twelve eminent citizens, representing each of the races and all of the large interests in Bombay, who commanded the respect and enjoyed the confidence of the fanatical element of the people, and would be permitted to do many things and introduce innovations that would not be tolerated if suggested by foreigners, or the government.

After the special duty which they were organized to perform had been accomplished The Improvement Trust was made permanent as a useful agency to undertake works of public utility of a similar character which the government could not carry on. The twelve trustees serve without pay or allowances; not one of them receives a penny of compensation for his time or trouble, or even the reimbursement of incidental expenses made necessary in the performance of his duties. This is an exhibition of unusual patriotism, but it is considered perfectly natural in Bombay. To carry out the plans of the Trust, salaried officials are employed, and a large force is necessary. The trustees have assumed great responsibilities, and supply the place of a board of public works, with larger powers than are usually granted to such officials. The municipality has turned over to them large tracts of real estate, some of which has been improved with great profit; it has secured funds by borrowing from banks upon the personal credit of its members, and by issuing bonds which sell at a high premium, and the money has been used in the improvement of the city, in the introduction of sanitary reforms, in building model tenements for the poor, in creating institutions of public necessity or advantage and by serving the people in various other ways.

The street car system of Bombay belongs to an American company, having been organized by a Mr. Kittridge, who came over here as consul during President Lincoln's administration. Recognizing the advantage of street cars, in 1874 he interested some American capitalists in the enterprise, got a franchise, laid rails on a few of the principal streets and has been running horse cars ever since.

The introduction of electricity and the extension of the street railway system is imperatively needed. Distances are very great in the foreign section, and during the hot months, from March to November, it is impossible for white men to walk in the sun, so that everybody is compelled to keep or hire a carriage; while on the other hand the density of the population in other sections is so great as to be a continual and increasing public peril. Bombay has more than 800,000 inhabitants, two-thirds of whom are packed into very narrow limits, and in the native quarters it is estimated that there is one human being to every ten square yards of space. It will be realized that this is a dangerous condition of affairs for a city that is constantly afflicted with epidemics and in which contagious diseases always prevail. The extension of the street car service would do something to relieve this congestion and scatter many of the people out among the suburbs, but the Orientals always swarm together and pack themselves away in most uncomfortable and unhealthful limits, and it will always be a great danger when the plagues or the cholera come around. Multitudes have no homes at all. They have no property except the one or two strips of dirty cotton which the police require them to wear for clothing. They lie down to sleep anywhere, in the parks, on the sidewalks, in hallways, and drawing their robes over their faces are utterly indifferent to what happens. They get their meals at the cook shops for a few farthings, eat when they are hungry, sleep when they are sleepy and go through life without a fixed abode.

In addition to the street car company the United States is represented by the Standard Oil Company, the Vacuum Oil Company, and the New York Export and Import Company. Other American firms of merchants and manufacturers have resident agents, but they are mostly Englishmen or Germans.

There is, however, very little demand in India for agricultural implements, although three-fourths of the people are employed in tilling the soil. Each farmer owns or rents a very small piece of ground, hardly big enough to justify the use of anything but the simple, primitive tools that have been handed down to him through long lines of ancestors for 3,000 years. Nearly all his implements are home-made, or come from the village blacksmith shop, and are of the rudest, most awkward description. They plow with a crooked stick, they dig ditches with their fingers, and carry everything that has to be moved in little baskets on their heads. The harvesting is done with a primitive-looking sickle, and root crops are taken out of the ground with a two-tined fork with a handle only a foot long. The Hindu does everything in a squatting posture, hence he uses only short-handled tools. Fifty or seventy-five cents each would easily replace the outfit of three-fourths of the farmers in the empire. Occasionally there is a rajah with large estates under cultivation upon which modern machinery is used, but even there its introduction is discouraged; first, because the natives are very conservative and disinclined to adopt new means and new methods; and, second, and what is more important, every labor-saving implement and machine that comes into the country deprives hundreds of poor coolies of employment.

The development of the material resources of India is slowly going on, and mechanical industries are being gradually established, with the encouragement of the government, for the purpose of attracting the surplus labor from the farms and villages and employing it in factories and mills, and in the mines of southern India, which are supposed to be very rich. These enterprises offer limited possibilities for the sale of machinery, and American-made machines are recognized as superior to all others. There is also a demand for everything that can be used by the foreign population, which in India is numbered somewhere about a million people, but the trade is controlled largely by British merchants who have life-long connections at home, and it is difficult to remove their prejudices or persuade them to see the superiority of American goods. Nevertheless, our manufactories, on their merits, are gradually getting a footing in the market.

When Mark Twain was in Bombay, a few years ago, he met with an unusual experience for a mortal. He was a guest of the late Mr. Tata, a famous Parsee merchant, and received a great deal of attention. All the foreigners in the city knew him, and had read his books, and there are in Bombay hundreds of highly cultivated and educated natives. He hired a servant, as every stranger does, and was delighted when he discovered a native by the name of Satan among the numerous applicants. He engaged him instantly on his name; no other recommendation was necessary. To have a servant by the name of Satan was a privilege no humorist had ever before enjoyed, and the possibilities to his imagination were without limit. And it so happened that on the very day Satan was employed, Prince Aga Khan, the head of a Persian sect of Mohammedans, who is supposed to have a divine origin and will be worshiped as a god when he dies, came to call on Mr. Clemens. Satan was in attendance, and when he appeared with the card upon a tray, Mr. Clemens asked if he knew anything about the caller; if he could give him some idea who he was, because, when a prince calls in person upon an American tourist, it is considered a distinguished honor. Aga Khan is well known to everybody in Bombay, and one of the most conspicuous men in the city. He is a great favorite in the foreign colony, and is as able a scholar as he is a charming gentleman. Satan, with all the reverence of his race, appreciated the religious aspect of the visitor more highly than any other, and in reply to the question of his new master explained that Aga Khan was a god.

It was a very gratifying meeting for both gentlemen, who found each other entirely congenial. Aga Khan has a keen sense of humor and had read everything Mark Twain had written, while, on the other hand, the latter was distinctly impressed with the personality of his caller

That evening, when he came down to dinner, his host asked how he had passed the day:

"I have had the time of my life," was the prompt reply, "and the greatest honor I have ever experienced. I have hired Satan for a servant, and a God called to tell me how much he liked Huck Finn."

III

SERVANTS, HOTELS AND CAVE TEMPLES

Everybody who comes to India must have a personal servant, a native who performs the duty of valet, waiter and errand boy and does other things that he is told. It is said to be impossible to do without one and I am inclined to think that is true, for it is a fixed custom of the country, and when a stranger attempts to resist, or avoid or reform the customs of a country his trouble begins. Many of the Indian hotels expect guests to bring their own servants—to furnish their own chambermaids and waiters—hence are short-handed, and the traveler who hasn't provided himself with that indispensable piece of baggage has to look after himself. On the railways a native servant is even more important, for travelers are required to carry their own bedding, make their own beds and furnish their own towels. The company provides a bench for them to sleep on, similar to those we have in freight cabooses at home, a wash room and sometimes water. But if you want to wash your face and hands in the morning it is always better to send your servant to the station master before the trains starts to see that the tank is filled. Then a naked Hindu with a goatskin of water comes along, fills the tank and stands around touching his forehead respectfully every time you look his way until you give him a penny. The eating houses along the railway lines also expect travelers to bring their own servants, who raid their shelves and tables for food and drink and take it out to the cars. That is another of the customs of the country.

For these reasons a special occupation has been created, peculiar to India—that of travelers' servants, or "bearers" as they are called. I have never been able to satisfy myself as to the derivation of the name. Some wise men say that formerly, before the days of railroads, people were carried about in sedan chairs, as they are still in China, and the men who carried them were called "bearers;" others contend that the name is due to the circumstance that these servants bear the white man's burden, which is not at all likely. They certainly do not bear his baggage. They hire coolies to do it. A self-respecting "bearer" will employ somebody at your expense to do everything he can avoid doing and will never demean himself by carrying a trunk, or a bag, or even a parcel. You give him money to pay incidental expenses, for you don't want him bothering you all the time, and he hires other natives to do the work. But his wages are small. A first-class bearer, who can talk English and cook, pack trunks, look after tickets, luggage and other business of travel, serve as guide at all places of interest and compel merchants to pay him a commission upon everything his employer purchases, can be obtained for forty-five rupees, which is $15 a month, and keep himself. He gets his board for nothing at the hotels for waiting on his master, and on the pretext that he induced him to come there. But you have to pay his railway fare, third class, and give him $3 to buy warm clothing. He never buys it, because he does not need it, but that's another custom of the country. Then again, at the end of the engagement he expects a present—a little backsheesh

—two or three dollars, and a certificate that you are pleased with his services.

That is the cost of the highest priced man, who can be guide as well as servant, but you can get "bearers" with lesser accomplishments for almost any wages, down as low as $2 a month. But they are not only worthless; they actually imperil your soul because of their exasperating ways and general cussedness. You often hear that servants are cheap in India, that families pay their cooks $3 a month and their housemen $2, which is true; but they do not earn any more. One Swede girl will do as much work as a dozen Hindus, and do it much better than they, and, what is even more important to the housewife, can be relied upon. In India women never go out to service except as nurses, but in every household you will find not less than seven or eight men servants, and sometimes twenty, who receive from $1 to $5 a month each in wages, but the total amounts up, and they have to be fed, and they will steal, every one of them, and lie and loaf, and cause an infinite amount of trouble and confusion, simply because they are cheap. High-priced servants usually are an economy—good things always cost money, but give better satisfaction.

Another common mistake is that Indian hotel prices are low. They are just as high as anywhere else in the world for the accommodations. I have noticed that wherever you go the same amount of luxury and comfort costs about the same amount of money. You pay for all you get in an Indian hotel. The service is bad because travelers are expected to bring their own servants to answer their calls, to look after their rooms and make their beds, and in some places to wait on them in the dining-room. There are no women about the houses. Men do everything, and if they have been well trained as cleaners the hotel is neat. If they have been badly trained the contrary may be expected. The same may be said of the cooking. The landlord and his guest are entirely at the mercy of the cook, and the food is prepared according to his ability and education. You get very little beef because cows are sacred and steers are too valuable to kill. The mutton is excellent, and there is plenty of it. You cannot get better anywhere, and at places near the sea they serve an abundance of fish. Vegetables are plenty and are usually well cooked. The coffee is poor and almost everybody drinks tea. You seldom sit down to a hotel table in India without finding chickens cooked in a palatable way for breakfast, lunch and dinner, and eggs are equally good and plenty. The bread is usually bad, and everybody calls for toast. The deserts are usually quite good.

It takes a stranger some time to become accustomed to barefooted servants, but few of the natives in India of whatever class wear shoes. Rich people, business men, merchants, bankers and others who come in contact on equal terms with the foreign population usually wear them in the streets, but kick them off and go around barefooted as soon as they reach their own offices or their homes. Although a servant may be dressed in elaborate livery, he never wears shoes. The butlers, footmen, ushers and other servants at the government house in Calcutta, at the viceregal lodge at Simla, at the palace of the governor of Bombay, and the residences of the other high officials, are all barefooted.

Everybody with experience agrees that well-trained Hindu servants are quick, attentive and respectful and ingenious. F. Marion Crawford in "Mr. Isaacs" says: "It has always been a mystery to me how native servants manage always to turn up at the right moment. You say to your man, 'Go there and wait for me,' and you arrive and find him waiting; though how he transferred himself thither, with his queer-looking bundle, and his lota and cooking utensils and your best teapot wrapped up in a newspaper and ready for use, and with all the hundred and one things that a native servant contrives to carry about without breaking or losing one of them, is an unsolved puzzle. Yet there he is, clean and grinning as ever, and if he were not clean and grinning and provided with tea and cheroots, you would not keep him in your service a day, though you would be incapable of looking half so spotless and pleased under the same circumstances yourself."

Every upper servant in an Indian household has to have an under servant to assist him. A butler will not wash dishes or dust or sweep. He will go to market and wait on the table, but nothing more. A cook must have a coolie to wash the kitchen utensils, and wait on him. He will do nothing but prepare the food for the table. A coachman will do nothing but drive. He must have a coolie to take care of the horse, and if there are two horses the owner must hire another stable man, for no Hindu hostler can take care of more than one, at least he is not willing to do so. An American friend has told me of his experience trying to break down one of the customs of the East, and compelling one native to groom two horses. It is too long and tearful to relate here, for he was finally compelled to give in and hire a man for every horse and prove the truth of Kipling's poem:

"It is not good for the Christian race
To worry the Aryan brown;
  For the white man riles,
  And the brown man smiles,
And it weareth the Christian
  And the end of the fight
  Is a tombstone white
With the name of the late deceased.
  And the epitaph clear:
  A fool lies here,
Who tried to hustle the East."

That's the fate of everybody who goes up against established customs. And so we hired a "bearer."

There were plenty of candidates. They appeared in swarms before our trunks had come up from the steamer, and continued to come by ones and twos until we had made a selection. They camped outside our rooms and watched every movement we made. They sprang up in our way from behind columns and gate-posts whenever we left the hotel or returned to it. They accosted us in the street with insinuating smiles and politely opened the carriage door as we returned from our drives. They were of all sizes and ages, castes and religions, and, strange to say, most of them had become Christians and Protestants from their strong desire to please. Each had a bunch of "chits," as they call them—recommendations from previous employers, testifying to their intelligence, honesty and fidelity, and insisted upon our reading them. Finally, in self-defense, we engaged a stalwart Mohammedan wearing a snow-white robe, a monstrous turban and a big bushy beard. He is an imposing spectacle; he moves like an emperor; his poses are as dignified as those of the Sheik el Islam when he lifts his hands to bestow a blessing. And we engaged Ram Zon Abdullet Mutmammet on his shape.

It was a mistake. Beauty is skin deep. No one can judge merit by outside appearances, as many persons can ascertain by glancing in a mirror. Ram Zon, and that was what we called him for short, was a splendid illusion. It turned out that he could not scrape together enough English to keep an account of his expenditures and had to trust to his memory, which is very defective in money matters. He cannot read or write, he cannot carry a message or receive one; he is no use as a guide, for, although information and ideas may be bulging from his noble brow, he lacks the power to communicate them, and, worse than all, he is surly, lazy and a constitutional kicker. He was always hanging around when we didn't want him, and when we did want him he was never to be found.

Ram had not been engaged two hours before he appeared in our sitting room, enveloped in a dignity that permeated the entire hotel, stood erect like a soldier, brought his hand to his forehead and held it there for a long time—the salute of great respect—and gave me a sealed note, which I opened and found to read as follows:

"Most Honored Sir:—I most humbly beg to inform you this to your kind consideration and generousitee and trusting which will submit myself to your grant benevolence for avoid the troublesomeness to you and your families, that the servant Ram Zon you have been so honorable and benovelent to engage is a great rogue and conjurer. He will make your mind buzzling and will steal your properties, and can run away with you midway. In proof you please touch his right hand shoulder and see what and how big charm he has. Such a bad temperature man you have in your service. Besides he only grown up taller and looks like a dandee as it true but he is not fit to act in case not to disappeared. I beg of you kindly consult about those matters and select and choose much experienced man than him otherwise certainly you could be put in to great danger by his conjuring and into troubles.

"Hoping to excuse me for this troubles I taking, though he is my caste and countryman much like not to do so, but his temperature is not good therefore liable to your honourablesness, etc., etc."

When I told Ram about this indictment, he stoutly denied the charges, saying that it was customary for envious "bearers" to say bad things of one another when they lost good jobs. We did not feel of his right arm and he did not try to conjure us, but his temperature is certainly very bad, and he soon became a nuisance, which we abated by paying him a month's wages and sending him off. Then, upon the recommendation of the consul we got a treasure, although he does not show it in his looks.

The hotels of India have a very bad name. There are several good ones in the empire, however, and every experienced traveler and every clubman you meet can tell you the names of all of them. Hence it is not impossible to keep a good hotel in India with profit. The best are at Lucknow and Darjeeling. Those at Caucutta are the worst, although one would think that the vice-regal capital would have pride enough to entertain its many visitors decently.

Bombay at last has such a hotel as ought to be found in Calcutta and all the other large cities, an architectural monument, and an ornament to the country. It is due to the enterprise of the late Mr. J. N. Tata, a Parsee merchant and manufacturer, and it is to be hoped that its success will be sufficient to stimulate similar enterprises elsewhere. It would be much better for the people of India to coax tourists over here by offering them comforts, luxuries and pleasures than to allow the few who do come, to go away grumbling. The thousands who visit Cairo every winter are attracted there by the hotels, for no city has better ones, and no hotels give more for the money. Hence they pay big profits, and are a source of prosperity to the city, as well as a pleasure to the idle public.

The most interesting study in Bombay is the people, but there are several excursions into the country around well worth making, particularly those that take you to the cave temples of the Hindus, which have been excavated with infinite labor and pains out of the solid rock. With their primitive tools the people of ancient times chiseled great caverns in the sides of rocky cliffs and hills and fashioned them after the conventional designs of temples, with columns, pillars, vaulted ceilings, platforms for their idols and pulpits for their priests. The nearest of these wonderful examples of stone cutting is on an island in the harbor of Bombay, called Elephanta, because at one time a colossal stone elephant stood on the slope near the landing place, but it was destroyed by the Portuguese several centuries ago. The island rises about 600 feet above the water, its summit is crowned with a glorious growth of forest, its sides are covered with dense jungles, and the beach is skirted by mangrove swamps. You get there by a steam launch provided by the managers of your hotel, or by Cook & Sons, the tourist agents, whenever a sufficiently large party is willing to pay them for their trouble. Or if you prefer a sail you can hire one of the native boats with a peculiar rigging and usually get a good breeze in the morning, although it is apt to die down in the afternoon, and you have to take your chances of staying out all night. The only landing place at Elephanta Island is a wall of concrete which has been built out across the beach into four or five feet of water, and you have to step gingerly lest you slip on the slime. At the end of the wall a solid stairway cut in the hillside leads up to the temple. It was formerly used daily by thousands of worshipers, but in this degenerate age nobody but tourists ever climb it. Every boat load that lands is greeted by a group of bright-eyed children, who follow the sahibs (gentlemen) and mem-sahibs (ladies) up the stairs, begging for backsheesh and offering for sale curios beetles and other insects of brilliant hues that abound on the island. Coolies are waiting at the foot of the stairs with chairs fastened to poles, in which they will carry a person up the steep stairway to the temple for 10 cents. Reaching the top you find a solid fence with a gateway, which is opened by a retired army officer who has been appointed custodian of the place and collects small fees, which are devoted to keeping the temples clean and in repair.

The island is dedicated to Siva, the demon god of the Hindus, and it is therefore appropriate that its swamps and jungles should abound with poisonous reptiles and insects. The largest of the several temples is 130 feet square and from 32 to 58 feet high, an artificial cave chiseled out of the granite mountain side. The roof is sustained by sixteen pilasters and twenty-six massive fluted pillars. In a recess in the center is a gigantic figure of Siva in his character as The Destroyer. His face is turned to the east and wears a stern, commanding expression. His head-dress is elaborate and crowned by a tiara beautifully carved. In one hand he holds a citron and in the other the head of a cobra, which is twisted around his arm and is reaching towards his face. His neck is adorned with strings of pearls, from which hangs a pendant in the form of a heart. Another necklace supports a human skull, the peculiar symbol of Siva, with twisted snakes growing from the head instead of hair. This is the great image of the temple and represents the most cruel and revengeful of all the Hindu gods. Ten centuries ago he wore altogether a different character, but human sacrifices have always been made to propitiate him. Around the walls of the cave are other gods of smaller stature representing several of the most prominent and powerful of the Hindu pantheon, all of them chiseled from the solid granite. There are several chambers or chapels also for different forms of worship, and a well which receives its water from some mysterious source, and is said to be very deep.

The Portuguese did great damage here several centuries ago in a war with India, for they fired several cannon balls straight into the mouth of the cave, which carried away several of the columns and destroyed the ornamentation of others, but the Royal Asiatic Society has taken the trouble to make careful and accurate repairs.

Although the caves at Elephanta are wonderful, they are greatly inferior in size and beauty to a larger group at Ellora, a day's journey by train from Bombay, and after that a carriage or horseback ride of two hours. There are 100 cave temples, carved out of the solid rock between the second and the tenth centuries. They are scattered along the base of a range of beautifully wooded hills about 500 feet above the plain, and the amount of labor and patience expended in their construction is appalling, especially when one considers that the men who made them were without the appliances and tools of modern times, knew nothing of explosives and were dependent solely upon chisels of flint and other stones. The greatest and finest of them is as perfect in its details and as elaborate in its ornamentations as the cathedrals at Milan or Toledo, except that it has been cut out of a single piece of stone instead of being built up of many small pieces.

The architect made his plans with the most prodigal detail and executed them with the greatest perfection. He took a solid rock, an absolute monolith, and chiseled out of it a cathedral 365 feet long, 192 feet wide and 96 feet high, with four rows of mighty columns sustaining a vaulted roof that is covered with pictures in relief illustrating the power and the adventures and the achievements of his gods. It would accommodate 5,000 worshippers. Around the walls he left rough projections, which were afterward carved into symbolical figures and images, eight, ten and twelve feet high, of elephants lions, tigers, oxen, rams, swans and eagles, larger than life. Corner niches and recesses have been enriched with the most intricate ornamentation, and in them, still of the same rock, without the introduction of an atom of outside material, the sculptors chiseled the figures of forty or more of the principal Hindu deities. And on each of the four sides is a massive altar carved out of the side of the cliff with the most ornate and elaborate traceries and other embellishment.

Indeed, my pen is not capable of describing these most wonderful achievements of human genius and patience. But all of them have been described in great detail and with copious illustrations in books that refer to nothing else. I can only say that they are the most wonderful of all the human monuments in India.

> "From one vast mount of solid stone
> A mighty temple has been cored
> By nut-brown children of the sun,
> When stars were newly bright, and blithe
> Of song along the rim of dawn—
> A mighty monolith."

The thirty principal temples are scattered along the rocky mountain side within a distance of two miles, and seventy-nine others are in the immediate neighborhood. The smallest of the principal group is 90 feet long, 40 feet wide, with a roof 40 feet high sustained by thirty-four columns. They are all alike in one particular. No mortar was used in their construction or any outside material. Every atom of the walls and ceilings, the columns, the altars and the images and ornaments stands exectly where the Creator placed it at the birth of the universe.

There are several groups of cave temples in the same neighborhood. Some of them were made by the Buddhists, for it seems to have been fashionable in those days to chisel places of worship out of the rocky hillsides instead of erecting them in the open air, according to the ordinary rules of architecture. There are not less than 300 in western India which are believed to have been made within a period of a thousand years. Archæologists dispute over their ages, just as they disagree about everything else. Some claim that the first of the cave temples antedates the Christian era; others declare that the oldest was not begun for 300 years after Christ, but to the ordinary citizen these are questions of little significance. It is not so important for us to know when this great work was done, but it would be extremely gratifying if somebody could tell us who did it—what genius first conceived the idea of carving a magnificent house of worship out of the heart of a mountain, and what means he used to accomplish the amazing results.

We would like to know for example, who made the designs of the Vishwa Karma, or carpenter's cave, one of the most exquisite in India, a single excavation 85 by 45 feet in area and 35 feet high, which has an arched roof similar to the Gothic chapels of England and a balcony or gallery over a richly sculptured gateway very similar to the organ loft of a modern church. At the upper end, sitting cross-legged in a niche, is a figure four feet high, with a serene and contemplative expression upon its face. Because it has none of the usual signs and symbols and ornaments that appertain to the different gods, archæologists have pronounced it a figure of the founder of the temple, who, according to a popular legend, carved it all with his own hands, but there is nothing to indicate for whom the statue was intended, and the various stories told of it are pure conjectures that only exasperate one who studies the details. Each stroke of the chisel upon the surface of the interior was as delicate and exact as if a jewel instead of a granite mountain was being carved.

There are temples to all of the great gods in the Hindu catalogue; there are several in honor of Buddha, and others for Jain, all more or less of the same design and the same style of execution. Those who care to know more about them can find full descriptions in Fergusson's "Indian Architecture."

South of Bombay, on the coast, is the little Portuguese colony of Goa, the oldest European settlement in India. You will be surprised to know that there are four or five of these colonies belonging to other European governments within the limits of British India, entirely independent of the viceroy and the authority of Edward VII. The French have two towns of limited area in Bengal, one of them only an hour's ride from Calcutta. They are entirely outside of the British jurisdiction and under the authority of the French Republic, which has always been respected. The Dutch have two colonies in India also, and Goa, the most important of all, is subject to Portugal. The territory is sixty-two miles long by forty miles wide, and has a population of 446,982. The inhabitants are nearly all Roman Catholics, and the archbishop of Goa is primate of the East, having jurisdiction over all Roman Catholics between Cairo and Hong-Kong.

More than half of the population are converted Hindus, descendants of the original occupants of the place, who were overcome by the Duke of Albuquerque in 1510, and after seventy or eighty years of fighting were converted by the celebrated and saintly Jesuit missionary, St. Francis Xavier. He lived and preached and died in Goa, and was buried in the Church of the Good Jesus, which was erected by him during the golden age of Portugal—for at one time that little kingdom exercised a military, political, ecclesiastical and commercial influence throughout the world quite as great, comparatively speaking, as that of Great Britain to-day. Goa was then the most important city in the East, for its wealth and commerce rivaled that of Genoa or Venice. It was as large as Paris or London, and the viceroy lived in a palace as fine as that occupied by the king. But very little evidence of its former magnificence remains. Its grandeur was soon exhausted when the Dutch and the East India Company came into competition with the Portuguese. The Latin race has never been tenacious either in politics or commerce. Like the Spaniards, the Portuguese have no staying power, and after a struggle lasting seventy years, all of the wide Portuguese possessions in the East fell into the hands of the Dutch and the British, and nothing is now left but Goa, with its ruins and reminiscences and the beautiful shrine of marble and jasper, which the Grand Duke of Tuscany erected in honor of the first great missionary to the East.

IV

THE EMPIRE OF INDIA

India is a great triangle, 1,900 miles across its greatest length and an equal distance across its greatest breadth. It extends from a region of perpetual snow in the Himalayas, almost to the equator. The superficial area is 1,766,642 square miles, and you can understand better what that means when I tell you that the United States has an area of 2,970,230 square miles, without counting Alaska or Hawaii. India is about as large as that portion of the United States lying east of a line drawn southward along the western boundary of the Dakotas, Kansas and Texas.

The population of India in 1901 was 294,361,056 or about one-fifth of the human race, and it comprises more than 100 distinct nations and peoples in every grade of civilization from absolute savages to the most complete and complex commercial and social organizations. It has every variety of climate from the tropical humidity along the southern coast to the frigid cold of the mountains; peaks of ice, reefs of coral, impenetrable jungles and bleak, treeless plains. One portion of its territory records the greatest rainfall of any spot on earth; another, of several hundred thousand square miles, is seldom watered with a drop of rain and is entirely dependent for moisture upon the melting snows of the mountains. Twelve thousands different kinds of animals are enumerated in its fauna, 28,000 plants in its flora, and the statistical survey prepared by the government fills 128 volumes of the size of our census reports. One hundred and eighteen distinct languages are spoken in various parts of India and fifty-nine of these languages are spoken by more than 100,000 people each. A large number of other languages and dialects are spoken by different tribes and clans of less than 100,000 population. The British Bible Society has published the whole or parts of the Holy Scriptures in forty-two languages which reach 220,000,000 people, but leave 74,000,000 without the Holy Word. In order to give the Bible to the remainder of the population of India it would be necessary to publish 108 additional translations, which the society has no money and no men to prepare. From this little statement some conception of the variety of the people of India may be obtained, because each of the tribes and clans has its own distinct organization and individuality, and each is practically a separate nation.

Language.	Spoken by	Language.	Spoken by
Hindi	85,675,373	Malayalam	5,428,250
Bengali	41,343,762	Masalmani	3,669,390
Telugu	19,885,137	Sindhi	2,592,341
Marathi	18,892,875	Santhal	1,709,680
Punjabi	17,724,610	Western Pahari	1,523,098
Tamil	15,229,759	Assamese	1,435,820
Gujarathi	10,619,789	Gond	1,379,580
Kanarese	9,751,885	Central Pahari	1,153,384
Uriya	9,010,957	Marwadi	1,147,480
Burmese	5,926,864	Pashtu	1,080,931

The Province of Bengal, for example, is nearly as large as all our North Atlantic states combined, and contains an area of 122,548 square miles. The Province of Rajputana is even larger, and has a population of 74,-744,886, almost as great as that of the entire United States. Madras has a population of 38,000,000, and the central provinces 47,000,000, while several of the 160 different states into which India is divided have more than 10,000,000 each.

The population is divided according to religions as follows:

Hindus	207,146,422	Sikhs	2,195,268
Mohammedans.	62,458,061	Jains	1,334,148
Buddhists	9,476,750	Parsees	94,190
Animistic	8,711,360	Jews	18,228
Christians	2,923,241		

It will be interesting to know that of the Christians enumerated at the last census 1,202,039 were Roman Catholics, 453,612 belonged to the established Church of England, 322,586 were orthodox Greeks, 220,863 were Baptists, 155,455 Lutherans, 53,829 Presbyterians and 157,847 put themselves down as Protestants without giving the sect to which they adhere.

The foreign population of India is very small. The British-born number only 96,653; 104,583 were born on the continent of Europe, and only 641,854 out of nearly 300,000,000 were born outside the boundaries of India.

India consists of four separate and well-defined regions: the jungles of the coast and the vast tract of country known as the Deccan, which make up the southern half of the Empire; the great plain which stretches southward from the Himalayas and constitutes what was formerly known as Hindustan; and a three-sided tableland which lies between, in the center of the empire, and is drained by a thousand rivers, which carry the water off as fast as it falls and leave but little to refresh the earth. This is the scene of periodical famine, but the government is pushing the irrigation system so rapidly that before many years the danger from that source will be much diminished.

The whole of southern India, according to the geologists, was once covered by a great forest, and indeed there are still 66,305,506 acres in trees which are carefully protected. The black soil of that region is proverbial for its fertility and produces cotton, sugar cane, rice and other tropical and semi-tropical plants with an abundance surpassed by no other region. The fruit-bearing palms require a chapter to themselves in the botanies, and are a source of surprising wealth. According to the latest census the enormous area of 546,224,964 acres is under cultivation, which is an average of nearly two acres per capita of population, and probably two-thirds of it is actually cropped. About one-fourth of this area is under irrigation and more than 22,000,000 acres produce two crops a year.

Most of the population is scattered in villages, and the number of people who are not supported by farms is much smaller than would be supposed from the figures of the census. A large proportion of the inhabitants returned as engaged in trade and other employments really belong to the agricultural community, because they are the agents of middlemen through whose hands the produce of the farms passes. These people live in villages among the farming community. In all the Empire there are only eight towns with more than 200,000 inhabitants; only three with more than 500,000, and only one with a million, which is Calcutta. The other seven in order of size are Bombay, Madras, Hyderabad, Lucknow, Rangoon, Benares and Delhi. There are only twenty-nine towns with more than 100,000 inhabitants; forty-nine with more than 50,000; 471 with more than 10,000; 877 with more than 5,000, and 2,134 organized municipalities with a population of 1,000 or more. These municipalities represent an aggregate population of 29,244,221 out of a total of 294,361,056, leaving 265,134,722 inhabitants scattered upon farms and in 729,752 villages. The city population, however, is growing more rapidly than that of the country, because of the efforts of the government to divert labor from the farms to the factories. In Germany, France, England and other countries of Europe and in the United States the reverse policy is pursued. Their rural population is drifting too rapidly to the cities, and the cities are growing faster than is considered healthful. In India, during the ten years from 1891 to 1901 the city population has increased only 2,452,083, while the rural population has increased only 4,567,032.

The following table shows the number of people supported by each of the principal occupations named:

Agriculture	191,691,731
Earth work and general labor (not agriculture)	17,953,261
Producing food, drink and stimulants	16,758,726
Producing textile fabrics	11,214,158
Personal, household and sanitary	10,717,500
Rent payers (tenants)	106,873,575
Rent receivers (landlords)	45,810,673
Field laborers	29,325,985
General laborers	16,941,026

Cotton weavers	5,460,515
Farm servants	4,196,697
Beggars (non-religious)	4,222,241
Priests and others engaged in religion	2,728,812
Workers and dealers in wood, bamboo, etc.	2,499,531
Barbers and shampooers	2,331,598
Grain and pulse dealers	2,264,481
Herdsmen (cattle, sheep and goats)	2,215,791
Indoor servants	2,078,018
Washermen	2,011,624
Workers and dealers in earthen and stone ware	2,125,225
Shoe, boot and sandal makers	1,957,291
Shopkeepers	1,839,958
Workers and dealers in gold and silver	1,768,597
Cart and pack animal owners	1,605,529
Iron and steel workers	1,475,883
Watchmen and other village servants	1,605,118
Grocery dealers	1,587,225
Sweepers and scavengers	1,518,482
Fishermen and fish curers	1,280,358
Fish dealers	1,269,435
Workers in cane and matting	1,290,961
Bankers, money lenders, etc.	1,200,998
Tailors, milliners and dressmakers	1,142,153
Officers of the civil service	1,043,872
Water carriers	1,089,574
Oil pressers	1,055,933
Dairy men, milk and butter dealers	1,013,000

The enormous number of 1,563,000, which is equal to the population of half our states, are engaged in what the census terms "disreputable" occupations. There are about eighty other classes, but none of them embraces more than a million members.

Among the curiosities of the census we find that 603,741 people are engaged in making and selling sweetmeats, and 550,241 in selling cardamon seeds and betel leaves, and 548,829 in manufacturing and selling bangles, necklaces, beads and sacred threads. There are 497,509 teachers and professors, 562,055 actors, singers and dancers, 520,044 doctors and 279,646 lawyers.

The chewing of betel leaves is one of the peculiar customs of the country, even more common than tobacco chewing ever was with us. At almost every street corner, in the porticos of the temples, at the railway stations and in the parks, you will see women and men, squatting on the ground behind little trays covered with green leaves, powdered nuts and a white paste, made of the ashes of cocoanut fiber, the skins of potatoes and a little lime. They take a leaf, smear it with the lime paste, which is intended to increase the saliva, and then wrap it around the powder of the betel nut. Natives stop at these stands, drop a copper, pick up one of these folded leaves, put it in their mouths, and go off chewing, and spitting out saliva as red as blood. Strangers are frequently attracted by dark red stains upon pavements and floors which look as if somebody had suffered from a hemorrhage or had opened an artery, but they are only traces of the chewers of the betel nut. The habit is no more harmful than chewing tobacco. The influence of the juice is slightly stimulating to the nerves, but not injurious, although it is filthy and unclean.

It is a popular impression that the poor of India live almost exclusively upon rice, which is very cheap and nourishing, hence it is possible for a family to subsist upon a few cents a day. This is one of the many delusions that are destroyed when you visit the country. Rice in India is a luxury that can be afforded only by the people of good incomes, and throughout four-fifths of the country is sold at prices beyond the reach of common working people. Sixty per cent. of the population live upon wheat, barley, fruit, various kinds of pulses and maize. Rice can be grown only in hot and damp climates, where there are ample means of irrigation, and only where the conditions of soil, climate and water supply allow its abundant production does it enter into the diet of the working classes. Three-fourths of the people are vegetarians, and live upon what they produce themselves.

The density of the population is very great, notwithstanding the enormous area of the empire, being an average of 167 to the square mile, including mountains, deserts and jungles, as against 21.4 to the square mile in the United States. Bengal, the province of which Calcutta is the capital, on the eastern coast of India, is the most densely populated, having 588 people to the square mile. Behar in the south has 548, Oudh in the north 531; Agra, also in the north, 419, and Bombay 202. Some parts of India have a larger population to the acre than any other part of the world. The peasants, or coolies, as they are called, are born and live and die like animals. Indeed animals seldom are so closely herded together, or live such wretched lives. In 1900, 54,000,000 people were more or less affected by the famine, and 5,607,000 were fed by the government for several months, simply because there was no other way for them to obtain food. There was no labor they could perform for wages, and those who were fortunate enough to secure employment could not earn enough to buy bread to satisfy the hunger of their families. It is estimated that 30,000,000 human beings starved to death in India during the nineteenth century, and in one year alone, the year in which that good woman, Queen Victoria, assumed the title of empress, more than 5,000,000 of her subjects died from hunger. Yet the population without immigration is continually increasing from natural causes. The net increase during the ten years from 1891 to 1901 was 7,046,385. The struggle for life is becoming greater every year; wages are going down instead of up, notwithstanding the rapid increase of manufacturing industries, the extension of the railway system and other sources of wealth and employment that are being rapidly developed.

More than 200,000,000 persons in India are living upon less than 5 cents a day of our money; more than 100,000,000 are living upon less than 3 cents; more than 50,000,000 upon less than 1 cent and at least two-thirds of the entire population do not have food enough during any year of their lives to supply the nourishment demanded by the human system. As I have already shown, there are only two acres of land under cultivation for each inhabitant of India. This includes gardens, parks and pastures, and it is not evenly distributed. In many parts of the country, millions are compelled to live upon an average of one-fourth of an acre of land and millions more upon half an acre each, whereas an average of five acres of agricultural land per capita of population is believed to be necessary to the prosperity of a nation.

Few countries have such an enormous birth rate and death rate. Nowhere else are babies born in such enormous numbers, and nowhere does death reap such awful harvests. Sometimes a single famine or plague suddenly sweeps millions into eternity, and their absence is scarcely noticed. Before the present sanitary regulations and inspections were introduced the death rate was nearly double what it is now; indeed, some experts estimate that it must have been several times as great, but no records were kept in some of the provinces, and in most of them, they were incomplete and inaccurate. India is now in a healthier condition than ever before, and yet the death rate varies from 31.10 per 1,000 in the cold provinces of Agra and Oudh to 82.7 per 1,000 in the tropical regions of Behar. In Bombay last year the rate was 70.07 per 1,000; in the central provinces 56.75; in the Punjab, which has a wide area in northwestern India, it was 47.7 and in Bengal 36.63.

The birth rate is almost as large, the following table being reported from the principal provinces named:

	Births per 1,000 pop.		Births per 1,000 pop.
Behar	50.5	Burmah	37.4
Punjab	48.4	Bombay	36.3
Agra	48.9	Assam	35.4
Central provinces	47.3	Madras	31.3
Bengal	42.9		

Even with the continual peril from plague and famine, the government does not encourage emigration, as you think would be considered a wise policy, but retards it by all sorts of regulations and restrictions, and it is difficult to drive the Hindus out of the wretched hovels in which they live and thrive and breed like rats or rabbits. The more wretched and comfortless a home, the more attached the natives are to it. The less they have to leave the more reluctant they are to leave it, but the same rule applies to every race and every nation in the south of

Europe and the Turkish Empire, in Syria, Egypt, the East India Islands, and wherever the population is dense and wages are low. It is the semi-prosperous middle class who emigrate in the hope of bettering their condition.

There is less emigration from India than from any other country. During the last twenty years the total number of persons emigrating from the Indian Empire was only 316,349, less than come to the United States annually from Italy, and the statistics show that 138,660 of these persons returned to their former homes during that period, leaving the net emigration since 1882 only 177,689 out of 300,000,000 of population. And most of these settled in other British colonies. We have a few Hindu merchants and Parsees in the United States, but no coolies whatever. The coolies are working classes that have gone to British Guiana, Trinidad, Jamaica and other West Indies, Natal, East Africa, Fiji and other British possessions in the Pacific. There has been a considerable flow of workmen back and forth between India and Burma and Ceylon, for in those provinces labor is scarce, wages are high and large numbers of Hindus are employed in the rice paddies and tea plantations.

The government prevents irregular emigration. It has a "protectorate of emigrants" who is intrusted with the enforcement of the laws. Natives of India are not permitted to leave the country unless they are certain of obtaining employment at the place where they desire to go, and even then each intending emigrant must file a copy of his contract with the commissioner in order that he may be looked after in his new home, for the Indian government always sends an agent to protect the interests of its coolies to every country where they have gone in any considerable numbers. Every intending emigrant must submit to a medical examination also, for the navigation laws prohibit vessels from taking aboard any native who does not show a certificate from an official that he is in full possession of his health and faculties and physically fit to earn his living in a strange country. Vessels carrying emigrants are subject to inspection, and are obliged to take out licenses, which require them to observe certain rules regarding space occupied, ventilation, sanitation and the supply of food and water. Most of the emigrants leaving India go out under contract and the terms must be approved by the agent of the government.

The fact that the government and the benevolent people of Europe and America have twice within the last ten years been compelled to intervene to save the people of India trom perishing of starvation has created an impression that they are always in the lowest depths of distress and continually suffering from any privations. This is not unnatural, and might under ordinary circumstances be accepted as conclusive proof of the growing poverty of the country and the inability of the people to preserve their own lives. Such a conclusion, however, is very far from the fact, and every visitor to India from foreign lands has a surprise awaiting him concerning its condition and progress. When three-fifths of a population of 300,000,000 have all their eggs in one basket and depend entirely upon little spots of soil for sustenance, and when their crops are entirely dependent upon the rains, and when for a succession of years the rains are not sufficient, there must be failures of harvest and a vast amount of suffering is inevitable. But the recuperative power of the empire is astonishing.

Although a famine may extend over its total length and breadth one season, and require all the resources of the government to prevent the entire population from perishing, a normal rainfall will restore almost immediate prosperity, because the soil is so rich, the sun is so hot, and vegetation is so rapid that sometimes three and even four crops are produced from the same soil in a single year. All the people want in time of famine is sufficient seed to replant their farms and food enough to last them until a crop is ripe. The fact that a famine exists in one part of the country, it must also be considered, is no evidence that the remainder of the empire is not abounding in prosperity, and every table of statistics dealing with the material conditions of the country shows that famine and plague have in no manner impeded their progress. On the other hand they demonstrate the existence of an increased power of endurance and rapid recuperation, which, compared with the past, affords ground for hope and confidence of an even more rapid advance in the future.

Comparing the material condition of India in 1904 with what it was ten years previous, we find that the area of soil under cultivation has increased 229,000,000 acres. What we call internal revenue has increased 17 per cent during the last ten years; sea borne foreign commerce has risen in value from £130,500,000 to £163,750,000; the coasting trade from £48,500,000 to £63,000,000, and the foreign trade by land from £5,500,000 to £9,000,000. Similar signs of progress and prosperity are to be found in the development of organized manufactures, in the increased investment of capital in commerce and industry, in dividends paid by various enterprises, in the extended use of the railways, the postoffice and the telegraph. The number of operatives in cotton mills has increased during the last ten years from 118,000 to 174,000, in jute mills from 65,000 to 114,000, in coal and other mines from 35,000 to 95,000, and in miscellaneous industries from 184,000 to 500,000. The railway employes have increased in number from 284,000 to 357,000 in ten years.

A corresponding development and improvement is found in all lines of investment. During the ten years from 1894 to 1904 the number of joint stock companies having more than $100,000 capital has increased from 950 to 1,366, and their paid up capital from £17,750,000 to £24,500,000. The paid in capital of banks has advanced from £9,000,000 to £14,750,000; deposits have increased from £7,500,000 to £23,650,000, and the deposits in postal savings banks from £4,800,000 to £7,200,000, which is an encouraging indication of the growth of habits of thrift. The passenger traffic on the railways has increased from 123,000,000 to 195,000,000, and the freight from 20,000,000 to 34,000,000 tons. The number of letters and parcels passing through the postoffice has increased during the ten years from 340,000,000 to 560,000,000; the postal money orders from £9,000,000 to £19,000,000, and the telegraph messages from 3,000,000 to 5,000,000 in number.

The income tax is an excellent barometer of prosperity. It exempts ordinary wage earners entirely—persons with incomes of less than 500 rupees, a rupee being worth about 33 cents of our money. The whole number of persons paying the income tax has increased from 354,594 to 495,605, which is about 40 per cent in ten years, and the average tax paid has increased from 37.09 rupees to 48.68 rupees. The proceeds of the tax have increased steadily from year to year, with the exception of the famine years.

There are four classifications of taxpayers, and the proportion paid by each during the last year, 1902, was as follows:

	Per cent.
Salaries and pensions	29.07
Dividends from companies and business	7.22
Interest on securities	4.63
Miscellaneous sources of income	59.08

The last item is very significant. It shows that nearly 60 per cent of the income taxpayers of India are supported by miscellaneous investments other than securities and joint stock companies. The item includes the names of merchants, individual manufacturers, farmers, mechanics, professional men and tradesmen of every class.

The returns of the postal savings banks show the following classes of depositors:

	Number.
Wage earners	352,349
Professional men with fixed incomes	233,108
Professional men with variable incomes	58,130
Domestics, or house servants	151,204
Tradesmen	32,065
Farmers	12,387
Mechanics	27,450

The interest allowed by the savings bank government of India is 3½ per cent.

Considering the awful misfortunes and distress which the country has endured during the last ten years, these facts are not only satisfactory but remarkable, and if it can progress so rapidly during times of plague and famine, what could be expected from it during a cycle of seasons of full crops.

During the ten years which ended with 1894 the seasons were all favorable, generally speaking, although local failures of harvests occurred here and there in districts of several provinces, but they were not sufficient in area, duration or intensity to affect the material conditions of the people. The ten succeeding years, however, ending with 1904 witnessed a succession of calamities that were unprecedented either in India or anywhere else on earth, with the exception of a famine that occurred in the latter part of the eighteenth century. Those ten years not only saw two of the worst famines, but repeated visitations of widespread and fatal epidemics. It is estimated that during the ten years ending December, 1903, a million and a half of deaths were caused by the bubonic plague alone, and that the mortality from that pestilence was small in comparison with that caused by cholera, fever and famine. The effects of those epidemics had been to hamper trade, to alarm and demoralize the people, to obstruct foreign commerce, prevent investments and the development of material resources. Yet during the years 1902 and 1903 throughout all India there was abundant prosperity. This restoration of prosperity is most noticeable in several of the districts that suffered most severely from famine. To a large measure the agricultural population have been restored to their normal condition.

It is difficult in a great country like India where wages are so small and the cost of living is so insignificant compared with our own country, to judge accurately of the condition of the laboring classes. The empire is so vast and so diverse in all its features that a statement which may accurately apply to one province will misrepresent another. But, taking one consideration with another, as the song says, and drawing an average, it is plainly evident that the peasant population of India is slowly improving in condition. The scales of wages have undoubtedly risen; there has been an improvement in the housing and the feeding of the masses; their sanitary condition has been radically changed, although they have fought against it, and the slow but gradual development of the material resources of the country promises to make the improvement permanent.

The chief source of revenue in India from ancient times has been a share in the crops of the farmers. The present system has been handed down through the centuries with very little modification, and as three-fifths of the people are entirely and directly dependent upon the cultivation of the land, the whole fabric of society has been based upon that source of wealth. The census gives 191,691,731 people as agriculturists, of whom 131,000,000 till their own or rented land, 18,750,000 receive incomes as landlord owners and the remainder are agricultural laborers. The landlord caste are the descendants of hereditary chiefs, of former revenue farmers and persons of importance to whom land grants were made in ancient times. Large tracts of land in northern India are owned by municipalities and village communities, whose officials receive the rents and pay the taxes. Other large tracts have been inherited from the invaders and conquerors of the country. It is customary in India for the landlord to receive his rent in a part of the crop, and the government in turn receives a share of this rent in lieu of taxes. This is an ancient system which the British government has never interfered with, and any attempt to modify or change it would undoubtedly be resisted. At the same time the rents are largely regulated by the taxes. These customs, which have come down from the Mogul empire, have been defined and strengthened by time and experience. Nearly every province has its own and different laws and customs on the subject, but the variation is due not to legislation, but to public sentiment. The tenant as well as the landlord insists that the assessments of taxes shall be made before the rent rate is determined, and this occurs in almost every province, although variations in rent and changes of proprietorship and tenantry very seldom occur. Wherever there has been a change during the present generation it has been in favor of the tenants. The rates of rent and taxation naturally vary according to the productive power of the land, the advantages of climate and rainfall, the facilities for reaching market and other conditions. But the average tax represents about two-thirds of a rupee per acre, or 21 cents in American money.

We have been accustomed to consider India a great wheat producing country, and you often hear of apprehension on the part of American political economists lest its cheap labor and enormous area should give our wheat growers serious competition. But there is not the slightest ground for apprehension. While the area planted to wheat in India might be doubled, and farm labor earns only a few cents a day, the methods of cultivation are so primitive and the results of that cheap labor are comparatively so small, that they can never count seriously against our wheat farms which are tilled and harvested with machinery and intelligence. No article in the Indian export trade has been so irregular or has experienced greater vicissitudes than wheat. The highest figure ever reached in the value of exports was during the years 1891-92, when there was an exceptional crop, and the exports reached $47,500,000. The average for the preceding ten years was $25,970,000, while the average for the succeeding ten years, ending 1901-02, was only $12,740,000. This extraordinary decrease was due to the failure of the crop year after year and the influence of the famines of 1897 and 1900. The bulk of the wheat produced in India is consumed within the districts where it is raised, and the average size of the wheat farms is less than five acres. More than three-fourths of the India wheat crop is grown on little patches of ground only a few feet square, and sold in the local markets. The great bulk of the wheat exported comes from the large farms or is turned in to the owners of land rented to tenants for shares of the crops produced.

The coal industry is becoming important. There are 329 mines in operation, which yielded 7,424,480 tons during the calendar year of 1902, an increase of nearly 1,000,000 tons in the five years ending 1903. It is a fair grade of bituminous coal and does well for steaming purposes. Twenty-eight per cent of the total output was consumed by the local railway locomotives in 1902, and 431,552 tons was exported to Ceylon and other neighboring countries. The first mine was opened in India as long ago as 1820, but it was the only one worked for twenty years, and the development of the industry has been very slow, simply keeping pace with the increase of railways, mills, factories and other consumers. But the production is entirely sufficient to meet the local demand, and only 23,417 tons was imported in 1902, all of which came as ballast. The industry gives employment to about 98,000 persons. Most of the stock in the mining companies is owned by private citizens of India. The prices in Calcutta and Bombay vary from $2.30 to $2.85 a ton.

India is rich in mineral deposits, but few of them have been developed, chiefly on account of the lack of capital and enterprise. After coal, petroleum is the most important item, and in 1902 nearly 57,000,000 gallons was refined and sold in the India market, but this was not sufficient to meet half the demand, and about 81,000,000 gallons was imported from the United States and Russia.

Gold mining is carried on in a primitive way in several of the provinces, chiefly by the washing of river sand. Valuable gold deposits are known to exist, but no one has had the enterprise or the capital to undertake their development, simply because costly machinery is required and would call for a heavy investment. Most of the gold washing is done by natives with rude, home-made implements, and the total production reported for $1902 was 517,639 ounces, valued at $20 an ounce. This, however, does not tell more than half the story. It represents only the amount of gold shipped out of the country, while at least as much again, if not more, was consumed by local artisans in the manufacture of the jewelry which is so popular among the natives. When a Hindu man or woman gets a little money ahead he or she invariably buys silver or gold ornaments with it, instead of placing it in a savings bank or making other investments. Nearly all women and children that you see are loaded with silver ornaments, their legs and feet as well as their hands and arms, and necklaces of silver weighing a pound or more are common. Girdles of beautifully wrought silver are sometimes worn next to the bare skin by ordinary coolies working on the roads or on the docks of the rivers, and in every town you visit you will find hundreds of shops devoted to the sale of silver and gold adornments of rude workmanship but put metal. The upper classes invest their savings in gold and precious stones for similar reasons. There is scarcely a family of the middle class without a jewel case containing many articles of great value, while both the men and women of the rich and noble castes own and wear on ceremonial occasions amazing collections of precious stones and gold ornaments which have been handed down by their ancestors who invested their surplus wealth in them at a time when no safe securities were to be had and savings banks had not been introduced into India. A large proportion of the native gold is consumed by local artisans in the manufacture of these ornaments, and is not counted in the official returns. An equal amount, perhaps, is worked up into gold foil and used for gilding temples, palaces and the houses of the rich. Like all orientals, the Indians are very fond of gilding, and immense quantities of pure gold leaf are manufactured in little shops that may be seen in every bazaar you visit.

India now ranks second among the manganese ore producing countries of the world, and has an inexhaustible supply of the highest grade. The quality of the ores from the central provinces permits their export in the face of a railway haul of 500 miles and sea transportation to England, Belgium, Germany and the United States, but, speaking generally, the mineral development of India has not yet begun.

V

TWO HINDU WEDDINGS

There was a notable wedding at Baroda, the capital of one of the Native States of the same name, while we were in India, and the Gaikwar, as the ruling prince is called, expressed a desire for us to be present. He has a becoming respect for and appreciation of the influence and usefulness of the press, and it was a pleasure to find so sensible a man among the native rulers. But, owing to circumstances over which we had no control, we had to deny ourselves the gratification of witnessing an event which few foreigners have ever been allowed to see. It is a pity winter is so short in the East, for there are so many countries one cannot comfortably visit any other time of year.

Baroda is a non-tributary, independent native state of the first rank, lying directly north of the province of Bombay, and its ruler is called a "gaikwar," which signifies "cowherd," and the present possessor of that title is one of the biggest men in the empire, one of the richest and one of the greatest swells. He is entitled to a salute of twenty-one guns, an honor conferred upon only two other native princes, the Maharajah of Mysore and the Nizam of Hyderabad. He is one of the ablest and one of the most progressive of the native princes. His family trace their descent back to the gods of mythology, but he is entirely human himself, and a handsome man of middle age. When we saw him for the first time he had half a dozen garlands of flowers hanging around his neck, and three or four big bouquets in his hand, which, according to the custom of the country, had been presented to him by affectionate friends. It was he who presented to the City of Bombay the beautiful statue of Queen Victoria which ornaments the principal public square. It is one of the finest monuments to be seen anywhere, and expressed his admiration of his empress, who had shown particular interest in his career. The present gaikwar was placed upon the throne in 1874 by Lord Northbrook, when he was Viceroy of India, to succeed Malhar Rao, one of those fantastic persons we read about in fairy stories but seldom find in real life. For extravagant phantasies and barbaric splendors he beat the world. He surpassed even those old spendthrifts of the Roman Empire, Nero, Caligula and Tiberius. He spent a million of rupees to celebrate the marriage ceremonies of a favorite pigeon of his aviary, which was mated with one belonging to his prime minister. But the most remarkable of his extravagant freaks was a rug and two pillow covers of pearls, probably the greatest marvel of all fabrics that were ever woven since the world was made.

The carpet, ten feet six inches by six feet in size, is woven entirely of strings of perfect pearls. A border eleven inches wide and a center ornament are worked out in diamonds. The pillow covers are three feet by two feet six inches in size. For three years the jewel merchants of India, and they are many, were searching for the material for this extraordinary affair. It cost several millions of dollars and was intended as a present for a Mohammedan lady of doubtful reputation, who had fascinated His Highness. The British Resident at his capital intervened and prohibited the gift on the ground that the State of Baroda could not afford to indulge its ruler in such generosity, and that the scandal would reflect upon the administration of the Indian Empire. The carpet still belongs to the State and may be seen by visitors upon a permit from one of the higher authorities. It is kept at Baroda in a safe place with the rest of the state jewels, which are the richest in India and probably the most costly belonging to any government in the world.

The regalia of the gaikwar intended for state occasions, which was worn by him at the wedding, is valued at $15,000,000. He appeared in it at the Delhi durbar in 1903. It consists of a collar and shoulder pieces made of 500 diamonds, some of them as large as walnuts. The smallest would be considered a treasure by any lady in the land. The border of this collar is made of three bands of emeralds, of graduated sizes, the outer row consisting of jewels nearly an inch square. From the collar, as a pendant, hangs one of the largest and most famous diamonds in the world, known as the "Star of the Deccan." Its history may be found in any work on jewels. There is an aigrette to match the collar, which His Highness wears in his turban.

This is only one of several sets to be found in the collection, which altogether would make as brave a show as you can find at Tiffany's. There are strings of pearls as large as marbles, and a rope of pearls nearly four feet long braided of four strands. Every pearl is said to be perfect and the size of a pea. The rope is about an inch in diameter. Besides these are necklaces, bracelets, brooches, rings and every conceivable ornament set with jewels of every variety, which have been handed down from generation to generation in this princely family for several hundred years. One of the most interesting of the necklaces is made of uncut rubies said to have been found in India. It has been worn for more than a thousand years. These jewels are kept in a treasure-room in the heart of the Nazar Bgah Palace, guarded night and day by a battalion of soldiers. At night when the palace is closed half a dozen huge cheetahs, savage beasts of the leopard family, are released in the corridors, and, as you may imagine, they are efficient watchmen. They would make a burglar very unhappy. During the daytime they are allowed to wander about the palace grounds, but are carefully muzzled.

Malhar Rao built a superb palace at a cost of $1,500,000 which is considered the most perfect and beautiful example of the Hindu-Saracenic order of architecture in existence, and its interior finish and decoration are wonderful for their artistic beauty, detail and variety. In front of the main entrance are two guns of solid gold, weighing two hundred and eighty pounds each, and the carriages, ammunition wagons and other accoutrements are made of solid silver. The present Maharajah is said to have decided to melt them down and have them coined into good money, with which he desires to endow a technical school.

Behind the palace is a great walled arena in which previous rulers of Baroda have had fights between elephants, tigers, lions and other wild beasts for the amusement of their court and the population generally. And they remind you of those we read about in the Colosseum in the time of Nero and other Roman emperors. Baroda has one of the finest zoological gardens in the world, but most of the animals are native to India. It is surrounded by a botanical garden, in which the late gaikwar, who was passionately fond of plants and flowers, took a great deal of interest and spent a great deal of money.

He built a temple at Dakor, a few miles from Baroda, which cost an enormous sum of money, in honor of an ancient image of the Hindu god, Krishna. It has been the resort of pilgrims for hundreds of years, and is considered one of the most sacred idols of India. In addition to the temple he constructed hospices for the shelter and entertainment of pilgrims, who come nowadays in larger numbers than ever, sometimes as many as a hundred thousand in a year, and are all fed and cared for, furnished comfortable clothing and medical attendance, bathed, healed and comforted at the expense of His Highness, whose generosity and hospitality are not limited to his own subjects. The throne of the idol Krishna in that temple is a masterpiece of wood carving and bears $60,000 worth of gold ornaments. Artists say that this temple, although entirely modern, surpasses in the beauty of its detail, both in design and workmanship, any of the old temples in India which people come thousands of miles to see.

Fate at last overtook the strange man who did all these things and he came to grief. Indignant at Colonel Phayre, the British Resident, for interfering with his wishes in regard to the pearl carpet and some other little fancies, he attempted to poison him in an imperial manner. He caused a lot of diamonds to be ground up into powder and dropped into a cup of pomolo juice, which he tried to induce his prudent adviser to drink. Ordinary drug store poison was beneath him. When Malhar Rao committed a crime he did it, as he did everything else, with royal splendor. He had tried the same trick successfully upon his brother and predecessor, Gaikwar

Khande Rao, the man who built a beautiful sailors' home at Bombay in 1870 to commemorate the visit of the Duke of Edinburgh to India. Colonel Phayre suspected something wrong, and declined to drink the toast His Highness offered. The plot was soon afterward discovered and Viceroy Lord Northbrook, who had tolerated his tyranny and fantastic performances as long as possible, made an investigation and ordered him before a court over which the chief justice of Bengal presided. The evidence disclosed a most scandalous condition of affairs throughout the entire province. Public offices were sold to the highest bidder; demands for blackmail were enforced by torture; the wives and daughters of his subjects were seized at his will and carried to his palace whenever their beauty attracted his attention. The condition of the people was desperate. In one district there was open rebellion; discontent prevailed everywhere and the methods of administration were infamous. It was shown that a previous prime minister had been poisoned by direct orders of his chief and that with his own hands the gaikwar had beaten one of his own servants to death. Two Hindu judges of the court voted for acquittal, but the remainder found him guilty. As the judgment was not unanimous, Mahal Rao escaped the death penalty which he deserved, and would have suffered but for the sympathy of his judicial co-religionists. He was deposed and sent to prison, and when an investigation of his finances was made, it was found that during the last year of his reign he had wasted $3,500,000 in gifts to his favorites, in gratifying his whims and fancies, and for personal pleasures. All of which was wrung from the people by taxation.

After his conviction the widow of his brother and predecessor, Khande Rao, whom he had poisoned, was allowed to exercise the right of adoption, and her choice fell upon the present gaikwar, then a lad of eleven, belonging to a collateral branch of the family. He was provided with English tutors and afterward sent to England to complete his education. He proved a brilliant scholar, an industrious, earnest, practical man, and, as I have said, Queen Victoria took a great personal interest in him. When he came to the throne in 1874, he immediately applied himself with energy and intelligence to the administration of the government and surrounded himself with the best English advisers he could get. Since his accession the condition of Baroda has entirely changed and is in striking contrast with that which existed under his predecessors. Many taxes have been abolished and more have been reduced. Public works have been constructed everywhere; schools, colleges, hospitals, asylums, markets, water works, electric lighting plants, manufactories and sanitary improvements have been introduced, competent courts have been established and the province has become one of the most prosperous in India.

Baroda is called "The Garden of India." It occupies a fine plain with rich alluvial soil, well watered, and almost entirely under cultivation. It produces luxurious crops of grain, cotton, sugar, tobacco and other staples, and the greater part of them are turned from raw material into the finished product in factories scattered throughthe state. We were advised that Baroda is the best place in India to study the native arts and fabrics. The manufacturing is chiefly controlled by Parsees, descendants of Persian fugitives who fled to India and settled in Baroda more than a thousand years ago, and in their temple at Navasari, a thriving manufacturing town, the sacred fire has been burning uninterruptedly for five hundred years. The City of Baroda has about 125,000 population. The principal streets are lined with houses of teakwood, whose fronts are elaborately carved. Their like cannot be seen elsewhere. The maharajah keeps up the elephant stables of his predecessor in which are bred and kept the finest animals in India. He also breeds the best oxen in the empire.

Through the good offices of Mr. Fee, our consul at Bombay, we received invitations to a Hindu wedding in high life. The groom was a young widower, a merchant of wealth and important commercial connections, a graduate of Elphinstone College, speaks English fluently, and is a favorite with the foreign colony. The bride was the daughter of a widow whose late husband was similarly situated, a partner in a rich mercantile and commission house, well known and respected. The family are liberal in their views, and the daughter has been educated at one of the American mission schools, although they still adhere to Hinduism, their ancestral religion. The groom's family are equally liberal, but, like many prominent families of educated natives, do not have the moral courage or the independence to renounce the faith in which they were born. The inhabitants of India are the most conservative of all peoples, and while an educated and progressive Hindu will tell you freely that he does not believe in the gods and superstitions of his fathers, and will denounce the Brahmins as ignorant impostors, respect for public opinion will not permit him to make an open declaration of his loss of faith. These two families are examples, and when their sons and daughters are married, or when they die, observe all the social and religious customs of their race and preserve the family traditions unbroken.

The home of the bridegroom's family is an immense wooden house in the native quarter, and when we reached it we had to pass through a crowd of coolies that filled the street. The gate and outside walls were gayly decorated with bunting and Japanese lanterns, all ready to be lighted as soon as the sun went down. A native orchestra was playing doleful music in one of the courts, and a brass band of twenty pieces in military uniforms from the barracks was waiting its turn. A hallway which leads to a large drawing-room in the rear of the house was spread with scarlet matting, the walls were hung with gay prints, and Japanese lanterns were suspended from the ceiling at intervals of three or four feet. The first room was filled with women and children eating ices and sweetmeats. Men guests were not allowed to join them. It was then half past four, and we were told that they had been enjoying themselves in that innocent way since noon, and would remain until late in the evening, for it was the only share they could have in the wedding ceremonies. Hindu women and men cannot mingle even on such occasions.

The men folks were in the large drawing-room, seated in rows of chairs facing each other, with an aisle four or five feet wide in the center. There were all sorts and conditions of men, for the groom has a wide acquaintance and intimate friends among Mohammedans, Jains, Parsees, Roman Catholics, Protestants and all the many other religions in Bombay, and he invited them to his marriage. Several foreign ladies were given seats in the place of honor at the head of the room around a large gilt chair or throne which stood in the center with a wreath of flowers carelessly thrown over the back. There were two American missionaries and their wives, a Jesuit priest and several English women.

Soon after we were seated there was a stir on the outside and the groom appeared arrayed in the whitest of white linen robes, a turban of white and gold silk, an exquisite cashmere shawl over his shoulders, and a string of diamonds around his neck that were worth a rajah's ransom. His hands were adorned with several handsome rings, including one great emerald set in diamonds, so big that you could see it across the room. Around his neck was a garland of marigolds that fell to his waist, and he carried a big bridal bouquet in his hand. As soon as he was seated a group of nautch dancers, accompanied by a native orchestra, appeared and performed one of their melancholy dances. The nautches may be very wicked, but they certainly are not attractive in appearance. Their dances are very much like an exercise in the Delsarte method of elocution, being done with the arms more than with the legs, and consisting of slow, graceful gesticulations such as a dreamy poet might use when he soliloquizes to the stars. There is nothing sensuous or suggestive in them. The movements are no more immodest than knitting or quilting a comfortable—and are just about as exciting. Each dance is supposed to be a poem expressed by gesture and posturing—the poetry of motion—a sentimental pantomime, and imaginative Hindus claim to be able to follow the story. The orchestra, playing several queer looking fiddles, drums, clarinets and other instruments, is employed to assist in the interpretation, and produces the most dreary and monotonous sounds without the slightest trace of theme or melody or rhythm. While I don't want to be irrev-

NAUTCH DANCERS

erent, they reminded me of a slang phrase you hear in the country about "the tune the old cow died of." Hindu music is worse than that you hear in China or Japan, because it is so awfully solemn and slow. The Chinese and Japanese give you a lot of noise if they lack harmony, but when a Hindu band reaches a fortissimo passage it sounds exactly as if some child were trying to play a bagpipe for the first time.

When I made an observation concerning the apparent innocence and unattractiveness of the nautch girls to a missionary lady who sat in the next seat, she looked horrified, and admonished me in a whisper that, while there was nothing immodest in the performance, they were depraved, deceitful and dissolute creatures, arrayed in gorgeous raiment for the purpose of enticing men. And it is certainly true that they were clad in the most dazzling costumes of gold brocades and gauzy stuffs that floated like clouds around their heads and shoulders, and their ears, noses, arms, ankles, necks, fingers and toes were all loaded with jewelry.

But their costumes were not half as gay as those worn by some of the gentlemen guests. The Parsees wore black or white with closely buttoned frocks and caps that look like fly-traps; the Mohammedans wore flowing robes of white, and the Hindus silks of the liveliest patterns and the most vivid colors. No ballroom belle ever was enveloped by brighter tinted fabrics than the silks, satins, brocades and velvets that were worn by the dignified Hindu gentlemen at this wedding, and their jewels were such as our richest women wear. A Hindu gentleman in full dress must have a necklace, an aigrette of diamonds, a sunburst in front of his turban, and two or three brooches upon his shoulders or breast. And all this over bare legs and bare feet. They wear slippers or sandals out of doors, but leave them in the hallway or in the vestibule, and cross the threshold of the house in naked feet. The bridegroom was bare legged, but had a pair of embroidered slippers on his feet, because he was soon to take a long walk and could not very well stop to put them on without sacrificing appearances.

They brought us trays of native refreshments, while the nautch girls danced, handed each guest a nosegay and placed a pair of cocoanuts at his feet, which had some deep significance—I could not quite understand what. The groom did not appear to be enjoying himself. He looked very unhappy. He evidently did not like to sit up in a gilded chair so that everybody could stare and make remarks about him, for that is exactly what his guests were doing, criticising his bare legs, commenting upon his jewels and guessing how much his diamond necklace cost. He was quite relieved when a couple of gentlemen, who seemed to be acting as masters of ceremonies, placed a second garland of flowers around his neck—which one of them whispered to me had just come from the bride, the first one having been the gift of his mother—and led him out of the room like a lamb to the slaughter.

When we reached the street a procession of the guests of honor was formed, while policemen drove the crowd back. First came the military band, then the masters of ceremonies—each having a cane in his hand, with which he motioned back the crowd that lined the road on both sides six or eight tiers deep. Then the groom marched all alone with a dejected look on nis face, and his hands clasped before him. After him came the foreign guests, two and two, as long as they were able to keep the formation, but after going a hundred feet the crowd became so great and were so anxious to see all that was going on, that they broke the line and mixed up with the wedding party, and even surrounded the solitary groom like a bodyguard, so that we who were coming directly after could scarcely see him. The noisy music of the band had aroused the entire neighborhood, and in the march to the residence of the bride's family we passed between thousands of spectators. The groom was exceedingly nervous. Although night had fallen and the temperature was quite cool, the perspiration was rolling down his face in torrents, and he was relieved when we entered a narrow passage which had been cleared by the policemen.

The bride's house was decorated in the same manner as the groom's, and upon a tray in the middle of a big room a small slow fire of perfumed wood was burning. The groom was led to the side of it, and stood there, while the guests were seated around him—hooded Hindu women on one side and men and foreign ladies on the other. Then his trainers made him sit down on the floor, cross-legged, like a tailor. Hindus seldom use chairs, or even cushions. Very soon four Brahmins, or priests, appeared from somewhere in the background and seated themselves on the opposite side of the fire. They wore no robes, and were only half dressed. Two were naked to the waist, as well as barefooted and barelegged. One, who had his head shaved like a prize fighter and seemed to be the officiating clergyman, had on what looked like a red flannel shirt. He brought his tools with him, and conducted a mysterious ceremony, which I cannot describe, because it was too long and complicated, and I could not make any notes. A gentleman who had been requested to look after me attempted to explain what it meant, as the ceremony proceeded, but his English was very imperfect, and I lost a good deal of the show trying to clear up his meaning. While the chief priest was going through a ritual his deputies chanted mournful and monotonous strains in a minor key—repetitions of the same lines over and over again. They were praying for the favor of the gods, and their approval of the marriage.

After the groom had endured it alone for a while the bride was brought in by her brother-in-law, who, since the death of her father, has been the head of the household. He was clad in a white gauze undershirt, with short sleeves, and the ordinary Hindu robe wrapped around his waist, and hanging down to his bare knees. The bride had a big bunch of pearls hanging from her upper lip, gold and silver rings and anklets upon her bare feet, and her head was so concealed under wrappings of shawls that she would have smothered in the hot room had not one of her playmates gone up and removed the coverings from her face. This playmate was a lively matron of 14 years, a fellow pupil at the missionary school, who had been married at the age of 9, so she knew all about it, and had adopted foreign manners and customs sufficiently to permit her to go about among the guests, chatting with both gentlemen and ladies with perfect self-possession. She told us all about the bride, who was her dearest friend, received and passed around the presents as they arrived, and took charge of the proceedings.

The bride sat down on the floor beside the husband that had been chosen for her and timidly clasped his hand while the priests continued chanting, stopping now and then to breathe or to anoint the foreheads of the couple, or to throw something on the fire. There were bowls of several kinds of food, each having its significance, and several kinds of plants and flowers, and incense, which was thrown into the flames. At one time the chief priest arose from the floor, stretched his legs and read a long passage from a book, which my escort said was the sacred writing in Sanskrit laying down rules and regulations for the government of Hindu wives. But the bride and groom paid very little attention to the priests or to the ceremony. After the first embarrassment was over they chatted familiarly with their friends, both foreign and native, who came and squatted down beside them. The bride's mother came quietly into the circle after a while and sat down beside her son-in-law—a slight woman, whose face was entirely concealed. When the performance had been going on for about an hour four more priests appeared and took seats in the background. When I asked my guardian their object, he replied, sarcastically, that it was money, that they were present as witnesses, and each of them would expect a big fee as well as a good supper.

"Poor people get married with one priest," he added, "but rich people have to have many. It costs a lot of money to get married."

Every now and then parcels were brought in by servants, and handed to the bride, who opened them with the same eagerness that American girls show about their wedding presents, but before she had been given half a chance to examine them they were snatched away from her and passed around. There were enough jewels to set the groom up in business, for all the relatives on both sides are rich, several beautifully embroidered shawls, a copy of Tennyson's poems, a full set of Ruskin's works, a flexible covered Bible from the bride's school teacher, and other gifts too numerous to mention. The ceremony soon became tedious and the crowded room was hot and stuffy. It was an ordeal for us to stay as long as we did, and we endured it for a couple of hours, but it was ten times worse for the bride and groom, for they had to sit on the floor over the fire, and couldn't even stretch their legs. They told us that it would take four hours more to finish the ritual. So we asked our hosts to excuse us, offered our sympathy and congratulations to the happy couple, who laughed and joked with us in English, while the priests continued to sing and pray.

VI

THE RELIGIONS OF INDIA

The most interesting of all the many religious sects in India are the Parsees, the residue of one of the world's greatest creeds, descendants of the disciples of Zoroaster, and the Persian fire worshipers, who sought refuge in India from the persecution of the all-conquering Mohammedans about the seventh century. They have not increased and probably have diminished in numbers, but have retained the faith of their fathers undefiled, which has been described as "the most sublime expression of religious purity and thought except the teachings of Christ." It is a curious fact, however, that although the Parsees are commercially the most enterprising people in India, and the most highly educated, they have never attempted to propagate or even to make known their faith to the world. It remained for Anquetil Duperron, a young Frenchman, a Persian scholar, to translate the Zend Avesta, which contains the teachings of Zoroaster, and may be called the Parsee bible. And even now the highest authority in Parsee theology and literature is Professor Jackson, who holds the chair of oriental languages in Columbia University, New York. At this writing Professor Jackson is in Persia engaged upon investigations of direct interest to the Parsees, who have the highest regard and affection for him, and perfect confidence in the accuracy of his treatment of their theology in which they permit him to instruct them.

The Parsees have undoubtedly made more stir in the world in proportion to their population than any other race. They are a small community, and number only 94,000 altogether, of whom 76,000 reside in Bombay. They are almost without exception industrious and prosperous, nearly all being engaged in trade and manufacturing, and to them the city of Bombay owes the greatest part of its wealth and commercial influence.

While the Parsees teach pure and lofty morality, and are famous for their integrity, benevolence, good thoughts, good works and good deeds, their method of disposing of their dead is revolting. For, stripped of every thread of clothing, the bodies of their nearest and dearest are exposed to dozens of hungry vultures, which quickly tear the flesh from the bones.

In a beautiful grove upon the top of a hill overlooking the city of Bombay and the sea, surrounded by a high, ugly wall, are the so-called Towers of Silence, upon which these hideous birds can always be seen, waiting for their feast. They roost upon palm trees in the neighborhood, and, often in their flight, drop pieces of human flesh from their beaks or their talons, which lie rotting in the fields below. An English lady driving past the Towers of Silence was naturally horrified when the finger of a dead man was dropped into her carriage by one of those awful birds; and an army officer told me, that he once picked up by the roadside the forearm and hand of a woman which had been torn from a body only a few hours dead and had evidently fallen during a fight between the birds. The reservoir which stores the water supply of Bombay is situated upon the same hill, not more than half a mile distant, and for obvious reasons had been covered with a roof. Some years ago the municipal authorities, having had their attention called to possible pollution of the water, notified the Parsees that the Towers of Silence would have to be removed to a distance from the city, but the rich members of that faith preferred to pay the expense of roofing over the reservoir to abandoning what to them is not only sacred but precious ground. The human mind can adjust itself to almost any conditions and associations, and a cultured Parsee will endeavor to convince you by clever arguments that their method is not only humane and natural, but the best sanitary method ever devised of disposing of the dead.

Funeral ceremonies are held at the residence of the dead; prayers are offered and eulogies are pronounced. Then a procession is formed and the hearse is preceded by priests and followed by the male members of the family and by friends. The body is not placed in a coffin, but is covered with rich shawls and vestments. When the gateway of the outer temple is reached, priests who are permanently attached to the Towers of Silence and reside within the inclosure, meet the procession and take charge of the body, which is first carried to a temple, where prayers are offered, and a sacred fire, kept continually burning there, is replenished. While the friends and mourners are engaged in worship, Nasr Salars, as the attendants are called, take the bier to the ante-room of one of the towers. There are five, of circular shape, with walls forty feet high, perfectly plain, and whitewashed. The largest is 276 feet in circumference and cost $150,000. The entrance is about fifteen or twenty feet from the ground and is reached by a flight of steps. The inside plan of the building resembles a circular gridiron gradually depressed toward the center, at which there is a pit, five feet in diameter. From this pit cement walks radiate like the spokes of a wheel, and between them are three series of compartments extending around the entire tower. Those nearest the center are about four feet long, two feet wide and six inches deep. The next series are a little larger, and the third, larger still, and they are intended respectively for men, women and children.

When the bearers have brought the body into the anteroom of the tower they strip it entirely of its clothing. Valuable coverings are carefully laid away and sent to the chamber of purification, where they are thoroughly fumigated, and afterward returned to the friends. The cotton wrappings are burned. The body is laid in one of the compartments entirely naked, and in half an hour the flesh is completely stripped from the bones by voracious birds that have been eagerly watching the proceedings from the tops of the tall palms that overlook the cemetery. There are about two hundred vultures around the place; most of them are old birds and are thoroughly educated. They know exactly what to expect, and behave with greatest decorum. They never enter the tower until the bearers have left it, and usually are as deliberate and solemn in their movements as a lot of undertakers. But sometimes, when they are particularly hungry, their greed gets the better of their dignity and they quarrel and fight over their prey.

After the bones are stripped they are allowed to lie in the sun and bleach and decay until the compartment they occupy is needed for another body, when the Nasr Salars enter with gloves and tongs and cast them into the central pit, where they finally crumble into dust. The floor of the tower is so arranged that all the rain that falls upon it passes into the pit, and the moisture promotes decomposition. The bottom of the pit is perforated and the water impregnated with the dust from the bones is filtered through charcoal and becomes thoroughly disinfected before it is allowed to pass through a sewer into the bay. The pits are the receptacles of the dust of generations, and I am told that so much of it is drained off by the rainfall, as described, that they have never been filled. The carriers are not allowed to leave the grounds, and when a man engages in that occupation he must retire forever from the world, as much as if he were a Trappist monk. Nor can he communicate with anyone except the priests who have charge of the temple.

The grounds are beautifully laid out. No money or labor has been spared to make them attractive, and comfortable benches have been placed along the walks where relatives and friends may sit and converse or meditate after the ceremonies are concluded. The Parsees are firm believers in the resurrection, and they expect their mutilated bodies to rise again glorified and incorruptible. The theory upon which their peculiar custom is based is veneration for the elements. Fire is the chief object of their worship, and they cannot allow it to be polluted by burning the dead; water is almost as sacred, and the soil of the earth is the source of their food, their strength and almost everything that is beautiful. Furthermore, they believe in the equality of all creatures before God, and hence the dust of the rich and the poor mingles in the pit.

Parsee temples are very plain and the form of worship is extremely simple. None but members of the faith are admitted. The interior of the temple is almost empty, except for a reading desk occupied by the priest. The walls are without the slightest decoration and are usually whitewashed. The sacred fire, the emblem of spiritual life, which is never extinguished, is kept in a small recess in a golden receptacle, and is attended by priests without interruption. They relieve each other every two hours, but the fire is never left alone.

The Mohammedans have many mosques in Bombay, but none of them is of particular interest. The Hindu or Brahmin temples are also commonplace, with two exceptions. One of them, known as the Monkey Temple, is covered with carved images of monkeys and other animals. There are said to be 300 of them, measuring from six inches to two feet in height. The other is the "Walkeshwar," dedicated to the "Sand Lord" occupying a point upon the shore of the bay not far from the water. It has been a holy place for many centuries. The legend says that not long after the creation of the world Rama, one of the most powerful of the gods, while on his way to Ceylon to recover Stia, his bride, who had been kidnaped, halted and camped there for a night and went through various experiences which make a long and tedious story, but of profound interest to Hindu theologians and students of mythology. The temple is about 150 years old, but does not compare with those in other cities of India. It is surrounded by various buildings for the residence of the Brahmins, lodging places for pilgrims and devotees, which are considered excellent examples of Hindu architecture. Several wealthy families have cottages on the grounds which they occupy for a few days each year on festival occasions or as retreats.

Upon the land side of the boulevard which skirts the shore of the bay, not far from the university of Bombay, is the burning ghat of the Hindus, where the bodies of their dead are cremated in the open air and in a remark-

BODY READY FOR THE FUNERAL PYRE—BOMBAY BURNING GHATS

ably rude and indifferent manner. The proceedings may be witnessed by any person who takes the trouble to visit the place and has the patience to wait for the arrival of a body. It is just as public as a burial in any cemetery in the United States. Bodies are kept only a few hours after death. Those who die at night are burned the first thing in the morning, so that curious people are usually gratified if they visit the place early. Immediately after a poor Hindu sufferer breathes his last the family retire and professional undertakers are brought in. The latter bathe the body carefully, dress it in plain white cotton cloth, wrap it in a sheet, with the head carefully concealed, place it upon a rude bier made of two bamboo poles and cross pieces, with a net work of ropes between, and four men, with the ends of the poles on their shoulders, start for the burning ghat at a dog trot, singing a mournful song. Sometimes they are followed by the sons or the brothers of the deceased, who remain through the burning to see that it is properly done, but more often that duty is entrusted to an employe or a servant or some humble friend of the family in whom they have confidence. Arriving at the burning ghat, negotiations are opened with the superintendent or manager, for they are usually private enterprises or belong to corporations and are conducted very much like our cemeteries. The cheapest sort of fire that can be provided costs two rupees, which is sixty-six cents in American money, and prices range from that amount upwards according to the caste and the wealth of the family. When a rich man's body is burned sandal-wood and other scented fuel is used and sometimes the fire is very expensive. After an agreement is reached coolies employed on the place make a pile of wood, one layer pointing one way and the next crossed at right angles, a hole left in the center being filled with kindling and quick-burning reeds. The body is lifted from the bier and placed upon it, then more wood is piled on and the kindling is lit with a torch. If there is plenty of dry fuel the corpse is reduced to ashes in about two hours. Usually the ashes are claimed by friends, who take them to the nearest temple and after prayers and other ceremonies cast them into the waters of the bay.

The death rate in Bombay is very large. The bubonic plague prevails there with a frightful mortality. Hence cremation is safer than burial. In the province of Bombay the total deaths from all diseases average about 600,000 a year, and you can calculate what an enormous area would be required for cemeteries. In 1900, on account of the famine, the deaths ran up to 1,318,783, and in 1902 they were more than 800,000. Of these 128,259 were from the plague, 13,600 from cholera, 5,340 from smallpox, and 2,212 from other contagious diseases. Hence the burning ghats were very useful, for at least 80 percent of the dead were Brahmins and their bodies were disposed of in that way.

It is difficult to give an accurate idea of Brahminism in a brief manner, but theoretically it is based upon the principles set forth in a series of sacred books known as the Vedas, written about 4,000 years ago. Its gods were originally physical forces and phenomena—nature worship,—which was once common to all men, the sun, fire, water, light, wind, the procreative and productive energies and the mystery of sex and birth, which impressed with wonder and awe the mind of primitive humanity. As these deities became more and more vague and indefinite in the popular mind, and the simple, instinctive appeal of the human soul to a Power it could not see or comprehend was gradually debased into what is now known as Brahminism, and the most repugnant, revolting, cruel, obscene and vicious rites ever practiced by savages or barbarians. There is nothing in the Vedas to justify the cruelties of the Hindu gods and the practices of the priests. They do not authorize animal worship, caste, child-marriage, the burning of widows or perpetual widowhood, but the Brahmins have built up a stupendous system of superstition, of which they alone pretend to know the mystic meaning, and their supremacy is established. Thus the nature worship of the Vedas has disappeared and has given place to terrorism, demon worship, obscenity, and idolatry.

The three great gods of the Hindus are Siva, Vishnu and Brahma, with innumerable minor deities, some 30,000,000 altogether, which have been created during emergencies from time to time by worshipers of vivid imaginations. When we speak of Hinduism or Brahminism as a religion, however, it is only a conventional use of a term, because it is not a religion in the sense that we are accustomed to apply that word. In all other creeds there is an element of ethics; morality, purity, justice and faith in men, but none of these qualities is taught by the Brahmins. With them the fear of unseen powers and the desire to obtain their favor is the only rule of life and the only maxim taught to the people. And it is the foundation upon which the influence and power of the Brahmins depend. The world and all its inhabitants are at the mercy of cruel, fickle and unjust gods; the gods are under the influence of the Brahmins; hence the Brahmins are holy men and must be treated accordingly. No Hindu will offend a Brahmin under any circumstances, lest his curse may call down all forms of misfortune. A Hindu proverb says:

"What is in the Brahmin's books, that is in the Brahmin's heart. Neither you nor I knew there was so much evil in the world."

The power of the priests or Brahmins over the Hindus is one of the phenomena of India. I do not know where you can get a better idea of their influence and of the reverence that is paid to them than in "Kim," Rudyard Kipling's story of an Irish boy who was a disciple of an old Thibetan lama or Buddhist monk. That story is appreciated much more keenly by people who have lived or traveled in India, because it appeals to them. There is a familiar picture on every page, and it is particularly valuable as illustrating the relations between the Brahmins and the people. "These priests are invested," said one of the ablest writers on Indian affairs, "with a reverence which no extreme of abject poverty, no infamy of private conduct can impair, and which is beyond anything that a mind not immediately conversant with the fact can conceive. They are invariably addressed with titles of divinity, and are paid the highest earthly honors. The oldest and highest members of other castes implore the blessing of the youngest and poorest of theirs; they are the chosen recipients of all charities, and are allowed a license in their private relations which would be resented as a deadly injury in any but themselves."

This reverence is largely due to superstitions which the Brahmins do their best to cultivate and encourage. There are 30,000,000 gods in the Hindu pantheon, and each attends to the affairs of his own particular jurisdiction. Most of them are wicked, cruel and unkind, and delight in bringing misfortunes upon their devotees, which can only be averted by the intercession of a priest. Gods and demons haunt every hill and grove and gorge and dark corner. Their names are usually unknown, but they go on multiplying as events or incidents occur to which the priests can give a supernatural interpretation. These gods are extremely sensitive to disrespect or neglect, and unless they are constantly propitiated they will bring all sorts of disasters. The Brahmin is the only man who knows how to make them good-natured. He can handle them exactly as he likes, and they will obey his will. Hence the superstitious peasants yield everything, their money, their virtue, their lives, as compensation for the intercession of the priests in their behalf.

The census of 1901 returned 2,728,812 priests, which is an average of one for every seventy-two members of the Hindu faith, and it is believed that, altogether, there are more than 9,000,000 persons including monks, nuns, ascetics, fakirs, sorcerers, chelas, and mendicants or various kinds and attendants employed about the temples who are dependent upon the public for support. A large part of the income of the pious Hindu is devoted to the support of priests and the feeding of pilgrims. Wherever you see it, wherever you meet it, and especially when you come in contact with it as a sightseer, Brahminism excites nothing but pity, indignation and abhorrence.

Buddhism is very different, although Buddha lived and died a Hindu, and the members of that sect still claim that he was the greatest, the wisest and the best of all Brahmins. No two religions are so contradictory and incompatible as that taught by Buddha and the modern teachings of the Brahmins. The underlying principles of Buddha's faith are love, charity, self-sacrifice, unselfishness, universal brotherhood and spiritual and physical purity. He believed in none of the present practices of the Hindu priests. There is a striking resemblance between the teachings of Buddha and the teachings of Christ. Passages in the New Testament, reporting the words of the Savior, seem like plagiarisms from the maxims of Buddha, and, indeed, Buddhist scholars tell of a myth concerning a young Jew who about five centuries after Buddha, and twenty centuries ago, came from Syria with a caravan and spent several years under instruction in a Buddhist monastery in Thibet. Thus they account for the silence of the scriptures concerning the doings of Christ between the ages of 12 and 20, and for the similarity between his sermons and those preached by the founder of their religion. Buddha taught that good actions bring happiness and bad actions misery; that selfishness is the cause of sin, sorrow and suffering, and that the abolition of self, sacrifices for others and the suppression of passions and desires is the only true plan of salvation. He died 543 years before Jesus was born, and within the next two centuries his teachings were accepted by two-thirds of the people of India, but by the tenth century of our era they had been forgotten, and a great transformation had taken place among the Indo-Ayran races, who began to worship demons instead of angels and teach fear instead of hope, until now there are practically no Buddhists in India with the exception of the Burmese, who are almost unanimous in the confession of that faith. It is a singular phenomenon that Buddhism should so disappear from the land of its birth, although 450,000,000 of the human race still turn to its founder with pure affection as the wisest of teachers and the noblest of ideals.

The teachings of Buddha survive in a sect known as

the Jains, founded by Jina, or Mahavira, a Buddhist priest, about a thousand years ago, as a protest against the cruel encroachments of the Hindus. Jina was a Perfect One, who subdued all worldly desires; who lived an unselfish life, practiced the golden rule, harmed no living thing, and attained the highest aim of the soul, right knowledge, right conduct, temperance, sobriety, chastity and a Holy Calm.

There are now 1,334,148 Jains in India, and among them are the wealthiest, most highly cultured and most charitable of all people. They carry their love of life to extremes. A true believer will not harm an insect, not even a mosquito or a flea. All Hindus are kind to animals, except when they ill treat them through ignorance, as is often the case. The Brahmins represent that murder, robbery, deception and every other form of crime and vice may be committed in the worship of their gods. They teach that the gods themselves are guilty of the most hideous depravity, and that the sacrifice of wives, children, brothers, sisters and friends to convenience or expediency for selfish ends is justifiable. Indeed, the British government has been compelled to interfere and prohibit the sacrifice of human life to propitiate the Hindu gods. It has suppressed the thugs, who, as you have read, formerly went about the country killing people in order to acquire holiness; it has prohibited the awful processions of the car of Juggernaut, before which hysterical fanatics used to throw their own bodies, and the bodies of their children, to be crushed under the iron wheels, in the hope of pleasing some monster among their deities. The suppression of infanticide, which is still encouraged by the Brahmins, is now receiving the vigilant attention of the authorities.

Every effort has been made during the last fifty years to prevent the awful cruelties to human beings that formerly were common in Hindu worship, but no police intervention has ever been necessary to protect dumb animals; nobody was ever punished for cruelty to them; on the contrary, animal worship is one of the most general of practices among the Hindus, and many beasts and reptiles are sacred. But the Jains go still further and establish hospitals for aged and infirm animals. You can see them in Bombay, in Delhi, Lucknow, Calcutta and other places where the Jains are strong. Behind their walls may be found hundreds of decrepit horses, diseased cows and bullocks, many dogs and cats and every kind of sick, lame and infirm beast. Absurd stories are told strangers concerning the extremes to which this benevolence is carried, and some of them have actually appeared in published narratives of travel in India. One popular story is that when a flea lights upon the body of a Jain he captures it carefully, puts it in a receptacle and sends it to an asylum where fat coolies are hired to sit around all day and night and allow fleas, mosquitoes and other insects to feed upon them. But although untrue, these ridiculous stories are valuable as illustrating the principles in which the Jains believe. They are strict vegetarians. The true believers will not kill an animal or a fish or a bird, or anything that breathes, for any purpose, and everybody can see that they strictly practice what they preach.

His most gracious majesty, King of Great Britain and Ireland and Emperor of India, has more Mohammedan subjects than the Great Turk or any other ruler. They numbered 62,458,061 at the last census. They are a clean, manly, honorable and industrious portion of the population. Commercially they do not rank as high as the Parsees, who number only 94,190, or the Jains, who number 1,334,148, but are vastly superior to the Hindus from any point of view. They are not so ignorant nor so filthy nor so superstitious nor so submissive to their priests. They are self-respecting and independent, and while the believers in no other creed are more scrupulous in the performance of their religious duties, they are not in any measure under the control or the dictation of their mullahs. They have their own schools, called kuttebs, they take care of their own poor very largely; drunkenness and gambling are very rare among them. They are hospitable, kind to animals and generous. The difference between the Mohammedans and the Hindus may be seen in the most forcible manner in their temples. It is an old saying that while one god created all men, each man creates his own god, and that is strikingly true among the ignorant, superstitious people of the East. The Hindu crouches in a shadow to escape the attention of his god, while the Mohammedan publicly prays to his five times a day in the nearest mosque, and if no mosque is near he kneels where he stands, and takes full satisfaction in a religion of hope instead of fear.

From the political standpoint the Mohammedans are a very important factor in the situation in India. They are more independent than the Hindus; they occupy a more influential position than their numbers entitle them to; they have most profound pride in their religion and race, and in their social and intellectual superiority, and the more highly they are educated the more manly, self-reliant and independent they become, and the feeling between the Mohammedans and the Hindus is bitterly hostile. So much so as to make them a bulwark of the government. Several authorities told me that Mohammedans make the best officials in the service and can be trusted farther than any other class, but, speaking generally, Islam has been corrupted and debased in India just as it has been everywhere else.

One of the results of this corruption is the sect known as Sikhs, which numbers about 2,195,268. It thrives best in the northern part of India, and furnishes the most reliable policemen and the best soldiers for the native army. The Sikhs retain much that is good among the teachings of Mohammed, but have a bible of their own, called the Abi-granth, made up of the sermons of Nanak, the founder of the sect, who died in the year 1530. It is full of excellent moral precepts; it teaches the brotherhood of man, the equality of the sexes; it rejects caste, and embraces all of the good points in Buddhism, with a pantheism that is very confusing. It would seem that the Sikhs worship all gods who are good to men, and reject the demonology of the Hindus. They believe in one Supreme Being, with attributes similar to the Allah of the Mohammedans, and recognize Mohammed as his prophet and exponent of his will. They have also adopted several Hindu deities in a sort of indirect way, although the Sikhs strictly prohibit idolatry. Their worship is pure and simple. Their temples are houses of prayer, where they, meet, sing hymns, repeat a ritual and receive pieces of "karah prasad," a consecrated pastry, which means "the effectual offering." They are tolerant, and not only admit strangers to their worship, but invite them to participate in their communion.

The morning we arrived in Agra we swallowed a hasty breakfast and hurried off to the great mosque to witness the ceremonies of what might be termed the Mohammedan Easter, although the anniversary has an entirely different significance. The month of Ramadan is spent by the faithful followers of the Prophet in a long fast, and the night before it is broken, called Lailatul-Kadr, or "night of power," is celebrated in rejoicing, because it is the night on which the Koran is supposed to have come down from heaven. In the morning following, which is as much a day of rejoicing as our Christmas, the men of Islam gather at the mosques and engage in a service of thanksgiving to Allah for the blessings they and their families have enjoyed during the year past, and pray for a repetition of the same mercies for the year to come. This festival is called the "Idu l-Fitr," and we were fortunate enough to witness one of the most impressive spectacles I have ever seen. Women never appear, but the entire male population, with their children assembled at the great park which surrounds the mosque, clad in festival attire, each bringing a prayer rug to spread upon the ground. About ten thousand persons of all ages and all classes came on foot and in all sorts of vehicles, with joyous voices and congratulations to each other that seemed hearty enough to include the whole world. Taking advantage of their good humor and the thankful spirits hundreds of beggars were squatting along the roadside and appealing to every passerby in pitiful tones. And nearly every one responded. Some people brought bags of rice, beans and wheat; others brought cakes and bread, but the greater number invested in little sea shells which are used in the interior of India as currency, and one hundred of them are worth a penny.

Rich people filled their pockets with these shells and scattered them by handsful among the crowd, and the shrieking beggars scrambled for them on the ground. There were long lines of food peddlers, with portable stoves, and tables upon which were spread morsels which the natives of India considered delicacies, but they were not very tempting to us. The food peddlers drove a profitable trade because almost every person present had been fasting for a lunar month and had a sharp appetite to satisfy. After the services the rich and the poor ate together, masters and servants, because Mohammed knew no caste, and it was an interesting sight to see the democratic spirit of the worshipers, for the rich and the poor, the master and the servant, knelt down side by side upon the same rug or strip of matting and bowed their heads to the ground in homage of the God that made them all. Families came together in carriages, bullock carts, on the backs of camels, horses, mules, donkeys, all the male members of the household from the baby to the grandfather, and were attended by all men servants of the family or the farm. They washed together at the basins where the fountains were spouting more joyously than usual, and then moved forward, laughing and chattering, toward the great mosque, selected places which seemed most convenient, spread their rugs, matting, blankets and sheets upon the ground, sat in long rows facing Mecca, and gossiped cheerfully together until the great high priest, surrounded by mullahs or lower priests, appeared in front of the Midrab, the place in every mosque from which the Koran is read, and shouted for attention.

Ram Zon, one of our "bearers," who is a Mohammedan, disappeared without permission or notice early in the morning, and did not report for duty that day. His piety was greater than his sense of obligation to his employers, and I saw him in the crowd earnestly going through the violent exercise which attends the worship of Islam.

MOHAMMEDANS AT PRAYER

When the hour for commencing the ceremony drew near the entire courtyard, several acres in extent, was covered with worshipers arranged in rows about eight feet apart from north to south, all facing the west, with their eyes toward Mecca in expectant attitudes. The sheikh has a powerful voice, and by long experience has acquired the faculty of throwing it a long distance, and, as he intoned the service, mullahs were stationed at different points to repeat his words so that everybody could hear. The first sound was a long wailing cry like the call of the muezzeins from the minarets at the hour of prayer. It was for the purpose of concentrating the attention of the vast audience which arose to its feet and stood motionless with hands clasped across their breasts. Then, as the reading proceeded, the great crowd, in perfect unison, as if it had practiced daily for months, performed the same motions one after the other. It was a remarkable exhibition of precision. No army of well drilled troops could have done better.

The following were the motions, each in response to the intonation of a prayer by the high priest:

1. Both hands to forehead, palms and fingers together, in the attitude of prayer.

2. Bend body forward at right angles, three times in succession, keeping hands in the same position.

3. Return to upright position, with hands lowered to the breast.

4. Bow head three times to the ground.

5. Rise and stand motionless with hands at sides.

6. Hands lifted to ears and returned to side, motions three times repeated.

7. Body at right angles again, with hands clasped at forehead.

8. Body erect, kneel and bow forward, touching the forehead three times to the earth.

9. Fall back upon knees and with folded hands.

10. Rise, stand at attention with clasped hands until the cry of the mullah announced that the ceremony was over; whereupon everybody turned to embrace his family and friends in a most affectionate manner, again and again. Some were crying, some were laughing, and all seemed to be in a state of suppressed excitement. Their emotions had been deeply stirred, and long fasting is apt to produce hysteria.

The boom of a cannon in a neighboring fortress, was a signal that the obligations of Ramadan had been fulfilled, that the fast was broken, and thousands of people rushed pell-mell to the eating stands to gorge themselves with sweetmeats and other food. The more dignified and aristocratic portion of the crowd calmly sat down again upon their rugs and mats and watched their servants unload baskets of provisions upon tablecloths, napkins and trays which they spread upon the ground. Not less than seven or eight thousand persons indulged in this picnic, but there was no wine or beer; nothing stronger than tea or coffee, because the Koran forbids it. And after their feast at the mosque the rest of the day was spent in rejoicing. Gay banners of all colors were displayed from the windows of Mohammedan houses, festoons of flowers were hung over the doors, and from the windowsills; boys were seen rushing through the streets loaded with bouquets sent from friend to friend with compliments and congratulations; firecrackers were exploded in the gardens and parks, and during the evening displays of fireworks were made to entertain the Moslem population, who were assembled in each other's houses or at their favorite cafes, or were promenading the streets, singing and shouting and behaving very much as our people do on the Fourth of July.

VII

HOW INDIA IS GOVERNED

The present form of government in India was adopted in 1858, after the terrible Sepoy mutiny had demonstrated the inability of the East India Company to control affairs. By an act of parliament all territory, revenues, tributes and property of that great corporation, which had a monopoly of the Indian trade, and, next to the Hanseatic League of Germany, was the greatest Trust ever formed, were vested in the Queen of Great Britain and Ireland, who in 1876 assumed the additional title of Empress of India. The title and authority were inherited by Edward VII. He governs through the Secretary of State for India, who is a Cabinet minister, and a Council of not less than ten members, nine of whom must have the practical knowledge and experience gained by a residence of at least ten years in India and not more than ten years previous to the date of their appointment. This Council is more of an advisory than an executive body. It has no initiative or authority, but is expected to confer with and review the acts of the Secretary of State for India, who can make no grants or appropriations from the revenues or decide any questions of importance without the concurrence of a majority of its members. The Council meets every week in London, receives reports and communications and acts upon them.

The supreme authority in India is the Viceroy, the

direct personal representative of the emperor in all his relations with his 300,000,000 Indian subjects; but, as a matter of convenience, he makes his reports to and receives his instructions from the Secretary of State for India, who represents that part of the empire both in the ministry and in parliament. The present viceroy is the Right Honorable George Nathaniel Curzon, who was raised to the peerage in October, 1898, as Baron Curzon of Kedleston. He is the eldest son of Lord Scarsdale, was born Jan. 11, 1859, was educated at Eton and Oxford; selected journalism as his profession; became correspondent of the London Times in China, India and Persia; was elected to parliament from Lancashire in 1886, and served until 1898; was private secretary to the Marquis of Salisbury, and under-secretary of state for India in 1891-92; under-secretary of state for foreign affairs in 1895-98; married Mary Leiter, daughter of Mr. L. Z. Leiter of Washington and Chicago, in 1895, and was appointed viceroy of India to succeed the Earl of Elgin, September, 1898.

There have been twenty-five viceroys or governors general of India since Warren Hastings in 1774, and the list includes some of the ablest statesmen in English history, but Lord Curzon is the only man in the list who has ever been his own successor. When his first term expired in September, 1903, he was immediately reappointed for another five years. Whether he continues through the second term depends upon certain contingencies, but it is entirely probable that he will remain, because he has undertaken certain reforms and enterprises that he desires to complete. His administration has been not only a conspicuous but a remarkable success. Although he has been severely criticised for his administrative policy and many of his official acts have been opposed and condemned, the sources from which the criticisms have come often corroborate the wisdom and confirm the success of the acts complained of. Lord Cornwallis was twice Governor General of India, but there was a long interval between his terms, the first beginning in 1786 and the second in 1805. He is the only man except Lord Curzon who has been twice honored by appointment to the highest office and the greatest responsibility under the British crown except that of the prime minister.

The Viceroy is assisted in the administration of the government by a cabinet or council of five members, selected by himself, subject to the approval of the king. Each member is assigned to the supervision of one of the executive departments,—finance, military, public works, revenue, agriculture and legislative. The viceroy himself takes personal charge of foreign affairs. The commander in chief of the army in India, at present Lord Kitchener, is ex-officio member of the council.

For legislative purposes the council is expanded by the addition of ten members, appointed by the Viceroy from among the most competent British and native residents of India upon the recommendation of provincial, industrial and commercial bodies. The remaining members are the heads of the various executive departments of the government. By these men, who serve for a period of five years, and whose proceedings are open to the public and are reported and printed verbatim, like the proceedings of Congress, the laws governing India are made, subject to the approval of the Viceroy, who retains the right of veto, and in turn is responsible to the British parliament and to the king.

Thus it will be seen that the system of government in

India is simple and liberal. The various industries and financial interests, and all of the great provinces which make up the empire, have a voice in framing the laws that apply to the people at large; but for convenience the territory is divided into nine great provinces, as follows:

Madras, with a governor whose salary is $40,000 a year.

Bombay, whose governor receives the same salary.

Bengal, with a lieutenant governor; salary, $33,000.

United Provinces, lieutenant governor; salary, $33,000.

Punjab, lieutenant governor; salary, $33,000.

Burma, lieutenant governor; salary, $33,000.

Assam, chief commissioner; salary, $16,500.

Central Provinces, chief commissioner, $16,500.

Northwestern Frontier Province, governed by an agent to the governor general, whose salary is $16,500.

The governors of Bombay and Madras are appointed by the king; the lieutenant governors and commissioners by the Viceroy. All of them have legislative councils and complete executive organizations similar to that of the general government at Calcutta. Each makes its own local laws and enjoys administrative independence similar to that of the states of the American Union, and is seldom interfered with by the Viceroy or the authorities in London, the purpose being to encourage home rule as far as possible. The provinces are divided into districts, which are the units of administration, and each district is under the control of an executive officer, who is responsible to the governor of the province.

Exclusive of the great provinces named are eighty-two of the ancient principalities, most of them retaining their original boundaries, governed by native chiefs, who are allowed more or less independence, according to their ability, wisdom and zeal. The control exercised by the central government varies in the different states, but there are certain general rules which are applied to all. The native princes have no right to make war or peace, or communicate officially with each other or with foreign governments except through the Viceroy. They are permitted to maintain a limited independent military force; they are allowed to impose a certain amount of taxes; no European is allowed to reside at their courts without their consent, but commerce, trade, industry, education, religious worship, the press and other rights and privileges are free to all just as much as in England or the United States. The native chiefs are not permitted to interfere with the judiciary, which has a separate and independent organization, as in Great Britain, with the Viceroy and the council of state corresponding to the House of Lords, as the highest court of appeal. Each native chief is "assisted" in his government by a "Resident," who is appointed by and reports to the Viceroy, and is expected to guide the policy and official acts of the native ruler with tact and delicacy. He remains in the background as much as possible, assumes no authority and exercises no prerogatives, but serves as a sort of ambassador from the Viceroy and friendly adviser to the native prince.

The following is a list of the ruling native princes in the order of their rank as recognized by the British government, and the salutes to which they are entitled:

Salute of twenty-one guns—
- Baroda, the Maharaja (Gaikwar) of.
- Hyderabad, the Nizam of.
- Mysore, the Maharaja of.

Salute of nineteen guns—
- Bhopal, the Begam (or Newab) of.
- Gwalior, the Maharaja (Singhai) of.
- Indore, the Maharaja (Holkar) of.
- Jammu and Kashmire, the Maharaja of.
- Kalat, the Khan of.
- Kolhapur, the Maharaja of.
- Mewar (Udaipur), the Maharaja of.
- Travancore, the Maharaja of.

Salute of seventeen guns—
- Bahawalpur, the Nawab of.
- Bharatpur, the Maharaja of.
- Bikanir, the Maharaja of.
- Bundi, the Maharao Raja of.
- Cochin, the Raja of.
- Cutch, the Rao of.
- Jeypore, the Maharaja of.
- Karauli, the Maharaja of.
- Kota, the Maharao of.
- Marwar (Jodhpur), the Maharaja of.
- Patiala, the Maharaja of.
- Rewa, the Maharaja of.
- Tonk, the Newab of.

Salute of fifteen guns—
- Alwar, the Maharaja of.
- Banswara, the Maharawal of.
- Datia, the Maharaja of.
- Dewas (senior branch), the Raja of.
- Dewas (junior branch), the Raja of.
- Dhar, the Raja of.
- Dholpur, the Maharaja Rana of.
- Dungarpur, the Maharawal of.

Idar, the Maharaja of.
Jaisalmir, the Maharawal of.
Khairpur, the Mir of.
Kishangarh, the Maharaja of.
Orchha, the Maharaja of.
Partabgarth, the Marharawat of.
Sikkam, the Maharaja of.
Sirohi, the Maharao of.

Salute of thirteen guns—
Benares, the Raja of.
Cooch Behar, the Maharaja of.
Jaora, the Nawab of.
Rampur, the Newab of.
Tippera, the Raja of.

Salute of eleven guns—
Agaigarh, the Maharaja of.
Baoni, the Newab of.
Bhaunagar, the Thakur Sahib of.
Bijawar, the Maharaja of.
Cambay, the Nawab of.
Chamba, the Raja of.
Charkhari, the Maharaja of.
Chhatarpur, the Raja of.
Faridkot, the Raja of.
Gondal, the Thakur Sahib of.
Janjira, the Newab of.
Jhabua, the Raja of.
Jahllawar, the Raj-Rana of.
Jind, the Raja of.
Gunagarth, the Newab of.
Kahlur, the Rajah of.
Kapurthala, the Raja of.

Mandi, the Raja of.
Manipur, the Raja of.
Morvi, the Thakur Sahib of.
Nabha, the Raja of.
Narsingarh, the Raja of.
Nawanagar, the Jam of.
Palanpur, the Diwan of.
Panna, the Maharaja of.
Porbandar, the Rana of.
Pudukota, the Raja of.
Radhanpur, the Newab of.
Rajgarth, the Raja of.
Rajpipla, the Raja of.
Ratlam, the Raja of.
Sailana, the Raja of.
Samthar, the Raja of.
Sirmur (Nahan), the Raja of.
Sitamau, the Raja of.
Suket, the Raja of.
Tehri (Garhwal), the Raja of.

The Viceroy has a veto over the acts of the native princes as he has over those of the provincial governors, and can depose them at will, but such heroic measures are not adopted except in extreme cases of bad behavior or misgovernment. Lord Curzon has deposed two rajahs during the five years he has been Viceroy, but his general policy has been to stimulate their ambitions, to induce them to adopt modern ideas and methods and to educate their people.

Within the districts are municipalities which have local magistrates and councils, commissioners, district and local boards and other bodies for various purposes similar to those of our county and city organizations. The elective franchise is being extended in more or less degree, according to circumstances, all over India, suffrage being conferred upon taxpayers only. The municipal boards have care of the roads, water supply, sewerage, sanitation, public lighting, markets, schools, hospitals and other institutions and enterprises of public utility. They impose taxes, collect revenues and expend them subject to the approval of the provincial governments. In all of the large cities a number of Englishmen and other foreigners are members of boards and committees and take an active part in local administration, but in the smaller towns and villages the government is left entirely to natives, who often show conspicuous capacity.

The policy of Lord Curzon has been to extend home rule and self-government as rapidly and as far as circumstances will justify. The population of India is a dense, inert, ignorant, depraved and superstitious mass of beings whose actions are almost entirely controlled by signs and omens, and by the dictation of the Brahmin priests. They are therefore not to be trusted with the control of their own affairs, but there is a gradual and perceptible improvement in their condition, which is encouraged by the authorities in every possible way. And as fast as they show themselves competent they are trusted with the responsibility of the welfare of themselves and their neighbors. The habitual attitude of the Hindu is crouching upon the ground. The British government is trying to raise him to a standing posture, to make him a man instead of the slave of his superstitions.

No one can visit India, no one can read its history or study its statistics, without admitting the success and recognizing the blessings of British occupation. The government has had its ups and downs. There have been terrible blunders and criminal mistakes, which we are in danger of repeating in the Philippine Islands, but the record of British rule during the last half-century—since the Sepoy mutiny, which taught a valuable lesson at an awful cost—has been an almost uninterrupted and unbroken chapter of peace, progress and good government. Until then the whole of India never submitted to a single ruler. For nearly a thousand years it was a perpetual battlefield, and not since the invasion of Alexander the Great have the people enjoyed such liberty or tranquillity as they do today. Three-eighths of the country still remains under the authority of hereditary native rulers with various degrees of independence. Foreigners have very little conception of the extent and the power of the native government. We have an indefinable impression that the rajah is a sensuous, indolent, extravagant sybarite, given to polo, diamonds and dancing girls, and amputates the heads of his subjects at pleasure; but that is very far from the truth. Many of the princes in the list just given, are men of high character, culture and integrity, who exercise a wise, just and patriarchal authority over their subjects. Seventeen of the rajputs (rashpootes, it is pronounced) represent the purest and bluest Hindu blood, for they are descended from Rama, the hero of the Ramayama, the great Hindu poem, who is generally worshiped as an incarnation of the god Bishnu; and their subjects are all their kinsmen, descended from the same ancestors, members of the same family, and are treated as such. Other rajahs have a relationship even more clannish and close, and most of them are the descendants of long lines of ancestors who have occupied the same throne and exercised the same power over the same people from the beginning of history. None of the royal families of Europe can compare with them in length of pedigree or the dimensions of their family trees, and while there have been bad men as well as good men in the lists of native rulers; while the people have been crushed by tyranny, ruined by extravagance and tortured by the cruelty of their masters, the rajahs of India have averaged quite as high as the feudal lords of Germany or the dukes and earls of England in ability and morality.

It has been the policy of Lord Curzon since he has been Viceroy to extend the power and increase the responsibility of the native princes as much as possible, and to give India the largest measure of home rule that circumstances and conditions will allow. Not long ago, at the investiture of the Nawab of Bahawalpur, who had succeeded to the throne of his father, the Viceroy gave a distinct definition of the relationship between the native princes and the British crown.

"It is scarcely possible," he said, "to imagine circumstances more different than those of the Indian chiefs now and what they were at the time Queen Victoria came to the throne. Now their sympathies have expanded with their knowledge and their sense of responsibility; with the degree of confidence reposed in them. They recognize their obligations to their own states and their duty to the imperial throne. The British crown is no longer an impersonal abstraction, but a concrete and inspiring force. The political system of India is neither feudalism nor federation. It is embodied in no constitution; it does not rest upon treaty, and it bears no resemblance to a league. It represents a series of relationships that have grown up between the crown and Indian princes under widely different historical conditions, but which in process of time have gradually conformed to a single type. The sovereignty of the crown is everywhere unchallenged. Conversely, the duties and the services of the state are implicitly recognized, and, as a rule, faithfully discharged. It is this happy blend of authority with free will, of sentiment with self-interest, of duties with rights, that distinguishes the Indian Empire under the British crown from any other dominion of which we read in history. The princes have gained prestige instead of losing it. Their rank is not diminished, and their privileges have become more secure. They have to do more for the protection they enjoy, but they also derive more from it; for they are no longer detached appendages of empire, but its participators and instruments. They have ceased to be architectural adornments of the imperial edifice, and have become the pillars that help to sustain the main roof."

At the same time Lord Curzon has kept a tight rein upon the rajahs and maharajas lest they forget the authority that stands behind them. He does not allow them to spend the taxes of the people for jewels or waste it in riotous living, and has the right to depose any of them for crime, disloyalty, misgovernment or any other cause he deems sufficient. The supreme authority of the British government has become a fact which no native state or ruler would for a moment think of disputing or doubting. No native chief fails to understand that his conduct is under scrutiny, and that if he committed a crime he would be tried and punished by the courts as promptly and as impartially as the humblest of his subjects. At the same time they feel secure in their authority and in the exercise of their religion, and when a native prince has no direct heir he has the right to select his successor by adoption. He may choose any child or young man among his subjects and if the person selected is of sound mind and respectable character, the choice is promptly ratified by the central government. There is no interference with the exercise of authority or the transaction of business unless the welfare of the people plainly requires it, and in such cases, the intervention has been swift and sure.

During the five years that he has been Viceroy, Lord Curzon has deposed two native rulers. One of them was the Rajah of Bhartpur, a state well-known in the history of India by its long successful resistance of the British treaty. In 1900 the native prince, a man of intemperate habits and violent passions, beat to death one of his personal servants who angered him by failing to obey orders to his satisfaction. It was not the first offense, but it was the most flagrant and the only one that was ever brought officially to the attention of the government. His behavior had been the subject of comment and the cause of scandal for several years, and he had received frequent warnings. Hence, when the brutal murder of his servant was reported at the government house, Lord Curzon immediately ordered his arrest and trial. He was convicted, sentenced to imprisonment for life, deprived of all his titles and authority, and his infant son was selected as his successor. During the minority of the young prince the government will be administered by native regents under British supervision.

In 1901 the uncle of the Maharaja of Panna died under mysterious circumstances. An investigation ordered by Lord Curzon developed unmistakable evidence that he had been deliberately poisoned. The rajah was suspended from power, was tried and convicted of the crime, and in April, 1902, was deposed, deprived of all honors and power and sentenced to imprisonment for life, while one of his subordinates who had actually committed the crime by his orders was condemned to death.

In January, 1903, the Maharaja of Indore, after testifying to his loyalty to the British crown by attending the durbar at Delhi, and after due notice to the viceroy, abdicated power in favor of his son, a boy 12 years old. The step was approved by Lord Curzon for reasons too many and complicated to be repeated here. During the minority of the young man the government will be conducted by native ministers under British supervision, and the boy will be trained and educated with the greatest care.

In 1894 the Maharaja of Mysore died, leaving as his heir an infant son, and it became necessary for the viceroy to appoint a regent to govern the province during his minority. The choice fell upon the boy's mother, a woman of great ability and intelligence, who justified the confidence reposed in her by administering the affairs of the government with great intelligence and dignity. She won the admiration of every person familiar with the facts. She gave her son a careful English education and a few months ago retired in his favor.

In several cases the privilege of adoption has been exercised by the ruling chief, and thus far has been confirmed by the British authority in every case.

There are four colleges in India exclusively for the education of native princes, which are necessary in that country because of the laws of caste. It is considered altogether better for a young prince to be sent to an English school and university, or to one of the continental institutions, where he can learn something of the world and come into direct association with young men of his own age from other countries, but, in many cases, this is impracticable, because the laws of caste will not permit strict Hindus to leave India and forbid their association with strangers. Even where no religious objections have existed, the fear of a loss of social dignity by contamination with ordinary people has prevented many native princes and nobles from sending their sons to ordinary schools. Hence princes, chiefs and members of the noble families in India have seldom been educated and until recently this illiteracy was not considered a discredit, because it was so common. To furnish an opportunity for the education of that class without meeting these objections, Lord Mayo, while viceroy, founded a college at Ajmer, which is called by his name. A similar institution was established at Lahore by Sir Charles Atchison, Lieutenant Governor of the Punjab in 1885. The corner stone was laid by the Duke of Connaught. A considerable part of the funds were contributed by the Punjab princes, and the balance necessary was supplied by the imperial government. Similar institutions have since been founded at Indore and Rajkot, and in the four schools about 300 of the future rulers of the native states are now receiving a healthy, liberal, modern education. The course of study has been regulated to meet peculiar requirements. It is not desired to make great scholars out of these young princes to fill their heads with useless learning, but to teach them knowledge that will be of practical usefulness when they assume authority, and to cultivate manly habits and pure tastes. Their physical development is carefully looked after. They play football, cricket and other games that are common at the English universities; they have gymnasiums and prizes for athletic excellence. They are taught English, French and the oriental languages; lower mathematics, geography, history and the applied sciences, particularly chemistry, electricity and engineering.

Lord Curzon has taken a deep interest in these institutions. He usually attends the graduating exercises and makes addresses to the students in presenting prizes or diplomas; and he gives them straight talks about the duties and the privileges of young men of their positions and responsibilities. He tells them that a rajah is worthless unless he is a gentleman, and that power can never safely be intrusted to people of rank unless they are fitted to exercise it. With a view of extending their training and developing their characters he has recently organized what is called the Imperial Cadet Corps, a bodyguard of the Viceroy, which attends him upon occasions of state, and is under his immediate command. He inspects the cadets frequently and takes an active personal interest in their discipline and education. The course of instruction lasts for three years, and is a modification of that given the cadets at West Point. The boys are taught military tactics, riding and the sciences. Very little attention is paid to higher mathematics of other studies except history, law and the modern languages. No one is eligible for admission to this corps except members of the families of the ruling native princes, and they must be graduates of one of the four colleges I have mentioned, under 20 years of age. There is great eagerness on the part of the young princess to join the dashing troop of horsemen. Four of the privates are now actual rulers of states with several millions of subjects and more than thirty are future maharajas. The honorary commander is the Maharaja Sir Pertas Singh, but the actual commander is a British major. It is proposed to offer commissions in the Indian army to the members of this corps at the close of their period of training, but that was not the chief purpose in Lord Curzon's mind when he suggested the organization. He desired to offer the most tempting inducement possible for the young princes to attend college and qualify themselves for their life work.

American visitors to India are often impressed with the presence of the same problems of government there that perplex our own people in the Philippines, and although England has sent her ablest men and applied her most mature wisdom to their solution, they are just as troublesome and unsettled as they ever were, and we will doubtless have a similar experience among our own colonial or, as they are called, insular possessions. There are striking coincidences. It makes one feel quite at home to hear Lord Curzon accused of the same errors and weaknesses that Judge Taft and Governor Wright have been charged with; and if those worthy gentlemen could get together, they might embrace with sympathetic fervor. One class of people in India declares that Lord Curzon sacrifices everything of value to the welfare of the natives; another class insists that he has his foot upon the neck of the poor Hindu and is grinding his brown face into the dust. In both England and India are organizations of good people who have conceived it to be their mission to defend and protect the natives from real or imaginary wrongs they are suffering, while there are numerous societies and associations whose business is to see that the Englishman gets his rights in India also.

It may console Lord Curzon to know that the criticisms of his policy and administration have been directed at every viceroy and governor general of India since the time of Warren Hastings, and they will probably be repeated in the future as long as there are men of different minds and dispositions and different ideas of what is right and proper.

England has given India a good government. It has accomplished wonders in the way of material improvements and we can say the same of the administration in the Philippine Islands, even for the short period of American occupation. Mistakes have been made in both countries. President Roosevelt, Secretary Taft, Governor General Wright and his associates would find great profit in studying the experience of the British. The same questions and the same difficulties that confront the officials at Manila have occurred again and again in India during the last 200 years, and particularly since 1858, when the authority and rights of the East India Company were transferred to the crown. And the most serious of all those questions is how far the native shall be admitted to share the responsibilities of the government. The situations are similar.

The population of India, like that of the Philippines, consists of a vast mixed multitude in various stages of civilization, in which not one man in fifty and not one woman in 200 can read or write.

Ninety per cent of the people, and the same proportion of the people of the Philippines, do not care a rap about "representative government." They do not know anything about it. They would not understand what the words meant if they ever heard them spoken. The small minority who do care are the "educated natives," who are just as human as the rest of us, and equally anxious to acquire money and power, wear a title, hold a government office and draw a salary from the public funds.

There are many most estimable Hindu gentlemen who do not come within this class, but I am speaking generally, and every person of experience in India has expressed the same opinion, when I say that a Hindu immediately becomes a politician as soon as he is educated. It he does not succeed in obtaining an office he becomes an opponent of the government, and more or less of an agitator, according to his ability and ambitions.

The universities of India turn out about five thousand young men every year who have been stuffed with information for the purpose of passing the civil service examinations, and most of them have only one aim in life, which is to secure government employment. As the supply of candidates is always much larger than the demand, the greater number fail, and, in their disappointment, finding no other profitable field for the exercise of their talents, become demagogues, reformers and critics of the administration. They inspire and maintain agitations for "home rule" and "representative government." They hold conventions, deliver lectures, write for the newspapers, and denounce Lord Curzon and his associates. If they were in the Philippine Islands they would organize revolutions and paper governments from places of concealment in the forests and mountains. They classify their emotions and desire for office under the name of patriotism, and some of them are undoubtedly sincere. If they had a chance they would certainly give their fellow countrymen the best government and the highest degree of happiness within their power. They call themselves "the people." But in no sense are they representatives of the great masses of the inhabitants. They have no influence with them and really care nothing about them. If the English were to withdraw from India to-day there would be perpetual revolution. If the Americans were to withdraw from Manila the result would be the same.

It should be said, however, that, with all their humbug about benevolence, the British have never had the presumption to assert that their occupation of India is exclusively for the benefit of the natives. They are candid enough to admit that their purpose is not entirely unselfish, and that, while they are promoting civilization and uplifting a race, they expect that race to consume a large quantity of British merchandise and pay good prices for it. The sooner such an understanding is reached in the Philippines the better. We are no more unselfish than the British, and to keep up the pretext of pure benevolence while we are in the Philippines for trade and profit also, is folly and fraud. It is neither fair nor just to the Filipinos nor to the people of the United States. At the same time the British authorities in India have given the natives a fair share of the offices and have elevated them to positions of honor, influence and responsibility. But they have discovered, as our people must also discover in the Philippines, that a civil service examination does not disclose all the qualities needed by rulers of men. The Hindu is very similar in character, disposition and talent to the Filipino; he has quick perceptions, is keen-witted, cunning and apt at imitations. He learns with remarkable ease and adapts himself to new conditions with great facility, but no amount of those qualities can make up for the manly courage, the sterling honesty, the unflinching determination and tireless energy of the British character. The same is true in the Philippine Islands.

At the last census only 864 Englishmen held active civil positions under the imperial government and 3,752 natives. The number of natives employed in the public service has been constantly increasing since 1879, while the number of Englishmen has been gradually growing less. No person other than a native of India can be appointed to certain positions under the government. Native officers manage almost all of the multifarious interests connected with the revenues, the lands, the civil courts and local administration. The duties of the civil courts throughout India, excepting the Court of Appeals, are almost entirely performed by native judges, who exercise jurisdiction in all cases affecting Europeans as well as natives, and the salaries they receive are very liberal. No country in the world pays better salaries than India to its judiciary. In Bengal a high court judge whether English or native, receives $16,000 a year, and the members of the lower courts are paid corresponding amounts.

It is asserted by prominent and unprejudiced members of the bar that nothing in the history of civilization has been more remarkable than the improvement that has taken place in the standard of morality among the higher classes of Indian officials, particularly among the judiciary. This is due in a great measure to the fact that their salaries have been sufficient to remove them from temptation, but a still greater influence has been the example of the irreproachable integrity of the Englishmen who have served with them and have created an atmosphere of honor and morality.

The English officials employed under the government of India belong to what is known as "The Covenanted Civil Service" the term "covenanted" having been inherited from the East India Company, which required its employes to enter into covenants stipulating that they would serve a term of years under certain conditions, including retirement upon half pay when aged, and pensions for their families after their death. Until 1853 all appointments to the covenanted service were made by nomination, but in that year they were thrown open to public competition of all British subjects without distinction of race, including natives of India as well as of England. The conditions are so exacting that few native Hindus are willing to accept them, and of the 1,067 men whose names were on the active and retired lists on the 31st of December, 1902, only forty were natives of India.

Lord Macaulay framed the rules of the competition and the scheme of examination, and his idea was to attract the best and ablest young men in the empire. Candidates who are successful are required to remain one year on probation, with an allowance of $500, for the purpose of preparing themselves for a second examination which is much more severe than the first. Having passed the second examination, they become permanent members of the civil service. They cannot be removed without cause, and are promoted according to length of service and advanced on their merits in a manner very similar to that which prevails in our army and navy. None but members of the covenanted service can become heads of departments, commissioners of revenue, magistrates and collectors, and there is a long list of offices which belong to them exclusively. Their service and assignment to duty is largely governed by their special qualifications and experience. They are encouraged to improve themselves and qualify themselves for special posts. A covenanted official who can speak the native languages, who distinguishes himself in literature or in oratory, who devises plans for public works, or distinguishes himself in other intellectual or official lines of activity is sure to be recognized and receive rapid advancement, while those who prefer to perform only the arduous duties that are required of them will naturally remain in the background. There is, and there always will be, more or less favoritism and partiality as long as human affections and personal regard influence official conduct, and I do not believe we would have it otherwise. We can admire the stern sense of justice which sends a son to the scaffold or denies a brother a favor that he asks, but we do not like to have such men in our families. There is undoubtedly more or less personal and political influence exercised in the Indian service, but I doubt if any other country is more free from those common and natural faults.

In addition to the covenanted service are the imperial service and the provincial service, which are recruited chiefly from the natives, although both are open to any subject of King Edward VII. All these positions are secured by competitive examinations, and, as I have already intimated, the universities of India have arranged their courses of study to prepare native candidates for them. This has been criticised as a false and injurious educational policy. The universities are called nurseries for the unnatural propagation of candidates for the civil service, and almost every young man who enters them expects, or at least aspires, to a government position. There is no complaint of the efficiency of the material they furnish for the public offices. The examinations are usually sufficient to disclose the mental qualifications of the candidates and are conducted with great care and scrupulousness, but they fail to discover the most essential qualifications for official responsibility, and the greater number of native appointees are contented to settle down at a government desk and do as little work as possible.

VIII

THE RAILWAYS OF INDIA

The railways of India are many and long and useful, but still very primitive in their appointments, having been built for utility and convenience, and not for comfort. The day will come, I suppose, when modern improvements will be introduced, and the long journeys which are necessary to reach any part of the vast empire will be made as pleasant and luxurious as transcontinental trips in the United States. Just now, however, the equipment is on a military basis of simplicity and severity. Passengers are furnished with what they need, and no more. They are hauled from one place to another at reasonable rates of speed; they are given shelter from the sun and the storms en route; a place to sit in the daytime and to lie down during the night; and at proper intervals the trains stop for refreshments—not very good or very bad, but "fair to middling," as the yankees say, in quality and quantity. It a traveler wants anything more he must provide it himself. People who live in India and are accustomed to these things are perfectly satisfied with them, although the tourist who has just arrived is apt to criticise and condemn for the first few days.

Every European resident of India who is accustomed to traveling by train has an outfit always ready similar to the kit of a soldier or a naval officer. It is as necessary as a trunk or a bag, an overcoat or umbrella, and consists of a roll of bedding, with sheets, blankets and pillows, protected by a canvas cover securely strapped and arranged so that when he wants to retire he need only unbuckle the straps and unroll the blankets on the bunk in the railway carriage. He also has a "tiffin basket," with a tea pot, an alcohol lamp, a tea caddy, plates and cups of granite ware, spoons, knives and forks, a box of sugar, a tin of jam, a tin of biscuits or crackers, and other concomitants for his interior department in case of an emergency; and, never having had anything better, he thinks the present arrangement good enough and wonders why Americans are dissatisfied. Persons of ordinary common sense and patience can get used to almost anything, and after a day of two travelers trained to the luxury of Pullman sleepers and dining cars adjust themselves to the primitive facilities of India without loss of sleep or temper, excepting always one condition: You are never sure "where you are at," so to speak. You never know what sort of accommodations you are going to have. There is always an exasperating uncertainty as to what will be left for you when the train reaches your place of embarkation.

Sleeping berths, such as they are, go free with first and second class tickets and every traveler is entitled to one bunk, but passengers at intermediate points cannot make definite arrangements until the train rolls in, no matter whether it is noonday or 2 o'clock in the morning. You can go down and appeal to the station master a day or two in advance and advise him of your wants and wishes, and he will put your name down on a list. If you are so fortunate as to be at the starting place of the train he will assign you a bunk and slip a card with your name written upon it into a little slot made for the purpose; the other bunks in the compartment will be allotted to Tom, Dick and Harry in the same manner. There are apartments reserved for ladies, too, but if you and your wife or family want one to yourselves you must be a major general, or a lieutenant governor, or a rajah, or a lord high commissioner of something or other to attain that desire. If they insist upon being exclusive, ordinary people are compelled to show as many tickets as there are bunks in a compartment, and the first that come have the pick, as is perfectly natural. The fellow who enters the train later in the day must be satisfied with Mr. Hobson's choice, and take what is left, even if it doesn't fit him. It the train is full, if every bunk is occupied, another car is hitched on, and he gets a lower, but this will not be done as long as a single upper is vacant. And the passengers are packed away as closely as possible because the trains are heavy and the engines are light, and the schedules must be kept in the running. A growler will tell you that he never gets a lower berth, that he is always crowded into a compartment that is already three-fourths occupied with passengers who are trying to sleep, but he forgets that they have more than he to complain of, and if he is a malicious man he can find deep consolation in the thought and make as great a nuisance of himself as possible. I do not know how the gentler sex behave under such circumstances, but I have heard stories that I am too polite to repeat.

There is no means of ventilation in the ceiling, but there is a frieze of blinds under it, along both sides of the car, with slats that can be turned to let the air in directly upon the body of the occupant of the upper berth, who is at liberty to elect whether he dies of pneumonia or suffocation. The gentleman in the lower berth has a row of windows along his back, which never fit closely but rattle like a snare drum, and have wide gaps that admit a forced draught of air if the night is damp or chilly. If it is hot the windows swell and stick so that you cannot open them, and during the daytime they rattle so loud that conversation is impossible unless the passengers have throats of brass like the statues of Siva. In India, during the winter season, there is a wide variation in the temperature, sometimes as much as thirty or forty degrees. At night you will need a couple of thick blankets; at noonday it is necessary to wear a pith helmet or carry an umbrella to protect the head from the sun, and as people do their traveling in the dry season chiefly, the dust is dreadful. Everything in the car wears a soft gray coating before the train has been in motion half an hour.

The bunks are too narrow for beds and too wide for seats. The act of rolling over in the night is attended with some danger and more anxiety, especially by the occupants of the upper berths. In the daytime you can sit on the edge like an embarrassed boy, with nothing to support your spine, or you can curl up like a Buddha on his lotus flower, with your legs under you; but that is not dignified, nor is it a comfortable posture for a fat man. Slender girls can do it all right; but it is impracticable for ladies who have passed the thirty-third degree, or have acquired embonpoint with their other graces. Or you can shove back against the windows and let your feet stick out straight toward the infinite. It isn't the fault of a railway corporation or the master mechanic of a car factory if they don't reach the floor. It is a defect for which nature is responsible. President Lincoln once said every man's legs ought to be long enough to reach the ground.

The cars are divided into two, three, or four compartments for first-class passengers, with a narrow little pen for their servants at the end which is absolutely necessary, because nobody in India travels without an attendant to wait upon him. His comfort as well as his social position requires it, and few have the moral courage to disregard the rule. To make it a little clearer I will give you a diagram sketched by your special artist on the spot.

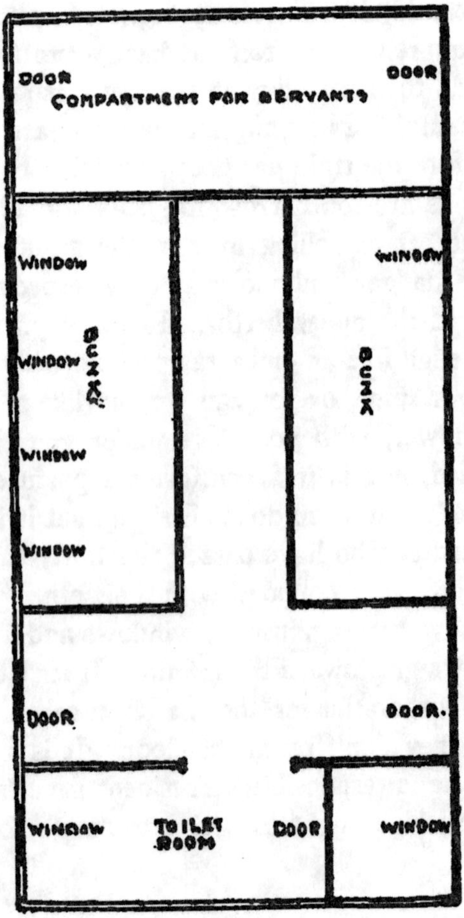

This is an excellent representation of a first-class railway carriage in India without meretricious embellishments.

The second-class compartments, for which two-thirds of the first-class rates are charged, have six narrow bunks instead of four, the two extras being in the middle supported by iron rods fastened to the floor and the ceiling. The woodwork of all cars, first, second, and third class, is plain matched lumber, like our flooring, painted or stained and varnished. The floor is bare, without carpet or matting, and around on the wall, wherever there is room for them, enormous hooks are screwed on. Over the doors are racks of netting. The bunks are plain wooden benches, covered with leather cushions stuffed with straw and packed as hard as tombstones by the weight of previous passengers. The ceiling is of boards pierced with a hole for a glass globe, which prevents the oil dripping upon your bald spot from a feeble and dejected lamp. It is too dim to read by and scarcely bright enough to enable you to distinguish the expression upon the lineaments of your fellow passengers. A scoop net of green cloth on a wire springs back over the light to cover it when you want to sleep: Sometimes it works and sometimes it doesn't. The toilet room is Spartan in its simplicity, and the amount of water in the tanks depends upon the conscientiousness of a naked heathen of the lowest caste, who walks over the roofs of the cars and is supposed to fill them from a pig skin suspended on his back. You furnish your own towel and the most untidy stranger in the compartment usually wants to borrow it, having forgotten to bring one himself. You acquire merit in heaven, as the Buddhists say, by loaning it to him, but it is a better plan to carry two towels, in order to be prepared for such an emergency.

As we were about starting upon a tour that required several thousand miles of railway travel and several weeks of time, the brilliant idea of avoiding all risks and anxiety by securing a private car was suggested, and negotiations were opened to that purpose, but were not concluded because of numerous considerations and contingencies which arose at every interview with the railway officials. They are not accustomed to such innovations and could not decide upon their own terms or ascertain, during the period before departure, what the connecting lines would charge us. There are private cars fitted up luxuriously for railway managers and high officials of the government, but they couldn't spare one of them for so long a time as we would need it. Finally somebody suggested a car that was fitted out for the Duke and Duchess of Connaught when they came over to the durbar at Delhi. It had two compartments, with a bathroom, a kitchen and servants' quarters, but only three bunks. They kindly offered to let us use it provided we purchased six first-class tickets, and were too obtuse to comprehend why he objected to paying six fares for a car that could not possibly admit more than three people. But that was only the first of several issues. At the next interview they decided to charge us demurrage at the rate of 16 cents an hour for all the time the car was not in motion, and, finally, at the third interview, the traffic manager said it would be necessary for us to buy six first-class tickets in order to get the empty car back to Bombay, its starting point, at the end of our journey. This brought the charges up to a total as large as would be necessary to transport a circus or an opera company, and we decided to take our chances in the regular way.

We bought some sheets and pillow cases, pillows and old-fashioned comfortables and blankets, and bespoke a compartment on the train leaving Bombay that night. Two hours before the time for starting we sent Thagorayas, our "bearer, down to make up the beds, which, being accustomed to that sort of business, he did in an artistic manner, and by allowing him to take command of the expedition we succeeded in making the journey comfortably and with full satisfaction. The ladies of our party were assigned to one compartment and the gentlemen to another, where the latter had the company of an engineer engaged upon the Bombay harbor improvements, and a very intelligent and polite Englishman who acts as "adviser" to a native prince in the administration of an interior province.

On the same train and next to our compartment was the private coach of the Gaikwar of Baroda, who was attended by a dozen or more servants, and came to the train escorted by a multitude of friends, who hung garlands of marigold about his neck until his eyes and the bridge of his nose were the only features visible. The first-class passengers came down with car loads of trunks and bags and bundles, which, to avoid the charge for extra luggage, they endeavored to stow away in their compartments. The third-class carriages were packed like sardines with natives, and up to the limit allowed by law, for, painted in big white letters, where every passenger and every observer can read it, is a notice giving the number of people that can be jammed into that particular compartment in the summer and in the winter. We found similar inscriptions on nearly all freight cars which are used to transport natives during the fairs and festivals that occur frequently—allowing fifteen in summer and twenty-three in winter in some of the cars, and in the larger ones thirty-four in winter and twenty-six in summer, to avoid homicide by suffocation.

The Gaikwar of Baroda in his luxurious chariot did not sleep any better than the innocent and humble mortals that occupied our beds. We woke up in the morning at Ahmedabad, got a good breakfast at the station, and went out to see the wonderful temples and palaces and bazaars that are described in the next chapter.

There are now nearly 28,000 miles of railway lines in India. On Jan. 1, 1903, the exact mileage under operation was 26,563, with 1,190 miles under construction. The latter was more than half completed during the year, and before the close of 1905, unless something occurs to prevent, the total will pass the thirty thousand mark. The increase has been quite rapid during the last five years, owing to the experience of the last famine, when it was demonstrated that facilities for rapid transportation of food supplies from one part of the country to another were an absolute necessity. It is usually the case that when the inhabitants of one province are dying of starvation those of another are blessed with abundant crops, and the most effective remedy for famine is the means of distributing the food supply where it is needed. Before the great mutiny of 1857 there were few railroads in India, and the lesson taught by that experience was of incalculable value. If re-enforcements could have been sent by rail to the beleaguered garrisons, instead of making the long marches, the massacres might have been prevented and thousands of precious lives might have been saved. In 1880 the system amounted to less than 10,000 miles. In 1896 it had been doubled; in 1901 it had passed the 25,000 mile mark, and now the existing lines are being extended, and branches and feeders are being built for military as well as famine emergencies. All the principal districts and cities are connected by rail. All of the important strategical points and military cantonments can be reached promptly, as necessity requires, and in case of a rebellion troops could be poured into any particular point from the farthermost limits of India within three or four days.

As I have already reminded you several times, India is a very big country, and it requires many miles of rails to furnish even necessary transportation facilities. The time between Bombay and Calcutta is forty-five hours by ordinary trains and thirty-eight hours by a fast train, with limited passenger accommodation, which starts from the docks of Bombay immediately after the arrival of steamers with the European mails. From Madras, the most important city of southern India, to Delhi, the most important in the north, sixty-six hours of travel are required. From Peshawur, the extreme frontier post in the north, which commands the Kyber Pass, leading into Afganistan, to Tuticorin, the southern terminus of the system, it is 3,400 miles by the regular railway route, via Calcutta, and seven days and night will be necessary to make the journey under ordinary circumstances. Troops could be hurried through more rapidly.

Nearly all the railways of India have either been built by the government or have been assisted with guarantees of the payment of from 3 to 5 per cent dividends. The government itself owns 19,126 miles and has guaranteed 3,866 miles, while 3,242 miles have been constructed by the native states. Of the government lines 13,441 miles have been leased to private companies for operation: 5,125 miles are operated by the government itself. Nearly three-fourths of the lines owned by native states have been leased for operation.

The total capital invested in railway property, to the end of 1902, amounted to $1,025,000,000, and during that year the average net earnings of the entire mileage amounted to 5.10 per cent of that amount. The surplus earnings, after the payment of all fixed charges and guarantees and interest upon bonds amounted to $4,233,080.

The number of passengers carried in 1902 was 197,749,567, an increase of 6,614,211 over the previous year. The aggregate freight hauled was 44,142,672 tons, an increase of 2,104,425 tons over previous year, which shows a healthy condition. During the last ten years the gross earnings of all the railways in India increased at the rate of 41 per cent.

Of the gross earnings 59 per cent. were derived from freight and the balance from passengers.

There is now no town of importance in India without a telegraph station. The telephone is not much used, but the telegraph lines, which belong to the government, more than pay expenses. There has been an enormous increase in the number of messages sent in the last few years by natives, which indicates that they are learning the value of modern improvements.

The government telegraph lines are run in connection with the mails and in the smaller towns the postmasters are telegraph operators also. In the large cities the telegraph offices are situated in the branch postoffices and served by the same men, so that it is difficult to divide the cost of maintenance. According to the present system the telegraph department maintains the lines, supplies all the telegraphic requirements of the offices and pays one-half of the salaries of operators, who also attend to duties connected with the postoffice. There were 68,084 miles of wire and 15,686 offices on January 1, 1904. The rate of charges for ordinary telegrams is 33 cents for eight words, and 4 cents for each additional word. Telegrams marked "urgent" are given the right of way over all other business and are charged double the ordinary rates. Telegrams marked "deferred" are sent at the convenience of the operator, generally during the night, at half of the ordinary rates. As a matter of convenience telegrams may be paid for by sticking postage stamps upon the blanks.

There are 38,479 postoffices in India and in 1902 545,364,313 letters were handled, which was an increase of 24,000,000 over the previous year and of 100,000,000 since 1896. The total revenues of the postoffice department were $6,785,880, while the expenditures were $6,111,070.

IX

THE CITY OF AHMEDABAD

Ahmedabad, capital of the province of Jujarat, once the greatest city of India, and formerly "as large as London," is the first stopping place on the conventional tour from Bombay through the northern part of the empire, because it contains the most perfect and pure specimens of Saracenic architecture; and our experience taught us that it is a place no traveler should miss. It certainly ranks next to Agra and Delhi for the beauty and extent of its architectural glories, and for other reasons it is worth visiting. In the eleventh century it was the center of the Eden of India, broad, fertile plains, magnificent forests of sweet-scented trees, abounding in population and prosperity. It has passed through two long periods of greatness, two of decay and one of revival. Under the rule of Sidh Rajah, "the Magnificent," one of the noblest and greatest of the Moguls, it reached the height of its wealth and power at the beginning of the fifteenth century. He erected schools, palaces and temples, and surrounded them with glorious gardens. He called to his side learned pundits and scholarly priests, who taught philosophy and morals under his generous patronage. He encouraged the arts and industries. His wealth was unlimited, and, according to local tradition, he lived in a style of magnificence that has never been surpassed by any of the native princes since. His jewels were the wonder of the world, and one of the legends says that he inherited them from the gods. But, unfortunately, his successors were weak and worthless men, and the glory of his kingdom passed gradually away until, a century later, his debilitated and indolent subjects were overcome and passed under the power of a Moslem who, in the earlier part of the sixteenth century, restored the importance of the province.

Ahmed Shah was his name.

He built a citadel of impregnable strength and imposing architecture and surrounded it by a city with broad streets and splendid buildings and called it after himself; for Ahmedabad means the City of Ahmed. Where his predecessor attracted priests and scholars he brought artists, clever craftsmen, skilled mechanics and artisans in gold, silver, brass and clay; weavers of costly fabrics with genius to design and skill to execute. Architects and engineers were sent for from all parts of the world, and merchants came from every country to buy wares. Thus Ahmedabad became a center of trade and manufacture, with a population of a million inhabitants, and was the richest and busiest city in the Mogul Empire. Merchants who had come to buy in its markets spread its reputation over the world and attracted valuable additions to its trades and professions. Travelers, scholars and philosophers came to study the causes of its prosperity, and marvelous stories are told by them in letters and books they wrote concerning its palaces, temples and markets. An envoy from the Duke of Holstein gives us a vivid account of the grandeur of the city and the splendor of the court, and tells of a wedding, at which the daughter of Ahmed Shah married the second son of the grand mogul. She carried to Delhi as her dower twenty elephants, a thousand horses and six thousand wagons loaded with the richest stuffs of whatever was rare in the country. The household of the rajah, he says, consisted of five hundred persons, and cost him five thousand pounds a month to maintain, "not comprehending the account of his stables, where he kept five hundred horses and fifty elephants." When this traveler visited the rajah he was sitting in a pavilion in his garden, clad in a white vestment, according to the Indian code, over which he had a cloak of gold "brocade," the ground color being carnation lined with white satin, and above it was a collar of sable, whereof the skins were sewed together so that the tails hung over down his back.

Among the manufacturers and business men of Ahmedabad in those days, as now, were many Jains—the Quakers of India—who belong to the rich middle class. They believe in peace, and are so tender-hearted that they will not even kill a mosquito or a flea. They are great business men, however, notwithstanding their soft hearts, and the most rapid money-makers in the empire. They built many of the most beautiful temples in India, in which they worship a kind and gentle god whose attributes are amiability, benevolence and compassion. The Jains of Ahmedabad still maintain a large "pinjrapol," or asylum for diseased and aged animals, with about 800 inmates, decrepit beasts of all species, by which they acquire merit with their god. And about the streets, and in the outskirts of the city, sitting on the tops of what look like telegraph poles, are pigeon houses; some of them ornamented with carving, other painted in gay colors and all of them very picturesque. These are rest houses for birds, which the Jains have built, and every day basins of food are placed in them for the benefit of the hungry.

In the groves outside of the city are thousands of monkeys, and they are much cleaner and more respectable in appearance than any you ever saw in a circus or a zoo. They are as large as Italian greyhounds, and of similar color, with long hair and uncommonly long tails, and so tame they will come up to strangers who know enough to utter a call that they understand. Our coachman bought a penny's worth of sweet bread in one of the groceries that we passed, and when we reached the first grove he uttered a cry similar to that which New England dairymen use in calling their cattle. In an instant monkeys began to drop from the limbs of trees that overhang the roadway, and came scampering from the corners, where they had probably been indulging in noonday naps. In two minutes he was surrounded by thirty-eight monkeys, which leaped and capered around like so many dogs as he held the sugar cake up in the air before them. It was a novel sight. These monkeys are fed regularly at the expense of the Jains, and none of God's creatures is too insignificant or irritating to escape their comprehensive benevolence.

One of the temples of the Jains, the Swamee Narayan, as they call it, on the outskirts of the city, is considered the noblest modern sacred building in all India. It is a mass of elaborate carving, tessellated marble floors and richly colored decorations, 150 feet long by 100 feet wide, with an overhanging roof supported by eighty columns, and no two of them are alike. They are masses of carving—figures of men and gods, saints and demons, animals, insects, fishes, trees and flowers, such as are only seen in the delirium of fever, are portrayed with the most exquisite taste and delicacy upon all of the surface exposed. The courtyard is inclosed by a colonnade of beautifully carved columns, upon which open fifty shrines with pagoda domes about twelve feet high, and in each of them are figures of Tirthankars, or saints of the calendar of the Jains. The temple is dedicated to Dharmamath, a sort of Jain John the Baptist, whose image, crowned with diamonds and other jewels, sits behind a beautiful gilded screen.

Ahmedabad now has a population of about 130,000. The ancient walls which inclose it are in excellent preservation and surround an area of about two square miles. There are twelve arched gateways with heavy teakwood doors studded with long brass spikes as a defense against elephants, which in olden times were taught to batter down such obstructions with their heads. The commerce of the city has declined of late years, but the people are still famous for objects of taste and ornament, and, according to the experts, their "chopped" gold is "the finest archaic jewelry in India," almost identical in shape and design with the ornaments represented upon sculptured images in Assyria. The goldsmiths make all kinds of personal adornments; necklaces, bracelets, anklets, toe, finger, nose and ear rings, girdles and arm-bands of gold, silver, copper and brass, and this jewelry is worn by the women of India as the best of investments. They turn their money into it instead of patronizing banks. As Mr. Micawber would have expressed it, they convert their assets into portable property.

The manufacture of gold and silver thread occupies the attention of thousands of people, and hundreds more are engaged in weaving this thread with silk into brocades called "kincobs," worn by rich Hindus and sold by weight instead of by measure. They are practically metallic cloth. The warp, or the threads running one way, is all either gold or silver, while the woof, or those running the other, are of different colored silks, and the patterns are fashioned with great taste and delicacy. These brocades wear forever, but are very expensive. A coat such as a rajah or a rich Hindu must wear upon an occasion of ceremony is worth several thousand dollars. Indeed, rajahs have had robes made at Ahmedabad for which the cloth alone cost $5,000 a yard. The skill of the wire drawers is amazing. So great is their delicacy of touch that they can make a thousand yards of silver thread out of a silver dollar; and if you will give one of them a sovereign, in a few moments he will reel off a spool of gold wire as fine as No. 80 cotton, and he does it with the simplest, most primitive of tools.

Nearly all the gold, silver and tin foil used in India is made at Ahmedabad, also in a primitive way, for the metal is spread between sheets of paper and beaten with a heavy hammer. The town is famous for its pottery also, and for many other manufactured goods.

The artisans are organized into guilds, like those of Europe in ancient times, with rules and regulations as strict as those of modern trades unions. The nagar-seth, or Lord Mayor, of Ahmedabad, is the titular head of all the guilds, and presides over a central council which has jurisdiction of matters of common interest. But each of the trades has its own organization and officers. Membership is hereditary; for in India, as in all oriental countries, it is customary for children to follow the trade or profession of their father. If an outsider desires to join one of the guilds he is compelled to comply with very rigid regulations and pay a heavy fee. Some of the guilds are rich, their property having been acquired by fines, fees and legacies, and they loan money to their own members. A serious crisis confronts the guilds of Ahmedabad in the form of organized capital and labor-saving machinery. Until a few years ago all of the manufacturing was done in the households by hand work. Within recent years five cotton factories, representing a capital of more than $2,500,000, have been established, and furnish labor for 3,000 men, women and children. This innovation was not opposed by the guilds because its products would come into direct competition only with the cotton goods of England, and would give employment to many idle people; but now that silk looms and other machinery are proposed the guilds are becoming alarmed and are asking where the intrusions are likely to stop.

The tombs of Ahmed, and Ganj Bhash, his chaplain, or spiritual adviser, a saintly mortal who admonished him of his sins and kept his feet in the path that leads to paradise, are both delightful, if such an adjective can apply, and are covered with exquisite marble embroidery, almost incredible in its perfection of detail. It is such as modern sculptors have neither the audacity or the imagination to design nor the skill or patience to execute. But they are not well kept. The rozah, or courtyard, in which the great king lies sleeping, surrounded by his wives, his children and other members of his family and his favorite ministers, is not cared for. It is dirty and dilapidated.

This vision of frozen music, as some one has described it, is a square building with a dome and walls of perforated fretwork in marble as delicate as Jack Frost ever traced upon a window pane. It is inclosed by a crumbling wall of mud, and can be reached only through a narrow and dirty lane obstructed by piles of rubbish, and the enjoyment of the visitor is sometimes destroyed and

HUTHI SINGH'S TOMB — AHMEDABAD

always seriously interfered with by the importunities of priests, peddlers and beggars who pursue him for backsheesh.

The lane from the mausoleum leads into the courtyard of the Jumma Musjid, a mosque erected by Ahmed Shah at the height of his power and glory. It is considered one of the most stately and satisfactory examples of Saracenic architecture.

The most beautiful piece of carving, however, in this great collection is a window in a deserted mosque called Sidi Sayid. Perhaps you are familiar with it. It has been photographed over and over again, and has been copied in alabaster, marble, plaster and wax; it has been engraved, photographed and painted, and is used in textbooks on architecture as an illustration of the perfection reached by the sculptors of India. The design is so complicated that I cannot describe it, but the central features are trees, with intertwining boughs, and the Hindu who made it could use his chisel with as free and delicate a hand as Raphael used his brush. Fergusson, who is recognized as the highest authority on architecture, says that it is "more like a work of nature than any other architectural detail that has yet been designed, even by the best masters of Greece or the middle ages." Yet the mosque which this precious gem made famous is abandoned and deserted, and the courtyard is now a cow pasture.

X

JEYPORE AND ITS MAHARAJA

A board of geographic names, similar to that we have in Washington, is badly needed in India to straighten out discrepancies in the nomenclature on the maps. I was told that only three towns in all the vast empire have a single spelling; all the rest have several; some have many; and the name of one town—I have forgotten which—is given in sixty-five different ways. Jeypore, for example, is given in fifteen. The sign over the entrance to the railway station reads "Jeypure;" on the lamps that light the platform it is painted "Jeypoor"; on the railway ticket it was "Jaypur"; on the bill of fare in the refreshment-room of the station it was "Jaipor"; on a telegram delivered by the operator at the station it was spelled "Jaiphur." If the employes about a single establishment in the town can get up that number of spells, what are we to expect from the rest of the inhabitants of a city of 150,000 people, and Jeypore is one of the simplest and easiest names in the gazetteer. The neighboring city of Jodpore, capital of the adjoining native state of Marwar, offers an even greater variety of orthoepy, for it appears in a different spelling on each of the three maps I carried around—a railway map, a government map, and the map in Murray's Guide Book. This is a fair illustration of the dissensions over nomenclature, which are bewildering to a stranger, who never knows when he gets the right spelling, and sometimes cannot even find the towns he is looking for.

Jodpore is famous for its forts, which present an imposing appearance from a wide spreading plain, as they are perched at the top of a rocky hill three hundred feet high, with almost perpendicular sides. The only way to reach it is by a zigzag road chiseled out of the cliff, which leads to a massive gateway. The walls are twenty-eight feet high, twenty-eight feet thick, and are crowned with picturesque towers. During ascent you are shown the impressions of the hands of the fifteen wives of one of the rajahs who were all burned in one grand holocaust upon his funeral pyre. I don't know why they did it, but the marks are there. Within the walls are some very interesting old palaces, built in the fifteenth century, of pure Hindu architecture, and the carvings and perforated marble work are of the most delicate and beautiful designs. The treasury, which contains the family jewels and plate, is the chief object of tourist curiosity, and they are a collection worth going far to see. The pearls and emeralds are especially fine, and are worth millions. The saddles, bridles, harness and other stable equipments are loaded with gold and silver ornaments set with precious stones, and the trappings for elephants are covered with the most gorgeous gold and silver embroidery.

About half a mile outside the city walls is a temple called the Maha Mandir, whose roof is supported by a hundred richly decorated columns. On each side of it are palaces intended exclusively for the use of spirits of former rulers of the country. Their beds are laid out with embroidery coverings and lace, sheltered by golden canopies and curtains of brocade, but are never slept in by living people, being reserved for the spirits of the dead. This is the only exhibition of the kind to be seen in India, and why the dead and gone rulers of Marwar should need lodgings when those of the other Indian states do not, is an unsolved mystery.

In the royal cemetery, three miles to the north, rows of beautiful but neglected cenotaphs mark the spots where the remains of each of some 300 rajahs were consumed with their widows. Some of them had more and some less, according to their taste and opportunities, and sutti, or widow burning, was enforced in Jodpore more strictly than anywhere else in India. You can imagine the thoughts this extraordinary place suggests. Within its walls, in obedience to an awful and relentless custom, not less than nine hundred or a thousand innocent, helpless women were burned alive, for these oriental potentates certainly must have allowed themselves at least three wives each. That would be a very moderate estimate. I have no doubt that some of them had forty, and perhaps four hundred, and we know that one had fifteen. But no matter how many times a rajah went to the matrimonial altar, every wife that outlived him was burned upon his funeral pyre in order that he might enjoy her society in the other world. Since widow burning was stopped by the British government in the sixties, the spirits of the rajahs of Jodpore have since been compelled to go to paradise without company. But they do not take any chances of offending the deities by neglect, for on a hill that overlooks their cemetery they have erected a sort of sweepstakes temple to Three Hundred Million Gods.

At the palace of the rajah of Ulwar, in a city of the same name, sometimes spelled Alwar and in forty other different ways, which lies about thirty miles north of

Jodpore, is another collection of jewels, ranked among the finest in India. The treasure-house contains several great chests of teakwood, handsomely carved and gilded, bound with gold and silver bands, and filled with valuable plate, arms, equipment, vessels and ornaments that have accumulated in the family during several centuries, and no matter how severe the plague or how many people are dying of famine, these precious heirlooms have never been disturbed. Perhaps the most valuable piece of the collection is a drinking cup, cut from a single emerald, as large as those used for after dinner coffee. There is a ruby said to be one of the largest in existence and worth $750,000; a yellow diamond valued at $100,000; several strings of almost priceless pearls and other jewels of similar value. There are caskets of gold and ivory in which hundreds of thousands of dollars' worth of jewels are imbedded, perfumery bottles of solid gold with the surfaces entirely incrusted with pearls and diamonds, and hung upon the walls around the apartment are shawls that are worth a thousand times their weight in gold. The saddles, harness and elephant trappings are much more beautiful and costly than those at Jodpore, and in the adjoining armory is a remarkable collection of swords and other weapons with hilts of gold, jade, enamel and jewels. A coat of mail worn by Bani Singh, grandfather of the present rajah, is made of solid gold, weighing sixteen and a half pounds, and is lavishly decorated with diamonds. The library is rich in rare oriental books and manuscripts wonderfully illuminated in colors and gold. It has a large collection of editions of the Koran in fifty or more different languages, and one manuscript book called "The Gulistan" is claimed to be the most valuable volume in India. The librarian insisted that it is worth 500,000 rupees, which is equivalent to about $170,000, and declared that the actual cost of the gold used in illuminating it was more than $50,000. It is a modern manuscript copy of a religious poem, made in 1848 by a German scribe at the order of the Maharaja Bani Singh. The miniatures and other pictures were painted by a native artist at Delhi, and the ornamental scroll work upon the margins of the pages and the initial letters were done by a resident of Ulwar.

Nearly all of the capitals of the provinces of Rajputana have similar treasures, the accumulations of centuries, and it seems like criminal negligence to keep such enormous sums of money tied up in jewels and useless ornaments when they might be expended or invested to the great advantage of the people in public works and manufactories. Some of the towns need such industries very badly because, off the farms, there is nothing in the way of employment for either men or women, and every branch of agriculture is overcrowded. One may moralize about these conditions as long as he likes; however, changes occur very slowly in India, and as Kipling so pertinently puts it in one of his poems, it's only a fool "Who tries to hustle the East."

Jeypore is the best, the largest and most prosperous of the twenty Rajput capitals, and is beyond comparison the finest modern city in India. It is also the busiest. Everybody seems to have plenty to do, and plenty to spend. The streets are as crowded and as busy as those of London or New York, with a bustling and stalwart race of men and women, happy and contented, and showing more energy than you often see in an oriental country. The climate is cool, dry and healthful. The city stands upon a sandy and arid plain, 1,600 feet above the sea,

STREET CORNER — JEYPORE, INDIA

surrounded by stony hills and wide wastes of desert, but even these natural disadvantages have contributed to its wealth and industries, for the barren hills are filled with deposits of fine clays, rare ores and cheap jewels like garnets, carbuncles and agates, which have furnished the people one of their most profitable trades. Out of this material they make an enamel which is famous everywhere, and has been the source of great gain and fame. It is shipped in large quantities to Europe, but the greater part is sold in the markets of India.

Jeypore is surrounded by a wall twenty feet high and nine feet thick, built within the last century, and hence almost in perfect condition. Indeed the town, unlike most of the Indian cities, is entirely without ruins, and you have to ride five miles on the back of an elephant in order to see one. The streets are wide and well paved, and laid out at exact angles. Four great thoroughfares 111 feet wide run at equal intervals at right angles with each other. All the other streets are fifty-five feet wide and the alleys are twenty-eight feet. Parks and public squares are laid out with the same regularity, and the houses are of uniform heights and generally after the same pattern. The façades are almost fantastic, being covered profusely with stucco and "ginger-bread work," so much that it is almost bewildering. The roofs are guarded by highly ornamental balustrades that look like perforated marble, but are only molded plaster; the windows are filled with similar material; the doorways are usually arched and protected with overhanging canopies, and the doors are painted with pictures in brilliant colors. The entire city has been "whitewashed" a bright rose color, every house having almost the same tint, which gives a peculiar appearance. There is nothing else like it in all the world. The outer walls of many of the houses are painted with pictures of animals and birds, trees, pagodas and other fantastic designs, and scenes like those on the drop curtains of theatres, which appear to have been done by unskilled amateurs, and the whole effect—the colors, the gingerbread work and the tints—reminds you of the frosted cakes and other table decorations you sometimes see in confectioners' windows at Christmas time. You wonder that the entire city does not melt and run together under the heat of the burning sun. The people wear colors even more brilliant than those of their houses, and in whichever direction you look you see continual streams passing up and down each broad highway like animated rainbows, broken here and there by trains of loaded camels, huge elephants with fanciful canopies on their backs and half-naked Hindus astride their heads, guiding them. Jeypore was the first place we found elephants used for business purposes, and they seemed to be quite numerous—more numerous than horses—and some of them were covered with elaborate trappings and saddles, and had their heads painted in gay tints and designs. That was a new idea also, which I had never seen before, and I was told that it is peculiar to Jeypore. The bullock carts, which furnish the only other means of transportation, are also gayly painted. The designs are sometimes rude and the execution bears evidence of having been done with more zeal than skill. The artist got the giddiest colors he could find, and laid them on without regard to time or expense. The wheels, bodies and tongues of the carts, and the canopies that cover those in which women are carried, are nightmares of yellows, greens, blues, reds and purples, like cheap wooden toys. Everything artificial at Jeypore is as bright and gay as dyes and paint can make it.

A great deal of cloth is manufactured there, both cotton and silk; most of it in little shops opening on the sidewalk, and it is woven and dyed by hand where everybody can see that the work is honestly done. As you walk along the business part of town you will see women and children holding long strips of red, green, orange, purple or blue cloth—sometimes cotton and sometimes silk, fresh from the vats of dye, out of the dust, in the sunshine, until the colors are securely fastened in the fibers. Even the men paint their whiskers in fantastic colors. It is rather startling to come up against an old gentleman with a long beard the color of an orange or a spitzenberg apple. You imagine they are lunatics, but they are only pious Mohammedans anxious to imitate the Prophet, who, according to tradition, had red whiskers.

About half of the space of the four wide streets is given up to sidewalk trading, and rows of booths, two or three miles in length, occupy the curbstones, with all kinds of goods; everything that anybody could possibly want, fruits, vegetables, groceries, provisions, boots and shoes, ready-made clothing, hats and caps, cotton goods and every article of wearing apparel you can think of, household articles, furniture, drugs and medicines, jewelry, stationery, toys—everything is sold by these sidewalk merchants, who squat upon a piece of matting with their stock neatly piled around them.

One feature of the street life in Jeypore, however, is likely to make nervous people apprehensive. The maharaja and other rich men keep panthers, leopards, wildcats and other savage beasts trained for tiger hunting and other sporting purposes, and allow their grooms to lead them around through the crowded thoroughfares just as though they were poodle dogs. It is true that the brutes wear muzzles, but you do not like the casual way they creep up behind you and sniff at the calves of your legs.

Siwai Madhao Singh, Maharaja of Jeypore, is one of the most interesting persons in India, and he represents the one hundred and twenty-third of his family, which is ants of the hero of a great Sanskrit epic called the Ramayana, while the emperor of Japan represents only the one hundred and twenty-third of his family, which is reckoned the oldest of royal blood. The poem consists of 24,000 stanzas, arranged in seven books, and describes the adventures and sets forth the philosophy of Rama, the seventh incarnation of Vishnu, one of the two greatest of the gods.

Siwai Madhao Singh is proud of his ancestry, proud of his ancient faith, proud of the traditions of his race, and adheres with scrupulous conservatism to the customs and the manners of his forefathers. At the same time he is very progressive, and Jeypore, his capital, has the best modern museum, the best hospital, the best college, the best industrial and art school, and the largest school for girls among all the native states of India, and is more progressive than any other Indian city except Calcutta and Bombay. The maharaja was selected to represent the native princes at the coronation of King Edward, and at first declined to go because he could not leave India for a foreign country without losing caste. When the reasons for his selection had been explained to him, and he was informed that his refusal must be construed as an act of disrespect to his sovereign, he decided that it was his duty to waive his religious scruples and other

MAHARAJA OF JEYPORE AND HIS PRIME MINISTER

objections and show his esteem and loyalty for the Emperor of India. But he could not go without great preparation. He undertook to protect himself as much as possible from foreign influences and temptations, and adhered as strictly as circumstances would allow to the requirements of his caste and religion. He chartered a ship to carry him from Bombay to London and back; loaded it with native food supplies sufficient to last him and his party for six months, and a six months' supply of water from the sacred Ganges for cooking and drinking purposes. His preparations were as extensive and complete as if he were going to etablish a colony on some desert island. He was attended by about 150 persons, including priests, who carried their gods, altars, incense, gongs, records, theological works, and all the appurtenances required to set up a Hindu temple in London. He had his own stewards, cooks and butchers—servants of every kind—and, of course, a good supply of wives and dancing girls. A temporary temple was set up on the dock in Bombay before sailing, and Rama, his divine ancestor, was worshiped continuously for two weeks by the maharaja's priests in order to secure his beneficent favor on the voyage. When London was reached the entire outfit was transferred to a palace allotted to his use, and such an establishment as he maintained there was never seen in the world's metropolis before.

Siwai Madhao Singh was received with distinguished honors by the king, the court, the ministry, the statesmen and the commercial and industrial interests of England. He was one of the most conspicuous persons at the coronation, and if he had been trained from childhood for the part he could not have conducted himself with greater grace and dignity. Everybody was delighted with him, and he was delighted with his reception. He returned to Jeypore filled with new ideas and inspired with new ambitions to promote the welfare of his people, and although he had previously shown remarkable capacity for government he feels that his experience and the knowledge he acquired during his journey were of inestimable value to him. One of the results is a determination to send his sons to England to be educated, because he feels that it would be an injustice to them and to the people over whom they must some time rule, to deprive them of the advantages offered by English institutions and by association with the people that he desires them to meet. Caste is no longer an objection. The maharaja has broken caste without suffering any disadvantage, and has discovered that other considerations are more important. He has learned by actual personal experience that the prejudices of his race and religion against travel and association with foreigners has done an immeasurable amount of injustice. He has seen with his own eyes how the great men of England live and prosper without caste, and is willing to do like them. They do not believe in it. They regard it as a narrow, unjust and inconvenient restriction, and he is partially convinced that they are right. The most distinctive feature of Hindu civilization thus received a blow from which it can never recover, because Siwai Madhao Singh is recognized as one of the ablest, wisest and most sincere of all the Hindu princes, and his influence in this and as in other things is almost unlimited. He expects to go to England again. He desires to visit other countries also, because he realizes that he can learn much that is of value to him and to his people by studying the methods and the affairs of foreign nations.

HALL OF THE WINDS — JEYPORE

In November, 1902, when Lord Curzon visited Jeypore, a banquet was given in his honor, at which the maharaja made a remarkable speech, alluding to his experience in England and the benefit he derived from that visit. In reply Lord Curzon said: "When I persuaded Your Highness to go to England as the chosen representative of Rajputana at the coronation of the king, you felt some hesitation as to the sharp separation from your home and from the duties and the practices of your previous life. But you have returned fortified with the conviction that dignity and simplicity of character, and uprightness and magnanimity of conduct are esteemed by the nobility and the people of England not less than they are here. I hope that Your Highness' example may be followed by those who come after you, and that it may leave an enduring mark in Indian history."

The palace and gardens of the maharaja cover one-seventh of the entire area of the city of Jeypore, and are inclosed within a mighty wall, which is entered through several stately gates. The only portion of the palace visible from the street is called the Hawal Mahal, or "Hall of the Winds," which Sir Edwin Arnold's glowing pen describes as "a vision of daring and dainty loveliness, nine stories of rosy masonry, delicate overhanging balconies and latticed windows, soaring tier after tier of fanciful architecture, a very mountain of airy and audacious beauty, through a thousand pierced screens and gilded arches. Aladdin's magician could have called into existence no more marvelous an abode, nor was the pearl and silver palace of the Peri more delicately charming."

Those who have had the opportunity to compare Sir Edwin Arnold's descriptions with the actual objects in Japan, India and elsewhere are apt to give a liberal allowance to his statements. He may be an accomplished poet, but he cannot see straight. He looks at everything through rose-colored magnifying glasses. The Hall of the Winds is a picturesque and unique piece of Hindu architecture. It looks like the frosting on a confectioners' cake. But it is six instead of nine stories in height, is made of the cheapest sort of stucco, and covered with deep pink calcimine. It is the residence of the ladies of the harem, or zenana, as that mysterious part of a household is called in India.

The palace of the maharaja is a noble building, but very ornate, and is furnished with the most tawdry and inappropriate French hangings and furniture. It is a pity that His Highness did not allow his own taste to prevail, and use nothing but native furniture and fabrics. His garden is lovely, being laid out in the highest style of Hindu landscape art. At the foot of the grounds is a great marble building, open on all sides, with a picturesque roof sustained by a multitude of columns, which is the public or audience hall, where His Highness receives his subjects and conducts affairs of ceremony. Behind it is a relic of some of his semi-barbarous ancestors in the form of a tank, in which a lot of loathsome crocodiles are kept for the amusement of people who like that sort of thing. They are looked after by a venerable, half-naked old Hindu, who calls them up to the terrace by uttering a peculiar cry, and, when they poke their ugly noses out of the water and crawl up the steps, teases them with dainty morsels he has obtained at the nearest slaughter-house. It is not a soul-lifting spectacle.

The stables are more interesting. The maharaja maintains the elephant stud of his ancestors, and has altogether about eighty monsters, which are used for heavy work about the palace grounds and for traveling in the country. In the stud are two enormous savage beasts, which fight duels for the entertainment of the maharaja and his guests. These duels take place in a paddock where horses are exercised. His Highness has erected a little kiosk, in which he can sit sheltered from the sun while the sport goes on. He also has a lot of leopards, panthers and cheetahs (Hindu wildcats), trained like dogs for hunting purposes, and are said to be as useful and intelligent as Gordon setters. He frequently takes a party of friends into the jungle for tiger shooting, and uses these tame beasts to scare up the game.

He is fond of horses and has 300 breeding mares and stallions kept in long stables opening upon the paddock in which they are trained. Each horse has a coolie to look after it, for no coolie could possibly attend to more than one. The man has nothing else to do. He sleeps on the straw in the stall of the animal, and seldom leaves it for a moment from the time he is assigned to the duty until his services are no longer required. The maharaja has spent a great deal of money and taken a great deal of pains to improve the stock of his subjects, both horses and cattle. He has an experimental farm for encouraging agriculture and teaching the people, and a horticultural garden of seventy acres, with a menagerie, in which are a lot of beautiful tigers captured by his own men upon his own estates within twelve miles of town. They catch a good many tigers alive, and one of his amiable habits is to present them to his friends and people whom he desires to honor.

In the center of the horticultural garden stands one of the noblest modern buildings in India, a museum which the maharaja established several years ago for the permanent exhibition of the arts and industries of his people, who are very highly skilled in metal and loom work of all kinds, in sculpture, enameling, in making jewelry of gold and silver, and varieties of glass work. At great expense he has assembled samples of similar work from other countries in order that his subjects may have the benefit of comparing it with their own, and in connection with the museum has established a school of art and industry. This at present has between five and six hundred students receiving instruction in the arts and industries in which the people of Jeypore have always excelled. The museum is called Albert Hall, in honor of the King of England, and the park is christened in memory of the late Earl of Mayo, who, while Viceroy of India, became an intimate friend and revered adviser of the father of the maharaja. An up-to-date hospital with a hundred beds is named Mayo Hospital.

The Maharaja's College is another institution which has been established by this public-spirited and progressive Hindu, who has done more for the education of his people than any other native prince. There are now about 1,000 students, with a faculty of eighty-two professors, including fifteen Englishmen and twelve Persians. The college is affiliated with the University of Calcutta, and has the best reputation of any institution of learning among the native states. But even higher testimony to the liberality and progressive spirit of this prince is a school for the education of women. It is only of recent years that the women in India were considered worth educating, and even now only about half a million in this vast country, with a female population of 150,000,000, can read and write. But the upper classes are gradually beginning to realize the advantage of educating their girls, and the Maharaja of Jeypore was one of the first to establish a school for that purpose, which now has between 700 and 800 girls under the instruction of English and native teachers.

We had great fun at Jeypore, and saw many curious and interesting things, for it is the liveliest and most attractive place we found in India, with the greatest number of novelties and distinctive local color. We went about day after day like a lot of lunatics, kodaks in hand, taking snap-shots at all the odd looking characters—and their name is legion—that we saw in the strees, and it was an unusual experience. Everybody hasn't an opportunity to photograph a group of elephants in full regalia carrying their owners' wives or daughters on shopping excursions or to visit friends—of course we didn't know which. And that is only one of the many unusual spectacles that visitors to Jeypore may see in every direction they choose to look. The gay raiment worn by the women and the men, the fantastic designs painted upon the walls of the houses and the bullock carts, are a never-ending delight, for they are absolutely unique, and the latter ought to be placed on pedestals in museums instead of being driven about for ordinary transportation purposes. The yokes of the oxen are carved with fanciful designs; everything is yellow or orange or red. Even the camels are draped with long nettings and fringes and tassels that reach from their humps to their heels. The decorative idea seems to prevail over everything in Jeypore. Nothing is without an ornament, no matter how humble its purpose or how cheap its material or mechanism, its owner embellishes as much as money and imagination will allow. Everything pays tribute to the esthetic sense of the people.

The bullocks are lean animals of cream color, with long legs, and trot over the road like horses, making four or five miles an hour. Instead of carrying a bit in their mouths, the reins are attached to a little piece of iron that passes through a hole in the cartilage of the nose, and the traces which draw the load spring from a collar that resembles a yoke. Most of the hauling is done by these animals. They are used for every purpose that we use horses and mules. Cows are never yoked. They are sacred. The religion of the Hindu prohibits him from subjecting them to labor. They are used for milking and breeding, and are allowed to run at large. Nobody dare injure a cow or even treat it unkindly. It would be as great a sin as kicking a congressman. A learned pundit told me the other day how it happened that cows became so highly esteemed in India. Of course he did not pretend to have been on the spot, but had formed a theory from reading, study and reflection, and by that same method all valuable theories are produced. He said that once upon a time cattle became scarce because of an epidemic which carried many of them off, and in order to recover their numbers and protect them from slaughter by the people some raja persuaded the Brahmins to declare them sacred. Everything that a Brahmin says goes in India, and the taboo placed upon those cows was passed along until it extended over the entire empire and has never been removed. I suppose we might apply the same theory to the sacred bulls of Egypt.

We took our first elephant ride one morning to visit Amber, the ancient but now deserted capital of the

ELEPHANT BELONGING TO THE MAHARAJAH OF JEYPORE

province of Jeypore, where tens of millions of dollars were wasted in the construction of splendid palaces and mansions that are now abandoned, and standing open and empty, most of them in good condition, to the enjoyment of tourists only and an occasional party of pilgrims attracted hither by sacred associations. The reason alleged for abandoning the place was the lack of pure water.

The maharaja usually furnishes elephants for visitors to his capital to ride around on. We are told that he delights to do it because of his good heart and the number of idle monsters in his stable who have to be exercised daily, and might as well be toting tourists about the country as wandering around with nobody on their backs. But a certain amount of ceremony and delay is involved in the transaction of borrowing an elephant from an Indian prince, hence we preferred to hire one from Mr. Zoroaster, who keeps a big shop full of beautiful brass and enamel work, makes Indian rugs and all sorts of things and exerts a hypnotic influence over American millionaires. One American millionaire, who was over there a few days ahead of us, evidently came very near buying out Mr. Zoroaster, who shows his order book with great pride, and a certain estimable American lady, who owns a university on the Pacific slope, recently bought enough samples of Indian art work from him to fill the museum connected with that institution. Mr. Zoroaster will show you the inventory of her purchases and the prices she paid, and will tell you in fervent tones what a good woman she is, and what remarkable taste she has, and what rare judgment she shows in the selection of articles from his stock to illustrate the industrial arts of India. He charged us fifteen rupees, which is equivalent to five dollars in American money, more or less, according to the fluctuations of exchange, for an elephant to carry us out to Amber, six miles and a half. We have since been told that we should have paid but ten rupees, and some persons assert that eight was plenty, and various other insinuations have been made concerning the way in which Mr. Zoroaster imposed upon innocent American globe trotters, and there was plenty of people who kept reminding us that we might have obtained an elephant for nothing. But Zoroaster is all right; his elephants are all right; the mahouts who steer them are all right, and it is worth fifteen rupees to ride to Amber on the back of a great, big clumsy beast, although you don't realize it at the time.

Beginners usually do not like the sensation of elephant riding. Young girls giggle, mature ladies squeal, middle-aged men grab hold of something firm and say nothing, while impenitent sinners often express themselves in terms that cannot properly be published. The acute trouble takes place just after mounting the beast and just before leaving the lofty perch occupied by passengers on his back. A saddle is placed upon his upper deck, a sort of saw-horse, and the lower legs stretch at an angle sufficiently obtuse to encompass his breadth of beam. This saw-horse is lashed to the hull with numerous straps and ropes and on top of it are placed rugs and cushions. Each saddle is built for four passengers, sitting dos-a-dos, back to back, two on a side, and a little shelf hangs down to support their feet. In order to diminish the climb the elephant kneels down in the road. A naked heathen brings a ladder, rests it against the side of the beast and the passengers climb up and take their seats in the saddle. Another naked heathen, who sits straddle the animal's neck, looks around at the load, inquires if everybody is ready, jabs the elephant under the ear with a sharpened iron prong and then the trouble begins. It is a good deal like an earthquake.

An elephant gets up one leg at a time, and during the process the passengers on the upper deck are describing parabolas, isosceles triangles and parallelepipedons in the circumambient atmosphere. There isn't much to hold on to and that makes it the more exciting. Then, when the animal finally gets under way, its movements are similar to those of an earthquake or a vessel without ballast in a first-class Hatteras gale. The irregularity and uncertainty of the motion excites apprehension, and as the minutes pass by you become more and more firmly convinced that something is wrong with the animal or the saddle or the road, and the way the beast wiggles his ears is very alarming. There is nobody around to answer questions or to issue accident-insurance policies and the naked heathen attendants talk no language that you know. But after a while you get used to it, your body unconsciously adjusts itself to the changes of position, and on the return trip, you have a pretty good time. You become so accustomed to the awkward and the irregular movements that you really enjoy the novelty and are perfectly willing to try it again.

But the most wonderful part of all is how the mahout steers the elephant. It is one of the mysteries that foreigners can never understand. He carries a goad in each hand—a rod of iron, about as big as a poker, with an ornamental handle generally embossed with silver or covered with enamel. One of the points curves around like half a crescent; the other is straight and both are sharpened to a keen point. When the mahout or driver wants the elephant to do something, he jabs one of the goads into his hide—sometimes one and sometimes the other, and at different places on the neck, under the ears, and on top of the head, and somehow or another the elephant understands what a jab in a particular place means and obeys cheerfully like the great, good-natured beast that he is. I have never been able to understand the system. Elephant driving is an occult science.

The road to Amber passes through an interesting part of the city of Jeypore and beyond the walls the broad highway is crowded with carts loaded with vegetables and other country produce coming into town and quite as many loaded with merchandise going the other way. Some of them are drawn by bullocks and some by camels; there are long caravans of camels with packs and paniers upon their backs. As you meet hundreds of pedestrians you will notice that the women all have baskets or packages upon their heads. The men never carry anything. On either side of the broad highway are cultivated gardens and gloomy looking houses and acres covered with ruins and crumbling tombs. The city of Amber, which, as I have already told you, was once the capital of the province and the scene of great splendor, as well as frequent strife, is now quite deserted. It once had 50,000 inhabitants, but now every house is vacant. Few of them even have caretakers. The beautiful palace with its marble coverings, mosaics and luxuriant gardens is occupied only by a number of priests and fakirs, who are supposed to spend their time in meditation upon heavenly things, and in obedience to an ancient custom they sacrifice a sheep or a goat in one of the temples every morning. Formerly human beings were slain daily upon this altar—children, young girls, women and peasants, who either offered themselves for the sake of securing advancement in reincarnation or were seized by the savage priests in the absence of volunteers. This was stopped by the British a century ago, and since then the blood of rams and goats has atoned for the sins of Jeypore.

XI

ABOUT SNAKES AND TIGERS

A gentleman in Bombay told me that 50,000 people are killed in India every year by snakes and tigers, and his extraordinary statement was confirmed by several officials and others to whom I applied for information. They declared that only about one-half of the deaths from such causes were ever reported; that the government was endeavoring to secure more complete and exact returns, and was offering rewards for the destruction of reptiles and wild animals. Under instructions from Lord Curzon the authorities of the central government at Calcutta gave me the returns for British India for the ten years from 1892 to 1902, showing a total of 26,461 human beings and 88,019 cattle killed by snakes and wild animals during the fiscal year 1901-2. This does not include the mortality from these causes in the eighty-two native states which have one-third of the area and one fourth of the population of the empire. Nor does it include thousands of cases in the more remote portions of the country, which are never reported to the authorities. In these remote sections, vast areas of mountains, jungles and swamps, the danger from such causes is much greater and deaths are more frequent than in the thickly settled portions; so that my friend's estimate was not far out of the way.

The official statistics for British India only (the native

states not included) for the ten years named are as follows:

KILLED BY WILD ANIMALS AND SNAKES.

	Persons	Cattle
1892	21,988	81,688
1893	24,016	90,253
1894	24,449	96,796
1895	25,190	100,107
1896	24,322	88,702
1897	25,242	84,187
1898	25,166	91,750
1899	27,585	98,687
1900	25,833	91,430
1901	26,461	88,019
Total ten years	250,252	907,619

Taking 1901 as a sample, I find that 1,171 persons were killed by tigers and 29,333 cattle; 635 persons and 37,473 cattle were killed by leopards; 403 human beings and 5,048 cattle were killed by wolves; 1,442 human beings and 9,123 cattle were killed by other wild animals, and 22,810 human beings and 5,002 cattle by snakes. This is about the average record for the ten years, although the number of persons killed by tigers in 1901-2 was considerably less than usual.

The largest sacrifice of life was in the Province of Bengal, of which Calcutta is the capital, and where the imperial authorities have immediate control of such affairs. The government offers a bounty of $1 for every snake skin, $5 for every tiger skin, and a corresponding amount for other animals. During 1901-2, 14,301 wild animals were reported killed and 96,953 persons received rewards. The number of snakes reported destroyed was 69,668 and 2,858 persons were rewarded. The total amount of rewards paid was $33,270, which is much below the average and the smallest amount reported for many years. During the last ten years the amount of rewards paid has averaged about $36,000 annually. The falling off in 1901-2 is due to the discovery that certain enterprising persons had gone into the business of breeding snakes for the reward, and had been collecting considerable sums from the government by that sort of fraud. Hereafter no one will be able to collect claims without showing satisfactory evidence that the snakes were actually wild when killed or captured. It is hardly necessary to say that no one has thus far been accused of breeding tigers for the bounty, although large numbers of natives are engaged in the business of capturing them for menageries and zoological gardens.

In the maharaja's park at Jeypore we saw a dozen or more splendid man-eating tigers, which, the keeper told us, had been captured recently only twelve miles from that city. His Highness keeps a staff of tiger hunters and catchers for amusement. He delights in shooting big game, and several times a year goes into the jungles with his native hunters and parties of friends and seldom returns without several fine skins to add to his collection. His tiger catchers remain in the woods all the time, and he has a pleasant way of presenting the animals they catch to friends in India, England and elsewhere. While we were in Jeypore I read in a newspaper that the Negus of Abyssinia had given Robert Skinner two fine lions to take home to President Roosevelt, and I am sure the maharaja of Jeypore would be very glad to add a couple of man-eating tigers if he were aware of Colonel Roosevelt's love for the animal kingdom. I intended to make a suggestion in that line to him, but there were so many other things to talk about that it slipped my mind.

The maharaja catches tigers in the orthodox way. He has cages of iron and the toughest kind of wood set upon wheels so that they can be hauled into the jungle by oxen. When they reach a suitable place the oxen are unhitched, the hunters conceal the wheels and other parts of the wagon with boughs and palm leaves. A sheep or a goat or some other animal is sacrificed and placed in the cage for bait and the door is rigged so that it will remain open in an inviting manner until the tiger enters and lifts the carcass from the lever. The instant he disturbs the bait heavy iron bars drop over the hole through which he entered and he is a prisoner at the mercy of his captors. Sometimes the scheme fails and the hunters lose their time and trouble and bait, but being men of experience in such affairs they generally know the proper place and the proper season to look for game. When the watchers notify them that the trap is occupied they come with oxen and haul it to town, where it is backed up against a permanent cage in the menagerie, the iron door is lifted, and the tiger is punched with iron bars until he accepts the quarters that have been provided for him, and becomes a prisoner for life.

It is a terrible thing when a hungry and ugly man-eater comes into a village, for the inhabitants are generally defenseless. They have no guns, because the government does not allow the natives to carry arms, and their only weapons are the implements of the farm. If they would clear out and scatter the number of victims would not be so large, but they usually keep together for mutual defense, and, as a consequence, the animal has them at his mercy. A man-eater that has once tasted human flesh is never satiated, and attacks one victim after another until he has made away with an entire village.

The danger from snakes and other poisonous reptiles is much greater than from tigers and other wild beasts, chiefly because snakes in India are sacred to the gods, and the government finds it an exceedingly delicate matter to handle the situation as the circumstances require. When a Hindu is bitten by a snake it is considered the act of a god, and the victim is honored rather than pitied. While his death is deplored, no doubt, he has been removed from an humble earthly sphere to a much more happy and honorable condition in the other world. Therefore, while it is scarcely true that the Hindus like to be killed by snake poison, they will do very little to protect themselves or cure the bites. Nor do they like to have the reptiles killed for fear of provoking the gods that look after them. The snake gods are numbered by hundreds of thousands, and shrines have been erected to them in every village and on every highway. If a pious Hindu peasant sees a snake he will seldom run from it, but will remain quiet and offer a prayer, and if it bites him and he dies, his heirs and relatives will erect a shrine to his memory. The honor of having a shrine erected to one's memory is highly appreciated. Hence death from snake poison is by no means the worst fate a Hindu can suffer. These facts indicate the difficulties the government officials meet in their endeavors to exterminate reptiles.

Snake charmers are found in every village. They are usually priests, monks or sorcerers, and may generally be seen in the neighborhood of Hindu temples and tombs. They carry from two to twenty hideous reptiles of all sizes in the folds of their robes, generally next to their naked bosoms, and when they see a chance of making a few coppers from a stranger they draw them out casually and play with them as if they were pets. Usually the fangs have been carefully extracted so that the snakes are really harmless. At the same time they are not agreeable companions. Sometimes snake charmers will allow their pets to bite them, and, when the blood appears upon the surface of the skin, they place lozenges of some black absorbent upon the wounds to suck up the blood and afterward sell them at high prices for charms and amulets.

When Mr. Henry Phipps of New York was in India he became very much interested in this subject. His sympathies were particularly excited by the number of poor people who died from snake bites and from the bites of wild animals, without medical attention. There is only one small Pasteur institute in India, and it is geographically situated so that it cannot be reached without several days' travel from those parts of the empire where snakes are most numerous and the mortality from animals is largest. With his usual modesty, without saying anything to anybody, Mr. Phipps placed $100,000 in the hands of Lord Curzon with a request that a hospital and Pasteur institute be established in southern India at the most accessible location that can be found for the treatment of such cases, and a laboratory established for original research to discover antidotes and remedies for animal poisons. After thorough investigation it was decided to locate the institute in the Province of Madras. The local government provided a site and takes charge of its maintenance, while the general government will pay an annual subsidy corresponding to the value of the services rendered to soldiers sent there for treatment.

While we were waiting at a railway station one morning a solemn-looking old man, who, from appearances, might have been a contemporary of Mahomet, or the nineteenth incarnation of a mighty god, squatted down on the floor and gazed upon us with a broad and benevolent smile. He touched his forehead respectfully and bowed several times, and then, having attracted attention and complied with the etiquette of his caste, drew from his breast a spry little sparrow that had been nestling between his cotton robe and his bare flesh. Stroking the bird affectionately and talking to it in some mysterious language, the old man looked up at us for approval and placed it upon the pavement. It greeted us cordially with several little chirps and hopped around over the stone to get the kinks out of its legs, while the old fakir drew from his breast a little package which he unfolded carefully and laid on the ground. It contained an assortment of very fine beads of different colors and made of glass. Taking a spool of thread from the folds of his robe, the old man broke off a piece about two feet long and, calling to the bird, began to whistle softly as his pet hopped over toward him. There was evidently a perfect understanding between them. The bird knew what was expected and proceeded immediately to business. It grasped the lower end of the thread in its little claws as its trainer held it suspended in the air with the other end wound around his forefinger, and swung back and forth, chirruping cheerfully. After swinging a little while it reached the top, and then stood proudly for a moment on the fakir's finger and acknowledged our applause. Then it climbed down again like a sailor or a monkey and dropped to the ground. I had never seen an exhibition so simple and yet unusual, but something even better was yet to come, for, in obedience to instruction, the little chap picked up the tiny beads one after another with his bill and strung them upon the thread, which it held with its tiny toes.

XII

THE RAJPUTS AND THEIR COUNTRY

In India, as everywhere else, the climate and physical features of the country have exercised a sharp and lasting influence upon the race that lives therein. The noblest characters, the brave, the strong, the enduring and the progressive come from the north, where the air is keen and encourages activity, while those who dwell in the south have hereditary physical and moral lassitude. The geographical names are typical of the people. They all mean something and have a poetical and oftentimes a political significance. "The Mountains of Strength" encompass a plateau called "The Abode of Princes," and beyond and behind them stretches a desert called the "Region of Death." This country is called the Rajputana—pronounced Raashpootana—and is composed of the most interesting of all the native states of India, twenty in number, with an area of 150,000 square miles and a population of more than 12,000,000. They are the only part of the empire where ancient political institutions and dynasties survive, and their preservation is due to the protection of the British authorities. Each prince is the hereditary chief of a military clan, the members of which are all descended from a common ancestor, and for centuries have been the lords of the soil. Many of the families are Mohammedans, and they are famous for their chivalry, their loyalty, their independence and love of the truth. These characteristics, I contend, are largely due to the climate and the topography of the territory in which they live.

Mount Abu, the sacred Olympus of western India, a huge heap of granite rising 5,650 feet above the sea, is in the center of Rajputana. It is called the "Pinnacle of the Saints," and upon its summit may be found the highest ideals of Indian ecclesiastical architecture in a group of five marble temples erected by peace-loving and life-protecting Jains, the Quakers of the East. These temples were built about a thousand years ago by three brothers, pious merchant princes, Vimala Sah, Tejpala and Vastupala. The material was carried more than 300 miles over mountains and across plains—an undertaking worthy of the ancient Egyptians. The columns and pillars, the cornices, the beams that support the roofs, the arches of the gateways, windows and doors, the sills and lintels, the friezes and wainscoting, all of the purest and daintiest marble, were chiseled by artists of a race whose creed pronounces patience to be the highest virtue, whose progenitor lived 8,000,000 years, and to whom a century is but a day. The purpose of the prayers of these people is to secure divine assistance in the suppression of all worldly desires, to subdue selfishness, to lift the soul above sordid thoughts and temptations. Therefore they built their temples amid the most beautiful scenery they could find. They made them cool and dark because of the heat and glare of this climate, with wide porticoes, overhanging eaves that shut out the sunshine and make the interior one great refreshing shadow, tempting the warm and weary to enter the cool twilight, for all the light they have is filtered through screens made of great sheets of fine-grained marble, perforated with tracery and foliage designs as delicate as Brussels lace.

In the center of this wonderful museum of sculpture, surrounded by a forest of carved columns, which in the minuteness and beauty of detail stand almost unrivaled even in this land of lavish labor and inexhaustible patience, sits the image of Parswanatha, the god of Peace and Plenty, a divinity that encourages love and gentleness and truth, to whom these temples were dedicated. He is seated upon an exquisite platform of alabaster, with legs crossed and arms folded, silent and immovable, engaged in the contemplation of the good and beautiful, and his lips are wreathed in a smile that comprehends all human beings and will last throughout eternity. Around this temple, as usual with the Jains, is a cloister—a wide colonnade supported by a double row of pillars. There are fifty-five cells opening upon it, but instead of being occupied by monks or priests, in each of them, upon a throne of lotus leaves, sits an exact miniature duplicate of the image of the same god, in the same posture, with the same expression of serene and holy calm. A number of young priests were moving about placing fresh flowers before these idols, and in the temple was a group of dusty, tired, hungry, half-naked and sore-footed pilgrims, who had come a long way with packs on their backs bearing their food and seeking no shelter but the shade of temples or trees. Here at last they found rest and relief and consolation, and it seems a beautiful religion that requires nothing more from its devotees.

The forty-eight columns which sustain the dome of this temple have been pronounced the most exquisite examples of carved marble in existence, and the highest authority on Indian architecture declares that the dome "in richness of ornament and delicacy of detail is probably unsurpassed in the world."

Facing the entrance to the temple is a square building, or portico, containing nine large white elephants, each carved from a monolith of marble. Originally they all had riders, intended to represent Vimala Sah, the Jain merchant, and his family going in procession to worship, but several of the figures have been broken entirely away and others have been badly damaged. These five temples, with their courtyards and cloisters, are said to have cost $90,000,000 and to have occupied fourteen years in building, from 1032 to 1046 A. D.

Mount Abu is the headquarters of the Rajputana administration, the hot weather station for the British troops, and the favorite summer resort of the European colonies of western India. The mountain is encircled with well-made roads, winding among the forests, and picturesque bridle paths. There are many handsome villas belonging to officials and private citizens, barracks, schools, asylums, clubs and other modern structures.

In several of the larger cities of the province can be found temples similar to those I have described; some of them of Saracenic architecture, equal to that of the Alhambra or the Persian palaces. The pure Hindu designs differ from the Saracenic as widely as the Gothic from the Romanesque, but often you find a mixture embracing the strongest features of both. The rich and the strong gave expression to their own sense of beauty and taste when by the erection of these temples they sought to honor and glorify the gods to whom they pray.

Ajmere, the winter capital of the governor general of Rajputana, is one of the oldest and most beautiful cities of western India, having been founded only a hundred years after the beginning of the Christian era, and occupying a picturesque position in an amphitheater made by the mountains, 3,000 feet above the sea. It is protected by a stone wall, with five gateways; many of the residences and most of the buildings are of stone, with ornamental façades, and some of them are of great antiquity. In the olden days it was the fashion to build houses to last forever. Ajmere has a population of about 70,000. It is surrounded by a fertile country, occupied by an industrious, wealthy, and prosperous people. The city is commanded by a fortress that crowns a noble hill called "The Home of the Stars," possesses a mosque that is one of the most successful combinations of Hindu and Saracenic architecture of which I have spoken, the conception of some unknown genius, combining the Mohammedan ideas of grandeur with Hindu delicacy of taste and prodigality of detail. In its decorations may be found some of the most superb marble embroidery that the imagination can conceive of. One of the highest authorities dates its erection as far back as the second century before Christ, but it is certainly of a much later date. Some architects contend that it belongs to the fourteenth century; it is however, considered the finest specimen of early Mohammedan architecture in existence. The mosque can be compared to a grand salon, open to the air at one side, the ceiling, fifty feet high, supported by four rows of columns, eighteen in each row, which are unique in design, and no two of them are alike. The designs are complex and entirely novel, and each is the work of a different artist, who was allowed entire liberty of design and execution, and endeavored to surpass his rivals.

There are several other mosques and temples of great beauty in Ajmere, and some of them are sacred places that attract multitudes of pilgrims, who are fed daily by the benevolence of rich contributors. Enormous rice puddings are cooked in eight enormous earthen caldrons, holding several bushels each, which are ready at noon every day. The composition contains rice, butter, sugar, almonds, raisins and spices, and to fill all of the eight pots costs about $70. The moment the pudding is cooked a bell is rung, and the pilgrims are allowed to help themselves in a grab-game which was never surpassed. Greedy creatures scald themselves in the pudding so badly that they sometimes carry the marks for life. It is counted a miracle caused by the intercession of the saints that no lives have ever been lost in these scrambles, although nearly every day some pilgrim is so badly burned that he has to be taken to a hospital. The custom is ancient, although I was not able to ascertain its origin or the reason why the priests do not allow the pudding to cool below the danger point before serving it.

Ajmere is the headquarters of one of the greatest railways in India, with extensive shops, employing several thousand natives and Europeans. The chief machinists, master mechanics and engineers are almost exclusively Scotchmen.

In this province may be found an excellent illustration of the effect of the policy of the British government toward the native princes. It had good material to work with, because the twenty independent Rajput princes are a fine set of men, all of whom trace their descent to the sun or the moon or to one of the planets, and whose ancestors have ruled for ages. Each family has a genealogical tree, with roots firmly implanted in mythology, and from the day when the ears of their infants begin to distinguish the difference in sounds, and their tongues begin to frame thoughts in words, every Rajput prince is taught the tables of his descent, which read like those in the Old Testament, and the names of his illustrious ancestors. Attached to each noble household is a chronicler or bard, whose business is to keep the family record straight, and to chant the epics that relate the achievements of the clan. As I have said, all the Rajput families are related and belong to the same caste, which has prevented them from diluting their blood by marriage with inferior families. It is his blood, and not the amount of his wealth or the extent of his lands, that ennobles a Rajput. Many of the noblest families are very poor, but the poorest retains the knowledge and the pride of his ancestors, which are often his only inheritance.

These characteristics and other social and religious customs make Rajputana one of the most romantic and fascinating spots in India, and perhaps there is no more interesting place to study the social, political and economical development of a people who once held that only two professions could be followed by a gentleman — war and government. But their ancient traditions have been thoroughly revised and modified to meet modern ideas. They have advanced in prosperity and civilization more rapidly than any other of the native states. Infanticide of girl babies was formerly considered lawful and generally practiced among them, and widows were always burned alive upon the funeral pyres of their husbands, but now the Rajput princes are building hospitals and asylums for women instead, bringing women doctors from Europe to look after the wives and daughters in their harems, and are founding schools for the education of girls.

About three miles from the center of Ajmere is Mayo

TOMB OF ETMAH-DOWLAH — AGRA

College, for the exclusive education of Rajput princes, and erected by them. The center building, of white marble, is surrounded by villas and cottages erected for the accommodation of the members of the princely families who are sent there. The villas are all of pure Hindu architecture, and there has been considerable rivalry among the different families to see which should house its cadets in the most elegant and convenient style. Hence, nowhere else in India can be found so many fine examples of modern native residence architecture. The young princes live in great style, each having a little court around him and a number of servants to gratify his wants. It is quite the usual arrangement for a college student to live in a palatial villa, with secretaries, aides-de-camp, equerries and bodyguards, for Indian princes are very particular in such matters, and from the hour of birth their sons are surrounded with as much ceremony as the King of Spain. They would not be permitted to attend the college if they could not continue to live in regal state. Some of them, only 10 or 12 years old, have establishments as large and grand as those of half the kings of Europe, and the Princes Imperial of England or of Germany live the life of a peasant in comparison.

XIII

THE ANCIENT MOGUL EMPIRE

The ancient Mogul Empire embraced almost as much of India as is controlled by the British today, and extended westward into Europe as far as Moscow and Constantinople. It was founded by a young warrior known as Timour the Tartar, or Tamerlane, as he is more frequently called in historical works. He was a native of Kesh, a small town fifty miles south of Samarkand, the capital of Bokhara, which was known as Tartary in those days. This young man conquered more nations, ruled over a wider territory and a larger number of people submitted to his authority than to any other man who ever lived, before or since. His expansion policy was more successful than that of Alexander the Great or Julius Cæsar or Charles V. or Napoleon, and he may properly be estimated as one of the greatest if not the very greatest and most successful soldier in all history. Yet he was not born to a throne. He was a self-made man. His father was a modest merchant, without wealth or fame. His grandfather was a scholar of repute and conspicuous as the first convert to Mohammedanism in the country in which he lived. Timour went into the army when he was a mere boy. There were great doings in those days, and he took an active part in them. From the start he seems to have been cast for a prominent role in the military dramas and tragedies being enacted upon the world's wide stage. He inherited a love of learning from his grandfather and a love of war as well as military genius from some savage ancestor. He rose rapidly. Other men acknowledged his superiority, and before he was 30 years old he found himself upon a throne and acknowledged to be the greatest soldier of his time. He came into India in 1398 and set up one of his sons on a throne at Delhi, where his descendants ruled until the great Indian mutiny of 1857—460 years. He died of fever and ague in 1405, and was buried at Samarkand, where a splendid shrine erected over his tomb is visited annually by tens of thousands of pilgrims, who worship him as divine.

Babar, sixth in descent from Timour, consolidated the states of India under a central government. His memoirs make one of the most fascinating books ever written. He lived a stirring and a strenuous life, and the world bowed down before him. His death was strangely pathetic, and illustrates the faith and the superstition of men mighty in material affairs but impotent before gods of their own creation. His son and the heir to his throne, Humayon, being mortally ill of fever, was given up to die by the doctors, whereupon the affectionate father went to the nearest temple and offered what he called his own worthless soul as a substitute for his son. The gods accepted the sacrifice. The dying prince began to recover and the old man sank slowly into his grave.

The empire increased in wealth, glory and power, and among the Mogul dynasty were several of the most extraordinary men that have ever influenced the destinies of nations. Yet it seems strange that from the beginning each successive emperor should be allowed to obtain the throne by treachery, by the wholesale slaughter of his kindred and almost always by those most shameful of sins—parricide and ingratitude to the authors of their being. Rebellious children have always been the curse of oriental countries, and when we read the histories of the Mogul dynasty and the Ottoman Empire and of the tragedies that have occurred under the shadows of the thrones of China, India and other eastern countries, we cannot but sympathize with the feelings of King Thebaw of Burma, who immediately after his coronation ordered the assassination of every relative he had in the world and succeeded in "removing" seventy-eight causes of anxiety.

Babar, the "Lion," as they called him, was buried at Kabul, the capital of Afghanistan, and was succeeded by Humayon, the son for whom he gave his life. The latter, on Sunday. Dec. 14, 1517, the day that Martin Luther delivered his great speech against the pope and caused the new word "Protestant"—one who protests—to be coined, drove Sikandar, the last of the Afghan dynasty, from India. When they found the body of that strenuous person upon the battle field, the historians say, "five or six thousand of the enemy were lying dead in heaps within a small space around him;" as if he had killed them all. The wives and slaves of Sikandar were captured. Humayon behaved generously to them, considering the fashion of those times, but took the liberty to detain their luggage, which included their jewels and other negotiable assets. In one of their jewel boxes was found a diamond which Sikandar had acquired from the sultan Alaeddin, one of his ancestors, and local historians, writing of it at the time, declared that "it is so valuable that a judge of diamonds valued it at half the daily expenses of the entire world." This was the first public appearance in good society of the famous Kohinoor, which, as everybody knows, is now the chief ornament in the crown of Edward VII., King of Great Britain and Ireland and Emperor of India. It is valued at £880,000, or $4,400,000 in our money. Queen Victoria never wore it. She had it taken from the crown and replaced by a paste substitute. This jewel thus became one of the heirlooms of the Moguls, who lived in such splendor as has never been seen since or elsewhere and could not be duplicated in modern times.

In the winter of 1555 Humayon was descending a stairway when his foot slipped and he fell headlong to the bottom. He was carried into his palace and died a few days later, being succeeded by his son, a boy of 13, who in many respects was the noblest of the Moguls, and is called in history Akbar the Great. He came to the throne in 1556, and his reign, which lasted until 1605, was almost contemporaneous with that of Queen Elizabeth. In reading his history one is impressed by the striking resemblance between him and the present Emperor of Germany. Beiram, who had been his father's prime minister, and whose clear intellect, iron will and masterful ability had elevated the house of Tamerlane to the glory and power it then enjoyed, remained with the young king as his adviser, and, owing to the circumstances, did not treat him with as much deference and respect as Akbar's lofty notions considered proper. The boy endured the slights for four years, and when he reached the age of 17 there occurred at the court of the Moguls an incident which was repeated several centuries later at Berlin, but it turned out differently.

Beiram, like Bismarck, submitted to the will of his young master, surrendered all insignia of authority, and started on a pilgrimage to Mecca, but before he left India his chagrin and indignation got the better of his judgment and he inspired an insurrection against the throne. He was arrested and brought back to Delhi, where, to his surprise, he was received with the greatest ceremony and honor. According to the custom of the time, nobles of the highest rank clothed him with garments from the king's wardrobe, and when he entered the royal presence Akbar arose, took him by the hand and led the astonished old man to a seat beside the imperial throne. Beiram, realizing the magnanimity of his boyish master, fell upon his knees, kissed the feet of the king, and between sobs begged for pardon. The king conferred the greatest possible honors upon him, but gave him no responsibility, and Beiram's proud and sensitive soul found relief in resuming his pilgrimage to Mecca. But he never reached that holy place. He died on the way by the hand of an Afghan noble, whose father, years before, he had killed in battle.

You must remember Akbar, because so many of the glories of Indian architecture, which culminate at Agra and Delhi, are due to his refined taste and appreciation for the beautiful, and I shall have a good deal to say about him, because he was one of the best men that ever wore a crown. He was great in every respect; he was great as a soldier, great as a jurist, great as an executive, broad-minded, generous, benevolent, tolerant and wise, an almost perfect type of a ruler, if we are to believe what the historians of his time tell us about him. He was the handsomest man in his empire; he excelled all his subjects in athletic exercises, in endurance and in physical strength and skill. He was the best swordsman and the best horseman and his power over animals was as complete as over men. And as an architect he stands unrivaled except by his grandson, who inherited his taste.

Although a pagan and without the light of the gospel, Akbar recognized the merits of Christianity and exemplified the ideals of civil and religious liberty which it teaches, and which are now considered the highest attribute of a well-ordered state. While Queen Elizabeth was sending her Catholic subjects to the scaffold and the rack, while Philip II. was endeavoring to ransom the souls of heretics from perdition by burning their bodies alive in the public plazas of his cities, and while the awful incident of St. Bartholomew indicated the religious condition of France, the great Mogul of Delhi called around his throne ministers of peace from all religions, proclaimed tolerance of thought and speech, freedom of worship and theological controversy throughout his dominions; he abolished certain Hindu practices, such as trials by ordeal, child marriage, the burning of widows and other customs which have since been revived, because he considered them contrary to justice, good morals and the welfare of his people, and displayed a cosmopolitan spirit by marrying wives from the Brahmin, Buddhist, Mohammedan and Christian faiths. He invited the Roman Catholic missionaries, who were enjoying great success at Goa, the Portuguese colony 200 miles south from Bombay, to come to Agra and expound their doctrines, and gave them land and money to build a church. His grandson and successor married a Catholic queen—a Portuguese princess.

But notwithstanding the just, generous and noble life of Akbar, he was overthrown by his own son, Selim, who took the high-sounding title Jehanghir, "Conqueror of the World," and he had been reigning but a short time when his own son, Kushru, endeavored to treat him in the same manner. The revolt was promptly quelled. Seven hundred of the supporters of the young prince were impaled in a row, and that reckless youth was conducted slowly along the line so that he could hear the dying reproaches of the victims of his misguided ambition. Other of his sons also organized rebellions afterward and "the conqueror of the world" had considerable difficulty in retaining his seat upon the throne, but he proved to be a very good king. He was just and tolerant, sober and dignified and scrupulous in observing the requirements of his position, and was entirely subject to the influence of a beautiful and brilliant wife.

His successor was Shah Jehan, one of the most interesting and romantic figures in Indian history, who began his reign by murdering his brothers. That precaution firmly established him upon the throne. He, too, was considered a good king, but his fame rests chiefly upon the splendor of his court and the magnificent structures he erected. He rebuilt the ancient City of Delhi upon a new site, adorned it with public buildings of unparalleled cost and beauty, and received his subjects seated upon the celebrated peacock throne, a massive bench of solid gold covered with mosaic figures of diamonds, rubies, pearls and other precious stones. It cost £6,500,000, which is $32,500,000 of our money, even in those times, when jewels were cheap compared with the prices of today. In 1729 Nadir Shah, the King of Persia, swooped down upon India and carried this wonder of the world to his own capital, together with about $200,000,000 in other portable property.

There are many good traits in the character of Shah Jehan. Aside from his extravagance, his administration was to be highly commended. Under his rule India reached the summit of its wealth and prosperity, and the people enjoyed liberty and peace, but retribution came at last, and his sons did unto him as he had done unto his father, and much more also. They could not wait until he was ready to relinquish power or until death took the scepter from his hand, but four of them rebelled against him, drove him from the throne and kept him a prisoner for the last eight years of his life. But scarcely had they overthrown him when they began to quarrel among themselves, and Aurangzeb, the fourth son, being the strongest among them, simplified the situation by slaughtering his three brothers, and was thus able to reign unmolested for more than half a century, until he died in 1707, 89 years old. His last days were embittered by a not unnatural fear that he would suffer the fate of his own father.

From the time that the Emperor Aurangzeb climbed to the throne of the Moguls upon the dead bodies of his father and three elder brothers, the glory and power of that empire began to decay. He reigned forty-nine years. His court was magnificent. At the beginning his administration was wise and just, and he was without question an able, brave and cultured king. But, whether as an atonement for his crimes or for some other reason, he became a religious fanatic, and after a few years the broad-minded policy of religious liberty and toleration, which was the chief feature of the reign of his father and his grandfather, was reversed, and he endeavored to force all of his subjects into the Mohammedan faith. He imposed a heavy head tax upon all who did not profess that faith; he excluded all but Moslems from the public service; he deprived "infidels," as they were generally termed, of valuable civil rights and privileges; he desecrated the shrines and destroyed the sacred images of the Hindus, and prohibited the religious festivals and other features of their worship. The motive of this policy was no doubt conscientious, but the effect was the same as that which has followed similar sectarian zeal in other countries. The history of the world demonstrates that religious intolerance and persecution always destroy prosperity. No nation ever prospered that prohibited freedom of worship. You will find a striking demonstration of that truth in Spain, in the Balkan states and in the Ottoman Empire, in modern times without going back to the Jews and other ancient races. The career of Aurangzeb is strikingly like that of Philip II. of Spain, and his character was similar to that of Louis XIV. of France, who was his contemporary. Both were unscrupulous, arrogant, egotistical and cruel kings; both were religious devotees and endeavored to compensate for a lack of morals by excessive zeal in persecuting heretics, and in promoting what they considered the interests of their church; and both created disaffection and provoked rebellion among their subjects, and undermined the power and authority of the dynasties to which they belonged.

It is needless to review the slow but gradual decay of the Great Mogul Empire. With the adoption of Aurangzeb's policy of intolerance it began to crumble, and none of his successors proved able to restore it. He died in 1707, and the throne of the Moguls was never again occupied by a man of force or notable ability. The history of the empire during the eighteenth century is merely a record of successive failures, of disintegration, of successful rebellions and of invasions by foreign foes, which stripped the Moguls of their wealth and destroyed their resources. First came the Persians; then the Afghans, who plundered the imperial capital, desecrated tombs and temples, destroyed the fortresses and palaces and left little but distress and devastation when they departed. One by one the provinces separated themselves from the empire and set up their own independence; until in 1804 the English took possession of the remnant and have maintained their authority ever since.

Within the wall of the great citadel at Delhi, for reasons of policy, the English allowed the great Mogul to maintain a fictitious court, and because the title continued to command the veneration of the natives, at state ceremonies the nominal successor of Timour the Tartar was allowed to sit upon a throne in the imperial hall of audience and receive the homage of the people. But the Moguls were not allowed to exercise authority and were idle puppets in the hands of their advisers until the great mutiny of 1857 brought the native soldiers into the palace crying:

"Help, oh King, in our Fight for the Faith."

It is not necessary to relate the details of that awful episode of Indian history, but it will do no harm to recall what we learned in our school days of the principal incidents and refer to the causes which provoked it. From the beginning of the British occupation of India there had been frequent local uprisings caused by discontent or conspiracy, but the East India Company, and the officials of the British government who supported it, had perfect confidence in the loyalty of the sepoys—the native soldiers who were hired to fight against their fellow countrymen for so much pay. They were officered by Englishmen, whose faith in them was only extinguished by assassination and massacre. The general policy and the genera. results of British administration have been worthy of the highest commendation, but there have been many blunders and much injustice from time to time, due to individuals rather than to the nation. A weak and unwise man in authority can do more harm in a year than can be corrected in a century. Several so-called "reforms" had been introduced into the native army; orders had been issued forbidding the use of caste marks, the wearing of earrings and other things which Englishmen considered trivial, but were of great importance to the Hindus. Native troops were ordered over the sea, which caused them to lose their caste; new regulations admitted low-caste men to the service; the entire army was provided with a new uniform with belts and cockades made from the skins of animals which the Hindus considered sacred, and cartridges were issued which had been covered with lard to protect them from the moisture of the climate, and, as everybody knows, the flesh of swine is the most unclean thing in existence to the pious Hindu. All these things, which the stubborn, stupid Englishmen considered insignificant, were regarded by the sepoys as deliberate attacks upon their religion, and certain conspirators, who had reasons for desiring to destroy British authority, used them to convince the native soldiers that the new regulations were a long-considered and deliberate attempt to deprive them of their caste and force them to become Christians. Unfortunately the British officers in command refused to treat the complaints seriously, and laughed in the faces of their men, which was insult added to injury, and was interpreted as positive proof of the evil intentions of the government.

This situation was taken advantage of by certain Hindu princes who had been deprived of power or of pensions previously granted. Nana Sahib, the deposed raja of Poona, was the leader, and the unsuspecting authorities allowed him to travel about the country stirring up discontent and conspiring with other disloyal native chiefs for a general uprising and massacre, which, according to their programme, occurred in northern India during the summer of 1857. If the British had desired to play into the hands of the conspirators they could not have adopted a policy more effective in that direction. Utterly unconscious of danger and unsuspicious of the conspiracies that were enfolding them, they relieved city after city of its guard of English troops and issued arms and ammunition in unusual and unnecessary quantities to the sepoys, at whose mercy the entire foreign population was left.

The outbreak occurred according to the programme of Nana Sahib, who proved to be a leader of great ability and strategic skill, and in nearly every city of northern India, particularly at Delhi, Lucknow, Cawnpore and other places along the Ganges, men, women and children, old and young, in the foreign colonies were butchered in cold blood. In Agra 6,000 foreigners gathered for protection in the walls of the great fort, and most of them were saved. Small detachments of brave soldiers under General Havelock, Sir Henry Lawrence, Sir Colin Campbell, Sir Hugh Rose, Lord Napier and other leaders fought their way to the rescue, and the conspiracy was finally crushed, but not without untold suffering and enormous loss of life.

On the evening of May 11, 1857, about fifty foreigners, all unarmed civilians, were brought into the palace at Delhi, and by order of Bahander Shah, the Mogul whom the mutineer leaders had proclaimed Emperor of India, were thrust into a dungeon, starved for five days and then hacked to pieces in the beautiful courtyard. The new emperor, a weak-minded old man with no energy or ability, and scarcely intellect enough to realize his responsibilities, pronounced judgment and issued the orders prepared for him by the conspirators by whom he was surrounded. But retribution was swift and sure. A few weeks later when the British troops blew in the walls of the palace citadel after one of the most gallant assaults ever recorded in the annals of war, the old man, with two of his sons, fled to the tomb of Humayon, who occupied the Mogul throne from 1531 to 1556, as if that sanctuary would be revered by the British soldiers.

This tomb is one of the most notable buildings in India. It stands on the bank of the Jumna River, about five miles from the present city of Delhi. It is an octagonal mass of rose-colored sandstone and white marble, decorated with an ingenuity of design and delicacy of execution that have never been surpassed, and is crowned by a marble dome of perfect Persian pattern, three-fourths the diameter of that of St. Paul's Cathedral of London, and almost as large as that of the Capitol at Washington. In this splendid mausoleum, where twelve of his imperial ancestors sleep, the Last of the Moguls endeavored to conceal himself and his sons, but Colonel Hodson, who commanded a desperate volunteer battalion of foreigners whose property had been confiscated or destroyed by the mutineers, whose wives had been ravished and whose children had been massacred, followed the flying Mogul to the asylum he sought, and dragged him trembling and begging for mercy from among the tombs.

Hodson was a man of remarkable character and determination and was willing to assume responsibility, and

"Hodson's Horse," as the volunteer battalion was called, were the Rough Riders of the Indian mutiny. He took the aged king back to Delhi and delivered him to the British authorities alive, but almost imbecile from terror and excitement. The two princes, 19 and 22 years of age, he deliberately shot with his own revolver before leaving the courtyard of the tomb in which they were captured.

This excited the horror of all England. The atrocities of the mutineers were almost forgotten for the moment. That the heirs of the throne of the great Moguls should be killed by a British officer while prisoners of war was an offense against civilization and Christianity that could not be tolerated, although only a few weeks before these two same princes had participated in the cold-blooded butchery of fifty Christian women and children. There was a parliamentary investigation. Hodson explained that he had only a few men, too few to guard three prisoners of such importance; that he was surrounded by fifty thousand half-armed and excited natives, who would have exterminated his little band and rescued his prisoners if any one of their number had possessed sufficient presence of mind and courage to make the attempt. Convinced that he could not conduct three prisoners through that crowd of their adherents and sympathizers without sacrificing his own life and that of his escort, he took the responsibility of shooting the princes like the reptiles they were, and thus relieved the British government from what might have been a most embarrassing situation.

Hodson was condemned by parliament and public opinion, while the bloodthirsty old assassin he had captured was treated as gently and as generously as if he had been a saint. Bahandur Shah was tried and convicted of treason, but was acquitted of responsibility for the massacre on the ground that his act authorizing it was a mere formality, and that it would have occurred without his consent at any rate. Instead of hanging him the British government sent him in exile to Rangoon, where he was furnished a comfortable bungalow and received a generous pension until November, 1862, when he died. Bahandur Shah had a third son, a worthless drunken fellow, who managed to escape the consequences of his participation in the massacre and accompanied him into exile. He survived his father for several years and left a widow and several children at Rangoon, including a son, who inherited his indolence, but not his vices. The latter still lives there on a small pension from the British government, is idle, indifferent, amiable and well-liked. He goes to the races, the polo games and tennis matches, and takes interest in other sports, but is too lazy to participate. He has married a Burmese wife and they have several children, who live with him in the bungalow that was assigned to his grandfather when he was sent to Burma forty-five years ago, and, judging from appearances, it has not been repaired since. Although he is perfectly harmless, the Last of the Moguls is required to report regularly to the British commandant and is not allowed to leave Burma, even if he should ever desire to do so.

XIV

THE ARCHITECTURE OF THE MOGULS

Although the Moguls have vanished, their glory remains in the most sublime and beautiful monuments that were ever erected by human hands, and people come from the uttermost parts of the earth to admire them. In the form of fortresses, palaces, temples and tombs they are scattered pretty well over northern India, and the finest examples may be found at Agra, a city of 200,000 inhabitants, only a short ride from Delhi, the Mogul capital. Agra was their favorite residence. Akbar the Great actually removed the seat of government there the latter part of the sixteenth century, and expended genius and money until he made it the most beautiful city in India and filled it with the most splendid palaces that were ever seen. Shah Jehan, his grandson, who was a greater man than he, and lived and reigned nearly a hundred years after him, even surpassed him in architectural ambition and accomplishments. Jehan built the fort at Agra, and the best specimens of his architectural work are within its walls, erected between 1630 and 1637, and he was confined within them, the prisoner of his son Aurangzeb, for seven years before his death, from 1658 to 1665.

The fortress at Agra is probably the grandest citadel ever erected. It surpasses in beauty and strength the Kremlin at Moscow, the Tower of London, the citadel at Toledo and every other fortress I know of. Nothing erected in modern times can compare with it. Although it would be a poor defense and protection against modern projectiles, it was impregnable down to the mutiny of 1857. The walls are two miles and a quarter in circumference; they are protected by a moat 30 feet wide and 35 feet deep; they are 70 feet high and 30 feet thick, and built of enormous blocks of red sandstone. There are two entrances, both very imposing, one called the Delhi Gate and the other the Elephant Gate, where there used to be two large stone elephants, but they were removed many years ago. Within the walls is a collection of the most magnificent oriental palaces ever erected, with mosques, barracks, arsenals, storehouses, baths and other buildings for residential, official and military purposes, all of them on the grandest scale. Since the British have had possession they have torn down many of the old buildings and have erected unsightly piles of brick and stone in their places, but while such vandalism cannot be condemned in terms too strong, the world should be grateful to them for leaving the most characteristic and costly of the Mogul residences undisturbed. A small garrison of English soldiers is quartered in the fortress at present, just enough to protect it and keep things in order, but there is room for several regiments, and during the mutiny of 1857 more than 6,000 foreigners, refugees from northern India, found refuge and protection here.

Although the palaces seem bare and comfortless to us to-day, and we wonder how people could ever be contented to live in them, we are reminded that when they were actually occupied the open arches were hung with curtains, the marble floors were spread with rugs and covered with cushions, and the banquet halls were furnished with sumptuous services of gold, silver and linen. The Moguls were not ascetics. They loved luxury and lived in great magnificence with every comfort and convenience that the ingenuity and experience of those days could contrive. It is never safe to judge of things by your own standard. You may always be sure that intelligent people will adapt themselves in the best possible manner to their conditions and environment. Those who live in the tropics know much better how to make themselves comfortable than friends who visit them from the arctic zone. Wise travelers will always imitate local habits and customs so far as they are able to do so. While these wonderful compositions of carved marble seem cold and comfortless as they stand empty to-day, we must not forget that they were very different when they were actually inhabited. Some idea of the luxury of the Mogul court may be gained from an account given by M. Bernier, a Frenchman who visited Agra in 1663 during the reign of Shah Jehan. He says:

"The king appeared sitting upon his throne, in the bottom of the great hall of the Am-kas, splendidly appareled. His vest was of white satin, flowered and raised with a very fine embroidery of gold and silk. His turban was of cloth-of-gold, having a fowl wrought upon it like a heron, whose foot was covered with diamonds of an extraordinary bigness and price, with a great oriental topaz, which may be said to be matchless, shining like a little sun. A collar of big pearls hung about his neck down to his stomach, after the manner that some of the heathens wear their great beads. His throne was supported by six pillars, or feet, said to be of massive gold, and set with rubies, emeralds and diamonds. I am not able to tell you aright either the number or the price of this heap of precious stones, because it is not permitted to come near enough to count them and to judge of their water and purity. Only this I can say: that the big diamonds are there in confusion, and that the throne is estimated to be worth four kouroures of roupies, if I remember well. I have said elsewhere that a roupie is almost equivalent to half a crown, a lecque to a hundred thousand roupies and a kourour to a hundred lecques, so that the throne is valued at forty millions of roupies, which are worth about sixty millions of French livres. That which I find upon it best devised are two peacocks covered with precious stones and pearls. Beneath this throne there appeared all the Omrahs, in splendid apparel, upon a raised ground covered with a canopy of purified gold, with great golden fringes and inclosed by a silver balistre. The pillars of the hall were hung with tapestries of purified gold, having the ground of gold; and for the roof of the hall there was nothing but great canopies of flowered satin, fastened with great red silken cords that had big tufts of silk mixed with threads of gold."

The gem of the architectural exhibition at Agra, always exempting the Taj Mahal, is the "Pearl Mosque," so called because it is built of stainless white marble, without the slightest bit of color within except inscriptions from the Koran here and there inlaid in precious stones. It was the private chapel of the Moguls, as you might say; was built between 1648 and 1655, and has been pronounced by the highest authority to be the purest and most elegant example of Saracenic architecture in existence. No lovelier sanctuary was ever erected in honor of the Creator. One of the inscriptions tells us that it was intended to be "likened to a mansion of paradise or to a precious pearl." It is built after the usual fashion, a square courtyard paved with white marble and surrounded by a marble colonnade of exquisite arches, supported by pillars of perfect grace. The walls upon three sides are solid; the western side, looking toward Mecca, being entirely open, a succession of arches supported by columns exquisitely carved. And the roof is crowned with a forest of minarets and three white marble domes. In the center of the courtyard is a marble tank thirty-seven feet square and three feet deep, in which the faithful performed their ablutions before going to prayer.

Near by the mosque is the Diwan-i-'Am, or Hall of Public Audience, 201 feet square, in which the Moguls received their subjects and held court. The roof is supported by nine rows of graceful columns cut from red sandstone and formerly covered with gold. The rest of the building is marble. The throne stood upon a high platform in an alcove of white marble, richly decorated, and above it are balconies protected by grilles or screens behind which the sultanas were permitted to watch the proceedings. Back of the audience-room is a great quadrangle, planted with trees, flowers and vines. White marble walks radiate from a marble platform and fountain basin in the center, and divide the garden into beds which, we are told, were filled with soil brought from Cashmere because of its richness. And even to-day gardeners say that it is more productive than any found in this part of the country. Around this court were the apartments of the zenana, or harem, occupied by the mother, sisters, wives and daughters of the sultan who were more or less prisoners, but had considerable area to wander about in, and could sit in the jasmine tower, one of the most exquisite pieces of marble work you can imagine, and on the flat roofs of the palaces, which were protected by high screens, and enjoy views over the surrounding country and up and down the Jumna River. From this lofty eyrie they could witness reviews of the troops and catch glimpses of the gay cavalcades that came in and out of the fortress, and in a small courtyard was a bazar where certain favored merchants from the city were allowed to come and exhibit goods to the ladies of the court. But these were the only glimpses female royalty ever had of the outer world.

No man was ever admitted to the zenana except the emperor. All domestic work was done by women, who were watched on the outside by eunuchs and then by soldiers. They had their own place of worship, the "Gem Mosque" they called it, a beautiful little structure erected by Shah Jehan, and afterward used as his prison.

The baths are of the most sumptuous character. The walls are decorated with raised foliage work in colors, silver and gold, upon a ground of mirrors, and the ceiling is finished with pounded mica, which has the effect of silver. Fronting the entrance of the bathrooms are rows of lights over which the water poured in broad sheets into a basin, then, running over a little marble causeway, fell over a second cluster of lights into another basin, and then another and another, five in succession, so that many ladies were able to bathe in these fascinating fountains at the same time. Below the baths we were shown some dark and dreary vaults. In the center of the most gloomy of them there is a pit—a well—which, the guide told us, has its outlet in the bottom of the river, three-quarters of a mile away. Over this pit hangs a heavy beam of wood very highly carved, and in the center is a groove from which dangles a silken rope. Here, according to tradition, unfaithful inmates of the harem were hanged, and when life was extinct the cord was cut and the body fell into the pit, striking the keen edge of knives at frequent intervals, so that it finally reached the river in small fragments, which were devoured by fishes or crocodiles, or if they escaped them, floated down to the sea. After each execution a flood of water was turned from the fountains into the pit to wash away the stains.

But let us turn from this terrible place to the jasmine tower containing apartments of the chief sultana, which overhangs the walls of the fort and is surpassingly beautiful: a series of rooms entirely of marble—roof, walls and floor—and surrounded by a broad marble veranda supported by noble arches springing from graceful, slender pillars arranged in pairs and protected by a balustrade of perforated marble. One could scarcely imagine anything more dainty than these lacelike screens of stone extremely simple in design and exquisite in execution. The interior walls are incrusted with mosaic work of jasper, carnelian, lapis-lazuli, agate, turquoise, bloodstone, malachite and other precious materials in the form of foliage, flowers, ornamental scrolls, sentences from the Koran in Arabic letters and geometrical patterns. The decoration is as beautiful and as rich as the Taj Mahal, so far as it goes, and was done by the same artists.

There is a broad field for the imagination to range about in and picture this palace when it was a paradise of luxury and splendor, filled with gorgeous and costly hangings, draperies, rugs, couches and cushions. The writers of the time tell us that the sultanas had 5,000 women around them who were divided into companies. First were the three chief wives, next in rank were 300 concubines and the remainder were dancing girls, musicians, artists, embroiderers, seamstresses, hair dress-ers, cooks and other servants. The mother of the Mogul was always the head of the household. The three empresses were subject to her authority, according to the oriental custom, and while they might stand first in the affections of the Mogul they were subordinate to his mother, who conducted affairs about the harem, we are told, with the same regularity and strictness that were found in the executive departments of the state. Each of the wives received an allowance according to her rank. If she had a child, especially a son, she was immediately promoted to the highest rank, given larger and better quarters, provided with many more servants and furnished with a much larger allowance in money.

The apartments of the emperor are quite plain when compared with the adjoining suite of the favorite sultana, but are massive, dignified and appropriate for a sovereign of his wealth and power, and everything is finished with that peculiar elegance which is only found in the East. In all the great cluster of buildings there is nothing mean or commonplace. Every apartment, every corridor, every arch and every column is perfect and a wonder of architectural design, construction and decoration.

From the emperor's apartments you may pass through a stately pavilion to a large marble courtyard. Upon one side of it, next to the wall that overhangs the river, is a slab of black marble known as "The Black Marble Throne." And upon this he used to sit when hearing appeals for justice from his subjects or other business of supreme importance. Upon the opposite side of the court is a white marble slab upon which the grand vizier sat and to the east is a platform where seats were provided for the judges, the nobles and the grandees of the court.

In this pavilion have occurred some of the most exciting scenes in Indian history.

Perhaps you would like to know something about the women who lived in these wonderful palaces, and are buried in the beautiful tombs at Agra. They had their romances and their tragedies, and although the Mohammedan custom kept them closely imprisoned in the zenanas, they nevertheless exerted a powerful influence in arranging the destinies of the Mogul empire. The most notable of the women, and one who would have taken a prominent part in affairs in whatever country or in whatever generation it had pleased the Almighty to place her, was Nur Jehan, sultana of the Mogul Jehanghir. She lived in the marble palace of Agra from 1556 to 1605; a woman of extraordinary force of character, the equal of Queen Elizabeth in intellect and of Mary Stuart in physical attractions, and her life was a mixture of romance and tragedy. Her father, Mizra Gheas Bey, or Itimad-Ud Daula, as he was afterward known, was grand vizier cf the Mogul empire during the latter part of the reign of Akbar the Great. An obscure but ambitious Persian scholar, hearing of the generous patronage extended to students by Emperor Akbar in India, he started from Teheran to Delhi overland, a distance of several thousand miles. He had means enough to buy a donkey for his wife to ride, and trudged along with a caravan on foot beside the animal to protect her and the panniers which contained all their earthly possessions. The morning after the caravan reached Kandahar, Turkestan, a daughter was born to the wife of Mirza, and was, naturally, a great source of anxiety and embarrassment to him, but the principal merchant of the caravan, struck with the beauty of the child and with sympathy for the mother, provided for their immediate needs, took them with him to Agra and there used his good offices with the officials in behalf of the father, who was given employment under the government. His ability and fidelity were soon recognized. He was promoted rapidly, and finally reached the highest office in the gift of the Mogul—that of prime minister of the empire—which he filled with conspicuous ability, wisdom and prudence for many years. As his daughter grew to girlhood she attracted the attention of Prince Jehanghir, who became violently in love with her, and, to prevent complications, the emperor caused her to be married to Shir Afghan Kahn, a young Persian of excellent family, who was made viceroy of Bengal, and took his wife with him to Calcutta.

Several years later, when Jehanghir ascended the throne, he had not forgotten the beautiful Persian, and sent emissaries to Calcutta to arrange with her husband for a divorce so that he might take her into his own harem. Shir Afghan refused, and the king ordered his assassination. Nur Jehan undoubtedly loved her husband, and sincerely mourned him. She repelled the addresses of the emperor, and for several years earned her living by embroidery and painting silks. One day the emperor surprised her in her apartment. He was the only man in India who had the right to intrude upon his lady subjects, but seems to have used it with rare discretion. When she recognized her visitor she bowed her head to the floor nine times in accordance with the custom of the country; and although she was wearing the simplest of garments, she had lost none of her beauty or graces, and treated the Mogul with becoming modesty and dignity. When he reproached her for her plain attire she replied:

"Those born to servitude must dress as it shall please them whom they serve. Those women around me are my servants and I lighten their bondage by every indulgence in my power; and I, who am your slave, O Emperor of the World, am willing to dress according to your pleasure and not my own."

This significant retort pleased His Majesty immensely, and, with the facilities that were afforded emperors in those days, he had her sent at once to the imperial harem, where she was provided with every possible comfort and luxury and was promoted rapidly over the other women. She received the title Nur Jehan Begam (Light of the World). The Emperor granted her the right of sovereignty in her own name; her portrait was placed upon the coin of the country; and after several years her power became so great that the officials would not obey any important order from his majesty unless it bore her indorsement. He willingly submitted to her judgment and counsel. She repressed his passions, caprices and prejudices, and when any matter of serious importance arose in the administration of affairs, it was submitted to her before action was taken. Her beauty and her graces were the theme of all the poets of India, and her goodness, the kindness of her heart and her unbounded generosity are preserved by innumerable traditions. She was the godmother of all orphan girls and provided their dowers when they were married, and it is said that during her reign she procured good husbands for thousands of friendless girls who otherwise must have spent their lives in slavery. Thus the child of the desert became the most powerful influence in the East, for in those days the authority of the Mogul extended from the Ganges to the Bosporus and the Baltic Sea.

Nur Jehan took good care of her own family. Her father continued to occupy the office of grand vizier until his death, and her brother, Asaf Khan, became high treasurer of the empire and father-in-law of the Mogul. Other relatives were placed in remunerative and influential positions. But at last she made a blunder, and failed to secure the crown for her son, Sheriar, who, being a younger member of the family, was not entitled to it, and Shah Jehan, the oldest son of the Mogul by another wife, succeeded him to the throne.

Shah Jehan promptly murdered his ambitious brother, as was the amiable custom of those days, but treated his father's famous widow with great respect and generosity. He presented her with a magnificent palace, gave her an allowance of $1,250,000 a year and accepted her pledge that she would interfere no longer in politics. She survived nineteen years and devoted her time and talents thereafter and several millions of dollars to the construction of a tomb to the memory of her father, which still stands as one of the finest of the group of architectural wonders of Agra. It is situated in a walled garden on the bank of the River Jumna about a mile and a half from the hotels, and is constructed entirely of white marble. The sides are of the most beautiful perforated work, and the towers are of exquisite design. Much of the walls are covered with the Florentine mosaic work similar to that which distinguishes the Taj Mahal.

Shah Jehan, the greatest of all the Moguls, had many wives, and three in particular. One of them was a Hindu, of whom we know very little; another was a Mohammedan, the daughter of Asaf Khan, high treasurer of the empire and the niece of Nur Jehan. She is the woman who sleeps in the Taj Mahal, the most beautiful of all human structures. The third was Miriam, a Portuguese Christian princess, who never renounced her religion, and built a Roman Catholic Church in a park outside the walls of Agra in connection with a palace provided for her special residence. This marriage was brought about through the influence of the governor of the Portuguese colony at Goa, 200 miles south of Bombay, and illustrates the liberality of Shah Jehan in religious matters. He not only tolerated, but invited Catholic missionaries to come into his empire and preach their doctrines, and although we know very little of the experience of the Sultana Miriam, and her life must have been rather lonely and isolated, yet the king did not require her to remain in the harem with his other wives, but gave her an independent establishment a considerable distance from the city, where she was attended by ladies of her own race and religion. Her palace has disappeared, but the church she built is still standing, and her tomb is preserved. By successive changes they have passed under the control of the Church of England and her grounds are now occupied by an orphanage under the superintendence of a Mr. Moore, who has 360 young Hindus under his care. The fathers and mothers of most of them died during the famine and he is teaching them useful trades. We stopped to talk to some of the children as we drove about the place, but did not get much information. The boys giggled and ran away and the workmen were surprisingly ignorant of their own affairs, which, I have discovered, is a habit Hindus cultivate when they meet strangers.

Akbar the Great is buried in a coffin of solid gold in a mausoleum of exquisite beauty about six miles from Agra on the road to Delhi. It is another architectural wonder. Many critics consider it almost equal to Taj Mahal. It is reached by a lovely drive along a splendid road that runs like a green aisle through a grove of noble old trees whose boughs are inhabited by myriads of parrots and monkeys. The mausoleum is quite different from any other that we have seen, being a sort of pyramid of four open platforms, standing on columns. These are of red sandstone and the fourth, where rests the tomb of the great Mogul, of marble. The lower stories are frescoed and decorated elaborately in blue and gold. The fourth or highest platform is a beautiful little cloister of the purest white. No description in words could possibly do it justice or convey anything like an accurate idea of its beauty. Imagine, if you can, a platform eighty feet from the ground reached by beautiful stairways and inclosed by roofless walls of the purest marble that was ever quarried. These walls are divided into panels. Each panel contains a slab of marble about an inch thick and perforated like the finest of lace. The divisions and frame work, the base and frieze are chiseled with embroidery in stone such as can be found nowhere else. There is no roof but the sky. In the center of this lofty chamber stands a solid block of marble which is covered with inscriptions from the Koran in graceful, flowing Persian text. Sealed within that cenotaph are the remains of the great Akbar.

About three feet from his head stands a low marble column exquisitely carved. It is about four feet high, and in the center of the top is a defect, a rough hole, which seems to have been left there intentionally. When the mighty Akbar died, his son and successor, the Emperor Jehanghir, imbedded in the center of that column, where it might be admired by the thousands of people who came to the tomb every day, the Kohinoor, then the most valued diamond in the world and still one of the most famous of jewels, and chief ornament in the British crown. It was one of the most audacious exhibitions of wealth and recklessness ever made, but the stone remained there in the open air, guarded only by the ordinary custodian of the tomb, from 1668 to 1739, when Nadir, Shah of Persia, invaded India, captured Delhi, sacked the palaces of the moguls, and carried back to his own country more than $300,000,000 worth of their treasures.

XV

THE MOST BEAUTIFUL OF BUILDINGS

Once upon a time there lived an Arab woman named Arjumand Banu. We know very little about her, except that she lived in Agra, India, and was the Sultana of Shah Jehan, the greatest of the Mogul emperors. She must have been a good woman and a good wife, because, after eighteen years of married life, and within twelve months after his accession to the throne, in 1629, she died in giving birth to her fourteenth baby. And her husband loved her so much that he sheltered her grave with a mausoleum which, without question or reservation, is pronounced by all architects and critics to be the most beautiful building in the world—the most sublime and perfect work of human hands.

It is called the Taj Mahal, which means "The Crown of the Palaces," and is pronounced Taash Mahal, with the accent on the last syllable of the last word. Its architect is not definitely known, but the design is supposed to have been made by Ustad Isa, a Persian, who was assisted by Geronino Verroneo, an Italian, and Austin de Bordeaux, a Frenchman. They are credited with the mosaics and other decorations. Austin designed and made the famous peacock throne at Delhi. Governor La Fouche of that province, who has carefully restored the park that surrounds the building, and is keeping things up in a way that commands hearty commendation, has

THE TAJ MAHAL

the original plans and specifications, which were discovered among the archives of the Moguls in Delhi after the mutiny of 1857. The records show also that the tomb cost more than $20,000,000 of American money, not including labor, for like those other famous sepulchers, the pyramids of Egypt, this wonderful structure was erected by forced labor, by unpaid workmen, who were drafted from their shops and farms by order of the Mogul for that purpose, and, according to the custom of the time, they were compelled to support themselves as well as their families during the period of their employment. Thousands of those poor, helpless creatures died of starvation and exhaustion; thousands perished of disease, and thousands more, including women and children, suffered untold distress and agony, all because one loving husband desired to do honor to the favorite among his many wives. The workmen were changed at intervals, 20,000 being constantly employed for twenty-two years upon this eulogy in marble. The descendants of some of the artists engaged upon its matchless decoration still live in Agra and enjoy a certain distinction because of their ancestry. Forty or fifty of them were employed by Governor La Fouche in making repairs and restorations in 1902, and a dozen or more are still at work. It is customary in that country for sons to follow the occupations of their fathers.

The road to the Taj Mahal from the City of Agra crosses the River Jumna, winds about among modern bungalows in which British officials and military officers reside, alternating with the ruins of ancient palaces, tombs, temples and shrines which are allowed to deface the landscape. Some of the fields are cultivated, and in December, when we were there, the business of the farmers seemed chiefly to be that of hoisting water from wells to irrigate their crops. They have a curious method. A team of oxen hoists the buckets with a long rope running over a pulley, and every time they make a trip along the well-worn pathway they dump a barrel or more or much needed moisture into a ditch that feeds the thirsty ground.

The roadway is well kept. It was made several centuries ago, and was put in perfect order in 1902 on account of the Imperial durbar at Delhi, which brought thousands of critical strangers to see the Taj Mahal, which really is the greatest sight in India, and is more famous than any other building, except perhaps Westminster Abbey and St. Peter's Cathedral at Rome. The road leads up to a superb gateway of red sandstone inlaid with inscriptions from the Koran in white marble, and surmounted by twenty-six small marble domes, Moorish kiosks, arches and pinnacles. This gateway is considered one of the finest architectural monuments in all India. Bayard Taylor pronounced it equal to the Taj itself.

You pass under a noble arch one hundred and forty feet high and one hundred and ten feet wide, which is guarded by a group of Moslem priests and a squad of native soldiers who protect the property from vandals. Having passed this gateway you find yourself at the top of a flight of wide steps overlooking a great garden, which was originally laid out by the Mogul Shah Jehan and by Lord Curzon's orders was restored last year as nearly as possible to its original condition and appearance. About fifty acres are inclosed by a high wall of a design appropriate to its purpose. There are groups of cypress equal in size and beauty to any in India; groves of orange and lemon trees, palms and pomegranates, flowering plants and shrubs, through which winding walks of gravel have been laid. From the steps of the gateway to the tomb is a vista about a hundred feet wide paved with white and black marble with tessellated designs, inclosed with walls of cypress boughs. In the center are a series of tanks, or marble basins, fed from fountains, and goldfish swim about in the limpid water. This vista, of course, was intended to make the first view as impressive as possible, and it is safe to say that there is no other equal to it. At the other end of the marble-paved tunnel of trees, against a cloudless sky, rises the most symmetrical, the most perfect, perhaps the only faultless human structure in existence. At first one is inclined to be a little bewildered, a little dazed, as if the senses were paralyzed, and could not adjust themselves to this "poem in marble," or "vision in marble," or "dream in marble," as poets and artists have rhapsodized over it for four centuries.

No building has been more often described and sketched and painted and photographed. For three hundred and fifty years it has appeared as an illustration in the chapter on India in geographies, atlases and gazetteers; it is used as a model in architectural text-books, and of course is reproduced in every book that is written about India. It has been modeled in gold, silver, alabaster, wax and every other material that yields to the sculptor's will, yet no counterfeit can ever give a satisfactory idea of its loveliness, the purity of the material of which it is made, the perfection of its proportions, the richness of its decorations and the exquisite accuracy achieved by its builders. Some one has said that the Moguls designed like giants and finished like jewelers, and that epigram is emphasized in the Taj Mahal. Any portion of it, any feature, if taken individually, would be enough to immortalize the architect, for every part is equally perfect, equally chaste, equally beautiful.

I shall not attempt to describe it. You can find descriptions by great pens in many books. Sir Edwin Arnold has done it up both in prose and poetry, and sprawled all over the dictionary without conveying the faintest idea of its glories and loveliness. It cannot be described. One might as well attempt to describe a Beethoven symphony, for, if architecture be frozen music, as some poet has said, the Taj Mahal is the supremest and sublimest composition that human genius has produced. But, without using architectural terms, or gushing any more about it, I will give you a few plain facts.

The Taj Mahal stands, as I have already told you, at the bottom of a lovely garden surrounded by groves of cypress trees, on the bank of the River Jumna, opposite the great fortress of Agra, where, from the windows of his palace, the king could always see the snowwhite domes and minarets which cover the ashes of his Arab wife. Its base is a marble terrace 400 feet square, elevated eighteen feet above the level of the garden, with benches arranged around so that one can sit and look and look and look until its wonderful beauty soaks slowly into his consciousness; until the soul is saturated. Rising from the terrace eighteen feet is a marble pedestal or platform 313 feet square, each corner being marked with a marble minaret 137 feet high; so slender, so graceful, so delicate that you cannot conceive anything more so. Within their walls are winding staircases by which one can reach narrow balconies like those on lighthouses and look upon the Taj from different heights and study its details from the top as well as the bottom. The domes

INTERIOR OF TAJ MAHAL

that crown these four minarets are exact miniatures of that which covers the tomb.

On the east and on the west sides of the terrace are mosques built after Byzantine designs of deep red sandstone, which accentuates the purity of the marble of which the tomb is made in a most effective manner. At any other place, with other surroundings, these mosques would be regarded worthy of prolonged study and unbounded admiration, but here they pass almost unnoticed. Like the trees of the gardens and the river that flows at the foot of the terrace, they are only an humble part of the frame which incloses the great picture. They are intended to serve a purpose, and they serve it well. In beauty they are surpassed only by the tomb itself.

One of the mosques has recently been put in perfect repair and the other is undergoing restoration, by order of Lord Curzon, who believes that the architectural and archæological monuments of ancient India should be preserved and protected, and he is spending considerable government money for that purpose. This policy has been criticised by certain Christian missionaries, who, like the iconoclasts of old, would tear down heathen temples and desecrate heathen tombs. Many of the most beautiful examples of ancient Hindu architecture have already been destroyed by government authority, and the material of which they were built has been utilized in the construction of barracks and fortresses. You may not perhaps believe it, but there are still living in India men who call themselves servants of the Lord, who would erase every other monument that is in any way associated with pagan worship or traditions. They would destroy even the Taj Mahal itself, and then thank God for the opportunity of performing such a barbarous act in His service.

Midway between the two red mosques rises a majestic pile of pure white marble 186 feet square, with the corners cut off. It measures eighty feet from its pedestal to its roof, and is surmounted by a dome also eighty feet high, measuring from the roof, and fifty-eight feet in diameter. Upon the summit of the dome is a spire of gilded copper twenty-eight feet high, making the entire structure 224 feet from the turf of the garden to the tip of the spire. All of the domes are shaped like inverted turnips after the Byzantine style. Four small ones surround the central dome, exact duplicates and one-eighth of its size, and they are arranged upon arches upon the flat roof of the building. From each of the eight angles of the roof springs a delicate spire or pinnacle, an exact duplicate of the great minarets in the corners, each sixteen feet high, and they are so slender that they look like alabaster pencils glistening in the sunshine. The same duplication is carried out through the entire building. The harmony is complete. Every tower, every dome, every arch, is exactly like every other tower, dome and arch, differing only in dimensions.

The building is entered on the north and south sides through enormous pointed arches of perfect proportions reaching above the roof and at each corner of the frames that inclose them is another minaret, a miniature of the rest. Each of the six faces of the remainder of the octagon is pierced by two similar arches, one above the other, opening upon galleries which serve to break the force of the sun, to moderate the heat and to subdue the light. They form a sort of colonnade around the building above and below, and are separated from the rotunda by screens of perforated alabaster, as exquisite and delicate in design and execution as Brussels point lace. The slabs of alabaster, 12 by 8 feet in size, are pierced with filigree work finely finished as if they were intended to be worn as jewels upon the crown of an empress. I am told that there is no stone work to compare with this anywhere else on earth. Hence it was not in Athens, nor in Rome, but in northern India that the chisel of the sculptor attained its most perfect precision and achieved its greatest triumphs. All of the light that reaches the interior is filtered through this trellis work.

The rotunda is unbroken, fifty-eight feet in diameter and one hundred and sixty feet from the floor to the apex of the dome. Like every other part of the building, it is of the purest white marble, inlaid with mosaics of precious stones. The walls, the pillars, the wainscoting and the entire exterior as well as the interior of the building are the same. You have doubtless seen brooches, earrings, sleeve-buttons and other ornaments of Florentine mosaic, with floral and other designs worked out with different colored stones inlaid on black or white marble. You can buy paper weights of that sort, and table tops which represent months of labor and the most exact workmanship. They are very expensive because of the skill and the time required to execute them. Well, upon the walls of the tomb of the Princess Arjamand are about two acres of surface covered with such mosaics as fine and as perfect as if each setting were a jewel intended for a queen to wear—turquoise, coral, garnet, carnelian, jasper, malachite, agate, lapis lazuli, onyx, nacre, bloodstone, tourmaline, sardonyx and a dozen other precious stones of different colors. The guide book says that twenty-eight different varieties of stone, many of them unknown to modern times, are inlaid in the walls of marble.

The most beautiful of these embellishments are inscriptions, chiefly passages from the Koran and tributes of praise to "The Exalted One of the Palace" who lies buried there, worked out in Arabic and Persian characters, which are the most artistic of any language, and lend themselves gracefully to decorative purposes. The ninety-nine names of God, which pious Mussulmans love to inscribe, appear in several places. Over the archway of the entrance is an inscription in Persian characters which reads like a paraphrase of the beatitudes:

"Only the Pure in Heart can Enter the Garden of God."

This arch was once inclosed by silver doors, which were carried off by the Persians when they invaded India and sacked the palaces of Agra in 1739.

There is no wood or metal in this building; not a nail or a screw or a bolt of any sort. It is entirely of marble, mortised and fastened with cement.

The acoustic properties of the rotunda are remarkable and a sound uttered by a human voice will creep around its curves repeating and repeating itself like the vibrations of the gongs of Burmese temples, until it is lost in a whisper at the apex of the dome. I should like to hear a violin there or a hymn softly sung by some great artist.

In the center of the rotunda Shah Jehan and his beloved wife are supposed to lie side by side in marble caskets, inlaid with rich gems and embellished by infinite skill with lacelike tracery. But their bodies are actually buried in the basement, and, the guides assert, in coffins of solid gold. She for whom this tomb was built occupies the center. Her lord and lover, because he was a man and an emperor, was entitled to a larger sarcophagus, a span loftier and a span longer. Both of the cenotaphs are embellished with inlaid and carved Arabic inscriptions. Upon his, in Persian characters, are written these words:

"His Majesty, King of Kings, Lord of Lords, Shadow of Allah, whose Court is now in Heaven; Saith Jesus, on whom be peace, This World is a Bridge; Pass thou over it, Build not upon it! It lasteth but an Hour; Devote its Minutes to thy Prayers; for the Rest is Unseen and Unknown!"

No other person has such a tomb as this; nor pope, nor potentate, nor emperor. Nowhere else have human pride and wealth and genius struggled so successfully against the forgetfulness of man. The Princess Arjamand has little place in history, but a devoted, loving husband has rescued her name from oblivion, and has immortalized her by making her dust the tenant of the most majestic and beautiful of all human monuments.

Everybody admits that the Taj Mahal is the noblest tribute of affection and the most perfect triumph of the architectural art in existence, and the beautiful edifices in the fort at Agra, which we also owe to Shah Jehan, the greatest of the Moguls, have already been mentioned but I am conscious that my words are weak. It is not possible to describe them accurately. No pen can do them justice. The next best work in India, a group of buildings second only to those in Agra, and in many respects their equal, are credited to Akbar the Great, grandfather of Shah Jehan. He reigned from 1556 to 1605. They may be found at Fattehpur-Sikir (the City of Victory), twenty-two miles from Agra on the Delhi road, occupying a rocky ridge, surrounded by a stone wall with battlements and towers. The emperor intended these palaces to be his summer residence, and was followed there by many of the rich nobles of the court, who built mansions and villas of corresponding size and splendor to gratify him and their own vanity—but all its magnificence was wasted, strange to say. The city was built and abandoned within fifty years. Perhaps Akbar became tired of it, but the records tell us that it was impossible to secure a water supply sufficient for the requirements of the population and that the location was exceedingly unhealthy because of malaria. Therefore the king and the court, the officials of the government, with the clerks and servants, the military garrison and the merchants who supplied their wants, all packed up and moved away, most of them going back to Agra, where they came from, leaving the glorious marble palaces without tenants and allowing them to crumble and decay.

Abandoned cities and citadels are not unusual in India. I have already told you of one near Jeypore where even a larger population were compelled to desert their homes and business houses for similar reasons—the lack of a sufficient water supply, and there are several others in different parts of India. Some of them are in a fair state of preservation, others are almost razed to the ground, and their walls have been used as quarries for building stone in the erection of other cities. But nowhere can be found so grand, so costly and so extensive a group of empty and useless palaces as at Fattehpur-Sikri.

The origin of the town, according to tradition, is quite interesting. When Akbar was returning from one of his military campaigns he camped at the foot of the hill and learned that a wise and holy Brahmin named Shekh Selim

Chishli, who resided in a cave among the rocks, exercised powerful influence among the Hindu deities. Akbar was a Mohammedan, but of liberal mind, and had not the slightest compunction about consulting with a clergyman of another denomination. This was the more natural because his favorite wife was a Hindu princess, daughter of the Maharaja of Jeypore, and she was extremely anxious to have a child. She had given birth to twins some years previous, but to her deep grief and that of the emperor, they had died in infancy.

The holy man on the hill at Fattehpur was believed to have tremendous influence with those deities who control the coming of babies into this great world; hence the emperor and his sultana visited Shekh Selim in his rock retreat to solicit his interposition for the birth of a son. Now, the hermit had a son only 6 months old, who, the evening after the visit of the emperor, noticed that his father's face wore a dejected expression. Having never learned the use of his tongue, being but a few months old, this precocious child naturally caused great astonishment when, by a miracle, he sat up in his cradle and in language that an adult would use inquired the cause of anxiety. The old man answered:

"It is written in the stars, oh, my son, that the emperor will never have an heir unless some other man will sacrifice for him the life of his own heir, and surely in this wicked and selfish world no one is capable of such generosity and patriotism."

"If you will permit me, oh, my father," answered the baby, "I will die in order that his majesty may be consoled."

The hermit explained that for such an act he could acquire unlimited merit among the gods, whereupon the obliging infant straightened its tiny limbs and expired. Some months after the sultana gave birth to a boy, who afterward became the Emperor Jehanghir.

Akbar, of course, was gratified and to show his appreciation of the services of the hermit decided to make the rocky ridge his summer capital. He summoned to his aid all the architects and artists and contractors in India, and a hundred thousand mechanics, stone cutters, masons and decorators were kept busy for two scores of years erecting the palaces, tombs and temples that now testify with mute eloquence to the genius of the architects and builders of those days. It is shown by the records that this enterprise cost the taxpayers of India a hundred millions of dollars, and that did not include the wages of the workmen, because most of them were paid nothing. In those days almost everything in the way of government public works was carried on by forced labor. The king paid no wages. The material was expensive. Very little wood was used. The buildings are almost entirely of pure white marble and red sandstone. They had neither doors nor windows, but only open arches which were hung with curtains to secure privacy, and light was admitted to the interior through screens of marble, perforated in beautiful designs. The entrance to the citadel is gained through a gigantic gateway, one of the noblest portals ever erected. It was intended as a triumphal arch to celebrate the victory of Akbar over the Afghans, and to commemorate the conquest of Khandesh, and this is recorded in exquisite Persian characters upon its frontal and sides. Compared with it the arches of Titus and Constantine in Rome and the Arc de Triomphe in Paris are clumsy piles of masonry. There is nothing to be

TOMB OF SHEIK-SALIM — FATTEHPUR

compared with it anywhere in Europe, and the only structure in India that resembles it in any way may be found among the ruins in the neighborhood of Delhi.

Through this majestic portal you enter a quadrangle about six hundred feet square, inclosed by a lofty cloister which Bishop Heber pronounced the finest that was ever erected. He declared that there was no other quadrangle to be compared to it in size or proportions or beauty. In the center of this wonderful inclosure is a building that resembles a miniature temple. It is not large, and its low roof and far projecting eaves give it the appearance of a tropical bungalow. It is built of the purest marble. No other material was used in its contruction. There is not a nail or a screw or an ounce of metal of any kind in its walls, and very little cement or mortar was used. Each piece of stone fits the others so perfectly that there was no need of bolts or anything to hold it in place. It stands upon a pedestal four feet high and is crowned with a low white dome of polished metal. The walls of this wonderful building are pillars of marble inclosing panels of the same material sawed in very thin slabs and perforated in exquisite geometrical patterns. No two panels are alike; there is no duplication of design on the pillars; every column is different; every capital and every base is unique. We are told that it was customary in the days of the Moguls to assign a section of a building to an artist and allow him to exercise his skill and genius without restriction, of course within certain limits. Notwithstanding this diversity of design, the tomb of Shekh Selim, of which I have attempted to give you an idea, is an ideal of perfect harmony, and every stroke of the chisel was as precise as if the artist had been engraving a cameo. It was erected by Akbar and his Queen,

Luquina, as a token of gratitude to the old monk who brought them an heir to their throne, but, unfortunately this heir was an ungrateful chap and treated his father and mother very badly.

Another tomb of equal beauty but smaller dimensions, is also a tribute of respect and affection. Under this marble roof lies all that remains of that extraordinary baby who gave his life to gratify the king.

Surrounding the quadrangle are the apartments of the emperor, the residences of his wives and the offices in which he conducted official business. They are all built of marble of design and beauty similar to those within the walls of the fort at Agra. One of them, known as the Hall of Records, is now used for the accommodation of visitors because there is no hotel and very little demand for one. The only people who ever go to Fattehpur Sikri are tourists, and they take their own bedding and spread it on the marble floor. It is a long journey, twenty-six miles by carriage, and it is not possible to make it and return on the same day.

The Imperial Hall of Audience, where Akbar was accustomed to sit in his robes of state each day to receive the petitions and administer justice to his subjects, is a splendid pavilion of red sandstone with fifty-six columns covered with elaborate carving in the Hindu style. Here he received ambassadors from all parts of the earth because the glory of his court and the liberality of his policy gave him universal reputation. Here Jesuit missionaries gave him the seeds of the tobacco plant which they brought from America, and within a few miles from this place was grown the first tobacco ever produced in India. The hookah, the big tobacco pipe, with a long tube and a bowl of perfumed water for the smoke to pass through, is said to have been invented at Fattehpur Sikri by one of Akbar's engineers.

Connected by a marble corridor with the palace, and also with the Hall of Public Audience, is a smaller pavilion, where, according to the custom of the times, the emperor was in the habit of receiving and conferring with his ministers and other officials of his government, with ambassadors and with strangers who sought his presence from curiosity or business reasons. This diwan-i-khas, or privy chamber, is pointed out as the place where the emperor held his celebrated religious controversies. We are told that for several years Jesuit missionaries were invited there and encouraged to explain the dogmas and doctrines of their faith to the nobles and the learned pundits of the Indian Empire, often in the presence of the Mogul, who took part in the discussions.

When his majesty was tired of business and wanted relaxation he ordered his servants to remove the silken rug and cushions upon which he sat to a little marble portico on the other side of the palace, where the pavement of the court was laid in alternate squares of black and white marble. This was known as the imperial puchisi board, and we are told that his majesty played a game resembling chess with beautiful slave girls dressed in costume to represent the men upon the board. Here he sat for hours with his antagonists, and was so proud of his skill that expert puchisi players from all parts of the empire were summoned to play with him.

At the other end of the inclosure is a large building known as the mint, where the first rupees were coined. They were cubes of gold, covered with artistic designs and with Persian inscriptions reading "God is great.

Mighty is His Glory." The largest coin was called a "henseh" and was worth about $1,000 in our money. And there were several other denominations, in the forms of cubes, and they bore similar pious inscriptions.

The residences of the women of the court and the ministers and other high officials were of corresponding splendor and beauty. There is nothing on our side of the world or in Europe to compare with them in beauty of design, costliness of material and lavishness of decoration. The grandest palaces of the European capitals are coarse and clumsy beside them, and the new library at Washington, which we consider a model of architectural perfection, can be compared to these gems of Hindu architects as cotton duck to Brussels lace.

The palaces, temples and tombs in northern India are unequaled examples of the architectural and decorative arts. Nothing more beautiful or more costly has ever been built by human hands than the residences and the sepulchers of the Moguls, while their audience chambers, their baths and pavilions are not surpassed, and are not even equaled in any of the imperial capitals of Europe. The oriental artists and architects of the Mohammedan dynasties lavished money upon their homes and tombs in the most generous manner, and the refinement of their taste was equal to their extravagance. And where do you suppose they obtained all the money for these buildings, which cost millions upon millions of dollars? The architectural remains of Akbar and Shah Jehan, the two most splendid of the Moguls, represent an expenditure of several hundred millions, even though the labor of construction was unpaid, and where did they get the funds to pay for them? Lieutenant Governor La Touche, who has been collecting the records of the Mogul dynasty and having them carefully examined, discovers that their revenues average about $100,000,000 a year for a hundred years or more. In 1664 the land taxes amounted to £26,743,000, in 1665 they amounted to £24,056,000, while in 1697, during the reign of the Mogul Aurangzeb, they reached their highest figure, which was £38,719,000.. With these funds they were required to keep up their palaces, pay their officials, maintain their armies and provide for the luxurious tastes of their courtiers.

XVI

THE QUAINT OLD CITY OF DELHI

Wherever the viceroy may hold court, wherever the government may sit, Delhi always has been and always will be the capital of India, for have not the prophets foretold that the gilded marble palaces of the Moguls will stand forever? Although Benares and Lucknow have a larger population, Delhi is regarded as the metropolis of Northern India, and in commerce and manufactures stands fourth in the list of cities, Bombay, Calcutta and Madras only surpassing it in wealth, industry and trade. If you will look at the map for a moment you will notice its unusually favorable location, both from a commercial and military standpoint. It occupies a central place in northern India, has railway connections with the frontier and is equidistant from Bombay and Calcutta, the principal ports of the empire. It receives raw materials from the northern provinces and from mysterious regions beyond the boundary. Its cunning artisans convert them into finished products and ship them to all the markets of the world. Being of great strategic importance, a large military garrison is maintained there, and the walls of an ancient fort shelter arsenals filled with guns and magazines filled with ammunition, which may be promptly distributed by railway throughout the empire on demand. It is the capital of one of the richest and most productive provinces, the headquarters of various departments of the government, the residence of a large foreign colony, civil, military and commercial; it has the most learned native pundits in India; it has extensive missionary stations and educational institutions, and is the center and focus of learning and all forms of activity. It is a pity and a disgrace that Delhi has no good hotels. There are two or three indifferent ones, badly built and badly kept. They are about as good as the average in India, but ought to be a great deal better, for if travelers could find comfortable places to stop Delhi might be made a popular resort.

Travelers complain also of the pestiferous peddlers who pursue them beyond the limit of patience. We were advised by people who know India not to buy anything until we reached Delhi, because that city has the best shops and the best bazaars and produces the most attractive fabrics, jewelry and other articles which tourists like to take home to their friends. And we found within a few moments after our appearance there that we would have no difficulty in obtaining as many things as we wanted. We arrived late at night, and when we opened the doors of our chambers the next morning we found a crowd of clamoring merchants in the corridor waiting to seize us as we came out. And wherever we went—in temples, palaces, parks and in the streets—they followed us with their wares tied up in bundles and slung over their backs. When we drove out to "The Ridge," where the great battles took place during the mutiny of 1857, to see a monument erected in memory of the victims of Indian treachery, two enterprising merchants followed us in a carriage and interrupted our meditations by offering silks, embroideries and brass work at prices which they said were 20 per cent lower than we would have to pay in the city. When we went into the dining-room of the hotel we always had to pass through a throng of these cormorants, who thrust jewelry, ivory carvings, photographs, embroideries, cashmere shawls, silks and other goods in our faces and begged us to buy them. As we rode through the streets they actually ran at the sides of the carriage, keeping pace with the horses until we drove them off by brandishing parasols, umbrellas and similar weapons of defense. We could not go to a mosque or the museum without finding them lying in wait for us, until we became so exasperated that homicide would have been justifiable. That is the experience of every traveler, especially Americans, who are supposed to be millionaires, and many of our fellow countrymen spend their money so freely as to excite the avarice of the Delhi tradesmen. And indeed it is true that their goods are the most attractive, although their prices are higher than you have to pay in the smaller towns of India, where there is less demand.

The principal business section, called Chandni Chauk, which means Silver street, has been frequently described as one of the most picturesque and fascinating streets in the world. It is about a mile long and seventy-five feet broad. In the center are two rows of trees, between which for several hundred years was an aqueduct, but it is now filled and its banks are used as a pathway, the principal promenade of the town. But a stranger cannot walk there in peace, for within five minutes he is hemmed in and his way is blocked by merchants, who rush out from the shops on both sides with their hands filled with samples of goods and business cards and in pigeon English entreat him to stop and see what they have for sale. Sometimes it is amusing when rival merchants grapple with each other in their frantic efforts to secure customers, but such unwelcome attentions impair the pleasure of a visit to Delhi.

The shops on both sides of the Chandni Chauk are full of wonderful loom and metal work, jewelry, embroidery, enamel, rugs, hangings, brocades, shawls, leather work, gems and carved ivory and wood. Delhi has always been famous for carvings, and examples of engraving on jade of priceless value are often shown. Sometimes a piece of jade can be found in a curio shop covered with relief work which represents the labor of an accomplished artist for years. In the days of the Moguls these useless ornaments were very highly regarded. Kings and rich nobles used to have engravers attached to their households. Artists and their families were always sure of a comfortable home and good living, hence time was no object. It was not taken into consideration. They were indifferent whether they spent five months or five years in fashioning a block of ivory or engraving a gem for their princely patrons. The greatest works of the most accomplished artists of the Mogul period are now nearly all in the possession of native princes and rich Hindus, and if one comes into the market it is snapped up instantly by collectors in Europe and the United States. Some of the carved ivory is marvelous. An artist would spend his entire life covering a tusk of an elephant with carvings of marvelous delicacy and skill; and even to-day the ivory carvers of Delhi produce wonderful results and sell them at prices that are absurdly small, considering the labor they represent.

Akbar the Great, who sat upon the Mogul throne the latter half of the sixteenth century, was a sensible man, and endeavored to divert the skill and taste of the artisans of his empire into more practical channels. Instead of maintaining artists to carve ivory and jade he established schools and workshops for the instruction of spinners, weavers and embroiderers, and offered high prices for fine samples of shawls and other woolen fabrics, weapons, pottery and similar useful articles. He purchased the rich products of the looms for the imperial wardrobe and induced the native princes to imitate his example. He organized guilds among his workmen, and secured the adoption of regulations which served to maintain a high standard, and permitted none but perfect products to be placed upon the market.

The descendants of the master workmen educated under this policy are still living and following the trades of their ancestors in Delhi, and there may be found the finest gold and silver cloth and the most elaborate embroidery produced in the world. The coronation robe of Queen Alexandra of England, which is said to have been of surpassing richness and beauty, was woven and embroidered in a factory upon the Chandni Chauk, and the merchant who made it is constantly receiving orders from the different courts of Europe and from the leading dressmakers of London, Paris and Vienna. He told us that Mrs. Leland Stanford had commissioned him to furnish the museum of her university in California the finest possible samples of different styles of Indian embroidery, and his workmen were then engaged in producing them. Her contract, he said, amounted to more than $60,000. Lady Curzon is his best customer, for she not only orders all of the material for her state gowns from him, but has brought him enough orders from the ladies of the British court to keep his shop busy for five years. He told us that Lady Curzon designed the corona-

A CORNER IN DELHI

tion robe of Queen Alexandra; he declared that she had the rarest taste of any woman he knew, and that she was the best dressed woman in the world—an opinion shared by other good judges.

He spread upon the floor wonderful samples of the skill and taste of his artists, brocades embroidered with jewels for the ceremonial robes of native princes; silks and satins whose surface was concealed by patterns wrought in gold and silver thread. And everything is done by men. Women do not embroider in India. He keeps eighty men embroiderers constantly employed, and pays them an average of 18 cents a day. The most famous of his artists, those who design as well as execute the delicate and costly garnishings, the men who made the coronation robe of the British queen, receive the munificent compensation of 42 cents a day. That is the maximum paid for such work. Apprentices who do the filling in and coarser work and have not yet acquired sufficent skill and experience to undertake more important tasks are paid 8 cents a day and work twelve hours for that.

Delhi is the principal distributing point for the famous Cashmere shawls which are woven of the hair of camels, goats and sheep in the province of Cashmere, which lies to the northward about 300 miles. They are brought packed in panniers on the backs of camels. I was told at Delhi that the foreign demand for Cashmere shawls has almost entirely ceased, that a very few are shipped from India nowadays because in Europe and America they are no longer fashionable. Hence prices have gone down, the weavers are dependent almost entirely upon the local market of India, and one can obtain good shawls for very low prices—about half what they formerly cost.

In northern India every Hindu must have a shawl; it is as necessary to him as a hat or a pair of boots to a citizen of Chicago or New York, and it is customary to invest a considerable part of the family fortune in shawls. They are handed down from generation to generation, for they never wear out; the older they are the more valuable they are considered. You often see a barefooted, bare-legged peasant with his head wrapped in a Cashmere shawl that would bring a thousand dollars in a London auction-room. It is considered absolutely essential for every young man to wear one of those beautiful fabrics, and if there is none for him in the family he saves his earnings and scrimps and borrows and begs from his relations until he gets enough money together to buy one. Most of the shawls are of the Persian pattern familiar to us. The groundwork is a solid color (white and yellow seem to be the most popular), and there are a good many of blue, green, orange and pink. A crowd of Hindus in this part of the country suggest a kaleidoscope as they move about with their brilliant colored shawls upon their shoulders.

The amount and fineness of embroidery upon the border and in the corners of shawls give them their value, and sometimes there is an elaborate design in the center. The shawl itself is so fine that it can be drawn through a finger ring or folded up and stowed away in an ordinary pocket, but it has the warmth of a Scotch blanket. Shawls are woven and embroidered in the homes of the people of Cashmere, and are entirely of hand work. There are no factories and no steam looms, and every stitch of the decoration is made with an ordinary needle by the fingers of a man. Women do not seem to have acquired the accomplishment.

A great deal of fun used to be made at the expense of Queen Victoria, who was in the habit of sending a Cashmere shawl whenever she was expected to make a wedding present, and no doubt it was rather unusual for her to persist in forcing unfashionable garments upon her friends. But there is another way of looking at it. The good queen was deeply interested in promoting the native industries of India, and bought a large number of shawls every year from the best artists in Cashmere. Up there shawl-makers have reputations like painters and orators with us, and if you would ask the question in Cashmere any merchant would give you the names of the most celebrated weavers and embroiderers. Queen Victoria was their most regular and generous patron. She not only purchased large numbers of shawls herself, but did her best to bring them into fashion, both because she believed it was a sensible practice, and would advance the prosperity of the heathen subjects in whom she took such a deep interest.

The arts and industries of India are very old. Their methods have been handed down from generation to generation, because sons are in the habit of following the trades of fathers, and they are inclined to cling to the same old patterns and the same old processes, regardless of labor-saving devices and modern fashions. Many people think this habit should be encouraged; that what may be termed the classic designs of the Hindus cannot be improved upon, and it is certainly true that all purely modern work is inferior. Lord and Lady Curzon have shown deep interest in this subject. Lord Curzon has used his official authority and the influence of the government to revive, restore and promote old native industries, and Lady Curzon has been an invaluable commercial agent for the manufacturers of the higher class of fabrics and art objects in India. She has made many of them fashionable in Calcutta and other Indian cities and in London, Paris and the capitals of Europe, and so great is her zeal that, with all her cares and responsibilities, and the demands upon her time, she always has the leisure to place orders for her friends and even for strangers who address her, and to assist the silk weavers, embroiderers and other artists to adapt their designs and patterns and fabrics to the requirements of modern fashions. She wears nothing but Indian stuffs herself, and there is no better dressed woman in the world. She keeps several of the best artists in India busy with orders from her friends, and is beginning to see the results of her efforts in the revival of arts that were almost forgotten.

The population of Delhi is about 208,000. The majority of the people, as in the other cities of northwestern India, are Mohammedans, descendants of the invaders of the middle ages, and the hostility between them and the Brahmins is quite sharp. The city is surrounded by a lofty wall six miles in circumference, which was built by Shah Jehan, the greatest of the Moguls, some time about 1630, and the modern town begins its history at that date. It has been the scene of many exciting events since then. Several times it has been sacked and its inhabitants massacred. As late as 1739 the entire population was put to the sword and everything of value within the walls was carried off by the Persians. In the center of the city still remains a portion of what was probably the most splendid palace that was ever erected. It is surrounded by a second wall inclosing an area 3,000 feet long by 1,500 feet wide, which was at one time filled with buildings of unique beauty and interest. They illustrated the imperial grandeur of the Moguls, whose style of living was probably more splendid than that of any monarchs of any nation before or since their time. Their extravagance was unbounded. Their love of display has never been surpassed, and while it is a question where they obtained the enormous sums of money they squandered in ceremonies and personal adornment, there is none as to the accuracy of the descriptions given to them. The fact that Nadir Shah, the Persian invader, was able to carry away $300,000,000 in booty of jewels and gold, silver and other portable articles of value when he sacked Delhi in 1739, is of itself evidence that the stories of the wealth and the splendor of the Moguls are not fables. It is written in the history of Persia that the people of that empire were exempt from taxation for three years because their king brought from Delhi enough money to pay all the expenses of his government and his army during that time. We are told that he stripped plates of gold from the walls of the palace of Delhi and removed the ceilings from the apartments because they were made of silver, and the peacock throne of itself was of sufficient value to pay the debts of a nation.

A considerable part of the palaces of the Moguls has been destroyed by vandals or removed by the British authorities in order to make room for ugly brick buildings which are used as barracks and for the storage of arms, ammunition and other military supplies. It is doubtful whether they could have secured uglier designs and carried them out with ruder workmanship. Writers upon Indian history and architecture invariably devote a chapter to this national disgrace for which the viceroys in the latter part of the nineteenth century were responsible, and they denounce it as even worse than the devastation committed by barbarian invaders. "Nadir Shah, Ahmed Khan and the Maratha chiefs were content to strip the buildings of their precious metals and the jeweled thrones," exclaims one eminent writer. "To the government of the present Empress of India was left the last dregs of vandalism, which after the mutiny pulled down these perfect monuments of Mogul art to make room for the ugliest brick buildings from Simla to Ceylon. The whole of the harem courts of the palace were swept off the face of the earth to make way for a hideous British barrack, without those who carried out this fearful piece of vandalism thinking it even worth while to make a plan of what they were destroying, or making any records of the most splendid palace in the world. Of the public parts of the palace, all that remain are the entrance hall, the Nobut Khana, the Dewani Aum, the Dewani Khas and the Rung Mahal, now used as a mess room, and one or two small pavilions. They are the gems of the palace, it is true, but without the courts and corridors connecting them they lose all their meaning and more than half their beauty. Being now situated in the midst of a British barrack yard, they look like precious stones torn from their settings in some exquisite piece of oriental jeweler's work and set at random in a bed of the commonest plaster."

It is only fair to say that no one appreciates this situation more keenly than Lord Curzon, and while he is too discreet a man to criticise the acts of his predecessors in office, he has plans to restore the interior of the fort to something like its original condition and has already taken steps to tear down the ugly brick buildings that deface the landscape. But something more is necessary. The vandalism still continues in a small way. While we were being escorted through the beautiful buildings by a blithe and gay young Irish soldier, I called his attention to several spots in the wall where bits of precious stone—carnelian, turquoise and agate—had been picked out and carried away as relics. The wounds in the wall were recent. It was perfectly apparent that the damage had been done that very day, but he declared that there was no way to prevent it; that he was the only custodian of the place; that there were no guards; that it was impossible for him to be everywhere at once, and that it was easy enough for tourists and other visitors to deface the mosaics with their pocket knives in one of the palaces while he was showing people through the others.

The mosaics which adorn the interior marble walls of the palaces are considered incomparable. They are claimed to be the most elaborate, the most costly and the most perfect specimens of the art in existence. The designs represents flowers, foliage, fruits, birds, beasts, fishes and reptiles, carried out with precious stones in the pure white marble with the skill and delicacy of a Neapolitan cameo cutter, and it is said that they were designed and done by Austin de Bordeaux, the Frenchman who decorated the Taj Mahal, and it was a bad man who did this beautiful work. History says that "after defrauding several of the princes of Europe by means of false gems, which he fabricated with great skill, he sought refuge at the court of the Moguls, where he was received with high favor and made his fortune."

The richest and the loveliest of the rooms in the palace is the Diwan-i-Khas, or Hall of Private Audience, which is built entirely of marble and originally had a silver ceiling. The walls were once covered with gold, and in the center stood the famous peacock throne. Over the north and south entrances are written in flowing Persian characters the following lines:

> If there be a Paradise on Earth
> It is This! It is This! It is This!

The building was a masterpiece of refined fancy and extravagance, and upon its decorations Austin de Bordeaux, whose work on the Taj Mahal pronounces him to be one of the greatest artists that ever lived, concentrated the entire strength of his genius and lavished the wealth of an empire. Mr. Tavernier, a French jeweler, who visited Delhi a few years after the palace was finished, estimated the value of the decorations of this one room at 27,000,000 francs.

One of the several thrones used by the Moguls on occasions of ceremony was a stool eighteen inches high and four feet in diameter chiseled out of a solid block of natural crystal. M. Tavernier asserts that it was the largest piece of crystal ever discovered, and that it was without a flaw. It was shattered by the barbarians during the invasion of the Marathas in 1789. But the peacock throne, which stood in the room I have just described, was even more wonderful, and stands as the most extraordinary example of extravagance on record.

A description written at the time says: "It was so called from its having the figures of two peacocks standing behind it, their tails being expanded, and the whole so inlaid with diamonds, sapphires, rubies, emeralds, pearls and other precious stones of appropriate colors as to represent life. The throne itself was six feet long by five feet broad. It stood upon six massive feet, which, like the body, were of solid gold, inlaid with rubies, emeralds and diamonds. It was surrounded by a canopy

HALL OF MARBLE AND MOSAICS IN THE PALACE OF THE MOGULS AT DELHI

of gold, supported by twelve pillars, all richly emblazoned with costly gems, and a fringe of pearls ornamented the borders of the canopy. Between the two peacocks stood a figure of a parrot of the ordinary size carved out of a single emerald. On either side of the throne stood an umbrella, one of the emblems of royalty. They were formed of crimson velvet, richly embroidered and fringed with pearls. The handles were eight feet high, of solid gold thickly studded with diamonds."

This throne, according to a medical gentleman named Bernier, the writer whose description I have quoted, was planned and executed under the direction of Austin de Bordeaux. It was carried away by Nadir Shah to Teheran in 1739, and what is left of it is still used by the Shah of Persia on ceremonial occasions. The canopy, the umbrellas, the emerald parrot and the peacocks have long ago disappeared.

The same splendor, in more or less degree, was maintained throughout the entire palace during the reign of the Moguls. The apartments of the emperor and those of his wives, the harem, the baths, the public offices, the quarters for his ministers, secretaries and attendants were all built of similar materials and decorated in the same style of magnificence. Some of the buildings are allowed to remain empty for the pleasures of tourists; others are occupied for military purposes, and the Rung Mahal, one of the most beautiful, formerly the residence of the Mogul's favorite wife, is now used for a messroom by the officers of the garrison. A writer of the seventh century who visited the place says: "It was more beautiful than anything in the East that we know of."

At one end of the group of the buildings is the Moti Majid, or Pearl Mosque, which answered to the private chapel of the Moguls, and has been declared to be "the daintiest building in all India." In grace, simplicity and perfect proportions it cannot be surpassed. It is built of the purest marble, richly traced with carving.

It is within the walls of this fort and among these exquisite palaces that the Imperial durbar was held on the 1st of January, 1903, to proclaim formally the coronation of King Edward VII., Emperor of India, and Lord Curzon, with remarkable success, carried out his plan to make the occasion one of extraordinary splendor. It brought together for the first time all of the native princes of India, who, in the presence of each other, renewed their pledges of loyalty and offered their homage to the throne. No spectacle of greater pomp and splendor has ever been witnessed in Europe or Asia or any other part of the world since the days of the Moguls. The peacock throne could not be recovered for the occasion, but Lord and Lady Curzon sat upon the platform where it formerly stood, and there received the ruling chiefs, nobles and princes from all the states and provinces of India. Lord Curzon has been criticised severely in certain quarters for the "barbaric splendor and barbaric extravagance of this celebration," but people familiar with the political situation in India and the temper of the native princes have not doubted for a moment the wisdom which inspired it and the importance of its consequences. The oriental mind is impressed more by splendor than by any other influence, and has profound respect for ceremonials. The Emperor of India, by the durbar, recognized those racial peculiarities, and not only gratified them but made himself a real personality to the native chiefs instead of an abstract proposition. It has given the British power a position that it never held before; it swept away jealousies and brought together ruling princes who had never seen each other until then. It broke down what Lord Curzon calls "the water-tight compartment system of India."

"Each province," he says, "each native state, is more or less shut off by solid bulkheads from its neighbors. The spread of railways and the relaxation of social restrictions are tending to break them down, but they are still very strong. Princes who live in the south have rarely ever in their lives seen or visited the states of the north. Perhaps among the latter are chiefs who have rarely ever left their homes. It cannot but be a good thing that they should meet and get to know each other and exchange ideas. To the East there is nothing strange, but something familiar and even sacred," continued Lord Curzon, "in the practice that brings sovereigns together with their people in ceremonies of solemnity. Every sovereign in India did it in the old days; every chief in India does it now; and the community of interest between the sovereign and his people, to which such a function testifies and which it serves to keep alive, is most vital and most important."

And the durbar demonstrated the wisdom of those who planned it. The expense was quite large. The total disbursements by the government were about $880,000, and it is probable that an equal amount was expended by the princes and other people who participated. That has been the subject of severe criticism also, because the people were only slowly recovering from the effect of an awful famine. But there is another point of view. Every farthing of those funds was spent in India and represented wages paid to workmen employed in making the preparations and carrying them into effect. No money went out of the country. It all came out of the pockets of the rich and was paid into the hands of the poor. What the government and the native princes and nobles expended in their splendid displays was paid to working people who needed it, and by throwing this large amount into circulation the entire country was benefited.

The extravagance of the Viceroy and Lady Curzon in their own personal arrangements has also been criticised, and people complain that they might have done great good with the immense sums expended in dress and entertainment and display, but it is easy to construe these criticisms into compliments, for everyone testifies that both the viceroy and his beautiful American wife performed their parts to perfection, and that no one could have appeared with greater dignity and grace. Every detail of the affair was appropriate and every item upon the programme was carried out precisely as intended and desired. Lord and Lady Curzon have the personal presence, the manners and all the other qualities required for such occasions.

Dr. Francois Bernier, the French physician who visited the Mogul court in 1658, and gives us a graphic description of the durbar and Emperor Aurangzeb, who reigned at that time, writes: "The king appeared upon his throne splendidly appareled. His vest was of white satin, flowered and raised with a very fine embroidery of gold and silk. His turban was of cloth of gold, having a fowl wrought upon it like a heron, whose foot was covered with diamonds of an ordinary bigness and price, with a great oriental topaz which may be said to be matchless, shining like a little sun. A collar of long pearls hung about his neck down to his stomach, after the manner that some heathens wear their beads. His throne was supported by six pillars of massive gold set with rubies, emeralds and diamonds. Beneath the throne there appeared the great nobles, in splendid apparel, standing upon a raised ground covered with a canopy of purple with great golden fringes, and inclosed by a silver balustrade. The pillars of the hall were hung with tapestries of purple having the ground of gold, and for the roof of the hall there was nothing but canopies of flowered satin fastened with red silken cords that had big tufts of silk mixed with the threads of gold hanging on them. Below there was nothing to be seen but silken tapestries, very rich and of extraordinary length and breadth."

XVII

THE TEMPLES AND TOMBS OF DELHI

Seven ancient ruined cities, representing successive periods and dynasties from 2500 B. C. to 1600 A. D., encumber the plains immediately surrounding the city of Delhi, within a radius of eighteen or twenty miles; and you cannot go in any direction without passing through the ruins of stupendous walls, ancient fortifications and crumbling palaces, temples, mosques and tombs. Tradition makes the original Delhi the political and commercial rival of Babylon, Nineveh, Memphis and Thebes, but the modern town dates from 1638, the commencement of the reign of the famous Mogul Shah Jehan, of whom I have written so much in previous chapters. About eleven miles from the city is a group of splendid ruins, some of the most remarkable in the world, and a celebrated tower known as the Kutab-Minar, one of the most important architectural monuments in India. You reach it by the Great Trunk Road of India, the most notable thoroughfare in the empire, which has been the highway from the mountains and northern provinces to the sacred River Ganges from the beginning of time, and, notwithstanding the construction of railroads, is to-day the great thoroughfare of Asia. If followed it will lead you through Turkestan and Persia to Constantinople and Moscow. Over this road came Tamerlane, the Tartar Napoleon, with his victorious army, and Alexander the Great, and it has been trodden by the feet of successive invaders for twenty or thirty centuries. To-day it leads to the Khyber Pass, the only gateway between India and Afghanistan, where the frontier is guarded by a tremendous force, and no human being is allowed to go either way without permits from the authorities of both governments. Long caravans still cross the desert of middle Asia, enter and leave India through this pass and follow the Grand Trunk Road to the cities of the Ganges. It is always thronged with pilgrims and commerce; with trains of bullock carts, caravans of camels and elephants, and thousands of pedestrians pass every milestone daily. Kipling describes them and the road in "Kim" in more graphic language than flows through my typewriter. In the neighborhood of Delhi the Grand Trunk Road is like the Appian Way of Rome, both sides being lined with the mausoleums of kings, warriors and saints in various stages of decay and dilapidation. And scattered among them are the ruins of the palaces of supplanted dynasties which appeared and vanished, arose and fell, one after another, in smoke and blood; with the clash of steel, the cries of victory and shrieks of despair.

In the center of the court of the ancient mosque of Kutbul Islam, which was originally built for a Hindu temple in the tenth century, stands a wrought-iron column, one of the most curious things in India. It rises 23 feet 8 inches above the ground, and its base, which is bulbous, is riveted to two stone slabs two feet below the surface. Its diameter at the base is 16 feet 4 inches and at the capital is 12 inches. It is a malleable forging of pure iron, without alloy, and 7.66 specific gravity. According to the estimates of engineers, it weighs about six tons, and it is remarkable that the Hindus at that age could forge a bar of iron larger and heavier than was ever forged in Europe until a very recent date. Its history is deeply cut upon its surface in Sanskrit letters. The inscription tells us that it is "The Arm of Fame of Raja Dhava," who subdued a nation named the Vahlikas, "and obtained, with his own arm, undivided sovereignty upon the earth for a long period." No date is given, but the historians fix its erection about the year 319 or 320 A. D. This is the oldest and the most unique of all the many memorials in India, and has been allowed to stand about 1,700 years undisturbed. An old prophecy declared that Hindu sovereigns would rule as long as the column stood, and when the empire was invaded in 1206 and Delhi became the capital of a Mohammedan empire, its conqueror, Kutb-ud-Din (the Pole Star of the Faith), originally a Turkish slave, defied it by allowing the pillar to remain, but he converted the beautiful Hindu temple which surrounded it into a Moslem mosque and ordered his muezzins to proclaim the name of God and His prophet from its roof, and to call the faithful to pray within its walls.

This Hindu temple, which was converted into a mosque, is still unrivaled for its gigantic arches and for the graceful beauty of the tracery which decorated its walls. Even in ruins it is a magnificent structure, and Lord Curzon is to be thanked for directing its partial restoration at government expense. The architectural treasures of India are many, but there are none to spare, and it is gratifying to find officials in authority who appreciate the value of preserving those that remain for the benefit of architectural and historical students. It it a pity that the original Hindu carvings upon the columns cannot be restored. There were originally not less than 1,200 columns, and each was richly ornamented with peculiar Hindu decorative designs. Some of them, in shadowy corners, are still almost perfect, but unfortunately those which are most conspicuous were shamefully defaced by the Mohammedan conquerors, and we must rely upon our imaginations to picture them as they were in their original beauty. The walls of the building are of purplish red standstone, of very fine grain, almost as fine as marble, and age and exposure seem to have hardened it.

In one corner of the court of this great mosque rises the Kutab Minar, a monument and tower of victory. It is supposed to have been originally started by the Hindus and completed by their Mohammedan conquerors. Another tower, called the Alai-Minar, about 500 feet distant, remains unfinished, and rises only eighty-seven feet from the ground. Had it been finished as intended, it would have been 500 feet high, or nearly as lofty as the Washington monument. According to the inscription, it was erected by Ala-din Khiji, who reigned from 1296 to 1316, and remains as it stood at his death. For some reason his successor never tried to complete it.

The Kutab Minar, the completed tower, is not only a notable structure and one of the most perfect in the world, second only in height to the Washington monument, but it is particularly notable for its geometrical proportions. Its height, 238 feet, is exactly five times the diameter of its base. It is divided into five stories each tapering in perfect proportions and being divided by projecting balconies or galleries. The first story, 95 feet in height, consists of twenty-four faces in the form of convex flutings, alternately semicircular and rectangular, built of alternate courses of marble and red sandstone. The second story is 51 feet high and the projections are all semicircular; the third story is 41 feet and the projections are all rectangular; the fourth, 26 feet high, is a plain cylinder, and the fifth or top story, 25 feet high, is partly fluted and partly plain. The mean diameter of each story is exactly one-fifth of its height, and the material is alternate courses of marble and red sandstone, the entire exterior surface being incrusted with inscriptions from the Koran, sculptured in sharp relief. It has been compared for beauty of design and perfection of proportions to the Campanile at Florence, but that is conventional in every respect, while the Kutab Minar is unique. The sculptures that cover its surface have been compared to those upon the column of Trajan in Rome and the Column Vendome in Paris, but they are intended to relate the military triumphs of the men in whose honor they were erected, while the inscription upon the Kutab Minar is a continuous recognition of the power and glory of God and the virtues of Mahomet, His prophet.

Whichever way you look, whichever way you drive, in that extraordinary place, you find artistic taste, the religious devotion, the love of conquest and the military genius of the Mohammedans combined and perpetuated in noble forms. The camel driver of Mecca, like the founder of Christianity, was a teacher of peace and an example of humility, but his followers have been famous for their pride, their brilliant achievements, their audacity and their martial violence and success. The fortresses scattered over the plain bear testimony to their fighting qualities, and are an expression of their authority and power; their gilded palaces and jeweled thrones testify to their luxurious taste and artistic sentiment, while the massive mausoleums which arise in every direction testify to their pride and their determination that posterity shall not forget their names. I have told you in a previous chapter about the tomb of Humayun, the son of Baber (the Lion of the Faith), who transmitted to a long line of Moguls the blood of conquerors. But it is only one of several noble examples of architecture and pretensions, and as evidence of the human sympathies of the man who built it, the tomb of his barber is near by.

About a mile across the plain is another group of still more remarkable sepulchers, about seven or eight miles from Delhi. They are surrounded by a grove of mighty trees, whose boughs overhang a crumbling wall intended to protect them. As we passed the portal we found ourselves looking upon a large reservoir, or tank, as they call them here, which long ago was blessed by Nizamu-Din, one of the holiest and most renowned of the Brahmin saints, so that none who swims in it is ever drowned. A group of wan and hungry-looking priests were standing there to receive us; they live on backsheesh and sleep on the cold marble floors of the tombs. No dinner bell ever rings for them. They depend entirely upon charity, and send out their chelas, or disciples, every morning to skirmish for food among the market men and people in the neighborhood. While we stood talking to them a group of six naked young men standing upon the cornice of a temple attracted our attention by their violent gesticulations, and then, one after another, plunged headlong, fifty or sixty feet, into the waters of the pool. As they reappeared upon the surface they swam to the marble steps of the pavilion, shook themselves dry like dogs and extended their hands for backsheesh. It was an entirely new and rather startling form of entertainment, but we learned that it was their way of making a living, and that they are the descendants of the famous men and women who occupy the wonderful tombs, and are permitted to live among them and collect backsheesh from visitors as they did from us. Several women were hanging around, and half a dozen fierce-looking mullahs, or Mohammedan priests, with their beards dyed a deep scarlet because the prophet had red hair.

The most notable of the tombs, the "Hall of Sixty-four Pillars," is an exquisite structure of white marble, where rests Azizah Kokal Tash, foster brother of the great Mogul Akbar. He was buried here in 1623, and around him are the graves of his mother and eight of his brothers and sisters. Another tomb of singular purity and beauty is that of Muhammud Shah, who was Mogul from 1719 to 1748—the man whom Nadir Shah, the Persian, conquered and despoiled. By his side lie two of his wives and several of his children.

The tomb of Jehanara, daughter of the great Emperor Shah Jehan, is a gem of architecture, a dainty bungalow of pure white marble. The roof is a low dome with broad eaves, and the walls are slabs of thin marble perforated in geometric designs like the finest lace. The inscription calls her "Heavenly Minded," and reminds us that "God is the Resurrection and the Life;" that it was her wish that nothing but grass might cover her dust, because "Such a pall alone was fit for the lowly dead," and closes with a prayer for the soul of her father. Notwithstanding her wishes, so expressed, the tomb cost $300,000, but such sentiments, which appear upon nearly all of the Mogul tombs, are not to be taken literally. The inscription over the entrance to one of the grandest in India, where lies "The Piercer of Battle Ranks," admits that "However great and powerful man may be in the presence of his fellow creatures; however wide his power

TOMB OF AMIR KHUSRAN — PERSIAN POET — DELHI

With panels of perforated marble

and influence, and however large his wealth, he is as humble and as worthless as the smallest insect in the sight of God." Human nature was the same among the Moguls as it is to-day, and the men who were able to spend a million or half a million dollars upon their sepulchers could afford to throw in a few expressions of humility.

The most beautiful of the tombs is that of Amir Khusrau, a poet who died at Delhi in 1315, the author of ninety-eight poems, many of which are still in popular use. He was known as "the Parrot of Hindustan," and enjoyed the confidence and patronage of seven successive Moguls. His fame is immortal. Lines he wrote are still recited nightly in the coffee-houses and sung in the harems of India, and women and girls and sentimental young men come daily to lay fresh flowers upon his tomb.

In the center of Delhi and on the highest eminence of the city stands the Jumma Musjid, almost unrivaled among mosques. There is nothing elsewhere outside of Constantinople that can compare with it, either in size or splendor, and we are told that 10,000 workmen were employed upon it daily for six years. It was built by Shah Jehan of red sandstone inlaid with white marble; is crowned with three splendid domes of white marble striped with black, and at each angle of the courtyard stands a gigantic minaret composed of alternate stripes of marble and red sandstone. There are three stately portals approached by flights of forty steps, the lowest of which is 140 feet long. Through stately arches you are led into a courtyard 450 feet square, inclosed by splendid arcaded cloisters. In the center of the court is the usual fountain basin, at which the worshipers perform their ablutions, and at the eastern side, facing toward Mecca, at the summit of a flight of marble steps, is the mosque,

260 feet long and 120 feet wide. The central archway is eighty feet high.

Over in one corner of the cloisters is a reliquary guarded by a squad of fierce-looking priests, which contains some of the most precious relics of the prophet in existence. They have a hair from his mustache, which is red; one of his slippers, the print of his foot in a stone, two copies of portions of the Koran—one of them written by his son-in-law, Imam Husain, very clear and well preserved, and the other by his grandson, Imam Hasan. Both are very beautiful specimens of chirography, and would have a high value for that reason alone, but obtained especial sanctity because of the tradition that both were written at the dictation of the Prophet himself, and are among the oldest copies of the Koran in existence.

XVIII

THUGS, FAKIRS, AND NAUTCH DANCERS

The most interesting classes among the many kinds of priests, monks and other people, who make religion a profession in India, are the thugs, fakirs and nautch girls, who are supposed to devote their lives and talents to the service of the gods. There are several kinds of fakirs and other religious mendicants in India, about five thousand in number, most of them being nomads, wandering from city to city and temple to temple, dependent entirely upon the charity of the faithful. They reward those who serve them with various forms of blessings; give them advice concerning all the affairs of life from the planting of their crops to the training of their children. They claim supernatural powers to confer good and invoke evil, and the curse of a fakir is the last misfortunte that an honest Hindu cares to bring upon himself, for it means a failure of his harvests, the death of his cattle by disease, sickness in his family and bad luck in everything that he undertakes. Hence these holy men, who are familiars of the gods, and are believed to spend most of their time communicating with them in some mysterious way about the affairs of the world, are able to command anything the people have to give, and nobody would willingly cross their shadows or incur their displeasure. The name is pronounced as if it were spelled "fah-keer."

These religious mendicants go almost naked, usually with nothing but the smallest possible breech clout around their loins, which the police require them to wear; they plaster their bodies with mud, ashes and filth; they rub clay, gum and other substances into their hair to give it an uncouth appearance. Sometimes they wear their hair in long braids hanging down their backs like the queue of a Chinaman; sometimes in short braids sticking out in every direction like the wool of the pickaninnies down South. Some of them have strings of beads around their necks, others coils of rope round them. They never wear hats and usually carry nothing but a small brass bowl, in imitation of Buddha, which is the only property they possess on earth. They are usually accompanied by a youthful disciple, called a "chela," a boy of from 10 to 15 years of age, who will become a fakir himself unless something occurs to change his career.

Many of the fakirs endeavor to make themselves look as hideous as possible. They sometimes whitewash their faces like clowns in circuses; paint lines upon their cheeks and draw marks under their eyes to give them an inhuman appearance. At certain seasons of the year they may clothe themselves in filthy rags for the time being as an evidence of humility. Most of them are very thin and spare of flesh, which is due to their long pilgrimages and insufficient nourishment. They sleep wherever they happen to be. They lie down on the roadside or beneath a column of a temple, or under a cart, or in a stable. Sometimes kindly disposed people give them beds, but they have no regular habits; they sleep when they are sleepy, rest when they are tired and continue their wanderings when they are refreshed.

About the time the people of the country are breakfasting in the morning the chela starts out with the brass bowl and begs from house to house until the bowl is filled with food, when he returns to wherever his master is waiting for him and they share its contents between them. Again at noon and again at night the chela goes out on similar foraging expeditions and conducts the commissary department in that way. The fakir himself is supposed never to beg; the gods he worships are expected to take care of him, and if they do not send him food he goes without it. It is a popular delusion that fakirs will not accept alms from anyone for any purpose, for I have considerable personal experience to the contrary. I have offered money to hundreds of them and have never yet had it refused. A fakir will snatch a penny as eagerly as any beggar you ever saw, and if the coin you offer is smaller than he expects or desires he will show his disapproval in an unmistakable manner.

The larger number of fakirs are merely religious tramps, worthless, useless impostors, living upon the fears and superstitions of the people and doing more harm than good. Others are without doubt earnest and sincere ascetics, who believe that they are promoting the welfare and happiness of their fellow men by depriving themselves of everything that is necessary to happiness, purifying their souls by privation and hardship and obtaining spiritual inspiration and light by continuous meditation and prayer. Many of these are fanatics, some are epileptics, some are insane. They undergo self-torture of the most horrible kinds and frequently prove their sincerity by causing themselves to be buried alive, by starving to death, or by posing themselves in unnatural attitudes with their faces or their arms raised to heaven until the sinews and muscles are benumbed or paralyzed and they fall unconscious from exhaustion. These are tests of purity and piety. Zealots frequently enter temples and perform such feats for the admiration of pilgrims and by-standers. Many are clairvoyants and have the power of second sight. They hypnotize subjects and go into trances themselves, in which condition the soul is supposed to leave the body and visit the gods. Some of the metaphysical phenomena are remarkable and even startling. They cannot be explained. You have doubtless read of the wonderful fakir, Ram Lal, who appears in F. Marion Crawford's story of "Mr. Isaacs," and there is a good deal concerning this class of people in Rudyard Kipling's "Kim." Those two, by the way, are universally considered the best stories of Indian life ever written. You will perhaps remember also reading of the astonishing performances of Mme. Blavatsky, who visited the United States some years ago as the high priestess of Theosophy. Her supernatural manifestations attracted a great deal of attention at one time, but she was finally exposed and denounced as a charlatan.

Among the higher class of fakirs are many extraordinary men, profound scholars, accomplished linguists and others whose knowledge of both the natural and the occult sciences is amazing. I was told by one of the highest officials of the Indian Empire of an extraordinary feat performed for his benefit by one of these fakirs, who in some mysterious way transferred himself several hundred miles in a single night over a country where there were no railroads, and never took the trouble to explain how his journey was accomplished.

The best conjurers, magicians and palmists in India are fakirs. Many of them tell fortunes from the lines of the hand and from other signs with extraordinary accuracy. Old residents who have come in contact with this class relate astounding tales. While at Calcutta a young lady at our hotel was incidentally informed by a fortune-telling fakir she met accidentally in a Brahmin temple that she would soon receive news that would change all her plans and alter the course of her life, and the next morning she received a cablegram from England announcing the death of her father. If you get an old resident started on such stories he will keep telling them all night.

Of course you have read of the incredible and seemingly impossible feats performed by Hindu magicians, of whom the best and most skillful belong to the fakir class. I have seen the "box trick," or "basket trick," as they call it, in which a young man is tied up in a gunny sack and locked up in a box, then at a signal a few moments after appears smiling at the entrance to your house, but I have never found anyone who could explain how he escaped from his prison. This was performed daily on the Midway Plaisance at the World's Fair at Chicago and was witnessed by thousands of people. And it is simple compared with some of the doings of these fakirs. They will take a mango, open it before you, remove the seeds, plant them in a tub of earth, and a tree will grow and bear fruit before your eyes within half an hour. Or, what is even more wonderful, they will climb an invisible rope in the open air as high as a house, vanish into space, and then, a few minutes after, will come smiling around the nearest street corner. Or, if that is not wonderful enough, they will take an ordinary rope, whirl it around their head, toss it into the air, and it will stand upright, as if fastened to some invisible bar, so taut and firm that a heavy man can climb it.

These are a few of the wonderful things fakirs perform about the temples, and nobody has ever been able to discover how they do it. People who begin an inquiry usually abandon it and declare that the tricks are not done at all, that the spectators are simply hypnotized and imagine that they have seen what they afterward describe. This explanation is entirely plausible. It is the only safe one that can be given, and it is confirmed by other manifestations of hypnotic power that you would not believe if I should describe them. Fakirs have hypnotized people I know and have made them witness events and spectacles which they afterward learned were transpiring, at the very moment, five and six thousand miles away. For example, a young gentleman, relating his experience, declared that under the power of one of these men he attended his brother's wedding in a London church and wrote home an account of it that was so accurate in its details that his family were convinced that he had come all the way from India without letting them know and had attended it secretly.

Many of the snake charmers to whom I referred in a previous chapter are fakirs, devoted to gods whose specialties are snakes, and pious Hindus believe that the deities they worship protect them from the venom of the reptiles. Sometimes you can see one of them at a temple deliberately permit his pets to sting him on the arm, and he will show you the blood flowing. Taking a little black stone from his pocket he will rub it over the wound and then rub it upon the head of the snake. Then he will rub the wound again, and again the head of the snake, all the time muttering prayers, making passes with his hands, bowing his body to the ground, and going through other forms of worship, and when he has concluded he will assure you that the bite of the snake has been made harmless by the incantation.

I have never seen more remarkable contortionists than the fakirs who can be always found about temples in Benares, and frequently elsewhere. They are usually very lean men, almost skeletons. As they wear no clothing, one can count their bones through the skin, but their muscles and sinews are remarkably strong and supple. They twist themselves into the most extraordinary shapes. No professional contortionist upon the vaudeville stage can compare with these religious mendicants, who give exhibitions in the open air, or in the porticos of the temples in honor of some god and call it worship. They acquire the faculty of doing their feats by long and tedious training under the instruction of older fakirs, who are equally accomplished, and the performances are actually considered worship, just as much as an organ voluntary, the singing of a hymn, or a display of pulpit eloquence in one of our churches. The more wonderful their feats, the more acceptable to their gods, and they go from city to city through all India, and from temple to temple, twisting their bodies into unnatural shapes and postures under the impression that they will thereby attain a higher degree of holiness and exalt themselves in the favor of heaven. They do not give exhibitions for money. They cannot be hired for any price to appear upon a public stage. Theatrical agents in London and elsewhere have frequently tempted them with fortunes, but they cannot be persuaded to display their gifts for gain, or violate their caste and the traditions of their profession.

There is a fearful sect of fakirs devoted to Siva and to Bhairava, the god of lunacy, who associate with evil spirits, ghouls and vampires, and practice hideous rites of blood, lust and gluttony. They tear their flesh with their finger-nails, slash themselves with knives, and occasionally engage in a frantic dance from which they die of exhaustion.

The nautches of India have received considerable attention from many sources. They are the object of the most earnest admonitions from missionaries and moralists, and no doubt are a very bad lot, although they do not look it, and are a recognized and respected profession among the Hindus. They are consecrated to certain gods soon after their birth; they are the brides of the impure and obscene deities of the Hindu pantheon, and are attached to their temples, receiving their support from the collections of the priests or the permanent endowments, often living under the temple roof and almost always within the sacred premises. The amount of their incomes varies according to the wealth and the revenues of the idol to which they were attached. They dance before him daily and sing hymns in his honor. The ranks of the nautch girls are sometimes recruited by the purchase of children from poor parents, and by the dedication of the daughters of pious Hindu families to that vocation, just as in Christian countries daughters are consecrated to the vocation of religion from the cradle and sons are dedicated to the priesthood and ministry. Indeed it is considered a high honor for the daughter of a Hindu family to be received into a temple as a nautch.

They never marry and never retire. When they become too old to dance they devote themselves to the training of their successors. They are taught to read and write, to sing and dance, to embroider and play upon various musical instruments. They are better educated than any other class of Hindu women, and that largely accounts for their attractions and their influence over men. They have their own peculiar customs and rules, similar to those of the geishas of Japan, and if a nautch is so fortunate as to inherit property it goes to the temple to which she belongs. This custom has become law by the confirmation of the courts. No nautch can retain any article of value without the consent of the priest in charge of the temple to which she is attached, and those who have received valuable gifts of jewels from their admirers and lovers are often compelled to surrender them. On the other hand, they are furnished comfortable homes, clothing and food, and are taken care of all of their lives, just the same as religious devotees belonging to any other sect. Notwithstanding their notorious unchastity and immorality, no discredit attaches to the profession, and the very vices for which they are condemned are considered acts of duty, faith and worship, although it seems almost incredible that a religious sect will encourage gross immorality in its own temples. Yet Hinduism has done worse things than that, and other of its practices are even more censurable.

Bands of nautches are considered necessary appurtenances of the courts of native Hindu princes, although they are never found in the palaces of Mohammedans. They are brought forward upon all occasions of ceremony, religious, official and convivial. If the viceroy visits the capital of one of the native states he is entertained by their best performances. They have a place on the programme at all celebrations of feast days; they appear at weddings and birthday anniversaries, and are quite as important as an orchestra at one of our social occasions at home. They are invited to the homes of native gentlemen on all great occasions and are treated with the utmost deference and generosity. They are permitted liberties and are accorded honors that would not be granted to the wives and daughters of those who entertain them, and stand on the same level as the Brahmin priests, yet they are what we would call women of the town, and receive visitors indiscriminately in the temples and other sacred places, according to their pleasure and whims.

A stranger in India finds it difficult to reconcile these facts, but any resident will assure you of the truth. The priests are said to encourage the attentions of rich young Hindus because of the gifts of money and jewels they are in the habit of showering upon nautches they admire, but each girl is supposed to have a "steady" lover, upon whom she bestows her affections for the time being. He may be old or young, married or unmarried, rich or poor, for as a rule it is to these women that a Hindu gentleman turns for the companionship which his own home does not supply.

There is a difference of opinion as to the beauty of the nautches. It is purely a matter of taste. There is no rule by which personal attractions may be measured, and doubtless there may be beautiful women among them, but, so far, I have never seen one. Their costumes are usually very elaborate, the materials being of the rarest and finest qualities and profusely embroidered, and their jewels are usually costly. Their manners are gentle, refined and modest; they are perfectly self-possessed under all circumstances, and, while their dancing would not be attractive to the average American taste, it is not immodest, and consists of a succession of graceful gestures and posturing which is supposed to have a definite meaning and express sentiments and emotions. Most of the dances are interpretations of poems, legends, stories of the gods and heroes of Indian mythology. Educated Hindus profess to be able to understand them, although to a foreigner they are nothing more than meaningless motions. I have asked the same question of several missionaries, but have never been able to discover a nautch dancer who has abandoned her vocation, or has deserted her temple, or has run away with a lover, or has been reached in any way by the various missions for women in India. They seem to be perfectly satisfied with their present and their future.

The greatest good women missionaries have done in India, I think, is in bringing modern medical science into the homes of the natives. No man is ever admitted to the zenanas, no matter what may happen, and thousands upon thousands, yes, millions upon millions, of poor creatures have suffered and died for lack of ordinary medical attention because of the etiquette of caste. American women brought the first relief, graduates from medical schools in Philadelphia, New York and Chicago, and now there are women physicians attached to all of the missions, and many of them are practicing independently in the larger cities. They are highly respected and exert a great influence.

Nizam-u-Din, one of the haliest of the Hindu saints, lies in a tomb of marble lace work and embroidery near Delhi; as exquisite a bit of architecture as you can imagine, so dainty in all its details that it ought to be the sepulcher of a fairy queen instead of that of the founder of the Thugs, the secret religious society of assassins which was suppressed and practically exterminated by the British authorities in the '60's and '70's. He died in

1652. He was a fanatic who worshiped the goddess Kali, the black wife of Siva, and believed that the removal of unbelievers from the earth was what we call a Christian duty. As Kali prohibited the shedding of blood, he trained his devotees to strangle their fellow beings without violating that prohibition or leaving any traces of their work, and sent out hundreds of professional murderers over India to diminish the number of heretics for the good and glory of the faith. No saint in the Hindu calendar is more generally worshiped or more profoundly revered unto the present day. His tomb is attended by groups of Brahmins who place fresh flowers upon the cenotaph every morning and cover it reverently with Cashmere shawls of the finest texture and pieces of rare embroidery.

India is the only country where crime was ever systematically carried on as a religious and legitimate occupation in the belief that it was right, for not only the Thugs, but other professional murderers existed for centuries, and still exist, although in greatly diminished numbers, owing to the vigilance of the police; not because they have become converted from the error of their ways. There are yet tribes of professional criminals who believe that, in following the customs and the occupation of their ancestors, they are acting in the only way that is right and are serving the gods they worship. Criminal organizations exist in nearly all the native states, and the government is just now making a special effort to stamp out professional "dacoits," who are associated for the purpose of highway robbery, cattle stealing and violence and carry on marauding expeditions from their headquarters continuously. They are just as well organized and as thoroughly devoted to their business as the gangs of highwaymen that used to make travel dangerous through Europe in the middle ages. And there are other criminal organizations with which it is even more difficult to deal. A recent report from the office of the home secretary says:

"We all know that trades go by castes in India; a family of carpenters will be a family of carpenters a century or five centuries hence, if they last so long; so with grain dealers, blacksmiths, leather-makers and every known trade. If we keep this in mind when we speak of 'professional criminals' we shall realize what the term really means. It means that the members of a tribe whose ancestors were criminals from time immemorial are themselves destined by the use of the caste to commit crime, and their descendants will be offenders against the law till the whole tribe is exterminated or accounted for in the manner of the Thugs. Therefore, when a man tells you he is a badhak, or a kanjar, or a sonoria, he tells you, what few Europeans ever thoroughly realize, that he is an habitual and avowed offender against the law, and has been so from the beginning and will be so to the end; that reform is impossible, for it is his trade, his caste—I may almost say, his religion—to commit crime."

The Thugs were broken up by Captain Sleeman, a brave and able British detective who succeeded in entering that assassination society and was initiated into its terrible mysteries. A large number of the leaders were executed from time to time, but the government, whose policy is always to respect religious customs of the Hindus, administered as little punishment as possible, and "rounding up" all of the members of this cult, as ranchmen would say, "corralled" them at the Town of Jabalpur, near the City of Allahabad, in northeastern India, where they have since been under surveillance. Originally there were 2,500, but now only about half of that number remain, who up to this date are not allowed to leave without a permit the inclosure in which they are kept.

One of the criminal tribes, called Barwars, numbers about a thousand families and inhabits forty-eight villages in the district of Gonda, in the Province of Oudh, not far from Delhi. They live quietly and honestly upon their farms during the months of planting and harvesting, but between crops they wander in small gangs over distant parts of the country, robbing and plundering with great courage and skill. They even despoil the temples of the gods. The only places that are sacred to them are the temple of Jaganath (Juggernaut), in the district of Orissa, and the shrine of a certain Mohammedan martyr. They have a regular organization under hereditary chiefs, and if a member of the clan gives up thieving he is disgraced and excommunicated. The plunder is divided pro rata, and a certain portion is set aside for their priests and as offerings to their gods.

There is a similar clan of organized robbers and murderers known as Sonoriaths, whose special business is to steal cattle, and the Mina tribe, which lives in the district of Gurgaon, on the frontier of the Punjab Province, has 2,000 members, given up entirely to robbery and murder. They make no trouble at home. They are honest in their dealings, peaceable, charitable, hospitable, and have considerable wealth, but between crops the larger portion of the men disappear from their homes and go into other provinces for the purpose of robbery, burglary and other forms of stealing. In the Agra Province are twenty-nine different tribes who from time immemorial have made crime their regular occupation and, like all those mentioned, look upon it as not only a legitimate but a religious act ordered and approved by the deities they worship.

Special laws have been enacted for restraining these castes or clans, and special police officers now exercise supervision over them. Every man is required to register at the police headquarters and receive a passport. He is required to live within a certain district, and cannot change his abode or leave its limits without permission. If he does so he is arrested and imprisoned. The authorities believe that they have considerably reduced the amount of crime committed by these clansmen, who are too cunning and courageous to be entirely suppressed. No amount of vigilance can prevent them from leaving their villages and going off into other provinces for criminal purposes, and the railways greatly facilitate their movements.

Nevertheless, if you will examine the criminal statistics of India you will be surprised at the small number of arrests, trials and convictions for penal offenses. The figures demonstrate that the people are honest and law abiding. There is less crime in India than in any other country in proportion to population, much less than in England or the United States. Out of a population of 300,000,000 people during the ten years from 1892 to 1902 there was an annual average of 1,015,550 criminal cases before the courts, and an average of 1,345,667 offenses against the criminal laws reported, while 870,665 persons were convicted of crime in 1902, with the following penalties imposed:

Death 500

Penal servitude	1,707
Imprisonment	175,795
Fines	628,092
Over two years' imprisonment	7,576
Between one and two years	39,067
Between fifteen days and one year	86,653
Under fifteen days	34,517

The following were the most serious crimes in 1902:

	Arrests.	Convictions.
Offenses against public peace	15,190	5,088
Murder	3,255	1,102
Assault	42,496	12,597
Dacoity or highway robbery	3,320	706
Cattle stealing	29,691	9,307
Ordinary theft	183,463	45,566
House-breaking	192,353	23,143
Vagrancy	25,212	18,877
Public nuisances	216,285	201,421

The following table will show the total daily average of prisoners, men and women, serving sentences for penal offenses in the prisons of India during the years named:

	Men.	Women.	Total.
1892	93,061	3,142	96,202
1893	91,976	2,988	94,964
1894	92,236	2,941	95,177
1895	97,869	3,216	101,085
1896	100,406	3,280	103,686
1897	109,989	3,277	113,266
1898	103,517	2,927	106,446
1899	101,518	2,773	104,292
1900	114,854	3,253	118,107
1901	108,258	3,124	111,382

Those who are familiar with criminal statistics in the United States and other countries, will, I am confident, agree with me that this is a most remarkable record for a population of 300,000,000, illiterate, superstitious, impregnated with false ideas of honor and morality, and packed so densely as the people of India are. The courts of justice have reached a high standard; the lower courts are administered almost exclusively by natives; the higher courts by English and natives together. No trial of importance ever takes place except before a mixed court, and usually the three great religions—Brahminism, Mohammedanism and Christianity—are represented on the bench.

One of the most difficult and delicate tasks of the British authorities has been to prevent infanticide, the murder of girl infants, because from time immemorial among all the races of India it has been practiced openly and without restraint and in many sections as a religious duty. And what has made it more difficult, it prevailed most extensively among the families of the highest rank, and among the natives, communities and provinces which were most loyal to the British crown. For example, the Rajputs, of whom I have written at length in a previous chapter, are the chivalry of India. They trace their descent from the gods, and are proud of their nobility and their honor, yet it has been the custom among them as far back as traditions run, to strangle more than half their girl babies at birth, and until this was stopped the records showed numbers of villages where there was not a single girl, and where there never had been one within the memory of man. As late as the census of 1869 seven villages were reported with 104 boys and one girl, twenty-three villages with 284 boys and twenty-three girls and many others in similar proportions. The statistics of the recent census of 1901, by the disparity between the sexes, show that this crime has not yet been stamped out. In the Rajputana Province, for example, there are 2,447,401 boys to 1,397,911 girls, and throughout the entire population of India there are 72,506,661 boys to 49,-516,381 girls. Among the Hindus of all ages there are 105,163,345 men to 101,945,387 women, and among the Sikhs, who also strangle their children, there are 1,241,-543 men to 950,823 women. Among the Buddhists, the Jains and other religions the ratio between the sexes was more even.

Sir John Strachy, in his admirable book upon India, says: "These people have gone on killing their children generation after generation because their forefathers did so before them, not only without a thought that there is anything criminal in the practice, but with the conviction that it is right. There can be little doubt that if vigilance were relaxed the custom would before long become as prevalent as ever." The measures taken by the government have been radical and stringent. A system of registration of births and deaths was provided by an act passed in 1870, with constant inspection and frequent enumeration of children among the suspected classes, and no efforts were spared to convince them that the government had finally resolved to prevent the practice and in doing so treated it as murder.

XIX

SIMLA AND THE PUNJAB

At Delhi the railway forks. One branch runs on to the frontier of Afghanistan via Lahore and Peshawur, and the other via Umballa, an important military post, to Simla, the summer capital and sanitarium of India. Because of the climate there must be two capitals. From October to April the viceroy occupies the government house at Calcutta with the civil and military authorities around him, but as soon as the summer heat sets in the whole administration, civil, military and judicial, removes to Simla, and everybody follows, foreign consuls, bankers, merchants, lawyers, butchers, bakers and candlestick makers, hotel and boardinghouse keepers, with their servants, coachmen and horses. The commander-in-chief of the army, the adjutant general and all the heads of the other departments with their clerks take their books and records along with them. The winter population of Simla is about 15,000; the summer population reaches 30,000. The exodus lasts about a month, during which time every railway train going north is crowded and every extra car that can be spared is borrowed from the other railways. The last of October the migration is reversed and everybody returns to Calcutta. This has been going on for nearly fifty years. The journey to Umballa is made by rail and thence by "dak-gherries," a sort of covered democrat wagon, "mailtongas," a species of cart, bullock carts, army wagons and carriages of every size and description, while the luggage is brought up the hills in various kinds of conveyance, much of it on the heads of coolies, both women and men. The distance, fifty-seven miles by the highway, is all uphill, but can be made by an ordinary team in twelve hours.

Long experience has taught the government officials how to make this removal in a scientific manner, and the records are arranged for easy transportation. The viceroy has his own outfit, and when the word is given the transfer takes place without the slightest difficulty or confusion. A public functionary leaves his papers at his desk, puts on his hat and walks out of his office at Calcutta; three days later he walks into his office at Simla, hangs his hat on a peg behind the door and sits down at his desk with the same papers lying in the same positions before him, and business goes on with the interruption of only three or four days at most. The migration makes no more difference to the administration than the revolutions of the earth. Formerly the various offices were scattered over all parts of Simla, but they have been gradually concentrated in blocks of handsome buildings constructed at a cost of several millions of dollars. The home secretary, the department of public works, the finance and revenue departments, the secretary of agriculture, the postmaster general and the secretary of war, each has quite as good an office for himself and his clerks as he occupies at Calcutta. There is a courthouse, a law library, a theatre and opera house, a number of clubs and churches, for the archbishop and the clergy follow their flocks, and the Calcutta merchants come along with their clerks and merchandise to supply the wants of their customers. It is a remarkable migration of a great government.

Although absolutely necessary for their health, and that of their families, it is rather expensive for government employes, or civil servants, as they are called in India, to keep up two establishments, one in Simla and one in Calcutta. But they get the benefit of the stimulating atmosphere of the hills and escape the perpetual Turkish bath that is called summer in Calcutta. Many of the higher officials, merchants, bankers, society people and others have bungalows at Simla furnished like our summer cottages at home. They extend over a long ridge, with beautiful grounds around them. It is fully six miles from one end of the town to the other, and the principal street is more than five miles long. The houses are built upon terraces up and down the slope, with one of the most beautiful panoramas of mountain scenery that can be imagined spread out before them. Deep valleys, rocky ravines and gorges break the mountainsides, which are clothed with forests of oak and other beautiful trees, while the background is a crescent of snowy peaks rising range above range against the azure sky. Many people live in tents, particularly the military families, and make themselves exceedingly comfortable. Simla is quite cold in winter, being 7,084 feet above the sea and situated on the thirty-second parallel of north latitude, about the same as Charleston, S. C., but in summer the climate is very fine.

The viceroy occupies a chateau called the Viceregal Lodge, perched upon a hill overlooking the town, and from his porches commands as grand a mountain landscape as you could wish to see. The Viceregal Lodge, like the government-house in Calcutta, was designed especially for its purpose and is arranged for entertainments upon a broad scale. The vice-queen takes the lead in social life, and no woman in that position has ever been more competent than Lady Curzon. There is really more society at Simla than in Calcutta. It is the Newport of India, but fortunately for the health of those who participate, it is mostly out of doors. The military element is large enough to give it an athletic and sporting character, and to the girls who are popular a summer at Simla is one prolonged picnic. There are races, polo, tennis, golf, drives, rides, walks, garden parties and all sorts of afternoon and morning functions. F. Marion Crawford describes the gayeties of Simla in "Mr. Isaacs," the first and best novel he ever wrote, and gives a graphic account of a polo match in which his hero was knocked off his horse and had his head bathed by the young lady he was in love with. Kipling has given us a succession of pictures of Simla society, and no novel of Indian life is without a chapter or two on it, because it is really the most interesting place in all the empire.

If you want to get a better idea of the place and its attractions than I can give, read "Mr. Isaacs." Many of its incidents are drawn from life, and the hero is a Persian Jew of Delhi, named Jacobs, whose business is to sell precious stones to the native princes. Crawford used to spend his summers at Simla when he was a reporter for the Allahabad Pioneer, and made Jacobs's acquaintance there. His Indian experiences are very interesting, and he tells them as well as he writes. When he was quite a young man he went to India as private secretary for an Englishman of importance who died over there and left him stranded. Having failed to obtain employment and having reached the bottom of his purse, he decided in desperation to enlist as a private soldier in the army, and was looking through the papers for the location of the recruiting officc when his eye was attracted by an advertisement from the Allahabad Pioneer, which wanted a reporter. Although he had never done any literary work, he decided to make a dash for it, and became one of the most successful and influential journalists in India until his career was broken in upon by the success of "Mr. Isaccs," his first novel, which was published in England and turned his pen from facts to fiction.

The railway journey from Delhi to Lahore is not exciting, although it passes through a section of great historical interest which has been fought over by contending armies and races for more than 3,000 years. Several of the most important battles in India occurred along the right of way, and they changed the dynasties and religions of the empire, but the plains tell no tales and show no signs of the events they have witnessed. Everybody who has read Kipling's stories will be interested in Umballa, although it is nothing but an important military post and railway junction. He tells you about it in "Kim," and several of his army stories are laid there. Sirhind, thirty-five miles beyond, was formerly one of the most flourishing cities in the Mogul Empire, and for a radius of several miles around it the earth is covered with ruins. It was the scene of successive struggles between the Hindus and the Sikhs for several centuries, and even to this day every Sikh who passes through Sirhind picks up and carries away a brick, which he throws into the first river he comes to, in hope that in time the detested city will utterly disappear from the face of the earth. Sirhind is the headquarters of American Presbyterian missionary work in the Punjab, as that part of India is called, and the headquarters of the largest irrigation system in the world, which supplies water to more than 6,000,000 acres of land.

Just before reaching Lahore we passed through Amritsar, a city which is famous for many things, and is the capital of the Sikhs, a religious sect bound together by the ties of faith and race and military discipline. They represent a Hindu heresy led by a reformer named Nanak Shah, who was born at Lahore in 1469 and preached a reformation against idolatry, caste, demon worship and other doctrines of the Brahmins. His theories and sermons are embraced in a volume known as the "Granth," the Sikh Bible, which teaches the highest standard of morality, purity and courage, and appeals especially to the nobler northern races of India. His followers, who were known as Sikhs, were compelled to fight for their faith, and for that reason were organized upon a military basis. Their leaders were warlike men, and when the Mogul power began to decay they struggled with the Afghans for supremacy in northern India. They have ever since been renowned for their fighting qualities; have always been loyal to British authority; for fifty years have furnished bodyguards for the Viceroy of India, the governors of Bombay, Bengal and other provinces, and so much confidence is placed in their coolness, courage, honesty, judgment and tact that they are employed as policemen in all the British colonies of the East. You find them everywhere from Tien-Tsin to the Red Sea. They are men of unusual stature, with fine heads and faces, full beards, serious disposition and military airs. They are the only professional fighters in the world. You seldom find them in any other business, and their admirers declare that no Sikh was ever convicted of cowardice or disloyalty.

Amritsar is their headquarters, their religious center and their sacred city. Their temples are more like Protestant churches than those of other oriental faiths. They have no idols or altars, but meet once a week for prayer and praise. Their preacher reads passages from the "Granth" and prays to their God, who may be reached through the intercession of Nanak Shah, his prophet and their redeemer. They sing hymns similar to those used in Protestant worship and celebrate communion by partaking of wafers of unleavened bread. Their congregations do not object to the presence of strangers, but usually invite them to participate in the worship.

The great attraction of Amritsar is "The Golden Temple" of the Sikhs which stands in the middle of a lake known as "The Pool of Immortality." It is not a large building, being only fifty-three feet square, but is very beautiful and the entire exterior is covered with plates of gold. In the treasury is the original copy of the "Granth" and a large number of valuable jewels which have been collected for several centuries. Among them is one of the most valuable strings of pearls ever collected.

The Punjab is a province of northern India directly south of Cashmere, east of Afghanistan and west of Thibet. It is one of the most enterprising, progressive and prosperous provinces, and, being situated in the temperate zone, the character of the inhabitants partakes of the climate. There is a great difference, morally, physically and intellectually, between people who live in the tropics and those who live in the temperate zone. This rule applies to all the world, and nowhere more than in India. Punjab means "five rivers," and is formed of the

Hindu words "punj ab." The country is watered by the Sutlej, the Beas, the Rabi, the Chenab and the Jhelum rivers, five great streams, which flow into the Indus, and thence to the Arabian Sea. Speaking generally, the Punjab is a vast plain of alluvial formation, and the eastern half of it is very fertile. The western part requires irrigation, the rainfall being only a few inches a year, but there is always plenty of water for irrigation in the rivers. They are fed by the melting snows in the Himalayas.

The City of Lahore, the capital of the Punjab, is a stirring, modern town, a railway center, with extensive workshops employing several thousand men, and early in the nineteenth century, under the administration of Ranjit Singh, one of the greatest of the maharajas, it acquired great commercial importance, but the buildings he erected are cheap and tawdry beside the exquisite architectural monuments of Akbar, Shah Jehan and other Moguls. The population of Punjab province by the census of 1901 is 20,330,339, and the Mohammedans are in the majority, having 10,825,698 of the inhabitants. The Sikhs are a very important class and number 1,517,019. There are only 2,200,000 Sikhs in all India, and those who do not live in this province are serving as soldiers elsewhere. The population of Lahore is 202,000, an increase of 26,000 during the last ten years.

When you come into a Mohammedan country you always find tiles. Somehow or another they are associated with Islam. The Moors were the best tilemakers that ever lived, and gave that art to Spain. In Morocco today the best modern tiles are found. The tiles of Constantinople, Damascus, Smyrna, Jerusalem and other cities of Syria and the Ottoman Empire are superior to any you can find outside of Morocco; and throughout

Bokhara, Turkestan, Afghanistan and the other Moslem countries of Asia tilemaking has been practiced for ages. In their invasion of India the Afghans and Tartars brought it with them, and, although the art did not remain permanently so far beyond the border as Delhi, you find it there, in the rest of the Punjab and wherever Mohammedans are in the majority.

Lahore is an ancient city and has many interesting old buildings. The city itself lies upon the ruins of several predecessors which were destroyed by invaders during the last twelve or fifteen centuries. There are some fine old mosques and an ancient palace or two, but compared with other Indian capitals it lacks interest. The most beautiful and attractive of all its buildings is the tomb of Anar Kali (which means pomegranate blossom), a lady of the Emperor Akbar's harem, who became the sweetheart of Selim, his son. She was buried alive by order of the jealous father and husband for committing an unpardonable offense, and when Selim became the Emperor Jehanjir he erected this wonderful tomb to her memory. It is of white marble, and the carvings and mosaic work are very fine. In striking contrast with it is a vulgar, fantastic temple covered inside and out with convex mirrors. In the center of the rotunda, upon a raised platform is carved a lotus flower, and around it are eleven similar platforms of smaller size. The guides tell you that upon these platforms the body of Ranjit Singh, the greatest of the maharajas, was burned in 1839, and his eleven wives were burned alive upon the platforms around him.

The Emperor Jehanjir is buried in a magnificent mausoleum in the center of a walled garden on the bank of the river five miles from Lahore, but his tomb does not compare in beauty or splendor with those at Agra and Delhi. There is a garden called "The Abode of Love," about six miles out of town, where everybody drives in the afternoon. It was laid out by the Mogul Shah Jehan in 1637 for a recreation ground for himself and his sultanas when he visited this part of the empire, and includes about eighty acres of flowers and foliage plants.

Modern Lahore is much more interesting than the ancient city. The European quarter covers a large area. The principal street is three miles long, shaded with splendid trees, and on each side of it are the public offices, churches, schools, hotels, clubs and the residences of rich people, which are nearly all commodious bungalows surrounded by groves and gardens. The native city is a busy bazaar, densely packed with gayly dressed types of all the races of Asia, and is full of dust, filth and smells. But the people are interesting and the colors are gay. It is sometimes almost impossible to pass through the crowds that fill the native streets, and whoever enters there must expect to be jostled sometimes by ugly-looking persons.

The fort is the center of activity. The ancient citadel has been adapted to modern uses and conveniences at the expense of its former splendor. The palaces and mosques, the baths and halls of audience of the Moguls have been converted into barracks, arsenals and storerooms, and their decorations have been covered with whitewash. The only object of interest that has been left is an armory containing a fine collection of ancient Indian weapons. But, although the city has lost its medieval picturesqueness, it has gained in utility, and has become the most important educational and industrial center of northern India. The university and its numerous affili-

"KIM," THE CHELA, AND THE OLD LAMA WHO SOUGHT THE WAY AND THE TRUTH AND THE LIGHT

ated schools, the law college, the college of oriental languages and the manual training school are all well attended and important, and the school of art and industry enjoys the reputation of being the most useful and the best-managed institution of the kind in the East, probably in all Asia, which is due to the zeal and ability of J. L. Kipling, father of Rudyard Kipling, who has spent the greater part of his life in making it what it is. He was also the founder of the museum or "Wonder-House," as the natives call it. It has the finest collection of Indian arts and industries in existence except that in South Kensington Museum, which Mr. Kipling also collected and installed. It was under the carriage of one of the great old-fashioned cannon that stand in front of this museum that "Kim" first encountered the aged Llama, and Kipling's father is the wise man who kept the "Wonder-House" and gave the weary pilgrim the knowledge and encouragement that sustained him in his search for The Way.

Rudyard Kipling was born in Bombay, where his father was principal of an art school, and was brought to Lahore when he was a child, so that he spent most of his younger life there. He was educated at the Lahore schools and university; he served for several years as a reporter of the Lahore newspaper, and there he wrote most of his short stories. "The Plain Tales From the Hills" and the best of his "Barrack-Room Ballads" were inspired by his youthful association with the large military garrison at this point. Here Danny Deever was hanged for killing a comrade in a drunken passion, and here Private Mulvaney developed his profound philosophy.

Lahore is the principal Protestant missionary center of northern India. The American Presbyterians are the oldest in point of time and the strongest in point of numbers. They came in 1849, and some of the pioneers are still living. They have schools and colleges, a theological seminary and other institutions, with altogether five or six thousand students, and are turning out battalions of native preachers and teachers for missionary work in other parts of India. The American Methodists are also strong and there are several schools maintained by British societies. Fifty years ago there was not a native Christian in all these parts, and the missionaries had to coax children into their schools by offering inducements in the form of food and clothing. Now by the recent census there are 65,811 professing Christians in the Punjab province, and the schools and native churches are nearly all self-supporting.

Lahore is an important market for native merchandise, and the distributing point for imported European goods as well as the native products, while Amritsar, the neighboring city, is the manufacturing center. Here come Cashmeris, Nepalese, Beluchis, Afghans, Persians, Bokharans, Khivans, Khokandes, Turcomans, Yarkandis, Cashgaris, Thibetans, Tartars, Ghurkhars, and other strange types of the human race in Asia, each wearing his native dress and bringing upon caravans of camels and elephants the handiwork of his neighbors. The great merchants of London, Paris, Vienna, New York and Chicago have buyers there picking up curious articles of native handiwork as well as staples like shawls from Cashmere and rugs and carpets from Amritsar. The finest carpets in India are produced at Amristar, and between 4,000 and 5,000 people are engaged in their manufacture. These operators are not collected in factories as with us, but work in their own homes. The looms are usually set up in the doorways, through which the only light can enter the houses, and as you pass up and down the streets you see women and men, even children, at work at the looms, for every member of the family takes a turn. As in China, Japan and other oriental countries, arts and industries are hereditary. Children always follow the trades of their parents, and all work is done in the households. The weavers of Amritsar to-day are making carpets and shawls upon the same looms that were used by their great-grandfathers—yes, their progenitors ten and twenty generations back—and are weaving the same patterns, and it is to be regretted that modern chemical dyes made in Paris, the United States and Germany are taking the place of the primitive native methods which produced richer and permanent colors.

The trade is handled by middlemen, who furnish materials to the weavers and pay them so much for their labor upon each piece. The average earnings seem to us ridiculously small. An entire family does not receive more than $3 or $4 a month while engaged in producing shawls that are sold in London and Paris for hundreds of pounds and rugs that bring hundreds of dollars, but it costs them little to live; their wants are few, they have never known any better circumstances and are perfectly contented. The middleman, who is usually a Persian Jew, makes the big profit.

Winter is not a good time for visiting northern India. The weather is too cold and stormy. The roads are frequently obstructed by snow, and the hotels are not built to keep people up to American temperature. We could not go to Cashmere at all, although it is one of the most interesting provinces of the empire, because the roads were blocked and blizzards were lurking about. There is almost universal misapprehension about the weather in India. It is certainly a winter country; it is almost impossible for unacclimated people to live in most of the provinces between March and November, and no one can visit some of them without discomfort from the heat at any season of the year. At the same time Cashmere and the Punjab province are comfortable no later than October and no earlier than May, for, although the sun is bright and warm, the nights are intensely cold, and the extremes are trying to strangers who are not accustomed to them. You will often hear people who have traveled all over the world say that they never suffered so much from the cold as in India, and it is safe to believe them. The same degree of cold seems colder there than elsewhere, because the mercury falls so rapidly after the sun goes down. However, India is so vast, and the climate and the elevations are so varied, that you can spend the entire year there without discomfort if you migrate with the birds and follow the barometer. There are plenty of places to see and to stay in the summer as well as in the winter.

We arrived in Bombay on the 12th of December, which was at least a month too late. It would have been better for us to have come the middle of October and gone immediately north into the Punjab province and Cashmere, where we would have been comfortable. But during the entire winter we were not uncomfortably warm anywhere, and even in Bombay, which is considered one of the hottest places in the world, and during the rainy season is almost intolerable, we slept under blankets every night and carried sun umbrellas in the daytime. At Jeypore, Agra, Delhi and other places the nights were as cold as they ever are at Washington, double blankets were necessary on our beds, and ordinary overcoats when we went out of doors after dark. Sometimes it was colder inside the house than outside, and in several of the hotels we had to put on our overcoats and wrap our legs up in steamer rugs to keep from shivering. At the same time the rays of the sun from 11 to 3 or 4 in the afternoon were intensely hot, and often seriously affect persons not acclimated. If we ever go to India again we will arrange to arrive in October and do the northern provinces before the cold weather sets in.

It's a pity we could not go to Cashmere, because everybody told us it is such an interesting place and so different from other parts of India and the rest of the world. It is a land of romance, poetry and strange pictures. Lalla Rookh and other fascinating houris, with large brown eyes, pearly teeth, raven tresses and ruby lips, have lived there; it is the home of the Cashmere bouquet, and the Vale of Cashmere is an enchanted land. Average Americans know mighty little about these strange countries, and it takes time to realize that they actually exist; but we find our fellow citizens everywhere we go. They outnumber the tourists from all other nations combined.

I notice that the official reports of the Indian government give the name as "Kashmir," and, like every other place over here, it is spelled a dozen different ways, but I shall stick to the old-fashioned spelling. It you want to know something about it, Cashmere has an area of 81,000 square miles, a population of 2,905,578 by the census of 1901, and is governed by a maharaja with the advice of a British "resident," who is the medium of communication between the viceroy and the local officials. The maharaja is allowed to do about as he pleases as long as he behaves himself, and is said to be a fairly good man.

The people are peaceful and prosperous; politics is very quiet; taxes are low; there is no debt, and a surplus of more than $3,000,000 in the treasury, which is an unusual state of affairs for a native Indian province. The exports have increased from $1,990,000 in 1892 to $4,465,000 in 1902, and the imports from $2,190,000 in 1892 to $4,120,000 in 1902. The country has its own coinage and is on a gold basis. The manufacturing industries are rapidly developing, although the lack of demand for Cashmere shawls has been a severe blow to local weavers, who, however, have turned their attention to carpets and rugs instead. Wool is the great staple, and from time immemorial the weavers of Cashmere have turned out the finest woolen fabrics in the world. They have suffered much from the competition of machine-made goods during the last half-century or more, and have been growing careless because they cannot get the prices that used to be paid for the finest products. In ancient times the making of woolen garments was considered just as much of an art in Cashmere as painting or sculpture in France and Germany, porcelain work in China or cloisonne work in Japan, and no matter how long a weaver was engaged upon a garment, he was sure to find somebody with sufficient taste and money to buy it. But nowadays, like everybody else who is chasing the nimble shilling, the Cashmere weavers are more solicitous about their profits than about their patterns and the fine quality of their goods. The lapse of the shawl trade has caused the government to encourage the introduction of the silk industry. A British expert has been engaged as director of sericulture, seedlings of the mulberry tree are furnished to villagers and farmers free of cost, and all cocoons are purchased by the state at good prices. The government has silk factories employing between 6,000 and 7,000 persons under the instruction of French and Swiss weavers.

XX

FAMINES AND THEIR ANTIDOTES

Famine is chronic in India. It has occurred at intervals for centuries past, as long as records have been kept, as long as man remembers, and undoubtedly will recur for centuries to come, although the authorities who are responsible for the well-being of the empire are gradually organizing to counteract forces of nature which they cannot control, by increasing the food supply and providing means for its distribution. But there must be hunger and starvation in India so long as the population remains as dense as it is. The reason is not because the earth refuses to support so many people. There is yet a vast area of fertile land untilled, and the fields already cultivated would furnish food enough for a larger population when normal conditions prevail, although there's but a bare half acre per capita. There is always enough somewhere in India for everybody even in times of sorest distress, but it is not distributed equally, and those who are short have no money to buy and bring from those who have a surplus. The export of grain and other products from India continues regularly in the lean as well as the fat years, but the country is so large, the distances so great, the facilities for transportation so inadequate, that one province may be exporting food to Europe because it has to spare, while another province may be receiving ships loaded with charity from America because its crops have failed and its people are hungry.

The health and happiness of three hundred million human souls in India and also of their cattle, their oxen, their sheep, their donkeys, their camels and their elephants are dependent upon certain natural phenomena over which neither rajah nor maharaja, nor viceroy, nor emperor, nor council of state has control, and before which even the great Mogul on his bejeweled throne stood powerless. It is possible to ameliorate the consequences, but it is not possible to prevent them.

Whether the crops shall be fat or lean, whether the people and the cattle shall be fed or hungry, depends upon the "monsoons," as they are called, alternating currents of wind, which bring rain in its season. All animal and vegetable life is dependent upon them. In the early summer the broad plains are heated by the sun to a temperature higher than that of the water of the great seas which surround them. In parts of northern India, around Delhi and Agra, the temperature in May and June is higher than in any other part of the empire, and is exceeded in few other parts of the world. This phenomenon remains unexplained. The elevation is about 2,100 feet above the sea; the atmosphere is dry and the soil is sandy. But for some reason the rays of the sun are intensely hot and are fatal to those who are exposed to them without sufficient protection. But this extreme heat is the salvation of the country, and by its own action brings the relief without which all animal and vegetable life would perish. It draws from the ocean a current of wind laden with moisture which blows steadily for two months toward the northwest and causes what is called the rainy season. That wind is called the southwest monsoon. The quantity of rain that falls depends upon the configuration of the land. Any cause which cools the winds from the sea and leads to the condensation of the vapor they carry—any obstacle which blocks their course—causes precipitation. Through all the northern part of India there is a heavy rainfall during April, May and June, the earth is refreshed and quantities of water are drained into reservoirs called "tanks," from which the fields are irrigated later in the summer.

The quantity of rainfall diminishes as the winds blow over the foothills and the mountains, and the enormous heights of the Himalayas prevent them from passing their snow-clad peaks and ridges. Hence the tablelands of Thibet, which lie beyond, are the dryest and the most arid region in the world.

As the sun travels south after midsummer the temperature falls, the vast dry tract of the Asiatic continent becomes colder, the barometric pressure over the land increases, and the winds begin to blow from the northeast, which are called the northeast monsoon, and cause a second rainy season from October to December. These winds, or monsoons, enable the farmers of India to grow two crops, and they are entirely dependent upon their regular appearance.

Over 80 per cent of the population are engaged in farming. They live from hand to mouth. They have no reserve whatever. If the monsoon fails nothing will grow, and they have no money to import food for themselves and their cattle from more fortunate sections. Hence they are helpless. As a rule the monsoons are very reliable, but every few years they fail, and a famine results. The government has a meteorological department, with observers stationed at several points in Africa and Arabia and in the islands of the sea, to record and report the actions of nature. Thus it has been able of late years to anticipate the fat and the lean harvests. It is possible to predict almost precisely several months in advance whether there will be a failure of crops, and a permanent famine commission has been organized to prepare measures of relief before they are needed. In other words, Lord Curzon and his official associates are reducing famine relief to a system which promotes economy as well as efficiency.

It is an interesting fact that the monsoon currents which cross the Indian Ocean from South Africa continue on their course through Australia after visiting India, and recent famines in the latter country have coincided with the droughts which caused much injury to stock in the former. Thus it has been demonstrated that both countries depend upon the same conditions for their rainfall, except that human beings suffer in India while only sheep die of hunger in the Australian colonies.

The worst famine ever known in India occurred in 1770, when Governor General Warren Hastings reported that one-third of the inhabitants of Bengal perished from hunger—ten millions out of thirty millions. The streets of Calcutta and other towns were actually blocked up with the bodies of the dead, which were thrown out of doors and windows because there was no means or opportunity to bury them. The empire has been stricken almost as hard during the last ten years. The development of civilization seems to make a little difference, for the famine of 1900-1901 was perhaps second in severity to that of 1770. This, however, was largely due to the fact that the population had not had time to recover from the famine of 1896-97, which was almost as severe, although everything possible was done to relieve distress and prevent the spread of plagues and pestilence that are the natural and unavoidable consequences of insufficient nourishment.

No precautions that sanitary science can suggest have been omitted, yet the weekly reports now show an average of twenty thousand deaths from the bubonic plague alone. The officials explain that that isn't so high a rate as inexperienced people infer, considering that the population is nearly three hundred millions, and they declare it miraculous that it is not larger, because the Hindu portion of the population is packed so densely into insanitary dwellings, because only a small portion of the natives have sufficient nourishment to meet the demands of nature and are constantly exposed to influences that produce and spread disease. The death rate is always very high in India for these reasons. But it seems very small when compared with the awful mortality caused by the frequent famines. The mind almost refuses to accept the figures that are presented; it does not seem possible in the present age, with all our methods for alleviating suffering, that millions of people can actually die of hunger in a land of railroads and steamships and other facilities for the transportation of food. It seems beyond comprehension, yet the official returns justify the acceptance of the maximum figures reported.

The loss of human life from starvation in British India alone during the famine of 1900-1901 is estimated at 1,236,855, and this is declared to be the minimum. In : country of the area of India, inhabited by a superstitious, secretive and ignorant population, it is impossible to compel the natives to report accidents and deaths, particularly among the Brahmins, who burn instead of bury their dead.

AN EKKA OR ROAD CART

Those who know best assert that at least 15 per cent of the deaths are not reported in times of famines and epidemics. And the enormous estimate I have given does not include any of the native states, which have one-third of the area and one-fourth of the population of the empire. In some of them sanitary regulations are observed, and statistics are accurately reported. In others no attempt is made to keep a registry of deaths, and there are no means of ascertaining the mortality, particularly in times of excitement. In these little principalities the peasants have, comparatively speaking, no medical attendance; they are dependent upon ignorant fakirs and sorcerers, and they die off like flies, without even leaving a record of their disappearance. Therefore the only way of ascertaining the mortality of those sections is to make deductions from the returns of the census, which is taken with more or less accuracy every ten years.

The census of 1901 tells a terrible tale of human suffering and death during the previous decade, which was marked by two famines and several epidemics of cholera, smallpox and other contagious diseases. Taking the whole of India together, the returns show that during the ten years from 1892 to 1901, inclusive, there was an increase of less than 6,000,000 instead of the normal increase of 19,000,000, which was to be expected, judging by the records of the previous decades of the country. More than 10,000,000 people disappeared in the native states alone without leaving a trace behind them.

The official report of the home secretary shows that Baroda State lost 460,000, or 19.23 per cent of its population.

The Rajputana states lost 2,175,000, or 18.1 per cent of their population.

The central states lost 1,817,000, or 17.5 per cent.
Bombay Province lost 1,168,000, or 14.5 per cent.
The central provinces lost 939,000, or 8.71 per cent.

These are the provinces that suffered most from the famine, and therefore show the largest decrease in population.

The famine of 1900-01 affected an area of more than four hundred thousand square miles and a population exceeding sixty millions, of whom twenty-five millions belong in the provinces of British India and thirty-five millions to the native states.

"Within this area," Lord Curzon says, "the famine conditions for the greater part of a year were intense. Outside it they extended with a gradually dwindling radius over wide districts which suffered much from loss of crops and cattle, if not from actual scarcity. In a greater or less degree in 1900-01 nearly one-fourth of the entire population of the Indian continent came within the range of relief operations.

"It is difficult to express in figures with any close degree of accuracy the loss occasioned by so widespread and severe a visitation. But it may be roughly put in this way: The annual agricultural product of India averages in value between two and three hundred thousand pounds sterling. On a very cautious estimate the production in 1899-1900 must have been at least one-quarter if not one-third below the average. At normal prices this loss was at least fifty million pounds sterling, or, in round numbers, two hundred and fifty million dollars in American money. But, in reality, the loss fell on a portion only of the continent, and ranged from total failure of crops in certain sections to a loss of 20 and 30 per cent of the normal crops in districts which are not reckoned as falling within the famine tract. If to this be added the value of several millions of cattle and other live stock, some conception may be formed of the destruction of property which that great drought occasioned. There have been many great droughts in India, but there have been no others of which such figures could have been predicated as these.

"But the most notable feature of the famine of 1900-01 was the liberality of the public and the government. It has no parallel in the history of the world. For weeks more than six million persons were dependent upon the charity of the government. In 1897 the high water mark of relief was reached in the second fortnight of May, when there were nearly four million persons receiving relief in British India. Taking the affected population as forty millions, the ratio of relief was 10 per cent. In one district of Madras and in two districts of the northwestern provinces the ratio for some months was about 30 per cent, but these were exceptional cases. In the most distressed districts of the central provinces 16 per cent was regarded in 1896-7 as a very high standard of relief. Now take the figures of 1900-01. For some weeks upward of four and a half million persons were receiving food from the government in British India, and, reckoned on a population of twenty-five millions, the ratio was 18 per cent, as compared with 10 per cent of the population in 1897. In many districts it exceeded 20 per cent. In several it exceeded 30 per cent. In two districts it exceeded 40 per cent, and in the district of Merwara, where famine had been present for two years, 75 per cent of the population were dependent upon the government for food. Nothing I could say can intensify the simple eloquence of these figures.

"The first thing to be done was to relieve the immediate distress, to feed the hungry, to rescue those who were dying of starvation. The next step was to furnish employment at living wages for those who were penniless until we could help them to get upon their feet again, and finally to devise means and methods to meet such emergencies in the future, because famines are the fate of India and must continue to recur under existing conditions.

"I should like to tell you of the courage, endurance and the devotion of the men who distributed the relief, many of whom died at their posts of duty as bravely and as uncomplainingly as they might have died upon the field of battle. The world will never know the extent and the number of sacrifices made by British and native officials. The government alone expended $32,000,000 for food, while the amount disbursed by the native states, by religious and private charities, was very large. The contributions from abroad were about $3,000,000, and the government loaned the farmers more than $20,000,000 to buy seed and cattle and put in new crops.

"So far as the official figures are concerned, the total cost of the famine of 1900 was as follows:

BRITISH INDIA	
Direct relief	$31,950,000
Loss of revenue	16,200,000
Loans to farmers and native states	21,300,000
NATIVE STATES	
Relief expenditure and loss of revenue	22,500,000
Total	$91,950,000

"Some part of these loans and advances will eventually be repaid. But it is not a new thing for the government of India to relieve its people in times of distress. The frequent famines have been an enormous drain upon the resources of the empire."

The following table shows the expenditures for famine relief by the imperial government of India during the last twenty-one years:

Five years, 1881-86	$ 25,573,885
Five years, 1886-91	11,449,190
Five years, 1891-96	21,631,900
1896-1897	8,550,705
1897-1898	19,053,575
1898-1899	5,000,000
1899-1900	10,642,235
1900-1901	20,829,335
1901-1902	5,000,000
Total (twenty-one years)	$127,730,825

Among the principal items chargeable to famine relief, direct and indirect, are the wages paid dependent persons employed during famines in the construction of railways and irrigation works, which, during the last twenty-one years, have been as follows:

	Direct famine relief.	Construction of railways.	Construction of irrigation works.
Five years, '81-'86	$ 379,760	$ 9,113,165	$3,739,790
1886-1891	277,030	666,665	1,384,570
1891-1896	411,065	12,056,505	921,675
1896-1897	6,931,750	....	156,100
1897-1898	17,752,025	....	125,055

1898-1899........	133,515	2,301,175	38,900
1899-1900........	10,375,590	....	119,650
1900-1901........	20,626,150	....	155,570
1901-1902........	2,645,905	....	353,465
Total (21 years)	$59,531,790	$24,137,610	$6,994,775

The chief remedies which the government has been endeavoring to apply are:

1. To extend the cultivated area by building irrigation works and scattering the people over territory that is not now occupied.

2. To construct railways and other transportation facilities for the distribution of food. This work has been pushed with great energy, and during the last ten years the railway mileage has been increased nearly 50 per cent to a total of more than 26,000 miles. About 2,000 miles are now under construction and approaching completion, and fresh projects will be taken up and pushed so that food may be distributed throughout the empire as rapidly as possible in time of emergency. Railway construction has also been one of the chief methods of relief. During the recent famine, and that of 1897, millions of coolies, who could find no other employment, were engaged at living wages upon various public works. This was considered better than giving them direct relief, which was avoided as far as possible so that they should not acquire the habit of depending upon charity. And as a part of the permanent famine relief system for future emergencies, the board of public works has laid out a scheme of roads and the department of agriculture a system of irrigation upon which the unemployed labor can be mobilized at short notice, and funds have been

set apart for the payment of their wages. This is one of the most comprehensive schemes of charity ever conceived, and must commend to every mind the wisdom, foresight and benevolence of the Indian government, which, with the experience with a dozen famines, has found that its greatest diffculty has been to relieve the distressed and feed the hungry without making permanent paupers of them. Every feature of famine relief nowadays involves the employment of the needy and rejects the free distribution of food.

3. The government is doing everything possible to encourage the diversification of labor, to draw people from the farms and employ them in other industries. This requires a great deal of time, because it depends upon private enterprise, but during the last ten years there has been a notable increase in the number of mechanical industries and the number of people employed by them, which it is believed will continue because of the profits that have been realized by investors.

4. The government is also making special efforts to develop the dormant resources of the empire. There has been a notable increase in mining, lumbering, fishing, and other outside industries which have not received the attention they deserved by the people of India; and, finally,

5. The influence of the government has also been exerted so far as could be to the encouragement of habits of thrift among the people by the establishment of postal savings banks and other inducements for wage-earners to save their money. Ninety per cent of the population of India lives from hand to mouth and depends for sustenance upon the crops raised upon little patches of ground which in America would be too insignificant for

consideration. There is very seldom a surplus. The ordinary Hindu never gets ahead, and, therefore, when his little crop fails he is helpless.

The munificence of Mr. Henry Phipps of New York has enabled the government of India to provide one of the preventives of famine by educating the people in agricultural science. A college, an experimental farm and research laboratory have been established on the government estate of Pusa, in southern Bengal, a tract of 1,280 acres, which has been used since 1874 as a breeding ranch, a tobacco experimental farm and a model dairy. No country has needed such an institution more than India, where 80 per cent of the population are engaged in agricultural pursuits, and most of them with primitive implements and methods. But the conservatism and the illiteracy, the prejudices and the ignorance of the natives make it exceedingly difficult to introduce innovations, and it is the conviction of those best qualified to speak that the only way of improving the condition of the farmer classes is to begin at the top and work down by the force of example. During a recent visit to India this became apparent to Mr. Phipps, who is eminently a practical man, and has been in the habit of dealing with industrial questions all of his life. He was brought up in the Carnegie iron mills, became a superintendent, a manager and a partner, and, when the company went into the great trust, retired from active participation in its management with an immense fortune. He has built a beautiful house in New York, has leased an estate in Scotland, where his ancestors came from, and has been spending a vacation, earned by forty years of hard labor, in traveling about the world. His visit to India brought him into a friendly acquaintance with Lord Curzon, in

A TEAM OF "CRITTERS"

whom he found a congenial spirit, and doubtless the viceroy received from the practical common sense of Mr. Phipps many suggestions that will be valuable to him in the administration of the government, and in the solution of the frequent problems that perplex him. Mr. Phipps, on the other hand, had his sympathy and interest excited in the industrial conditions of India, and particularly in the famine phenomena. He therefore placed at the disposal of Lord Curzon the sum of $100,000, to which he has since added $50,000, to be devoted to whatever object of public utility in the direction of scientific research the viceroy might consider most useful and expedient. In accepting this generous offer it appeared to His Excellency that no more practical or useful object could be found to which to devote the gift, nor one more entirely in harmony with the wishes of the donor, than the establishment of a laboratory for agricultural research, and Mr. Phipps has expressed his warm approval of the decision.

It is proposed to place the college upon a higher grade than has ever been reached by any agricultural school in India, not only to provide for a reform of the agricultural methods of the country, but also to serve as a model for and to raise the standard of the provincial schools, because at none of them are there arrangements for a complete or competent agricultural education. It is proposed to have a course of five years for the training of teachers for other institutions and the specialists needed in the various branches of science connected with the agricultural department, who are now imported from Europe. The necessity for such an education, Lord Curzon says, is constantly becoming more and more imperative. The higher officials of the government have long realized that there should be some institution in India where they can train the men they require, if their scheme of agricultural reformation is ever to be placed upon a practical basis and made an actual success. For those who wish to qualify for professorships or for research work, or for official positions requiring special scientific attainments, it is believed that a five years' course is none too long. But for young men who desire only to train themselves for the management of their own estates or the estates of others, a three years' course will be provided, with practical work upon the farm and in the stable.

The government has solved successfully several of the irrigation problems now under investigation by the Agricultural Department and the Geological Survey of the United States. The most successful public works of that nature are in the northern part of the empire. The facilities for irrigation in India are quite as varied as in the United States, the topography being similar and equally diverse. In the north the water supply comes from the melting snows of the Himalayas; in the east and west from the great river systems of the Ganges and the Indus, while in the central and southern portions the farmers are dependent upon tanks or reservoirs into which the rainfall is drained and kept in store until needed. In several sections the rainfall is so abundant as to afford a supply of water for the tanks which surpasses in constancy and volume that from any of the rivers. In Bombay and Madras provinces almost all of the irrigation systems are dependent upon this method. In the river provinces are many canals which act as distributaries during the spring overflow, carry the water a long distance and distribute it over a large area during the periods of inundation. In several places the usefulness of these canals has been increased by the construction of reservoirs which receive and hold the floods upon the plan proposed for some of our arid states.

In India the water supply is almost entirely controlled by the government. There are some private enterprises, but most of them are for the purpose of reaching land owned by the projectors. A few companies sell water to the adjacent farmers on the same plan as that prevailing in California, Colorado and other of our states. But the government of India has demonstrated the wisdom of national ownership and control, and derives a large and regular revenue therefrom. In the classification adopted by the department of public works the undertakings are designated as "major" and "minor" classes. The "major" class includes all extensive works which have been built by government money, and are maintained under government supervision. Some of them, classed as "famine protective works," were constructed with relief funds during seasons of famine in order to furnish work and wages to the unemployed, and at the same time provide a certain supply of water for sections of the country exposed to drought. The "minor" works are of less extent, and have been constructed from time to time to assist private enterprise.

The financial history of the public irrigation works of India will be particularly interesting to the people of the United States because our government is just entering upon a similar policy. The following statement is brought down to December 31, 1902:

Cost of construction	$125,005,705
Receipts from water rates (1902)	7,797,890
Receipts from land taxes (1902)	4,066,985

Total revenue from all sources (1902)......	11,864,875
Working expenses (1902)................	3,509,600
Net revenue (1902)....................	8,355,275
Interest on capital invested..............	4,720,615
Net revenue, deducting interest...........	3,634,660
Profit on capital invested, per cent........	6.97
Net profit to the government, per cent......	3.04

In addition to this revenue from the "major" irrigation works belonging to the government, the net receipts from "minor" works during the year 1902 amounted to $864,360 in American money.

In other words, the government of India has invested about $125,000,000 in reservoirs, canals, dams and ditches for the purpose of securing regular crops for the farmers of that empire who are exposed to drought, and not only has accomplished that purpose, but, after deducting 3½ per cent as interest upon the amount named, enjoys a net profit of more than $3,500,000 after the payment of running expenses and repairs. These profits are regularly expended in the extension of irrigation works.

In the Sinde province, which is the extreme western section of India, adjoining the colony of Beluchistan on the Arabian Sea, there are about 12,500,000 acres of land fit for cultivation. Of this a little more than 9,000,000 acres are under cultivation, irrigated with water from the Indus River, and the government system reaches 3,077,466 acres. Up to December 31, 1902, it had expended $8,830,000 in construction and repairs, and during that year received a net revenue of 8.5 per cent upon that amount over and above interest and running expenses.

In Madras 6,884,554 acres have been irrigated by the

government works at a cost of $24,975,000. In 1902 they paid an average net revenue of 9.5 per cent upon the investment, and the value of the crops grown upon the irrigated land was $36,663,000.

In the united provinces of Agra and Oudh in northern India the supply of water from the Himalayas is distributed through 12,919 miles of canals belonging to the government, constructed at a cost of $28,625,000, which irrigates 2,741,460 acres. In 1902 the value of the crops harvested upon this land was $28,336,005, and the government received a net return of 6.15 per cent upon the investment. The revenue varies in different parts of the provinces. One system known as the Eastern Jumna Canal, near Lucknow, paid 23 per cent upon its cost in water rents during that year. In other parts of the province, where the construction was much more expensive, the receipts fell as low as 2.12 per cent.

In the Punjab province, the extreme northwestern corner of India, adjoining Afghanistan on the west and Cashmere on the east, where the water supply comes from the melting snows of the Himalayas, the government receives a net profit of 10.83 per cent, and the value of the crop in the single year of 1902 was one and one-fourth times the total amount invested in the works to date.

This does not include a vast undertaking known as the Chenab Canal, which has recently been completed, and now supplies more than 2,000,000 acres with water. Its possibilities include 5,527,000 acres. As a combination of business and benevolence and as an exhibition of administrative energy and wisdom, it is remarkable, and is of especial interest to the people of the United

States because the conditions are similar to those existing in our own arid states and territories.

If you will take a map of India and run your eye up to the northwestern corner you will see a large bald spot just south of the frontier through which runs the river Chenab (or Chenaub)—the name of the stream is spelt a dozen different ways, like every other geographical name in India. This river, which is a roaring torrent during the rainy season and as dry as a bone for six months in the year, resembles several of our western rivers, particularly the North Platte, and runs through an immense tract of arid desert similar to those found in our mountain states. This desert is known as the Rechna Doab, and until recently was waste government land, a barren, lifeless tract upon which nothing but snakes and lizards could exist, although the soil is heavily charged with chemicals of the most nutritious character for plants, and when watered yields enormous crops of wheat and other cereals. Fifteen years ago it was absolutely uninhabited. To-day it is the home of about 800,000 happy and prosperous people, working more than 200,000 farms, in tracts of from five to fifty acres. The average population of the territory disclosed at the census of 1901 was 212 per square mile, and it is expected that the extension of the water supply and natural development will largely increase this average.

The colony has been in operation for a little more than eleven years. The colonists were drawn chiefly from the more densely populated districts of the Punjab province, and were attracted by a series of remarkable harvests, which were sold at exorbitant prices during the famine years. The land was given away by the government to actual settlers upon a plan similar to that of our homestead act, the settlers being given a guarantee of a certain amount of water per acre to a fixed price. The demand caused by the popularity of the colony has already exhausted the entire area watered by the canals, but an extension and enlargement of the system will bring more land gradually under cultivation, the estimates of the engineers contemplating an addition of 2,000,000 acres within the next few years.

The value of the crop produced in 1902 upon 1,830,525 acres of irrigated land in this colony was $16,845,000, irrigated by canals that cost $8,628,380, and the government enjoyed a net profit of 14.01 per cent that year upon its benevolent enterprise. Aside from the money value of the scheme, there is another very important consideration. More than half of the canals and ditches were constructed by "famine labor"—that is, by men and women (for women do manual labor in India the same as men) who were unable to obtain other employment and would have died of starvation but for the intervention of the government. Instead of being supplied with food at relief stations, these starving people were shipped to the Rechan Doab Desert and put to work at minimum wages.

You will agree with me that the government has a right to feel proud of its new colony, and its success has stimulated interest in similar enterprises in other parts of the empire. It has not only furnished employment to thousands of starving people, but by bringing under cultivation a large tract of barren land with a positive certainty of regular harvests it has practically insured that section of the country against future famines.

The following figures will show the rapid development of the colony from the first season of 1892-93 to the end of the season 1901, which is the latest date for which statistics can be obtained:

CAPITAL OUTLAY TO END OF YEAR

1892-93	£ 721,233	1897-98	£1,512,916
1893-94	878,034	1898-99	1,616,676
1894-95	995,932	1899-1900	1,677,982
1895-96	1,174,781	1900-01	1,725,676
1896-97	1,362,075		

ACRES IRRIGATED DURING THE YEAR

1892-93	157,197	1897-98	810,000
1893-94	270,405	1898-99	957,705
1894-95	269,357	1899-1900	1,353,223
1895-96	369,935	1900-01	1,830,525
1896-97	520,279		

NET REVENUE DURING THE YEAR

1892-93	£ 4,084	1897-98	£111,041
1893-94	3,552	1898-99	131,566
1894-95	9,511	1899-1900	155,302
1895-96	51,632	1900-01	421,812
1896-97	92,629		

RETURN ON CAPITAL OUTLAY, PER CENT

1892-93	0.57	1897-98	7.34
1893-94	0.40	1898-99	8.14
1894-95	0.96	1899-1900	9.26
1895-96	4.40	1900-01	14.01
1896-97	6.75		

The system of allotment of land may be interesting. As the area under irrigation was entirely open and unoccupied, few difficulties were met with, and the engineers were perfectly free in plotting the land. The entire area was divided into squares of 1,000 feet boundary on each side, and these squares were each divided into twenty-five fields which measure about one acre and are the unit of calculation in sales and in measuring water. Sixty squares, or 1,500 fields, compose a village, and between the villages, surrounding them on all four sides, are canals. Between the squares are ditches, and between the fields are smaller ditches, so that the water can be measured and the allowance made without difficulty. The government sells no smaller piece than a field of twenty-five acres, but purchasers can buy in partnership and afterwards subdivide it.

Each village is under the charge of a superintendent, or resident engineer, who is responsible to a superior engineer, who has charge of a number of villages. Each field is numbered upon a map, and a record is kept of the area cultivated, the character of the crops sown, the dates of irrigation and the amount of water allowed. Before harvest a new measurement is taken and a bill is given to the cultivator showing the amount of his assessment, which is collected when his crop is harvested. As there has never been a crop failure, this is a simple process, and in addition to the water rate a land tax of 42 cents an acre is collected at the same time and paid into the treasury to the credit of the revenue department, while the water rates are credited to the canal department.

The chief engineer fixes the volume of water to be furnished to each village and the period for which it is to remain flowing. The local superintendent regulates the amount allowed each cultivator, according to the crops he has planted. There are six rates, regulated by the crops, for some need more water than others, as follows:

Class. Crops.	Rate per acre.
1—Sugar cane	$2.50
2—Rice	2.10
3—Orchards, gardens, tobacco, indigo, vegetables and melons	1.66
4—Cotton, oil seeds, Indian corn and all cold weather crops, except grain and lentils	1.66
5—All crops other than specified above	.83
6—Single water to plow, not followed by a crop	.40

As I have shown you from the figures above, this enterprise has proved highly profitable to the government, and its management is entitled to the highest compliments.

The main canal was originally forty miles long, averaging 109 feet wide, with an average slope of one foot to the mile, and capable of carrying seven feet four inches of water, or 10,000 cubic feet, per second. Twenty-eight miles have since been enlarged to a width of 250 feet and the remaining twelve miles to a width of 150 feet. The canal has been deepened to nine feet six inches, and the intention is to deepen it one foot more. The banks of the main canal are twenty-five feet wide at the top and are built entirely of earth. A railway ninety-six miles long of three-foot gauge has been constructed down the main canal, which is a great convenience in shipping crops and pays a profit to the government. It was constructed by the canal engineers while the ditch was being dug. There are 390 miles of branch canals from thirty to fifty feet wide and from six to eight feet deep, and 2,095 miles of distributaries, or ditches running between villages and squares. The banks of the branches and ditches are all wide enough for highways, and thus enable the people to go from village to village and get their crops to market. Several towns of considerable size have already grown up; the largest, called Lyallpur, having about 10,000 inhabitants. It is the headquarters of the canal and also of the civil authorities; and scattered through the irrigated country are about 100 permanent houses used as residences and offices by the superintendents and engineers.

XXI

THE FRONTIER QUESTION

The most sensitive nerve in the British Empire terminates in Afghanistan, and the ghost of the czar is always dancing about the Khyber Pass, through which caravans laden with merchandise find their way across the mountains between India and the countries of Central Asia. Every time there is a stir in a clump of bushes, every time a board creaks in the floor, every time a footstep is heard under the window, the goose flesh rises on John Bull's back, and he imagines that the Great White Bear is smelling around the back door of his empire in India. Peshawur is the jumping-off place of the Northwest, the limit of British authority, the terminus of the railway system of India and the great gateway between that empire and Central Asia, through which everything must pass. It is to the interior of Asia what the Straits of Gibraltar are to the Mediterranean Sea, and the Dardanelles to the Black and Caspian seas. While there are 300 paths over the mountains in other directions, and it might be possible to cross them with an army, it has never been attempted and would involve dangers, expense and delays which no nation would undertake. The Khyber Pass has been the great and only route for ages whether for war or commerce. The masters of Central Asia, whether Persians, Greeks, Macedonians or Assyrians, have held it. Alexander the Great crossed it with his army. Timour the Tartar, whom we know better as Tamerlane, came through upon his all-conquering expedition when he subdued India to found the Mogul Empire, and if the Russians ever enter India by land they will come this way.

The pass is reached by crossing a stony plain ten miles from Peshawur, and winds through gorges and crevices in the mountains for thirty-three miles at an altitude averaging 7,000 feet above the sea. At one point the mountains close in to about 500 feet apart and the rocks rise in sheer precipices on either side; in other places the gorge widens to a mile or more and will average perhaps three-quarters of a mile the entire distance. It is a remarkable gateway, a natural barrier between hereditary enemies and easily defended from either side. Kabul, the capital of Afghanistan, is 180 miles from the western entrance to the defile.

The British fortifications are at Jamrud, nine miles from Peshawur, and the terminus of the railways, where a strong garrison is always kept. The pass itself is controlled by a powerful semi-independent native tribe called the Afridis, estimated at 20,000 strong, who receive subsidies from the British government and from the Ameer of Afghanistan to keep them good-natured on the pretext that they are to do police work and keep order in the pass. It is blackmail and bribery, but accomplishes its purpose, and the pass itself, with a strip of highlands and foothills on the Afghanistan side, is thus occupied by a neutral party, which prevents friction between the nations on either side of the border. The Afridis are fearless fighters, half-civilized, half-savage, and almost entirely supported by the subsidies they receive. Nearly all of the able-bodied men are under arms. A few, who are too old or too young to fight, remain at home and look after the cattle and the scraggy gardens upon the gravelly hillsides. The women are as hardy and as enduring as the men and are taught to handle the rifle. The British authorities are confident of the loyalty of the Afridis and believe that the present arrangement would be absolutely safe in time of war as it is in time of peace—that they would permit no armed body, whether Russians or Afghans, to cross the pass without the consent of both sides, as is provided by treaty stipulations.

The arrangement is as effective as it is novel and the Afridis carry out every detail conscientiously. The pass is open only two days in the week, on Tuesdays and Fridays. No one is permitted to cross or even enter it from either side except on those days. And even then travelers, tourists and others actuated by curiosity are not allowed to go through without permits. The caravans going both ways are required to camp under well-formed regulations at either entrance until daylight of Tuesday or Friday, when they are escorted through by armed bodies of Afridis horsemen. There is not the slightest danger of any sort to any one, but it is just as well to go through the ceremony, for it keeps the Afridis out of mischief and reminds them continually of their great responsibilities. These caravans are interesting. They are composed of long strings of loaded camels, ox-carts, mules and donkeys, vehicles of all descriptions and thousands of people traveling on foot, who come sometimes from as far west as the Ural Mountains and the banks of the Volga River. They come from Persia, from all parts of Siberia and from the semi-barbarous tribes who inhabit that mysterious region in central Asia, known as the "Roof of the World."

The camel drivers and the traders are fierce-looking men and extremely dirty. They have traveled a long way and over roads that are very dusty, and water is scarce the entire distance. They look as if they had never washed their faces or cut their hair, and their shaggy, greasy, black locks hang down upon their shoulders beneath enormous turbans. Each wears the costume of his own country, but they are so ragged, grimy and filthy that the romance of it is lost. The Afghans are in the majority. They are stalwart, big-bearded men, with large features, long noses and cunning eyes, and claim that their ancestors were one of the lost tribes of Israel. Their traditions, customs, physiognomy and dialects support this theory. Although they are Mohammedans, they practice several ancient Jewish rites. The American missionaries who have schools and churches among them are continually running up against customs and traditions which remind them forcibly of the Mosaic teachings. They have considerable literature, poetry, history, biography, philosophy and ecclesiastical works, and some of their priests have large libraries of native books, which, the missionaries say, are full of suggestions of the Old Testament.

One of the most successful missionaries in that part of the world was an apostate Polish Jew named Rev. Isidore Lowenthal, a remarkable linguist and a man of profound learning. He translated the Bible and several other religious books into Pashto, the language of the Afghans, and was convinced that he shared with them the same ancestry. A story that is invariably related to travelers up in that country refers to his untimely taking off, for he was accidentally shot by one of his household attendants, and his epitaph, after giving the usual statistical information, reads:

> He was shot accidentally by his chookidar.
> Well done, thou good and faithful servant.
> I am not ashamed of the gospel of Jesus Christ.

The Afghanistan question, is, so to speak, in statu quo. The ameer is friendly to the British, but asserts his independence with a great deal of firmness and vigor, and is an ever-present source of anxiety. He receives a subsidy of $600,000 from the British government, which is practically a bribe to induce him not to make friends with Russia, and yet there are continual reports concerning Russian intrigues in that direction. He declines to receive an English envoy and will not permit any Englishmen to reside at his court. The Indian government is represented at Kabul by a highly educated and able native Indian, who is called a diplomatic agent, and has diplomatic powers. He reports to and receives instructions from Lord Curzon directly, and is the only medium of communication between the ameer and the British government. The present ameer has been on the throne only since the death of his father, the ameer Abdur Rahman, in October, 1901, and for several months there was considerable anxiety as to what policy the young man, Habi Bullah Khan, would adopt. During the last three years of the old man's life he yielded his power very largely to his son, and selected him twenty wives from the twenty most influential families in the kingdom in order to strengthen his throne. Although Habi Bullah is not so able or determined as his father, he has held his position without an insurrection or a protest, and is no longer in danger of being overthrown by one of the bloody conspiracies which have interlarded Afghanistan history for the last two centuries.

The British were fortunate in having a viceroy at that critical period who was personally acquainted with the young ameer and a friend of his father. When Lord Curzon was a correspondent of the London Times, before he entered parliament, he visited Cabul and formed pleasant relations with the late ameer, who speaks of him in most complimentary terms in his recently published memoirs. The old man happened to die during the darkest period of the South African war, and Russia took occasion at that critical moment to demand the right to enter into independent diplomatic negotiations with Afghanistan for the survey of a railroad across that country. Only a few years before, Great Britain fought a war with Afghanistan and overthrew Shere Ali, the shah, because he received a Russian ambassador on a similar errand, after having refused to allow a British envoy to reside at his court or even enter his country. And there is no telling what might have happened had not Lord Curzon taken advantage of his personal relations and former friendship. Russia selected a significant date to make her demands. It was only a fortnight after the British repulse at Spion Kop, and Ladysmith was in a hopeless state of siege. Such situations have a powerful influence upon semi-civilized soldiers, who are invariably inclined to be friendly to those who are successful at arms. However, Lord Curzon had influence enough to hold the ameer to the British side, and the latter has ever since shown a friendly disposition to the British and has given the Russians no public encouragement.

The official report of the viceroy to the secretary of state for India in London, covering the ten years ending

Dec. 31, 1902, contains the following interesting paragraph concerning the greatest source of anxiety:

"Relations with Afghanistan have been peaceful throughout the decade. Although there is reason to believe that Afghan influence among the turbulent tribes on the northwestern frontier was at times the cause of restlessness and disorder, the Durand agreement of 1893, followed by the demarcation of the southern and nearly all the eastern Afghan boundary, set a definite limit to the legitimate interference of Afghanistan with the tribes included in the British sphere of influence. Under that agreement the annual subsidy paid by the British government to the ameer was increased from £80,000 to £120,-000. A further demarcation, which affected alike Afghanistan and the British sphere, was that which resulted from the Pamir agreement concluded with Russia in 1895. Russia agreed to accept the River Oxus as her southern boundary as far east as the Victoria Lake. Thence to the Chinese frontier a line was fixed by a demarcation commission. This arrangement involved an interchange of territories lying on the north and south bank of the Oxus respectively between Afghanistan and Bokhara, which was carried out in 1896. The Ameer of Afghanistan also undertook to conduct the administration of Wakkhan, lying between the new boundary and the Hindu Kush, in return for an increase of his subsidy.

"Under the strong rule of the late ameer the country for the most part enjoyed internal peace, but this was broken by the revolt of the Hazaras in 1892, which was severely suppressed. In 1895-96 Kafiristan, a region which the delimitation included in the Afghan sphere of influence, was subjugated. Political relations of the government of India with the late and with the present ameer have been friendly, and were undisturbed by the murder of the British agent at Kabul by one of his servants in 1895, an incident which had no political significance. In the year 1894-95 His Highness sent his second son, Shahzada Nasrulla Khan, to visit England as the guest of Her Majesty's government. The Ameer Abdur Rahman, G. C. B., died in October, 1901, and was peacefully succeeded by his eldest son, Habi Bullah Khan, G. C. M. G."

There is no doubt as to what Lord Curzon knows and believes concerning the aggressive policy of Russia in Asia, because, shortly before he was appointed viceroy of India, he wrote an article on that subject for a London magazine, which is still what editors call "live matter."

"The supreme interest," he said, "lies in the physical fact that it (the northwestern frontier) is the only side upon which India has been or ever can be invaded by land, and in the political fact that it confronts a series of territories inhabited by wild and turbulent, by independent or semi-independent tribes, behind whom looms the grim figure of Russia, daily advancing into clearer outline from the opposite or northwest quarter. It is to protect the Indian Empire, its peoples, its trades, its laboriously established government and its accumulated wealth from the insecurity and possible danger arising from a further Russian advance across the intervening space that the frontier which I am about to describe has been traced and fortified. Politicians of all parties have agreed that, while the territorial aggrandizement of Russia is permissible over regions where she replaces barbarism even by a crude civilization, there can be no excuse for allowing her to take up a position in territories acknowledging our sway, where she can directly menace

British interests in India, or indirectly impose an excessive strain upon the resources and the armed strength of our eastern dominions. The guardianship of the frontier is, therefore, an act of defense, not of defiance, and is an elementary and essential obligation of imperial statesmanship.

"Originally it was supposed that there were but three or four passes or cracks by which this mountain barrier was perforated, and that if British soldiers only stood sentinel at their exits an invader would have no other alternative but to come down and be annihilated. Modern surveys, however, have shown that the number of available passes is nearer 300 than three, a discovery which has suggested the policy of establishing friendly relations with the tribes who hold them, and thus acquiring an indirect control over their western mouths. For just as the main physical feature of the frontier is this mountain wall, with its narrow lateral slits, so the main political feature is the existence in the tracts of country thus characterized of a succession of wild and warlike tribes, owing allegiance to no foreign potentate, but cherishing an immemorial love for freedom and their native hills."

Although the idea of consolidating these border tribes into a single province, with an administrator and staff of officers of its own directly under the control of the viceroy, was first suggested by the late Lord Lytton, it has been the good fortune of Lord Curzon to carry it into effect, and it is considered one of the wisest and most notable events of his administration of Indian affairs. The new community, which is called the Northwest Frontier Province, was organized in February, 1901, and takes in the wide stretch of territory which is described by its name. It is directly governed by an agent of the governor general and a chief commissioner, who allow the widest liberty and jurisdiction to the local chiefs consistent with peace and good government. The new system has been working since 1902, and while it is yet too early to calculate the results, the improvement already noticed in the condition of affairs, peace, industry, morals, the increase of trade and the development of natural resources justifies the expectation that the semi-barbarous tribes will soon yield to the influences of civilization and settle down into industrious, law-abiding and useful citizens. At least their organization and discipline under the command of tactful and discreet English officers gives to India a frontier guard composed of 30,000 or 40,000 fearless fighters, who will be kept on the skirmish line and will prove invaluable through their knowledge of the country and the mountain trails in case of a border war. The military position of England has thus been strengthened immensely, and when the railways now being constructed in that direction are completed, so that regular British and native troops may be hurried to the support of the wild and warlike tribes whenever it is necessary, a constant cause of anxiety will be removed and the northwestern frontier will be thoroughly protected.

The problems connected with the aggressive policy of Russia on the Indian frontier are very serious from every point of view to every Englishman, and whenever the time comes, if it ever does come, the frontier will be defended with all the power of the British Empire. The aggressiveness of Russia has been felt throughout India much more than anyone can realize who has not lived there and come in contact with affairs. It has been like a dark cloud continually threatening the horizon; it has disturbed the finances of the country; it has entered into the consideration of every public improvement, and has, directly or indirectly, influenced the expenditure of every dollar, the organization of the army, the construction of fortifications and the maintenance of a fleet. The policy of Lord Curzon is to bring all the various frontier tribes, which aggregate perhaps 2,000,000, under the influence of British authority. To make them friends; to convince them that loyalty is to their advantage; to organize them so that they shall be a source of strength and not of weakness or peril; to teach them the blessings of peace and industry; to avoid unnecessary interference with their tribal affairs; to promote the construction of railways, highways and all facilities of communication; to extend trade, introduce schools and mechanical industries, and to control the traffic in arms and ammunition. The commercial and the military policies are closely involved and in a measure one is entirely dependent upon the other.

South of Afghanistan, and the westernmost territory under British control, is Baluchistan, whose western boundary is Persia and the Arabian Sea. It was formerly a confederation of semi-independent nomadic tribes under the Khan of Kalat, with a population of about a million souls, but twenty-six years ago, after the Afghan war of 1878, those tribes were taken under the protection of the Indian government and Sir Robert Sanderman, a wise, tactful and energetic man, assisted the native rulers to reorganize and administer their affairs. During that period the condition of the country has radically changed. British authority is now supreme, the primitive conditions of the people have been greatly improved, they have settled down almost universally in permanent towns and villages, many of them are cultivating the soil, producing valuable staples and improving their condition in every respect. The country consists largely of barren mountains, deserts and stony plains. Its climate is very severe. The summers are intensely hot and the winters intensely cold. The wealth of the people is chiefly in flocks and cattle, and they are now raising camels, which is a profitable business. The chief exports are wool and hides, which are all clear gain now that the cultivation of the fields provides sufficient wheat, barley, millet, potatoes and other vegetables to supply the wants of the people. Fruits grown in the valleys are superior to anything produced in other parts of Asia. The apples and peaches of Baluchistan are famous and are considered great delicacies in the Indian market. There is supposed to be considerable mineral in the mountains, although they have never been explored. Iron, lead, coal, asbestos, oil and salt have been found in abundance, and some silver.

The efforts of the government have been to direct the attention of the people to mechanical industries rather than to mining, because it is important to break them of their nomadic tendencies and accustom them to permanent homes and regular employment. They resemble the Bedouins of Arabia in many respects and prefer to follow their flocks and herds over the mountains rather than settle down in the towns. The men are hardy, brave, honest and intelligent, but are desperate fighters and of cruel disposition; the women resemble the Chinese more than the Arabs, and are bright, active and ingenuous. The sense of humor is highly developed and the laws of hospitality are similar to those of the Arabs.

Although the British agent in Baluchistan has autocratic powers whenever he finds it necessary to exercise them, the Khan of Kalat is allowed to govern the country in his own way, and to all appearances is the independent authority. He is given a subsidy of about $75,000 a year on his private account from the Indian government, and his official income averages about 500,000 rupees a year, which is equivalent to about $175,000. With this he pays the expenses of his government and maintains a bodyguard of about 250 native cavalry. Only once has the British government found it necessary to interfere in an arbitrary manner. On that occasion Khudadad, the late ruling khan, murdered his prime minister in a fit of passion, and upon investigation it was found that he had put to death also without trial a number of innocent subjects. The Viceroy of India permitted him to abdicate and gave him a generous allowance, which was much better treatment than the villain was entitled to. His son, Mir Mahmud, who succeeded him, turns out to be an excellent ruler. He is intelligent, conscientious, and has the welfare of his people at heart.

There is little of interest except the political question and the peculiar appearance of the people up in that particular part of India. It has been debatable ground as far back as the earliest days of Aryan colonization. Although Peshawur is regarded as a modern city, it is mentioned by the historians who wrote up the campaigns of Alexander the Great, and if you will go up there the guides will show you where he crossed the river. The city has a population of about 80,000, of which three-fourths are Moslems. They come from every part of Asia, and the streets and bazaars swarm with quaint costumes and strange faces unlike any you have ever seen before. And what strikes a traveler most forcibly is their proud demeanor, their haughty bearing and the independent spirit expressed by every glance and every gesture. They walk like kings, these fierce, intolerant sons of the desert, and their costumes, no matter how dirty and trail-worn they may be, add to the dignity and manliness of their deportment.

They are so different, these haughty Mohammedans, from the bare-legged, barefooted, cringing, crouching creatures you see farther south. It would seem impossible for these men to stoop for any purpose, but the Bengalese, the Hindustani and the rest of the population of the southern provinces, do everything on the ground. They never use chairs or benches, but always squat upon the floor, and all their work is done upon the ground. Carpenters have no benches, and if they plane a board they place it upon the earth before them and hold it fast with their feet. The blacksmith has his anvil on the floor; the goldsmith, the tailor and even the printer use the floor for benches, and it is the desk of the letter writer and the bookkeeper.

It looks queer to see a printer squatting before a case of type, and even queerer to see a person writing a letter with a block of paper spread out before him on the ground. But that is the Hindu custom. You find it everywhere throughout India, just as you will find everybody, men, women and children, carrying their loads, no matter how light or how heavy, upon their heads. If an errand boy is sent from a shop with a parcel he never touches it with his hands, but invariably carries it on top of his turban. One morning I counted seven young chaps with "shining morning faces" on their way to school, every one of them with his books and slate upon his head. The masons' helpers, who are mostly women, carry bricks and mortar upon their heads instead of in hods on their shoulders, and it is remarkable what heavy loads their spines will support. At the railway stations the luggage and freight is carried the same way. The necks and backs of the natives are developed at a very early age. If a porter can get assistance to hoist it to the top of his head he will stagger along under any burden all right. I have seen eight men under a grand piano and two men under a big American roller top desk, and in Calcutta, where one of the street railway companies was extending its tracks, I saw the workmen carry the rails upon their heads.

XXII

THE ARMY IN INDIA

The regular army in India is maintained at an average strength of 200,000 men. The actual number of names upon the pay rolls on the 31st of December, 1904, was 203,114. This includes several thousand non-fighting men, a signal corps, a number of officers engaged in semi-civil or semi-military duties, those on staff detail and those on leave of absence. The following is an exact statement:

BRITISH

Cavalry, three regiments	2,101	
Artillery, eighty-seven batteries	14,424	
Infantry, forty-five battalions	42,151	
Engineers, one battalion	204	
		58,880

NATIVES

Cavalry, forty regiments	24,608	
Artillery, fourteen batteries	6,235	
Infantry, 126 battalions	108,849	
Engineers, twenty-three battalions	3,925	
		143,617
Officers on staff duty		617
Grand total		203,114

This regular and permanent military force is supplemented by native armies in the various independent states, which are only indirectly under the command of the commander-in-chief and are not well organized, except in one or two of the provinces. There is a reserve corps consisting of 22,233 men who have served in the regular army and are now upon what we call the retired list. They may be called out at any time their services are needed. There is also a volunteer force numbering 29,500 men, including cavalry, artillery, infantry and marines, many of them under the command of retired officers of the regular army; and the employes of several of the great railroad companies are organized into military corps and drill frequently. There is also a military police under the control of the executive authorities of the several provinces, making altogether about 300,000 men capable of being mobilized on short notice in any emergency, about one-third of them being Englishmen and two-thirds natives.

In 1856, before the great mutiny, the British forces in India consisted of less than 40,000 Europeans and more than 220,000 natives, besides about 30,000 contingents, as they were called, maintained by the rulers of the native states and at their expense. The greater part of the artillery was manned by native soldiers under European officers. Three-fourths of the native soldiers participated in the mutiny. The Madras forces in southern India and the Sikhs in the Punjab were not only loyal but rendered valuable services in suppressing the revolt. On the reorganization of the army, after the mutiny was suppressed, it was decided that there should never be more than two natives to one European in the service; that the artillery should be manned by Europeans exclusively, and that all the arsenals and supply stations should be in their charge. Since the reorganization there has been an average of 60,000 British and 120,000 native troops in India. All the artillery has been manned by Europeans, the British troops have been garrisoned at stations where they can render the most prompt and efficient service, and all of the cantonments, as the European camps are called, all the fortresses and arsenals, are connected with each other and with Bombay and Calcutta by railway. When the mutiny broke out in 1857 there were only about 400 miles of railway in India, and it was a matter of great difficulty, delay and expense to move troops any distance. To-day India has nearly 28,000 miles of railway, which has all been planned and constructed as a part of the national defense system. In 1857 it took between three and four months for a relief party to reach Delhi from the seaboard. To-day ten times the force could be sent there from any part of India within as many days.

Another vital error demonstrated by the mutiny was the former plan of drawing soldiers from a single caste. They were all under the same influence; all had the same interests and were governed by the same prejudices, and could be easily united for the same purpose. Now caste is not recognized in the army. Recruits are drawn from every tribe and every caste, and men of different races, religions and provinces are thrown together in the same company and are not allowed to serve in the locality where they were enlisted. Enlistments are entirely voluntary. The natives are armed, equipped and clothed by the state, but provide their own food, for which they receive a proper allowance. This is necessary in order that they may regulate their own diet and obey the laws of their caste. There are also what are called "class company regiments," composed chiefly of men who are serving second enlistments. That is, men of the same race and caste are organized into separate companies, so that a regiment may have two companies of Sikhs, two companies of Brahmins, two companies of Rajputs, two companies of Mohammedans, two companies of Gurkhas and companies of other tribes or religious sects which neutralize each other and are inspired by active rivalry.

Race outbreaks and religious collisions very seldom occur in India these days, but the hostility between the several sects and races is very deep. The Mohammedan still dreams of the day when his race shall recover control of the Indian Empire and turn the Hindu temples into mosques. The Sikhs hate the Mohammedans as well as the Hindus. None of the sects is without its prejudices.

The most efficient section of the native army is composed of the Sikhs, the Gurkhas, who are enlisted in Nepaul, and the Pathans, who come from the hill tribes in the far northwest. These are all vigorous, hardy races, fearless, enduring and fond of military service. It would be difficult to find in any country better soldiers than they make, and their numerical strength in the Indian army could be doubled without difficulty in case more soldiers were needed.

All cities, towns and villages have regularly organized police forces, consisting entirely of natives and numbering about 700,000. In the larger cities and towns the chief officers are European, and throughout the entire country the preference in making appointments to this force is given to men who have served in the regular army. About 170,000 officers and men have this distinction and make very efficient police.

The supreme authority over the army in India is vested

by law in the viceroy and is exercised through a member of the council of state, known as the secretary of military affairs, who corresponds to our Secretary of War. The active command is in the person of the commander-in-chief, who is also a member of the council of state by virtue of his office. The present commander-in-chief is Lord Kitchener, the hero of Khartoum and of the recent Boer war. Lord Roberts was formerly in command of the Indian army. He served in that country for thirty-eight years in various capacities. He went as a youngster during the mutiny, was with the party that relieved Delhi, and saw his first fighting and got his "baptism of blood" upon the "ridge," which was the scene of the fiercest struggle between the English rescuers and the native mutineers. He has recently published a readable book giving an account of his experience during thirty-eight years of military service in India.

Lord Kitchener is assisted by four lieutenant generals, each having command of one of the four military divisions into which the empire is divided. The Calcutta division is under the command of General Sir Alfred Gaseley, who led the combined international forces to the relief of the besieged legations in Peking. There is a general staff similar to that recently organized in the United States army, which looks after the equipment, the feeding, the clothing and the transportation of the army with an enormous corps of clerks and subordinate officers.

The officers of the staff corps number 2,700, and are appointed from the line of the native army upon the merit system. Many of them were educated at the military colleges in England; many others have seen service in the regular army of great Britain, and have sought transfer because the pay is better and promotion is more rapid in the Indian than in the British army. However, before an officer is eligible for staff employment in India he must serve at least one year with a British regiment and one year with a native regiment, and must pass examinations in the native languages and on professional subjects. This is an incentive to study, of which many young officers take advantage, and in the Indian army list are several pages of names of officers who have submitted to examinations and have demonstrated their ability to talk, read and write one or more of the native tongues. The gossips say that during his voyage from London to Bombay two years ago Lord Kitchener shut himself up in his stateroom and spent his entire time refreshing his knowledge of Hindustani.

No officer is allowed a responsible command unless he can speak the native language of the district in which he is serving, and, as there are 118 different dialects spoken in India, some of the older officers have to be familiar with several of them. Such linguistic accomplishments are to the advantage of military officers in various ways. They are not only necessary for their transfer to staff duty, but insure more rapid promotion, greater responsibilities and render them liable at any time to be called upon for important service under the civil departments. Several thousand officers are now occupying civil and diplomatic posts, and are even performing judicial functions in the frontier provinces.

The armies of the native states look formidable on paper, but most of them are simply for show, and are intended to gratify the vanity of the Hindu princes who love to be surrounded by guards and escorted by soldiers with banners. Some of the uniforms of the native armies are as picturesque and artistic as those of the papal guards at the Vatican, and on occasions of ceremony they make a brave show, but with the exception of two or three of the provinces, the native forces would be of very little value in a war.

The military authorities of India are exceedingly proud of the morale and the hygienic condition of their troops, and the records of the judge advocates and medical departments show a remarkable improvement in these respects, which is largely due to the scientific construction of barracks, to the enforcement of discipline and regulations framed to suit climatic conditions, a better knowledge of the effect of food and drink and the close observance of the laws of hygiene. The climate is very severe, particularly upon Europeans, who must take care of themselves or suffer the consequences. The death rate in all armies in time of peace should be much lower than in the ordinary community, because recruits are required to submit to physical examinations, and none but able-bodied men are enlisted. The death rate in the army of the United States before our soldiers were sent to the Philippines was remarkably low, only three or four per 1,000 per year.

Some years ago in the army of India the mortality from disease was as high as sixty-nine per 1,000, but by the introduction of the reforms mentioned the rate had been reduced to nineteen per 1,000 in 1880, and for the last ten years has been less than sixteen per 1,000. According to the opinion of those best qualified to know, this is largely due to the introduction of what are known as Regimental Institutes, or Soldiers' Clubs, corresponding closely to the canteens which were abolished in our army a few years ago, but which are considered as important a part of the military organization in India as a hospital or arsenal. After fifty years of experience in India the British military authorities gave up the attempt to prohibit drinking in the army. Lord Kitchener says: "You might as well try to hasten the millennium." And for twenty years they have been using various measures, some of which have proved practicable and others impracticable, to promote temperance. The result is an almost unanimous conclusion upon the part of those who have given the subject study that the most effective means of preventing intemperance and promoting discipline and morals are the soldiers' institutes and clubs, in which liquor is sold in small quantities under strict regulations enforced by the enlisted men themselves. In other words, they have stopped trying to prohibit drinking because they found it was impossible, and are now trying to reduce it to the minimum. The placing of the regulation of the liquor traffic very largely with the men themselves, and removing the semblance of official interference of authority, is said to be one of the most effective arrangements, and the very fact that drinking is not forbidden and that liquor can be obtained at any moment within a few steps of the barracks is of itself a most wholesome influence, because it takes away the desire, and all the spirit of adventure and risk. As long as human nature is stubborn and contrary, men will do out of pure mischief what they are told must not be done. These matters have a deep interest for the viceroy, Lord Kitchener, the commander-in-chief, and other prominent officials of the army in India. Lord Kitchener takes an active part in the temperance work and in the administration of the soldiers' institutes, and has had an officer detailed to look after their arrangement and management. Not long ago the viceroy traveled seven hundred miles to deliver an address at an anniversary of the Army Temperance Association.

Colonel De Barthe, secretary of military affairs in the cabinet of the viceroy, to whom I was sent for information on this subject, said: "The lives of the British soldiers in India are very tedious and trying, especially during the hot summers, which, in the greater part of the empire, last for several months. The climate is enervating and is apt to reduce moral as well as physical vitality. There are few diversions. The native quarters of the large cities are dreadful places, especially for young foreigners. I cannot conceive of worse, from both a sanitary and a moral point of view. But they have a certain novelty; they are picturesque and oftentimes attractive and entertaining to homesick soldiers, who, as is natural, yield easily to temptations to dissipation.

"And the best remedy is to furnish counter attractions and give the men resorts that are comfortable and attractive, where they will not be subject to the restraint of authority or come in contact with their officers too often. The government, as well as philanthropic societies, is doing everything that it can to provide such places, to protect the enlisted man as far as possible from the temptations to which he is subjected, and to furnish him a loafing place where he will feel at home, where he may do as he likes to all reasonable limits, and where he can obtain a moderate amount of pure liquor without feeling that he is violating regulations and subjecting himself to punishment.

"We formerly had bars at which soldiers could buy pure liquor, instead of the poisonous stuff that is sold them in the native quarters of Indian cities, but we soon concluded that they defeated their own purposes. Being situated at convenient locations, soldiers would patronize them for the love of liquor, and induce others to do the same for the sake of companionship. This promoted intemperance, because the soldiers went to the bar only to drink, and for no other reason. There were no reading-rooms or loafing places or attractive surroundings, and they were not permitted to remain at the bar after they had been served with one drink.

"Those bars have been abolished, and, under the present system, an effort is being made to furnish homelike, attractive club-houses, where the enlisted men may pass their leisure time in comfortable chairs, with pleasant surroundings, games, newspapers, magazines, books, writing materials and a well-filled library. We give them a lunch-room and a bar which are much more attractive than any of the native bazaars can offer. They are allowed to drink liquor on the premises in moderation, and the regulations of the institute are enforced by a committee of the men themselves, which appeals to their honor, their pride and their love for their profession. A drunken enlisted man is quite as much of a humiliation to his comrades as a drunken officer would be to his associates, and the men feel quite as much responsibility in restraining each other and in preventing their comrades from getting into trouble as their officers—perhaps more. To this spirit, this esprit de corps, we appeal, and find after several years of experience that the institutes promote temperance, health, discipline and contentment among the men.

"The surgeons of the service will tell you, and their reports contain the details, that the largest amount of disease and the worst cases are due to contact with natives in the bazaars of the cities near which our barracks are located. It is impossible to keep the men out of them, and their visits can only be lessened by furnishing counter attractions. The soldiers' institutes have proved to be the strongest ever devised. Anyone who knows India can tell instantly where soldiers' institutes have not been established by examining the sick reports of the officers of the medical corps.

"You cannot prevent men from drinking any more than you can prevent them from swearing or indulging in any other vice," continued Colonel De Barthe, "but you can diminish the amount of vice by judicious measures, and that we believe is being done by our institutes, with their libraries, reading-rooms, lunch-rooms, cafes, amusement-rooms, bars, theaters for concerts, lectures and amateur dramatic performances. The government does not put in billiard tables or any other kind of games. We allow the men to do that for themselves, and they pay for them out of the profits of the bar. Nor do we furnish newspapers. We require the soldiers to subscribe for themselves. There is a good reason for this which should be obvious to everyone who has ever had experience in such matters. We furnish the building, provide the furniture, fuel, lights, fill the shelves of the library with excellent standard books of history, travels, biography, fiction and miscellaneous works, and have a way of shifting the books between stations occasionally, so that the men will not always have the same titles before their eyes. We furnish a piano for the amusement hall, and all of the permanent fixtures of the place, but the men are required to do their share, which gives them personal interest in the institute, increases their responsibility and takes away much of the official atmosphere. If we should provide magazines and newspapers they would not be so well satisfied with them. There would always be more or less grumbling and criticism. Hence it is better for them to make their own choice. If we should provide crockery and glassware for the refreshment-rooms it would be more frequently broken. The same rule prevails in other matters, and, what is still more important, we want to remove as much of the official relation as possible. The management of the institute is in the hands of soldiers, under the supervision of officers, who simply act as checks or as inspectors to see that things go straight.

"We encourage the men to organize singing clubs, amateur theatricals and other entertainments in which they take a great interest and considerable talent is sometimes developed. They have their own committees looking after these things, which is a healthful diversion; and the institute is the headquarters of all their sporting organizations and committees. The officers of the barracks never go there unless they are invited, but when the men give an entertainment every officer and his family attend and furnish as much assistance as possible."

Colonel De Barthe showed me the rules for the government of these institutes, which may be found in paragraph 658 of the Army Regulations for India, and begin with the words: "In order to promote the comfort and provide for the rational amusement of noncommissioned officers and men, to supply them with good articles at reasonable prices and to organize and maintain the means for indoor recreation, a regimental institute shall be provided," etc. It is then provided that there shall be a library, reading-rooms, games and recreation-rooms, a theater or entertainment hall, a refreshment-room and a separate room for the use of and under the exclusive jurisdiction of the Army Temperance Association. The reading-room is to be furnished with a library and the amusement-room with a piano; card playing is permitted in the recreation-room, but not for money or other stakes of value; the discussion of religious and political subjects within the institute is forbidden, and religious exercises are not allowed to be conducted in the building except in the room of the Army Temperance Association.

Every noncommissioned officer and private is entitled to the use of the institute except when excluded for profane or other improper language, for intoxication or other misconduct, for such time as the committee in charge shall deem advisable. The management of the institute is entrusted to several committees of non-commissioned officers and soldiers and an advisory committee of three or more officers. These committees have control of all supplies, receipts and expenditures, the preservation of order, the enforcement of the rules, and are enjoined to make the institute as attractive as possible. A committee of three, of whom the chairman must be a sergeant, is authorized to purchase supplies; an inventory of the stock must be taken once a month; there may be a co-operative store if deemed advisable by the commanding officer, at which groceries, provisions and general merchandise may be sold to the men at cost price; liquor may be sold in a separate room of limited dimensions, under the supervision of a committee of which a sergeant is chairman, and that committee, by assigning good reasons, has the power to forbid its sale to any person for any length of time. No spirituous liquor except rum can be kept or sold; that must be of the best quality and no more than one dram may be sold to any person within the hour, and only one quart of malt liquor. Beside these, aerated waters and other "soft drinks" must be provided, with coffee, tea, sandwiches and other refreshments as required. The profits of the institute may be devoted to the library, reading-room and recreation department, the purchase of gymnastic apparatus, etc., and articles for the soldiers' mess, and may be contributed to the widows and orphans' fund, if so determined by the patrons of the institution.

Those, in short, are the means used by the Indian government to promote temperance and morality in its army, and everyone who has experience and knowledge of the practical operation of such affairs approves them. In addition to the institutes described, the Army Temperance Association, which is entirely unofficial and composed of benevolent people in private life, has established in several of the large cities of India, where garrisons are stationed, soldiers' clubs, which also prove very efficacious. They are located in the bazaars and other parts of the cities frequented by soldiers and where the most mischief is usually done. They are clubs pure and simple, with reading and writing-rooms, games, music, restaurants, billiard-rooms and bars at which rum, beer, ale and other liquors are sold. There is also a devotional-room, in which religious meetings are held at stated times. These clubs are managed by private individuals in connection with committees of noncommissioned officers and enlisted men, and several of them represent investments of $15,000 and $20,000. In some cases a small membership fee is charged. They have proved very effective in catching human driftwood, and provide a place where men who are tempted may have another chance to escape the consequences. They are conducted upon a very liberal plan, and after pay day soldiers who start out for a debauch, as so many regularly do, are accustomed to leave their money and valuables with the person in charge before plunging into the sinks of vice, where so many men find pleasurc and diversion.

XXIII

MUTTRA, ALIGARH, LUCKNOW, CAWNPORE

On the way back from the frontier are plenty of delightful places at which the journey may be broken. You can have another glimpse of the most beautiful building in the world at Agra, and can take a day's excursion to Muttra, one of the seven sacred cities of India, the birthplace of Krishna, second in rank and popularity of the Hindu gods. The trains are conveniently arranged; they take you over from Agra in the morning and bring you back at night, which is well, because there is no hotel at Muttra, only what they call a dak bungalow, or lodging-house, provided by the municipal authorities for the shelter of travelers who have no friends to put them up. These dak bungalows are quite common in India, for comparatively few of the towns have hotels that a European or American would care to patronize. In Japan the native hotels are miracles of neatness and sweetness. In India, and the rest of Asia, they are, as far as possible, the reverse. I suppose it would be possible for a white man to survive a day or two in a native hotel, but the experience would not be classified as pleasure. Several of the native princes have provided dak bungalows for public convenience and comfort, and one or two are so hospitable as to furnish strangers food as well as lodging free of cost. The maharajas of Baroda, Jeypore, Bhartpur, Gwalior and several other provinces obey the scriptural injunction and have many times entertained angels unawares.

It is an ancient custom for the head of the state or the municipal authorities or the commercial organizations or the priests to provide free lodgings for pilgrims and strangers; indeed, there are comparatively few hotels at which natives are required to pay bills. When a Hindu arrives in a strange town he goes directly to the temple of his religion and the priest directs him to a place where he can stop. It is the development of ancient patriarchal hospitality, and the dak bungalow, which is provided for European travelers in all hotelless towns and cities, is simply a refinement of the custom. There are usually charges, but they are comparatively small. You are expected to furnish your own bedding, towels, etc., and there are no wire spring mattresses. Sometimes iron cots are provided and often bunks are built in the wall. If there are none all you have to do is to wrap the drapery of your couch around you and select a soft place on the floor. A floor does not fit my bones as well as formerly, but it is an improvement upon standing or sitting up. Usually the dak bungalows are clean. Occasionally they are not. This depends upon the character and industry of the person employed to attend them. The charges are intended to cover the expense of care and maintenance, and are therefore very moderate, and everybody is treated alike.

After a long, dusty drive in the suburbs of Delhi one day I crept into the grateful shade of a dak bungalow, found a comfortable chair and called for some soda to wash down the dust and biscuits to hold my appetite down until dinner time. I was sipping the cool drink, nibbling the biscuits and enjoying the breeze that was blowing through the room, when the attendant handed me a board about as big as a shingle with a hole drilled through the upper end so that it could be hung on a wall. Upon the board was pasted a notice printed in four languages, English, German, French and Hindustani, giving the regulations of the place, and the white-robed khitmatgar pointed his long brown finger to a paragraph that applied to my case. I paid him 10 cents for an hour's rest under the roof. It was a satisfaction to do so. The place was clean and neat and in every way inviting.

At many of the railway stations beds are provided by the firm of caterers who have a contract for running the refreshment-rooms. Most of the stations are neat and comfortable, and you can always find a place to spread your bedding and lie down. There is a big room for women and a big room for men. Sometimes cots are provided, but usually only hard benches around the walls. There are always washrooms and bathrooms adjoining, which, of course, are a great satisfaction in that hot and perspiring land. The restaurants at the railway stations are usually good, and are managed by a famous caterer in Calcutta, but the men who run the trains don't always give you time enough to eat.

On the passenger trains, ice, soda water, ginger ale, beer and other soft drinks are carried by an agent of the eating-house contractor, who furnishes them for 8 cents a bottle, and it pays him to do so, for an enormous quantity is consumed during the hot weather. The dust is almost intolerable and you cannot drink the local water without boiling and filtering it. The germs of all kinds of diseases are floating around in it at the rate of 7,000,000 to a spoonful. A young lady who went over on the ship with us didn't believe in any such non-

GROUP OF FAMOUS BRAHMIN PUNDITS

sense and wasn't afraid of germs. She drank the local water in the tanks on the railway cars and wherever else she found it, and the last we heard of her she was in a hospital at Benares with a serious case of dysentery.

Mark Twain says that there is no danger from germs in the sacred water of the Ganges, because it is so filthy that no decent microbe will live in it; and that just about describes the situation. It is a miracle that the deaths are so few. Millions of people fill their stomachs from that filthy stream day after day because the water washes away their sins, and I do not suppose there is a dirtier river in all the universe, nor one that contains more contagion and filth. It receives the sewage of several of the largest cities of India. Dead bodies of human beings as well as animals can be seen floating daily. From one end of it to the other are burning ghats where the bodies of the dead are soaked in it before they are placed upon the funeral pyres, and when the bones and flesh are consumed the ashes are cast upon the sacred stream. But the natives observe no sanitary laws, and the filth in which they live and move and have their being is simply appalling.

But I started out to tell you about Muttra, which is a very ancient place. It is mentioned by Pliny, the Latin historian, Ptolemy, the Egyptian geographer, and other writers previous to the Christian era, and is associated with the earliest Aryan migrations. Here Krishna, the divine herdsman, was born. He spent his childhood tending cattle in the village of Gokul, where are the ruins of several ancient temples erected in his honor, but, although he seems to have retained his hold upon the people, they have allowed them to crumble, and the profuse adornments of the walls and columns have been shamefully defaced. At one time it is said there were twenty great monasteries at that place, with several hundred monks, yet nothing is left of them but piles of stone and rubbish. All have been destroyed in successive wars, for Muttra has been the scene of horrible atrocities by the Mohammedans who have overrun the country during several invasions. Therefore most of the temples are modern, and they are too many to count. There is a succession of them on the banks of the river the whole length of the city, interspersed with hospices for the entertainment of pilgrims, and palaces of rich Hindus, who go there occasionally to wash away their sins, just as the high livers of London go to Homburg and Carlsbad to restore their digestions. One of the palaces connected with the temple, built of fine white stone in modern style, belongs to Lakshman Das, a Hindu who the guide told us is the richest man in India. The many merchants of Muttra all seem prosperous. The city is visited by hundreds of thousands of pilgrims every year, all of whom bring in more or less money, and the houses and shops are of a more permanent and imposing order of architecture than those of Delhi, Agra and other places. It has the appearance of being a rich community.

The shade trees along the streets swarm with monkeys and parrots, which are sacred, and when you go there you mustn't jump if a grinning monkey drops down upon your shoulders in a most casual manner and chatters in your ear. The animals are very tame. They are fed by the pilgrims, who gain great merit with the gods thereby, and the river is filled with sacred turtles, which are also objects of great interest and devotion.

Only two towns in India are more sacred than Muttra. One is Benares and the other is Jagernath, or Juggernaut, which is about 150 miles south of Calcutta on the shore of the Bay of Bengal. There is the great idol which we have all heard about from the missionaries, and, I regret to say, some have been guilty of a good deal of misrepresentation and exaggeration. When I was a boy I read in Sunday-school books the most heart-tearing tales about the poor heathen, who cast themselves down before the car of Juggernaut and were crushed to lifeless pulp under its monstrous wheels. This story has been told thousands of times to millions of horrified listeners, but an inquiry into the facts does not confirm it. It is true that on certain holy days the great image of Juggernaut, or Jagernath, whichever way you choose to spell it, and it weighs many tons, is placed upon a car and the car is drawn through the crowded streets by thousands of pilgrims, who cast flowers, rice, wheat, palm leaves, bamboo wisps, sweetmeats and other offerings in its way. Occasionally in the throng that presses around the image some one is thrown down and has the life trampled out of him; on several occasions people have been caught by the wheels or the frame of the car and crushed, and at rare intervals some hysterical worshiper has fallen in a fit of epilepsy or exhaustion and been run over, but the official records, which began in 1818, show only nine such occurrences during the last eighty-six years.

I have great respect for missionaries, but I wish some of them would be more charitable in disposition, a little more accurate in statement, and not print so much trash. In Muttra you have a good illustration of their usefulness. The American Methodists commenced work there in 1887. No educational or evangelical work had ever been attempted previous to that time, but the men and women who came were wise, tactful and industrious, and the result may be seen in a dozen or more schools, with several thousand pupils, a flourishing, self-supporting church, a medical mission, a deaconesses' home and training school, a printing establishment and bookshop which is self-supporting and a large number of earnest, intelligent converts. Wherever you go in heathen lands you will find that wisdom, judgment, tact and ability, when applied in any direction, always show good results, but all missionaries, I regret to say, are not endowed with those qualities or with what Rev. Dr. Hepburn of Japan calls "sanctified common sense," and the consequences are sometimes deplorable.

"By their works ye shall know them."

At Aligarh, a town of 50,000 inhabitants on the railway between Agra and Delhi, is a very rare and indeed a unique institution—a Moslem university and printing press—the only ones in India, and the only ones in the world established and conducted on modern lines. The university is modeled upon the English plan. It has an English president and dean and several English professors, all of them graduates of the University of Cambridge. The preparatory school has an English head master and assistant, and in the faculty is a professor of physical culture, who has brought manly sports among the students to a standard unequaled elsewhere in India. The Aligarh University has the best football team and the best cricket team in the empire.

This remarkable institution was founded in 1875 by Sir Syed Ahmed Khan, a Mohammedan lawyer and judge on the civil bench, for the education of his co-religionists in order that they may take places in the world beside the graduates of English and European universities and exercise a similar influence. He recognized that the

Moslem population of India must degenerate unless it was educated; that it could not keep pace with the rest of the world. He was shocked at the ignorance and the bigotry of his fellow Mohammedans and at their stubborn conservatism. He was a sincere believer in his own religion, and insisted that the faith of Islam, properly understood, was as much in the interest of truth and progress in every branch of human knowledge and activity as the Christian religion, and he devoted his entire fortune and collected contributions from rich Mohammedans for the establishment of a school that should be entirely up-to-date and yet teach the Koran and the ancient traditions of Islam. There are now about 500 students, who come from the most important families in India. They live together in dormitories built about the college, dine in the same refectory and enjoy a healthy, active college life. Foreign and Christian professors fill the chairs of science, mathematics and languages, while able mullahs give instruction in the Koran and direct the students in the daily exercise of the Mohammedan rites.

Sir Syed Ahmed Khan met with bitter opposition and animosity from the conservative element of his faith, and while some of his opponents admitted the purity and nobility of his motive, he was often accused of apostasy, but his noble life was spared until March, 1898, and he was permitted to see his institution enjoying great popularity and usefulness. There is at present a movement among the Mohammedans of India for the higher education of the members of that sect. It is the fruit of his labors and the men who are leading it are graduates of the Aligarh College.

Lucknow and Cawnpore are usually neglected by American travelers, but are sacred objects of pilgrimage to all Englishmen because of their terrible memories of the awful struggles of the mutiny of the sepoys, or native soldiers, in 1857, and their heroic defense and heroic relief by a handful of British troops under Sir Henry Havelock, General James Outram and Sir Colin Campbell. Although more has been written about Lucknow, yet the tragedy of Cawnpore is to me the more thrilling in several particulars, and that city was the scene of the greater agony.

Upon the shores of the Ganges River is a pretty park of sixty acres, in the center of which rises a mound. That mound covers the site of a well in which the bodies of 250 of the victims of the massacre were cast. It is inclosed by a Gothic wall, and in the center stands a beautiful figure of an angel in white marble by an Italian artist. Her arms are crossed upon her breast and in each hand she holds a palm branch. The archway is inscribed:

"These are They which Came
Out of Great Tribulation."

Chiseled in the wall that marks the circle of the well are these words:

"Sacred to the Perpetual Memory of a great Company of Christian people, chiefly Women and Children, who near this Spot were cruelly Murdered by the Followers of the Rebel Nana Dhundu Panth of Bithur, and cast, the Dying with the Dead, into the Well below on the XVth day of July, MDCCCLVII."

The story of Cawnpore has no parallel in history. It might have been repeated at Peking two or three years ago, for the conditions existed there. In the summer of 1857 sixty-one English artillerymen and about 3,000 sepoys were attached to the garrison at that place, where about 800 foreigners resided. Upon the 6th of June the native troops rose in mutiny, sacked the paymaster's office and burned several of the public buildings. The frightened foreigners fled into one of the larger buildings of the government, where they hastily threw up fortifications and resisted a siege for three weeks. Their position having become untenable, they arranged terms of capitulation with Nana Sahib, the leader of the mutiny, who had been refused the throne and the allowance paid by the British government to the late maharaja, although the latter had adopted him in legal form and had proclaimed him his heir. This was one of the principal reasons for the mutiny, and without considering the question of justice or injustice, Nana Sahib satiated his desire for vengeance under the most atrocious circumstances. Having accepted the surrender of the little garrison upon his personal assurances of their security and safe conduct to Allahabad, he placed the survivors, about 700 in number, in boats upon the Ganges River and bade them good-by. As soon as the last man was on board and the word was given to start down the stream, the blast of a bugle was heard. At that signal the crews of the boats leaped into the water, leaving the passengers without oars, and immediately the straw roofs of the boats burst into flames and showers of bullets were fired from lines of infantry drawn up on the banks. Most of those who jumped into the water to escape the flames were shot down by the bullets. And many who escaped both and endeavored to reach the shore were sabered by cavalrymen who awaited them. One boat load escaped.

The survivors of this incident, about 200 in number, were led back into the city, past their old homes, now in smoldering ruins, and were locked up in two rooms twenty feet long and ten feet wide. They had no beds, no furniture, no blankets, not even straw to lie upon. They were given one meal a day of coarse bread and water, and after suffering untold agonies for fifteen days were called out in squads and hacked to pieces by the ruffians of Nana's guard. Their bodies were cast into the well, which was afterward filled with earth and has since been the center of a memorial park.

The siege of Lucknow was somewhat different. When the mutiny broke out Sir Henry Lawrence, the governor, concentrated his small force of British soldiers, with eleven women and seven children, in his residency, which stood in the center of a park of sixty acres. It was a pretentious stone building, with a superb portico and massive walls, and protected by deep verandas of stone. Anticipating trouble, he had collected provisions and ammunition and was quite well prepared for a siege, although the little force around him was attacked by more than 30,000 merciless, bloodthirsty fanatics. The situation was very much as it was at Peking, only worse, and the terrific fire that was kept up by the sepoys may be judged by the battered stump of an old tree which still stands before the ruins of the residency. Although about three feet in diameter, it was actually cut down by bullets.

On the second day of the siege, while Sir Henry Lawrence was instructing Captain Wilson, one of his aids, as to the distribution of rations, a shell entered his apartment, exploded at his side and gave him a mortal wound. With perfect coolness and calm fortitude he appointed Major Banks his successor, instructed him in details as to the conduct of the defense, exhorted the soldiers of the garrison to their duty, pledged them never to treat with the rebels, and under no circumstances to surrender. He gave orders that he should be buried "without any fuss, like a British soldier," and that the only epitaph upon his tombstone should be:

"Here lies Henry Lawrence, Who Tried to do his Duty; May God have Mercy upon his soul."

He died upon the Fourth of July. Upon the 16th Major Banks, his successor in command, was killed and the authority devolved upon Captain Inglis, whose widow, the last survivor of the siege, died in London Feb. 4, 1904. The deaths averaged from fifteen to twenty daily, and most of the people were killed by an African sharp-shooter who occupied a commanding post upon the roof of a neighboring house and fired through the windows of the residency without ever missing his victim. The soldiers called him "Bob the Nailer." The latter part of August he was finally killed, but not until after he had shot dozens of men, women and children among the besieged. In order to protect themselves from his shots and those from other directions the windows of the residency were barricaded, which shut out all the air and ventilation, and the heat became almost intolerable. A plague of flies set in which was so terrible that the nervous women and children frequently became frantic and hysterical.

On the 5th of September a faithful native brought the first news that a relieving force under Sir Henry Havelock and General James Outram was nearing Lucknow. On the 25th Havelock fought his way through the streets of the city, which were packed with armed rebels, and on the 26th succeeded in reaching the residency. But, although the relief was welcome, and the sufferings of the besieged were for the moment forgotten, it was considered impracticable to attempt an evacuation because the whole party would have been massacred if they had left the walls. A young Irish clerk in the civil service, named James Kavanagh, undertook to carry a message to Sir Colin Campbell and succeeded in passing through the lines of the enemy. On the 16th of November Campbell fought his way through the streets with 3,500 men, and the relief of Lucknow was finally effected.

A few days later Sir Henry Havelock, the hero of the first relief, died from an attack of dysentery from which he had long been suffering, and his body was buried under a wide-spreading tree in the park. The tomb of Havelock is a sacred spot to all soldiers. A lofty obelisk marks the resting place of one of the noblest of men and one of the bravest and ablest of soldiers.

The residency is naturally a great object of interest, but the cemetery, gay with flowers and feathery bamboos, is equally so, because there lies the dust of 2,000 men and women who perished within the residency, in the attempts at relief and in other battles and massacres in that neighborhood during the mutiny.

Nana Sahib, who was guilty of these awful atrocities, was never punished. In the confusion and the excitement of the fighting he managed to make his escape, and mysteriously disappeared. It is now known that he took refuge in the province of Nepal, where he was given an asylum by the maharaja, and remained secretly under his protection, living in luxury for several years until his death. It is generally believed that the British authorities knew, or at least suspected, his whereabouts, but considered it wiser to ignore the fact rather than excite a controversy and perhaps a war with a powerful native province.

There is little of general interest in Cawnpore. Lucknow, however, is one of the most prosperous and busy towns in India. The people are wealthy and enterprising. It has probably more rich natives than any other city of India except Bombay, and their houses are costly and extravagant, but in very bad architectural taste. Millions of dollars have been spent in tawdry decorations and ugly walls, but they are partially redeemed by beautiful parks and gardens. Lucknow has the reputation of being the home of the Mohammedan aristocracy in India, and a large number of its wealthiest and most influential citizens belong to that faith. Their cathedral mosque is one of the finest in the country. The imambra connected with it is a unique structure and contains the largest room in the world without columns, being 162 feet long by 54 feet wide, and 53 feet high. It was built in 1784, the year of the great famine, in order to give labor and wages to a hungry people, and is one solid mass of concrete of simple form and still simpler construction.

The architect first made a mold or centering of timber, bricks and earth, which was covered with several layers of rubble and coarse concrete several feet in thickness. After it had been allowed a year or two to set and dry, the mold or centering was removed, and this immense structure, whose exterior dimensions are 263 by 145 feet, stood as solid as a rock, a single piece of cement literally cast in a mold, and, although it has been standing 125 years, it shows no signs of decay or deterioration. The word imambra signifies "the patriarch's palace." The big room is used for the celebration of the Moslem feast of Mohurram, which commemorates the martyrdom of the sons of Ali, the immediate descendants of Mahomet.

The royal palaces of Lucknow, formerly occupied by

the native kings, are considered the worst architecture of India, although they represent the expenditure of millions of dollars. But the hotels are the best in all the empire, except the new one of which I have spoken in Bombay. For this reason and because it is a beautiful city, travelers find it to their comfort and advantage to stop there for several days longer than they would stay elsewhere, and enjoy driving about the country visiting the different parks and gardens.

One of the most novel excursions in India may be made to the headquarters of the commissariat department of the army, about three miles out of town, where a herd of elephants is used for heavy lifting and transportation purposes. The intelligence, patience and skill of the great beasts are extraordinary. They are fed on "chow patties," a mixture of hay, grains and other forage, and are allowed a certain number for each meal. Each elephant always counts his as soon as they are delivered to him, and if spectators are present the guardkeepers frequently give them a short allowance, whereupon they make a terrible fuss until they get what they are entitled to.

There are some quaint customs among the farmers in that part of the country. The evil eye is as common and as much dreaded as in Italy, and people who are suspected of that misfortune are frequently murdered by unknown hands to rid the community of a common peril and nuisance.

Good and bad omens occur hourly; superstitions are as prevalent as in Spain. If a boy be born, for example, a net is hung over the doorway and a fire is lighted upon the threshold to prevent evil spirits from entering the house.

The commencement of the farming season is celebrated

TOMB OF AKBAR, THE GREAT MOGUL, AT AGRA

with ceremonies. The first furrow in the village is plowed by a committee of farmers from the neighborhood. The plow is first worshiped and decorated. The bullock or camel which draws it is covered with garlands of flowers, bright-colored pieces of cloth and rosettes of ribbon are braided into its tail and hung upon its horns. Behind the plow follows "the sower," who is also decorated with flowers and ornaments, has a red mark upon his forehead and his eyelids colored with lampblack. He drops seed into the furrow. Behind him comes a second man, who carefully picks up every grain that has fallen outside of the furrow. When the furrow is finished the farmers assemble at some house in the neighborhood and have a dinner of simple food. There are similar ceremonies connected with the harvest. Some of them are said to be inherited from their ancient Aryan ancestors; others are borrowed from the Arabs, Persians and Chinese.

XXIV

CASTE AND THE WOMEN OF INDIA

Everybody who keeps in touch with the slowly changing social conditions in India is convinced that the caste, the most important fetich of the Hindus, is gradually losing its hold, particularly upon the upper classes, because they cannot adjust it to the requirements of modern civilization and to the foreign customs they imitate and value so highly. Very high authorities have predicted in my hearing that caste will be practically obsolete within the next fifty years, and entirely disappear before the end of the century, provided the missionaries and other reformers will let it alone and not keep it alive by controversy. It is a sacred fetich, and when it is attacked the loyal Hindu is compelled to defend and justify it, no matter what his private opinion of its practicability and advantages may be, but, if foreigners will ignore it, the progressive, cultured Hindus will themselves discard it. The influences of travel, official and commercial relations, and social intercourse with foreigners, personal ambition for preferment in the military and the civil service, the adoption of modern customs and other agencies are at work undermining the institution, and when a Hindu finds that its laws interfere with his comfort or convenience, he is very certain to ignore them. The experience of the Maharaja of Jeypore, told in a previous chapter, is not unusual. His case is only one of thousands, for nearly every native prince and wealthy Hindu has broken caste again and again without suffering the slightest disadvantage, which has naturally made them indifferent.

Travelers see very little of this peculiar institution, and it is so complicated that they cannot comprehend it without months of study. They notice that half the men they meet on the streets have odd looking signs upon their foreheads. Ryas, our bearer, calls them "god marks," but they are entirely artificial, and indicate the particular deity which the wearer is in the habit of worshiping, as well as the caste to which he belongs. A white triangle means Krishna, and a red circle means Siva—the two greatest gods—or vice versa, I have forgotten which, and Hindus who are inclined to let their light shine before men spread on these symbols with great care and regularity. At every temple, every market place, at the places where Hindus go to bathe, at the railway stations, public buildings, in the bazaars, and wherever else multitudes are accustomed to gather, you will find Brahmins squatting on a piece of matting behind trays covered with little bowls filled with different colored ochers and other paints. These men know the distinctive marks of all the castes, and for small fees paint the proper signs upon the foreheads of their patrons, who wear them with great pride. You frequently see them upon children also; and on holidays and religious anniversaries, when the people come out for pleasure, or during special ceremonials at their temples, nearly everybody wears a "god mark," just as he would wear a badge denoting his regiment and corps at a Grand Army reunion.

The more you study the question of caste the more confusing it becomes, but it is interesting and important because it is the peculiar institution of India and is not found in any other country in the world. The number of castes is almost infinite. The 200,000,000 or more Hindus in this empire are divided into a vast number of independent, well-organized and unchangeable groups, which are separated by wide differences, who cannot eat together or drink from the same vessel or sit at the same table or intermarry. There have been, and still are, eminent and learned philosophers and social scientists who admire caste as one of the highest agencies of social perfection, and they argue that it alone has prevented the people of India from relapsing into barbarism, but foreigners in general and Christian missionaries in particular take a very different view, and many thoughtful and patriotic Hindus publicly declare that it is the real and only cause of the wretched condition of their people and the greatest obstacle to their progress. Mr. Shoshee Chunder Dutt, a very learned Hindu and author of a standard book entitled "India, Past and Present," declares that "civilization has been brought to a standstill by its mischievous restrictions, and there is no hope of its being remedied until those restrictions are removed."

It is curious to learn that the word "caste" is not Hindu at all, but Portuguese, and that instead of being an ancient feature of the Hindu religion, it is comparatively a modern idea.

The first form of religion in India was the worship of nature, and the chief gods of the people were the sun, fire, water and other natural phenomena, which were interpreted to the ignorant masses by priests, who gradually developed what is now called Brahminism, and, in the course of time, for social reasons, divided the people into four classes: First, the Brahmins, which include the priestly, the literary and the ruling portions of the population; second, the Kshatryas, or warriors, who were like the knighthoods of Europe in the middle ages; then the Vaisyas, or landòwners, the farming population, and those engaged in mercantile and manufacturing industries; and finally the Sudras, or servants who attended the other castes, toiled in the fields and did the heavy labor of the community.

Gradually these grand divisions became divided into sections or social groups. Trades, professions, tribes and clans, and particularly those who worshiped the same god, naturally drifted together and were watchful of their mutual interests. As there are as many gods in the Hindu pantheon as there are inhabitants of India, these religious associations are very numerous. Occupation is not a sign of caste. Every caste, and particularly the Brahmins, have members in every possible occupation. Nearly every cook in India is a Brahmin, which is a matter of almost imperative necessity, because no man can partake of food cooked or even touched by persons of lower caste. The Brahmins are also more numerous than any other caste. According to the recent census they number 14,888,000, adult men only being counted. The soldier caste numbers more than 10,000,000, the farmer caste and the leather workers have nearly as many. Nearly 20 per cent of the population of India is included in those four castes, and there are forty or fifty sub-castes, each having more than 1,000,000 members.

There are more than 1,800 groups of Brahmins, who have become so numerous and so influential that they are found everywhere. The number in the public service is very large, representing about 35 per cent of the entire mass of employes of the government in every capacity and station, and they have the largest proportion of educated men. It is a popular delusion that every Brahmin is a priest, when the fact is that they are so numerous that not more than a small percentage is employed in religious functions. But for more than 2,000 years they have maintained their superiority unchallenged. This is not only due to their pretensions, but to their intellectual force. They have been the priests, the writers, the rulers, the legislators of all India, because of their force of character and mental attainments, and will always preserve their supremacy through the same forces that enabled them to acquire it.

The laws of caste, as explained by Mr. Shoshee Chunder Dutt, the Hindu writer referred to above, provide:

1. That individuals cannot be married who do not belong to the same caste.

2. That a man may not sit down to eat with another who is not of his own caste.

3. That his meals must be cooked either by persons of his own caste or a Brahmin.

4. That no man of an inferior caste is to touch his cooked rations, or the dishes in which they are served, or even to enter his cook room.

5. That no water or other liquid contaminated by the touch of a man of inferior caste can be made use of—rivers, tanks and other large sheets of water being, however, held to be incapable of defilement.

6. That articles of dry food, excepting rice, wheat, etc., do not become impure by passing through the hands of a man of inferior caste so long as they remain dry, but cannot be taken if they get wet or greased.

7. That certain prohibited articles, such as cows' flesh, pork, fowls, etc., are not to be taken.

8. That the ocean or any other of the boundaries of India cannot be crossed over.

The only acts which now lead to exclusion from castes are the following:

1. Embracing Christianity or Mohammedanism.
2. Going to Europe, America or any other foreign country.
3. Marrying a widow.
4. Throwing away the sacred thread.
5. Eating beef, pork or fowl.
6. Eating food cooked by a Mohammedan, Christian or low caste Hindu.
7. Officiating as priest in the house of a low caste Sudra.
8. By a female going away from home for an immoral purpose.
9. By a widow becoming pregnant.

When a Hindu is excluded from caste his friends, relatives and fellow townsmen refuse to partake of his hospitality; he is not invited to entertainments in their houses; he cannot obtain wives or husbands for his children; even his own married daughters cannot visit him without running the risk of being excluded from caste; his priest and even his barber and washerman refuse to serve him; his fellow caste men ostracize him so completely that they refuse to assist him even in sickness or at the funeral of a member of his household. In some cases the man excluded from caste is debarred from the public temples.

To deprive a man of the services of his barber and his washerman is becoming more difficult these days, but the other penalties are enforced with more or less rigor.

They tell us that foreigners cannot appreciate the importance of caste. Murray's guide book warns the traveler to remember that fact, and says that the religion of the Hindu amounts to little more than the fear of demons, of the loss of caste and of the priests. Demons have to be propitiated, the caste rules are strictly kept and the priests presented with gifts. Great care has to be taken not to eat food cooked by a man of inferior caste; food cooked in water must not be eaten together by people of different castes, and castes are entirely separated with regard to marriage and trade. A sacred thread of cotton is worn by the higher castes. Washing in the sacred rivers, particularly the Ganges, and especially at Allahabad, Benares, Hardwar and other exceptionally holy spots, is of efficacy in preserving caste and cleansing the soul of impurities.

"The traveler should remember," says the guide book, "that all who are not Hindus are outcasts, contact with whom may cause the loss of caste to a Hindu. He should not touch any cooking or water holding utensil belonging to a Hindu, nor disturb Hindus when at their meals; he should not molest cows, nor shoot any sacred animal, and should not pollute holy places by his presence if any objection is made. The most sacred of all animals is the cow, then the serpent, and then the monkey. The eagle is the attendant of Vishnu, the bull of Siva, the goose of Brahma, the elephant of Indra, the tiger of Durga, the buffalo of Rama, the rat of Ganesh, the ram of Agni, the peacock of Kartikkeya, the parrot of Kama (the god of love), the fish, the tortoise and boar are incarnations of Vishnu, and the crocodile, cat, dog, crow, many trees, plants, stones, rivers and tanks are sacred."

Nevertheless, Brahmins are very clever in dodging an issue when it is necessary for their convenience. For example, when a modern water supply was introduced for the first time into a city of India the problem arose, How could the Hindus use water that came from hydrants, in face of the law which prohibited them drinking it from vessels which may have been touched by people of another caste? After much reflection and discussion the pundits decided that the payment of water rates should be considered an atonement for violating the ordinances of their religion.

There has been some improvement in the condition of women in India, and it is due almost entirely to the Christian missionaries who have brought about reforms which could not have occurred otherwise, although, at the same time, the spirit of modern progress has not been without its influence upon the native families. Remarkable instances have occurred in which native women have attained distinction in literature, scholarship and science. Several have passed university entrance examinations; a few have obtained degrees. In 1903 there were 264 women in collegiate institutions throughout the empire, more than has ever been known before. There has been a gradual increase in their number. In 1893-4 there were only 108; two years later there were 110. In 1898-9 the number jumped to 174, and in 1900-1 it reached 205, hence you will see that the advance has been normal and regular and there have been no steps backward. The greatest progress has been in the southern part of the empire, where women are less secluded and the prejudice against their education is not so strong. Nevertheless 99 per cent of the women of India are absolutely illiterate, and among the total of 144,409,000 only 1,433,000 can read and write; 75 per cent of them can do no more. If a census were taken of those who can read and understand an ordinary novel or a book of travel the total would be less than 250,000, and counted among the literates are all the girls now in school who have advanced as far as the first reader.

In the United Provinces, the richest and proudest of India, where the arts and sciences have advanced quite rapidly among men, only 56,000 women out of a total of 23,-078,000 can read and write, and that, as I said before, includes the girl children in the schools. In the Punjab Province, which lies in the north, out of a total of 12,-369,000 women and girls only 42,000 can read and write and at least 50 per cent of them are under 12 years of age. The total number of girls now attending school in India is only 446,282 out of a total population of 144,409,000 women, but even this small number shows most encouraging improvement during the last ten years. In 1893-4 the girls in school were only 375,868, but since then there has been a gradual increase every year—400,709 in 1897-8, 425,914 in 1899-1900 and 429,645 in 1900-01. In the Central Province, which ought to be one of the most progressive in India, out of a total female population of 23,078,000 only 20,821 girls altogether are in school.

But this does not fairly indicate the influence of women in India, where they take a larger and more active share in the responsibilities of the family and in the practical affairs of life than one would suppose. The mother of a family, if she is a woman of ability and character, is always the head of the household, and the most influential person in it, and as long as she lives she occupies the place of honor. Women often manage estates and commercial affairs, and several have shown remarkable executive ability and judgment. Several of the native states have been ruled by women again and again, and the Rannee of Sikkim is to-day one of the most influential persons in India, although she has never been outside of the town in which she lives.

An American lady told me of a remarkable interview she recently had with the granddaughter of Tipu, the native chief who, in the latter part of the eighteenth century, gave the English the hardest struggle they ever had in India. He was finally overcome and slain, and his territory is now under English rule, but his family were allowed a generous pension and have since lived in state with high-sounding titles. His granddaughter lives in a splendid palace in southern India, which she inherited from her father, and is now 86 years old. She cannot read or write, but is a women of extraordinary intelligence and wide knowledge of affairs, yet she has never been outside of the walls that surround her residence; she has never crossed the threshold of the palace or entered the garden that surrounds it since she was a child, and 90 per cent of her time, day and night, has been spent in the room in which she was born. Yet this woman, with a title and great wealth, is perfectly contented with her situation. She considers it entirely appropriate, and thinks that all the women in the world ought to live in the same way.

The influence she and other women of old-fashioned ideas and the conservative classes have is the chief obstacle to progress, for they are much more conservative than the men, and much more bigoted in their ideas. She does not believe that respectable women ought to go to school; she does not consider it necessary for them to read or write, and thinks that all women should devote themselves to the affairs of their households and bear children, duties which do not require any education. The missionaries who work in the zenanas, or harems, of India tell me that the prejudice and resistance they are compelled to overcome is much stronger and more intolerant among women than among men, for the former have never had an opportunity to see the outside of their homes; have never come in contact with foreigners and modern ideas, and are perfectly satisfied with their condition. They testify that Hindu wives as a rule are mere household drudges, and, with very rare exceptions, are patterns of chastity, industry and conjugal fidelity, and they are the very best of mothers.

Here and there a husband or a father is found who is conscious of the disadvantages under which the women of his family are laboring and would be glad to take upon himself the duty of instructing his wife and daughters, yet is prevented from doing so because the latter prefer to follow the example of their foremothers and remain ignorant.

While such conditions prevail it is impossible for the government to take any steps for the promotion of education among women, but a notable reform has been conducted by English women of India under the leadership of the Marchioness of Dufferin, Lady Curzon, and the wives of other viceroys, by supplying women doctors and hospitals, because, as you understand, men physicians are not permitted to enter zenanas except upon very rare occasions and then only in the most liberal of families. Nor are women allowed to be taken to hospitals. There are excellent hospitals and dispensaries in every part of India, but women are not permitted to participate in their benefits, and an untold amount of unnecessary suffering is the result. Some years ago, inspired by Lady Dufferin, an association was formed to provide women doctors, hospital nurses, and establish, under the direction of women exclusively, hospitals for the treatment of women and girls. This association is non-sectarian and no religious services or conversations are allowed. The movement has received active encouragement from both the imperial government and the local authorities, and by the latest returns is responsible for 235 hospitals and dispensaries, 33 women doctors with degrees from the highest institutions of Europe, 73 assistants, and 354 native students and trained nurses, who, during the year 1903, took care of nearly a million and a half of women and girls who needed treatment and relief. This does not include many similar institutions that are maintained by the various missionary boards for the same purpose. Taking both the civil and religious institutions together, the women of India are now well supplied with hospitals and asylums.

Scattered over the country under the care of zealous and devoted Christian women are a large number of homes for widows, and no one who has not lived in India can appreciate the importance of such institutions and the blessing they offer, for the situation of widows is pitiable. Formerly they were burned upon the funeral pyres of their husbands. It was an ancient custom, adopted from the Scythian tribes, who sacrificed not only the wives, but the concubines and slaves and horses upon the tombs of their dead lords.

The British government forbade "suttee," as widow burning was called, and although we hear that it is still practiced occasionally in remote parts of the empire, such an act would be punished as murder if the police were to learn of it. But the fate of some thousands of widows is worse than death, because among the superstitious

Hindus they are held responsible for the death of their husbands, and the sin must be expiated by a life of suffering and penance. As long as a widow lives she must serve as a slave to the remainder of the family, she must wear mourning, be tabooed from society, be deprived of all pleasures and comforts, and practice never-ending austerities, so that after death she may escape transmigration into the body of a reptile, an insect or a toad. She cannot marry again, but is compelled to remain in the house of her husband's family, who make her lot as unhappy and miserable as possible.

The Brahmins prohibit the remarriage of widows, but in 1856 Lord Canning legalized it, and that was one of the causes of the mutiny. The priests and conspirators told the native soldiers that it was only a step toward the abolition of all their rites and customs. The law, however, is a dead letter, and while there have been several notable marriages of widows, the husband and wife and the entire family have usually been boycotted by their relatives, neighbors and friends; husbands have been ruined in business and subjected to every humiliation imaginable.

If you will examine the census statistics you will be astonished at the enormous number of widows in India. Out of a total of 144,000,000 women in 1901, 25,891,936 were widows, of whom 19,738,468 were Hindus. This is accounted for by child marriage, for it is customary for children five years of age and upwards to become husbands and wives. At least 50 per cent of the adherents of Brahminism are married before they are ten years old and 90 per cent before they are fifteen. This also is an ancient custom and is due to several reasons. Fathers and mothers desire to have their children settled in life, as we say, as early as possible, and among the families of friends they are paired off almost as soon as they are born. The early marriage, however, is not much more than a betrothal, for after it takes place, usually with great ceremony, the children are sent back to their homes and remain under the care of their parents until they reach a proper age, when the wife is conducted with great rejoicing to the home of her husband, and what is equivalent to another marriage takes place. This occurs among the highly educated and progressive Hindus. They defend the custom as wise and beneficial on the theory that it is an advantage for husband and wife to be brought up together and have their characters molded by the same influences and surroundings. In that way, they argue, much unhappiness and trouble is prevented. But in India, as everywhere else, the mortality is greatest among children, and more than 70 per cent of the deaths reported are of persons under ten years of age. Those who are married are no more exempt than those who are not, which explains the number of widows reported, and no matter how young a girl may be when her husband dies she can never have a second.

Widowers are allowed to marry again and most of them do. There are only 8,110,084 widowers in all India as against nearly 26,000,000 widows.

Of course there are many native homes in which widows are treated kindly and receive the same attention and are allowed the same pleasures as the other women of the family, but those who understand India assert that they are exceptional, and hence asylums for those who are treated badly are very much needed. This is a matter with which the government cannot deal and the work is left entirely to the Christian missionaries, who establish homes and teach friendless widows to become self-supporting.

XXV

EDUCATION IN INDIA

Allahabad is the center of learning, the Athens in India, the seat of a native university, the residence of many prominent men, the headquarters of Protestant missionary work, the residence of the governor of the United Provinces, Sir James La Touche, one of the ablest and most progressive of the British officials in India. Allahabad was once a city of great importance. In the time of the Moguls it was the most strongly fortified place in India, but the ancient citadel has been torn down by the British and the palaces and temples it contained have been converted into barracks, arsenals and storehouses. Nowhere in India have so many beautiful structures been destroyed by official authority, and great regret is frequently expressed. Allahabad was also a religious center in ancient times and the headquarters of the Buddhist faith. The most interesting monument in the city is the Lat of Osoka, one of a series of stone columns erected by King Asoka throughout his domains about the year B. C. 260, which were inscribed with texts expressing the doctrines of Buddhism as taught by him. He did for that faith what the Emperor Constantine the Great did for Christianity; made it the religion of the state, appointed a council of priests to formulate a creed and prepare a ritual, and by his orders that creed was carved on rocks, in caves and on pillars of stone and gateways of cities for the education of the people. The texts or maxims embodied in the creed represent the purest form of Buddhism, and if they could be faithfully practiced by the human family this world would be a much better and happier place than it is.

Several handsome modern buildings are occupied by the government, the courts and the municipal officials, and the university is the chief educational institution of northern India. There are five universities in the empire —at Bombay, Calcutta, Lahore, Allahabad and Madras —and they are managed and conducted on a plan very different from ours, having no fixed terms or lectures, but having regular examinations open to all comers who seek degrees. The standard is not quite so high as that of our colleges and the curriculum is not so advanced. The students may come at 15 or 16 years of age and be examined in English, Latin, Greek history, geography, mathematics and the elements of science, the course being just a grade higher than that of our high schools, and get a degree or certificate showing their proficiency. They are very largely attended by natives who seek diplomas required for the professions and government employment. After two years' study in any regular course a student may present himself for an examination for a degree and is then eligible for a diploma in law, medicine, engineering and other sciences.

The slipshod systems pursued at these institutions have been severely criticised by scientific educators, but they seem to answer the purpose for which they are intended. It is often asserted that the colleges and universities in India do not cultivate a genuine desire for learning; that the education they furnish is entirely superficial, and that it is obtained not for its own sake, but because it is a necessary qualification for a government appointment or a professional career. It is asserted that no graduate of any of these institutions has ever distinguished himself for scholarship or in science, that no native of India educated in them has ever produced any original work of merit, and that no problem of political or material importance has ever been solved by a citizen of this empire. In 1902 Lord Curzon, who has taken a deep interest in this subject and is an enthusiastic advocate of public schools, appointed a commission to investigate the conduct and efficiency of the universities of India. The report was not enthusiastic or encouraging. It was entirely noncommittal. At the same time it must be said that the universities and colleges of India are a great deal better than nothing at all, and as there is no other provision for higher education they serve a very important purpose.

The deplorable illiteracy of the people of India is disclosed by the recent census. Ninety-five per cent of the men and more than 99 per cent of the women have never learned the first letter of the alphabet, and would not recognize their own name if written or printed. I have been told by ladies engaged in missionary and educational work that grown people of the lower classes cannot even distinguish one picture from another; that their mental perceptions are entirely blank, and that signs and other objects which usually excite the attention of children have no meaning whatever for them. The total number of illiterates recorded is 246,546,176, leaving 47,814,180 of both sexes unaccounted for, but of these only 12,097,530 are returned as able to read and write. The latest statistics show that 3,195,220 of both sexes are under instruction.

And even the percentages I have mentioned do not adequately represent the ignorance of the masses of the people, because more than half of those returned by the census enumerators as literates cannot read understandingly a connected sentence in a book or newspaper and can only write their own names. The other half are largely composed of foreigners or belong to the Brahmin castes. The latter are largely responsible for present conditions, because their long-continued enjoyment of a hereditary supremacy over the rest of the population has been due to their learning and to the ignorance of the masses belonging to other castes. They realize that they could never control any but an illiterate population. Hence the priests, who should be leaders in education, are, generally speaking, the most formidable opponents of every form of school.

The census shows that only 386,000 natives in the whole of India possess a knowledge of English, and this number includes all the girls, boys and young men under instruction.

The Parsees and Jains are more eager for learning than the Hindus, and are taking an active part in educational affairs. The Mohammedans are also realizing the importance of modern schools, and there is now quite an energetic movement among that sect. There is a school connected with almost every Jain temple. We visited one at Delhi. There were no benches or desks. The children, who were of all ages, from 4 years old upward, were squatting upon the floor around their masters, and were learning the ordinary branches taught in common schools, with the exception of one class over in a far corner of the room, which was engaged in the study of Sanskrit. It was explained to us that they were being trained for

AUDIENCE CHAMBER OF THE MOGUL — PALACE — AGRA

priests. Everybody was bare-footed and bare-legged, teachers and all, and every boy was studying out loud, repeating his lesson over and over as he committed it to memory. Some of the youngsters made their presence known by reading in very loud voices. A few of them had ordinary slates. Others used blocks of wood for the same purpose, but the most of them wrote their exercises upon pieces of tin taken from cans sent over by the Standard Oil Company. We went into a school one day where, for lack of slates and stationery, the children were copying their writing lessons in the sand on the floor. It was a new idea, but it answered the purpose. With little brushes they smoothed off a surface and formed letters as clearly as they could have been made upon a blackboard.

Bright colors are characteristic of the Hindus. Their garments are of the gayest tints; both the outer and inner walls of their houses are covered with rude drawings in colors; their carts are painted in fantastic designs; and their trunks are ornamented in a similar way. They are not always done in the highest form of art, but you may be sure that the colors are bright and permanent. Some people paint the hides of their horses and bullocks, especially on holidays, and their taste for art, both in design and execution, is much more highly developed than their knowledge of letters.

The present Indian educational system is about fifty years old, but popular education, as we use that term, was not introduced in a practical way until during the '80's. Up to that time nearly all the schools were conducted by missionaries and as private institutions. In 1858, when the government was transferred from the East India Company to the crown, there were only 2,000 public schools in all India, with less than 200,000 pupils, and even now with a population of 300,000,000 there are only 148,541 institutions of learning of all kinds, including kindergartens and universities, with a grand total of 4,530,412 pupils. Of these 43,160 are private institutions, with 638,999 pupils.

Education is not compulsory in India. The natives are not compelled to send their children to school and the officials tell me that if it were attempted there would be great trouble, chiefly because of the Brahmin priests, who, as I have already intimated, are decidedly opposed to the education of the masses. Normal schools have been established in every province for the training of teachers, with 31,114 young men and 2,833 young women as students. There has been a slight increase in the attendance at school during the last few years. In 1892 only 11.1 per cent of the children of school age were enrolled and the average attendance was a little over 7 per cent. In 1902 the enrollment had increased to 12.5 per cent of the school population, and the attendance to a little more than 8 per cent. Of the pupils in the public schools 509,525 were Brahmins and 2,269,930 non-Brahmins. In the private institutions 43,032 were Brahmins and the balance non-Brahmins.

There are several important art schools in India which have been established and are encouraged by the government for the purpose of encouraging the natives to pursue the industrial arts. Lord Curzon has taken a decided interest in this subject, and is doing everything in his power to revive the ancient art industries, such as brocade weaving, embroidery, carving, brass working, mosaic, lacquering, and others of a decorative character. The tendency of late years has been to increase the volume of the product at the sacrifice of the quality, and the foreign demand for Indian goods and the indifference of the buying public as to their excellence is said to have been very demoralizing upon the artisans.

From an artistic point of view, the manufactures of metal are the most important products of India; the wood carvers of ancient times surpassed all rivals and still have a well-deserved reputation. In every village may be found artists of great merit both in brass, copper, wood, silk and other industrial arts, but the quality of their work is continually deteriorating, and Lord Curzon and other sincere friends of India are endeavoring to restore it to the former high standard. For that purpose art schools have been established in Calcutta, Lahore, Bombay, Madras and other places, first to train the eyes and the hands of the young artisans, and, second, to elevate their taste and stimulate their ambition to excel in whatever line of work they undertake. There are several thousand young men in these schools who have shown remarkable talent and are beginning to make their influence felt throughout the country.

As you may imagine, it is very difficult to induce people to produce objects of high art when those which cost less labor and money can be sold for the same prices. As long as the foreign demand for Indian goods continues this tendency to cheapen the product will be noticed.

By the late census it appears that there were 2,590 publications in the native Indian languages during the year 1900, as against 2,178 during the previous year; 1,895 were books and 695 pamphlets; 1,616 of the books were original works and the remainder were translations; 832 were in the Bengali language and the remainder were divided among eighty-eight other languages, ninety-nine being in Sanskrit and 103 in Persian. Included in this list were poetry, fiction, works of travel, religious books, history, biography, philosophy and several on political economy. Among the Persian publications I noticed "A History of Russian Rule in Asia"; among the translations are Lord Lytton's "Last Days of Pompeii," several popular novels, and several of Shapespeare's plays. There was a history of England and a series of biographies entitled "Lives of Great Women," including those of Queen Victoria, Queen Elizabeth, Maria Theresa, Marie Antoinette, and the mother of Napoleon I.

Since 1902 there have been several movements among the Hindus and Mohammedan citizens of India looking to the advancement of their races and coreligionists. At Bombay, in December, 1903, was held a Mohammedan educational conference, and a committee was appointed to draw up a plan of permanent organization for the purpose of awakening among the members of that sect an interest in the advancement of women and the education of the masses. Representatives were present from nearly all of the provinces in which there is a Mohammedan population, and resolutions were passed declaring that, in the opinion of the conference, schools should be established throughout India to educate young women and children of both sexes in strict conformity with the customs and doctrines of Islam. It was asserted that such educational facilities are absolutely necessary to keep the children out of the public and Christian schools. The most notable feature of the conference, which marks an entirely new departure in the history of Islam, was the presence, unveiled and in modern dress, of Miss Sorabjee, a highly educated and accomplished member of that sect, who appeared daily upon the platform, participated in the debates and made a lengthy address upon the emancipation of women. She declared that in a population of 60,-000,000 Mohammedans only 4,000 girls are now attending school, which, she said, is a menace to civilization, a detriment to Islam and a disgrace to the members of that church. I was informed that this is the first time a Mohammedan woman ever made an address before a public assembly of Mohammedans, because the Koran does not permit women to appear in public and custom requires them to conceal their faces. Miss Sorabjee was, nevertheless, received with respect, and made a decidedly favorable impression upon the assembly, which was composed of men of culture and influence and true believers in the teachings of the Prophet.

Another notable feature of the conference was the unanimous recognition of the growing influence of Christianity in the Indian Empire, and the opinion that in order to preserve their faith the followers of Islam must imitate its example. Progressive Mohammedans have become convinced that not only their men but their women will insist upon having an education, and will seek it in the Christian schools if facilities are not furnished by members of their own religion. Aga Khan, a Mohammedan prince who presided over the gathering, explained that the conference was called in obedience to the spirit of progress, and as an indication that the Mohammedan section of the community was alive to the disadvantages under which the members of the faith were laboring, and to the need of educated men as leaders in society and commerce.

Mr. Tyabji, one of the judges of the Supreme Court of the Bombay presidency, took even more advanced ground and declared that the schools proposed by the conference must be far in advance of those heretofore provided by

Mohammedans, and teach English, French, German and the modern sciences as well as the maxims of the Koran. By that remark he uncovered the great defect of Mohammedan education, which is purely religious, with the exception of a single institution in northern India to which I refer in a previous chapter. The conservative element of the Moslem population holds that a knowledge of reading, writing and arithmetic is sufficient for members of that sect; hence in most of their schools they teach nothing except the Koran, which is the book of books, the law of laws, and contains knowledge sufficient for all mankind under all circumstances. Some progressive Mohammedans go a little too far in the other direction and would ignore all Arabic literature and leave all ecclesiastical affairs to the priests. The Arabic and Persian languages are rich in learning, poetry and general literature. But they are not cultivated, and are almost unknown to the Moslem priests, who are the school teachers of that faith to-day. They have left the revival of Arabic belles-lettres entirely to foreigners, and confine themselves to the Koran and the commentaries that have been prepared upon it. It is asserted that one can learn more of Arabian and Persian literature to-day in London, Oxford, Paris, Berlin or Zurich than is known in Constantinople or Cairo or any other Mohammedan city, and that Professor Max Muller of Oxford has done more to encourage its study than all the Mohammedan priests and professors in existence.

At almost the same time, although in another place, several of the leading thinkers and scholars of the Brahmin caste were discussing the same subject with the same purpose and from the same point of view. They have been endeavoring to inaugurate what they are pleased to call "the Renaissance of the Hindus." And there is also an active movement for a revival of Buddhism, although thus far it is confined to Japan and Ceylon. Buddhism is practically extinct in India. At the Hindu conference several thoughtful people expressed the view that something must be done to revive the vitality of that religion, because it is the faith of nearly 200,000,000 souls in India alone, over whom it is gradually losing its influence, because of the vigorous propaganda of the Christians. It was not admitted that the Hindus are adopting the Christian religion, but merely that they are losing confidence in their own and drifting toward materialism.

It is universally recognized among educated Brahmins that India is approaching a great religious crisis which demands the attention of all who are interested in the welfare of the people. The movement is slow, but quite obvious to all who are watching the development of reforms that have been proposed for the last fifteen or twenty years. It is based upon the fact that Brahminism, as taught at the temples of India to-day, does not satisfy or even appeal to educated men. At the same time it is insisted that true Hinduism has the same ideals and the same spiritual advantages that are offered by Christianity.

Experienced missionaries tell me there is a distinct tendency among educated Hindus to give up the old line of defense against the Christian religion, and, admitting the ethical purity and truth of the teachings of Christ, to attack some particular doctrine, some dogma over which Christians themselves have been in controversy, to elaborate the criticisms of Ingersoll and Bradlaugh, and to call attention to the failure of the Christians to realize their own ideals. This is very significant, but at the same time there is little encouragement or satisfaction in studying and tracing the various reforms that have been started from time to time among the Hindus. They have been many and frequent. New teachers are constantly arising, new organizations are being formed, and revivals of ancient precepts are occurring every year, but they do not endure. They are confined to limited circles, and none has yet penetrated to any extent into the dense mass of superstition, idolatry and ignorance which lays its offerings at the altars of cruel and obscene gods.

At one of Lady Curzon's receptions, among other notable men and women, I met Sir Nepundra Narayan Bhuf Bahadur, Maharaja of Cutch-Behar, and his wife, one of the few native women who dress in modern attire and appear in public like their European sisters. She is the daughter of one of the most famous of Indian reformers.

Early in the last century a scholar and patriot named Ramohun Roy, becoming dissatisfied with the teachings and habits of the Brahmins, renounced his ancestral religion and organized what was called "The Truth Seeking Society" for the purpose of reviving pure Hinduism. He proclaimed a theistic creed, taught the existence of one God, and the sin of idolatry. He declared for the emancipation of women, for charity to the poor and helpless, for the purity of life, and, altogether, his sermons and lectures are very similar to the teachings of the Unitarians in the United States. He was called the Theodore Parker of India, and attracted many followers. But before he had accomplished much he died, and his mantle fell upon Keshab Chunder Sen, a man of great learning, talent and worth, the son of one of the most conservative families of the Brahmin caste, born and brought up in a fetid atmosphere of superstition and idolatry. While attending school at Calcutta he was thrown in with European teachers and associates and, being of an inquisitive mind, undertook the study of religions other than his own. It naturally came about that he heard of the "Truth Seeking Society" and ultimately joined it, and by his force of character and ability became one of its leaders. Early in his career he concluded that the greatest weakness among the people of India is their treatment of their women, and he organized what was known as "The Indian Reform Association" for the purpose of promoting the education of women, preventing child marriage, relieving widows from their forlorn ostracism and securing for the daughters of Indian families the same legal and property rights that are enjoyed by the sons. The movement became quite popular and he gained considerable reputation. He went to England and Germany and delivered lectures and published several books. His agitation accomplished some practical results, and he secured the passage of several laws of importance establishing the civil rights of wives, widows and daughters.

In 1884 his daughter, a very brilliant and beautiful woman, married the Maharaja of Cutch-Behar, who was converted, joined the movement and became an active member of the society. Like many others of the princely families of India, he lays claim to divine origin, the founder of his dynasty having been a god. In 1772, the ruling rajah, having been attacked by more powerful neighbors, applied for protection to Warren Hastings, then governor of Bengal, and acknowledged subjection to the East Indian Company. The province of Cutch-Behar was thus one of the first to be absorbed by the British Empire, but it has ever since been governed by the native prince, who nominally owns all of the land in his territory and receives taxes in lieu of rent from his tenants, who are his subjects. His territory has a population of 650,000, of whom 427,000 are Hindus and 174,539 are Mohammedans. He is assisted in his government by a resident English adviser, appointed by the viceroy, and really has very little to do. He has a personal allowance of $150,000 for the support of himself and family, and inherited from his ancestors one of the most rare and valuable collections of jewels in India.

The present maharaja was born in 1863, educated in England, attained his majority in 1883, and has two sons, one of whom is a member of the Viceroy's Corps of Imperial Cadets, and the other acts as his father's secretary. The maharaja is considered one of the handsomest men in India, as he is one of the most accomplished and progressive, and his wife is as famous for her intellectual as for her physical attractions.

The late Jamsetjee Nusserwanji Tata of Bombay, a typical Parsee, amassed an enormous fortune as a merchant and manufacturer, won an enviable reputation for integrity, enterprise and public spirit, and for several years before his lamented death in 1904, was permitted to enjoy the gratification that men of his kind deserve after a long career of activity and usefulness. Having provided in a most ample manner for his own future wants, and intrusting his enormous business responsibilities to his sons, he devoted the rest of his life to travel and other pleasures, and a large portion of his fortune to benevolence. I have been frequently told that Mr. Tata in his time was the most enterprising man in India. He spent enormous sums in experiments for the development of the resources and industries of his country; some of which failed, but others have been eminently successful. He developed the cotton industry, perhaps more than any other man, and improved the staple by importing plants and seeds from Egypt. He was largely engaged in growing, preserving and exporting the fruits of India in order to furnish another occupation for the country people, and in a thorough exploration of its iron deposits, building furnaces, smelters, and mills with the hope of being able to supply the local markets with home made steel and iron. There is plenty of ore, plenty of coal and labor, and Mr. Tata was willing to pay the expense and do the work of a pioneer in order that his fellow countrymen may enjoy the wealth that lies dormant in their mountains.

He had cotton mills and other manufactories in various parts of India, but the greater part of his fortune was invested in the industries and real estate of his own province of Bombay. His residence was one of the largest and most beautiful palaces in that city, filled with works of art and trophies of travel. He was the owner of several of the finest business blocks, introduced modern apartment houses into Bombay, and built the modern hotel to which I have several times alluded. He supported several young Parsees in the technical schools and colleges of England, Germany and the United States. For years no less than six such students were selected annually to be educated at his expense, not only because he took a personal interest in the welfare of his co-religionists, but because he believed that young engineers, chemists, electricians and other practical scientists were needed to develop the resources of India.

Mr. Tata's latest act of benevolence, shortly before his death, was to place in the hands of a board of trustees, of whom the chancellor of the University of Bombay is chairman, real estate and securities valued at more than 3,500,000 of rupees, which is equivalent to about $1,250,000, the income from which, amounting to 120,000 rupees, or about $40,000 in our money, a year, is to be used for the establishment and perpetual maintenance of the Indian Research University, a name selected by a conference called together by the viceroy. This conference was composed of four directors of public instruction for the different provinces of India, the home secretary of the imperial government, the surgeon general of the army and several other gentlemen eminent in educational and public affairs. After a careful examination of all conditions they decided to locate the institution at the city of Bangalore, in the province of Mysore, in southern India, where the local government, as an inducement, donated 300 acres of land upon an eminence in a very favorable situation, and offered a contribution of 18,000 rupees a year toward the payment of the expenses, provided the money is used in such a way as to benefit the people of that province. It has also offered to defray a considerable part of the cost of erecting the necessary buildings.

XXVI

THE HIMALAYAS AND THE INVASION OF THIBET

Darjeeling is one of the most favored spots on earth, the loveliest place in India, and the favorite resort and sanitarium of the citizen element as distinguished from military and official circles. It is a hard journey, both going and coming, and a traveler gets impatient when he finds that it takes him from four o'clock in the afternoon of one day until nearly two o'clock of the next to make a journey of 246 miles. He leaves Calcutta with the thinnest clothing he can buy, but when he arrives there he is glad that he brought his overcoat and gloves, and pulls a second blanket over himself at night. At the same time it is not so cold in Darjeeling as one would expect from the altitude of 7,400 feet above the sea, and the latitude, which is about 27 degrees 50 minutes. You travel from four o'clock till seven upon a railway of ordinary gauge, cross the Ganges on a steamboat for an hour, taking your dinner while afloat; change into a three-foot gauge train until half-past four in the morning, when you are routed out, given a cup of coffee and a roll, and transferred to a baby carriage on wheels which crawls up the foothills of the Himalayas at the rate of six miles an hour.

The track is only two feet gauge, with forty-pound rails, which have been laid upon the ancient highway over which the caravans between China and India have passed for thirty centuries. It winds in and out of gorges and defiles and at several points the engineers have had to cut a foothold for it on the edges of tremendous precipices. It doubles on itself repeatedly, describes the letter S and the letter Z and the figure 8, and zigzags about so recklessly that the engineer puts his locomotive first at one end of the train and then at the other. Englishmen who write books on India assert that it is the grandest railway journey in the world, but we can show them several quite as picturesque and attractive in our own beloved Rocky Mountains. The only advantage they have over us there is the superior height of the mountains and the superior size of the trees. But you must remember that our country is young yet, and India is one of the oldest nations in the world.

The first few miles of track lie in a dense jungle, with vegetation of truly tropical luxuriance. Cane stalks grow fifty and sixty feet high, the grass is fifteen feet deep, beautiful bamboo trees, whose foliage is as fine as feathers, and palms which have plumage like a peacock and a bird of paradise, lift their proud and haughty heads above an impenetrable growth which, the guides tell us, is the home of tigers, rhinoceroses, panthers, bears, wild hogs, buffaloes, deer and all sorts of beasts, and snakes as big around as a barrel. Fern trees are lovely, and are found here in their greatest glory, but nevertheless we have foliage at home, and they are no more beautiful than our elms, oaks, and other trees that I might mention.

This is a great tea country, and the mountain sides have been cleared in many places for plantations. A tea planter in India is a heavy swell. He may be no more brilliant or intellectual or virtuous or handsome, but the fact that he grows tea instead of potatoes or wheat or sugar gives him a higher standing in the social scale. I was asking an explanation of this phenomenon from a very wise man the other day, and, although he insisted that his attention had never been called to it before, he was willing to admit that it was so, and he explained it on the theory that so many sons of dukes and earls and lords and the swagger set in England had come to India to engage in tea growing that they had created a caste of their own; so that whenever a man said he was a tea planter the public immediately assumed that his father belonged to the nobility and treated him accordingly. The tea planters usually live in good style. They have beautiful bungalows, gardens, lawns and groves, and although they complain of the depression of the industry, there is no evidence that they suffer for want of the necessities of life. In the Darjeeling district are about two hundred large plantations, employing from one to two thousand laborers each, and producing about 12,000,000 pounds a year. Most of the product is shipped to England.

They carry you up the mountains in tiny little cars seating six persons and open all around so that the passengers can take in all there is to see, and they have plenty of scenery. The trains are not allowed to run faster than six miles an hour as a precaution against accidents, which allows plenty of time to look about, and they twist around so that you can see things from various points of view. And if a passenger gets impatient or is in a hurry he can jump out of the car and walk ahead.

There is little doubt that the views from Darjeeling include the most majestic assemblage of mountains on the earth's surface. For a distance of 200 miles east and west there arise a succession of peaks not less than 22,000 feet high, and several of them more than 25,000. In the immediate vicinity and within sight are the highest mountains in the world. Everest, the king of mountains, which measures 29,200 feet, is only eighty miles distant; Kinchinjunga, which is forty-five miles distant, is 28,156 feet high, and also, in the immediate vicinity, are the following:

Janu	25,304	Kabru	24,015
Chumalari	23,943	Pauhanri	23,186
Donkia	23,176	Baudim	22,017
Narsingh	22,146	Kanhenjhan	22,500
Chomaino	23,300		

Between these mountain peaks is an almost continuous succession of snow fields and glaciers beyond all comparison. The snow line is 17,000 feet in midsummer, and in winter comes down to 12,000 and 15,000 feet, and when that altitude is reached snow is continuous and impassable. This is the highest and the most extensive of all mountain ranges. Along the northern frontier of India for 2,000 miles it stands like a vast hedge, the most formidable natural boundary in the world, nowhere lower than 17,000 feet, and impassable for armies the entire distance, with the exception of two gateways: Jeylup Pass here and at the Khyber Pass of which I told you in a previous chapter. There are passes over the snow, but their elevation is seldom less than 16,000 feet; the average elevation of the watershed exceeds 18,000 feet, and the great plateau of Thibet, which lies upon the other side, is between 15,000 and 16,000 feet above the sea.

This plateau, which is sometimes called the "Roof of the World," is 700 miles long and 500 miles wide, and could not be crossed by an army not only because of the winds and the cold, but also because there is very little water, no fuel and no supplies. No invading force could possibly enter India from the north if these passes were defended, because the inhospitable climate of Thibet would not sustain an army, and the enormous distance and altitude would make the transportation of supplies for any considerable force practically impossible. During the summer the plateau is covered with flocks and herds, but when the cold weather comes on the shepherds drive them into the foothills, where they find shelter. The width of the main range of the Himalayas will average about 500 miles between its northern and southern foothills; it embraces every possible kind of climate, vegetation and natural products, and is a vast reservoir from which four of the greatest rivers of the world flow across the plains of India, carrying the drainage from the melting snows, and without this reservoir northern India would be a hopeless and dreary desert.

There is a lively dispute among geographers, topographers and other learned pundits of the scientific bureaus of the Indian government as to whether Everest is really the king of the mountains. Other peaks in the group have their advocates, and over in Cashmere are several which lift their heads nearly as high as 30,000 feet, but few of them have been accurately measured, and the height of none can be determined with exactness. Mount Godwin, in Cashmere, is very near the height of Everest, and many claim that Kinchinjunga is even higher.

Darjeeling is a sanitarium of the greatest benefit to the people of India. The town is made up chiefly of hotels, hospitals and summer bungalows belonging to the mercantile class of Calcutta. Few officials except military officers ever go there. The official society follows the viceroy to Simla, where the summer is always gay, but those who seek health and rest only and are fond of nature ,prefer Darjeeling. The hotels are good, there are plenty of boarding houses, there are hospitals for all sorts of infirmities, and perhaps there is no other place in the world with such an ideal climate within a day's travel of the tropics. The hotels, villas, boarding houses, hospitals and asylums are scattered all over the hillside without regularity of arrangement. Wherever a level spot has been found some kind of a house has been erected, usually without any architectural taste, and the common use of corrugated iron for building material has almost spoiled the looks of the place. There is plenty of timber, and the great mountains are built of stone, so that there is no excuse for the atrocious structures that have been erected there.

Everybody who comes is expected to get up at half-past 3 in the morning in order to see the sun rise. Everything is arranged by the managers of the hotel. They have fixed the sunrise at that hour in order to compel their guests to make the greatest possible effort to see it because they will thus remember the incident, and the experience will remain longer in their memory. They give you a cup of coffee and a roll, and, if you insist upon it, you can get an egg, although the cook is not inclined to be obliging at that hour in the morning. They put you in a sort of sedan chair called a "dandy," and you are carried by four men seven miles up the mountains to a point 12,000 feet above the sea. From there you can look upon the most impressive spectacle that human eye has ever witnessed, the rising of the sun over an amphitheater surrounded by the highest group of peaks on the globe. Their snow-covered summits are illuminated gradually, beginning at the top, as if a search-light were slowly turned upon them. Mount Everest stands in the center, but is so much farther away that it does not seem so much higher than the rest.

There is little mountain climbing in India compared with the Alps, because the distances and the difficulties are so great. A Boston gentleman and his wife made the ascent of Mount Everest in 1904, and it is claimed that they went higher than anyone had ever gone before.

Darjeeling is not a large town, but it is filled with interesting people, and on Sunday a market is held in the principal bazaar which is declared to be the most picturesque and fascinating in all India. Throngs of natives in quaint costumes come from all parts of the country around, representatives of tribes which do not often stray so far away from their homes. They come from Nepaul, Thibet, Sikkim and the surrounding countries, and bring articles of home manufacture to exchange for "store goods." The features of the people are unmistakable testimony of their Mongolian origin. They are short of stature, with broad, flat faces, high cheek bones and bright, smiling eyes wide apart. The men grow no beards, but have long pigtails of coarse coal-black hair. The women are sturdy, good-natured and unembarrassed; they are adorned with a great quantity of jewelry, chiefly of silver, but often of gold. They wear circlets around their heads made of coral, turquoise, amber, agate, jade or other precious stones, with five or six necklaces and enormous girdles of the same material. Huge ear rings, four or five inches long, pull down the lobes of their ears. Their wrists are heavy with bracelets, their limbs with anklets, and their fingers are half hidden with rings. The entire fortune of a family is usually invested in personal adornments for the women members. They find this much safer than savings banks.

The attention of the world has recently been attracted in that direction because of an unusual and very significant movement of the Indian government, which, in the winter of 1904, took advantage of the embarrassments of Russia in the farther East, and sent a military expedition over the northern border on the pretext of escorting a diplomatic mission. Colonel Younghusband was sent as an envoy extraordinary—very extraordinary—for, with 2,500 British soldiers, he was instructed to make a treaty of commerce and good will with the Grand Lama of Thibet, and his orders were to stay at Lhassa until the treaty was negotiated and as much longer as was necessary to compel the Thibetans to respect its terms and carry out its stipulations. That means the permanent occupation of Lhassa by a British army and the opening of an unknown and mysterious region to trade.

Thibet is the unknown, mysterious country of the world, a land of desert and mountains inhabited by a primitive and bigoted people, who have for many years been under the protection of China, and paid tribute to the emperor until the late war with Japan in 1895. After the result of that conflict became known they seemed to lose their respect for and confidence in their protectors and have sent no envoys or money to Peking since. We know very little about Thibet. Foreigners are not permitted to enter the country, and only a few venturesome explorers have endured the hardships and faced the dangers of a visit to that forbidden land. Indeed, it is so perilous an undertaking that a skeptical public frequently takes the liberty to doubt the statements of the men who have gone there. But all agree that it is the hermit of nations, and its people are under the control of cruel and ignorant Buddhist priests, who endeavor to prevent them from acquiring any modern customs or ideas. One of the objects of Colonel Younghusband's expedition is to change this situation and persuade the ignorant and bigoted ecclesiastics who govern Thibet to open their gates and admit foreign merchants and foreign merchandise into that benighted country. There is considerable commerce, however. Parties of Thibetan traders are continually coming across the frontier into Darjeeling with all sorts of native products and may be seen in the market that is held every Sunday morning and during the weekdays in the bazaars of the city. After selling their goods they buy cottons, drugs, groceries, hardware and other European goods and take them back into their own country; but foreigners are not allowed to pass the line, and practically all of the trade of Thibet is monopolized by the Chinese, who sell the natives large quantities of cotton fabrics and other imported merchandise as well as tea, silk and other Chinese goods. This trade is supposed to be worth many millions of dollars, and the ability of India to furnish the tea and of England to furnish the manufactured goods that the inhabitants of Thibet may need is considered ample reason for sending the Younghusband expedition into that country. But there are other reasons quite as important.

Lying between Thibet and India is the independent state of Nepal, or Nepaul, the home of the Gurkhas, one of the finest fighting races in the world, and there are eighteen full regiments of them in the Indian army. The Gurkhas are a mountain people, industrious, temperate, hardy, brave, loyal, honest and without sense of fear. They are the main dependence of the Indian government among the native troops. Nepal has its own government and the people are proud of their independence.

While they are entirely friendly to Great Britain and have treaties with India under which the latter extends a protectorate over the province and enters into an offensive and defensive alliance, the Maharaja permits no British adviser to take part in his government and receives a representative of the viceroy only in the capacity of envoy or minister plenipotentiary. The latter dare not interfere with the administration of the government and never presumes to tender his advice to the native rulers unless it is asked. His duties are chiefly to keep the viceroy at Calcutta informed as to what is going on in the Nepal province and to cultivate the good will of the officials and the people.

There has never been a census of Nepal and the population has been variously estimated from 2,000,000 to 5,000,000. It is probably near the latter figure. The people are mostly engaged in raising cattle, sheep and goats and growing wheat, barley and other grains in the valleys. The principal exports, which amount to about $8,000,000 a year, are wool, hides and grain, and the imports, which amount to about $5,000,000, are cotton goods and other wearing apparel, iron and steel, cutlery and other manufactured merchandise.

The people of Nepal profess the Hindu faith and have close relations with the Brahmins at Benares, which is the Rome, or the Mecca, of Brahminism. They sometimes in the past have been bold enough to defy British authority, and, for example, protected Nana Sahib, the leader of the mutiny of 1857, and gave him an asylum when he fled from British vengeance. However amicable the relations between Nepal and the British government, the latter is scrupulously careful not to furnish any excuse for complaint or controversy, because a collision with this powerful people would not only result in the loss of the finest corps in the Indian army, but would make it extremely unpleasant for the people of Assam, Bengal, Oudh and the Punjab, which provinces lie next on the south.

One hundred years ago an army from Nepal invaded Thibet and sacked an important town. The Thibetans appealed to China, which had not yet lost its military vigor, and sent an army to invade Nepal. It came within eighteen miles of Gurkha, the capital, when the Nepals proposed a parley, paid a heavy indemnity and entered into a treaty of permanent peace, promising never to invade Thibet again. That was the last heroic act of the Chinese government, and then, in compliance with the terms of the treaty, all the passes through the Himalaya Mountains between the two countries were permanently closed by common consent, and in many cases were walled up with masonry, adding an artificial barrier to the natural wall. It was also agreed that there should be no communication across the border and that the inhabitants of both provinces would remain upon their own sides. This prohibition has been enforced until to-day, and has not been violated except by Buddhist priests and monks and a few venturesome explorers. No Englishman may even now enter Nepal or pass from Nepal into Thibet without permission from the authorities of both governments.

Mindful of the aggressive policy of Russia, which controls Turkestan, the country north of Thibet, the British government some years ago sent an envoy named McCauley to Lhassa, with the permission of the Chinese government, to open commercial relations with Thibet and find another market for the tea of Assam and the manufactured merchandise of India. But he was unable to do anything. He could not induce the priests, or lamas, who control the government, to negotiate with him. They would not respond to his advances and gave him plainly to understand that they did not care to improve their relations with India. Immediately after his departure the Thibetans began to fortify the passes over the mountains, and invaded the little province of Sikkim, which also adjoins Thibet. The British sent up troops and forbade the continuance of the work. The Thibetans withdrew to the interior and agreed to make a commercial treaty and open their market to Indian goods, promising to send a plenipotentiary to Calcutta for that purpose within six months; but he has never appeared, and frequent reminders from the British have passed without notice.

When Lord Curzon came to India he determined to reverse the policy of indifference which had been pursued by Lord Elgin, his predecessor. The opening of Thibet to Indian trade has been one of the principal features of his administrative programme. In 1900 he sent to Lhassa an ambassador in the person of Colonel Younghusband, a distinguished Asiatic traveler, who speaks the language of Thibet, to talk things over and persuade the Dailai Lama, as the chief ruler of Thibet is called, to carry out his promise about the treaties. The Grand Lama refused to receive Colonel Younghusband, and would have nothing whatever to do with him, rejecting his overtures without explanation and treating his messages with contempt.

While England was suffering the worst of the disasters of the recent war in South Africa the Russian government sent a secret embassy to Lhassa, carrying rich presents and large sums of money to the Grand Lama, for the ostensible purpose of securing permission to construct a branch from its Siberian Railway to Lhassa across Chinese Turkestan. The Grand Lama afterward sent an embassy to return the visit at St. Petersburg, which was received with great honors and presented with rich gifts. The Grand Lama, in recognition of these attentions, conferred upon the czar the title of "Lord and Guardian of the Gifts of Faith." It is the supreme Buddhist honor, and while the title is empty, it is particularly significant in this case, because it implies protection. It is believed that a secret treaty was made under which Russia promised to guarantee the independence of Thibet and protect that government against invasion in exchange for the privilege of constructing a railway line through its territory. The Thibetans are supposed to have accepted these terms because of their fear of China. Until 1895 Thibet was a province of the Chinese Empire, and paid tribute to the emperor every year, but since the war with Japan the Grand Lama has sent no messenger to Peking, has paid no tribute and has ignored the Chinese representative at Lhassa. The priests postponed negotiations on the pretext that it was necessary to consult Peking, and promised to send a mission to Calcutta within six months, but never have done so. In the meantime there has been continual friction on the border; the Indian authorities have repeatedly reminded the Grand Lama of his promise and its postponement, but he has stubbornly refused to communicate with them, and has even returned their communications unopened.

When the secret relations between Russia and Thibet were discovered the Chinese authorities were naturally indignant and the Indian authorities were alarmed. After a conference China granted permission for England to use whatever methods it thought best to bring the Grand Lama to terms. Thereupon Colonel Younghusband was sent to Lhassa again. The Grand Lama again refused to see him, declined to appoint an official to confer with him and returned his credentials unopened, and used other means to show his indifference and contempt for India and England.

When Younghusband returned to Calcutta and reported the failure of his mission and the insults offered him Lord Curzon decided that the time had come to act, and as soon as preparations could be made Colonel Younghusband started back to Lhassa escorted by 2,500 armed men and carrying provisions for two years. He was instructed to avoid collisions, to make friends with the people, to establish permanent posts on the line of march wherever he thought necessary and to remain at Lhassa until he secured a treaty opening the markets of Thibet to British merchants. The treaty is made, and by its terms the Thibetans are to pay England an indemnity of $3,750,000 to cover the cost of the expedition. Until the indemnity is paid the Indian troops will continue to occupy the Churubi Valley which leads to Lhassa.

Lord Curzon did not dispatch this expedition and undertake this strategic movement without considering the present situation of Russia. The czar took occasion to engage in negotiations not only with Thibet, but with Afghanistan also, at the very moment when England was suffering her most serious disasters and embarrassments of recent history, and is getting tit for tat. Before Colonel Younghusband's expedition was dispatched the British ambassador at St. Petersburg was instructed to inquire if the Russian government had any relations with

Thibet or any interests there, and was officially informed that it had not, hence the etiquette of the situation had been complied with and Lord Curzon was perfectly free to act.

XXVII

BENARES, THE SACRED CITY

No one can realize what an awful religion Brahminism is until he visits Benares, the most sacred city of India, upon the banks of the Ganges, the most sacred river, more holy to more millions of human souls than Mecca to the Moslem, Rome to the Catholic or Jerusalem to the Jew. This marvelous city it so holy that death upon its soil is equivalent to life eternal. It is the gate to paradise, the abundant entrance to everlasting happiness, and its blessings are comprehensive enough to include all races, all religions and all castes. It is not necessary to be a Brahmin or to worship Siva or Krishna or any other of the Hindu gods, nor even to believe in them. Their grace is sufficient to carry unbelievers to the Hindu heavens provided they die within the area inclosed by a boulevard encircling this city.

There are in Benares 2,000 temples and innumerable shrines, 25,000 Brahmin priests, monks, fakirs and ascetics, and it is visited annually by more than half a million pilgrims—a larger number than may be counted at Mecca or Jerusalem, or at any other of the sacred cities of the world. There are more than 500,000 idols established in permanent places for worship in Benares, representing every variety of god in the Hindu pantheon, so that all the pilgrims who go there may find consolation and some object of worship. There are twenty-eight sacred cows at the central temples, and perhaps 500 more at other places of worship throughout the city; the trees around the temple gardens swarm with sacred monkeys and apes; there are twenty-two places where the dead are burned, and the air of the city is always darkened during the daytime by columns of smoke that rise from the funeral pyres. No other city, not even London, has so many beggars, religious and otherwise; nowhere can so many pitiful spectacles of deformity and distress be seen; nowhere is such gross and repulsive obscenity and sensuality practiced—and all in the name of religion; nowhere are such sordid deceptions imposed upon superstitious believers, and nowhere such gloomy, absurd and preposterous methods used for consoling sinners and escaping the results of sin. Although Benares in these respects is the most interesting city in India, and one of the most interesting in the world, it is also the most filthy, repulsive and forbidding. Few people care to remain there more than a day or two, although to the ethnologist and other students, to artists and people in search of the picturesque, it has more to offer than can be found elsewhere in the Indian Empire.

Benares is as old as Egypt. It is one of the oldest cities in existence. It was already famous when Rome was founded; even when Joshua and his trumpeters were surrounding the walls of Jericho. It is the hope of every believer in Brahminism to visit Benares and wash away his sins in the water of the sacred Ganges; the greatest blessing he can enjoy is to die there; hence, the palaces, temples, and lodging-houses which line the river banks are filled with the aged relatives and friends of their owners and with pilgrims who have come from all parts of India to wait with ecstatic patience the summons of the angel of death in order to go straight to heaven.

Nothing in all their religion is so dear to devout Hindus as the Ganges. The mysterious cavern in the Himalayas which is supposed to be the source of the river is the most sacred place on earth. It is the fifth head of Siva, and for 1,600 miles to its delta every inch of the banks is haunted with gods and demons, and has been the scene of events bearing upon the faith of two-thirds of the people of India. The most pious act, and one that counts more than any other to the credit of a human soul on the great books above, is to make a pilgrimage from the source to the mouth of the Ganges. If you have read Kipling's story of "Kim," you will remember the anxiety of the old lama to find this holy stream, and to follow its banks. Pilgrims to Benares and other cities upon the Ganges secure bottles of the precious water for themselves and send them to friends and kindred in foreign lands. No river in all the world is so worshiped, and to die upon its sacred banks and to have one's body burned and his ashes borne away into oblivion upon its tawny current is the highest aspiration of hundreds of millions of people.

The Ganges is equally sacred to the Buddhist, and Benares is associated more closely with the career of Buddha than any other city. Twenty-five hundred years ago Buddha preached his first sermon there, and for ten centuries or more it was the headquarters of Buddhism. Buddha selected it as the center of his missionary work. He secured the support of its scholars, teachers and philosophers, and from there sent forth missionaries to China, Japan, Burmah, Ceylon, the Malay Peninsula, Siam, Thibet, and other countries until half the human race accepted him as divine, his teachings as the law of God, and Benares as the fountain of that faith. It is a

A HINDU ASCETIC — BENARES

tradition that one of the wise men who followed the Star of Bethlehem to the Child that was cradled in a manger was a learned pundit from Benares, and it is certainly true that the doctors of theology who have lived and taught in the temples and monasteries there have exercised a greater influence upon a larger number of men than those of any other city that ever existed. But in these modern days Benares is wholly given over to ignorance, superstition, vice, filth and idolatry. The pure and lofty doctrines of Buddha are no longer taught. The "Well of Knowledge" is a filthy, putrid hole filled with slime and rotting vegetation. Buddhism has been swept out of India altogether, and Brahminism is taught and practiced there in its most repulsive and depraved forms.

Occasionally some reformer appears who endeavors to rebuke the depravity and appeals to the thinking members of the Brahmin sect to restore the ancient philosophy and morality of their fathers. I saw such an one at Benares. He lives in a bare and comfortless temple surrounded by a garden; is entirely dependent upon charity; every mouthful of food that he eats is brought to him by his disciples. He spends his entire time, day and night, in contemplation; he sleeps when he is exhausted; he eats when food is handed him, and if he is neglected he starves until some thoughtful person brings him a bowl of rice or curry. He wears nothing but a single shirt of cotton; he owns nothing in all the world except a brass bowl, which is used for both food and drink, and a few relics of his predecessor and teacher whom he lived with and served and whose mantle fell upon him. To those who come to his temple with serious minds and anxious to know the truth, he talks freely, and his pride is gratified by having his visitors inscribe their names in a large book which is kept for that purpose. And contributions of money are very acceptable because they enable his disciples to circulate his thoughts and discourses in printed form. I noticed that most of the names in the visitors' book were those of Americans, and it occurred to me that his contemplations must be seriously disturbed by having so many of them intrude upon him. But he assured me that he was delighted to see every stranger who called; that it gratified him to be able to explain to American travelers the true principles of Brahminism and the correct doctrines of that sect. This was the more important, he said, because nearly every foreigner formed his impressions of Brahminism by what he saw and heard among the pilgrims about the temples.

It is only by contact with the crowds of eager pilgrims and devotees which throng the streets and temples of Benares that one may realize the vital force which Brahminism exercises in India. Next to Mohammedanism it is the livest and most influential and practical of all religions. The devotee lives and breathes and feels his faith. It enters every experience of his career, it governs every act, and compared with Brahminism, Christianity is perfunctory and exercises practically little control over its believers. Yet Christianity has come here, as it has entered all the other sacred cities of India, and under the very shadow of the Hindu holy of holies, within the circle that bounds the favored gate of heaven, it has set up and maintained several of the most prosperous and well attended schools in India. The government has established a college of high standard in a handsome gothic building, which many consider the best in India. And all agree that it is an admirable institution. It has about seven hundred students and teaches modern sciences which contradict every principle that the Brahmins propose. There is also a school there for the higher education of women with about 600 students, maintained by the Maharaja of Vizianagram, a learned and progressive Hindu prince, who has large estates in the neighborhood, and there are several other distinctly modern institutions in whose light Brahminism cannot live. They are growing and it is slowly decaying. The number of devotees and pilgrims who come there is still enormous, but those who have the best means of knowing declare that it is smaller every year. But while the decrease is comparatively small, its significance is great, and so great that prominent Brahmins have recently held a conference to consider what shall be done to protect the faith and defend it against the vigorous assaults of the school teachers, the missionaries and the materialists.

It does not take Hindus long to learn that the teachings of their priests do not conform to the conditions of modern civilization, and that their practices are not approved by those who believe in modern standards of morals. It is difficult for an educated man to adhere to or accept the teachings of the Hindu priests while their practices are absolutely repugnant to him. The church, therefore, if it may be called a church, must be reformed, and its practices must be revised, if the decay which is now going on is ever arrested.

Several religions have been born and bred and have died in Benares. Vedic, Moslem, Buddhist, Brahmin have been nursed and flourished and have decayed within the same walls. It is impossible to ascertain when the Ganges was first worshiped, or when people began to build temples upon its banks, or when Benares first became sacred. Water was one of the first objects worshiped; the fertilizing and life giving influence of a stream was one of the first phenomena of nature recognized. Ganga, the beautiful heroine of a Hindu legend, is supposed to have lived at the source of the water to which her name is given, and the river is often represented as flowing from the head of Siva, the chief deity of the Brahmins, the most repulsive, the most cruel, the most vicious of all the gods.

Siva is at once the generator and the destroyer. He represents time, the sun, water, fire and practically all the mysteries of nature, and Benares is the center of his influence and worship. The temple which attracts the most pilgrims is dedicated to him. The "Well of Knowledge," which is in the courtyard of the Golden Temple, is his chosen residence, and is resorted to by every pilgrim who drinks the putrid water from a ladle with which it is dipped up by the attendant priest. All around the Golden Temple are other temples and shrines dedicated to other gods, but Siva is supreme, and before his image is the kneeling bull, the common symbol of Phallic worship as represented in the legend of Europe. Siva's hair is a bunch of snakes, serpents wind around his neck, arms, waist and legs; a crescent is stamped upon his forehead, which was the chief symbol of the ancient cult of Arabia destroyed by Mohamet Aurangzeb, one of the Mogul emperors, who was a Mohammedan fanatic. He came here in the middle of his reign, destroyed half the Hindu temples and upon the ruins of the oldest and the finest shrine of Siva erected a mosque which still stands and its slender minarets almost pierce the sky. This mosque was thrust into the most sacred place of Hindu worship as an insult to the Brahmins, but the latter are more tolerant, and though they are very largely in the majority and control everything there, they permit it to stand untouched, but the worshipers of Islam are compelled to enter it through a side door. This, however, is due more to a desire to preserve the peace and prevent collisions between fanatics and fakirs than for any other reason.

The great temple of Siva, the Golden Temple, is not imposing. It is a small building with a low dome in the center and a smaller dome at each corner, above which rises an artistic tower. These and the roof are covered with beaten gold; hence the name of the temple. None but Hindus are permitted to cross the threshold, but strangers are permitted to block up the entrance and see everything that is going on inside. It is crowded with priests, pilgrims and sacred bulls and cows. The floor is covered with filth, the air is fetid and the atmosphere all around it reeks with offensive odors, suggesting all kinds of disease. There is always a policeman to protect strangers from injury or insult, and if you give the priests a little backsheesh they will look out for you.

Benares is the seventh city in size in India. Ten years ago it was fifth, but between the years 1891 and 1901 the population was reduced 10,000 inhabitants by cholera, famine and plague, and it dropped down two pegs in the list. It is a miracle that the entire population does not perish, because, notwithstanding the cautions and efforts of the government, every sanitary law is violated by thousands of people daily. The temples and other places frequented by pilgrims are filthy hotbeds of disease, and the water they drink from the holy wells is absolutely putrid, so that the odor can be detected a considerable distance. And yet half a million devotees from every part of India come here annually, and not only drink the poisonous stuff, but bathe in the polluted river and carry back to their homes bottles of it carefully corked and labeled, which the doctors tell us is an absolutely certain method of distributing disease. While almost all the large cities of India increased in population during the the last decade, Bombay and Benares fell off, the former from plagues and famine and the latter from all kinds of contagious and other diseases.

It is a city of great wealth and has many handsome and costly palaces and mansions which have been erected there by pious Hindu princes, rajahs, merchants, bankers and others who spend a part of each year within its sacred precincts, renewing their relations with the gods just as other people go to the springs and seashore to restore their physical vitality. The residential architecture is picturesque but not artistic. The houses are frequently of fantastic designs, and are painted in gay colors and covered with carvings that are often grotesque. They have galleries around them, and broad overhanging eaves to keep out the rays of the sun, and many of them are set in the midst of attractive groves and gardens. Some of the modern buildings are very fine. There is plenty of room for the display of landscape gardening as well as architecture, but the former has been neglected. The one thing that strikes a stranger and almost bewilders him is the vivid colors. They seem unnatural and inappropriate for a sacred city, but are not more incongruous than other features.

The streets in the outer part of the city are wide, well paved and well shaded. The business portion of the town, where the natives chiefly live, is a wilderness of narrow streets hemmed in with shops, factories, dwelling houses, temples, shrines, restaurants, cafes and boarding houses for pilgrims. Every shop is open to the street, and the shelves are bright with brass, silver and copper vessels and gaily painted images of the gods which are purchased by the pilgrims and other visitors. Benares is famous all over the world for its brass work and its silks. Half the shops in town are devoted to the sale of brass vessels of various kinds, chiefly bowls of many forms and styles which are required by the pilgrims in performing their religious duties. In addition to these there are a hundred different varieties of domestic and sacred utensils, many of them beautifully chased and engraved, and they are sold to natives at prices that seem absurd, but foreigners are expected to pay much more. Indeed, every purchase is a matter of prolonged negotiation. The merchant fixes his price very high and then lowers it gradually as he thinks discreet, according to the behavior of his customer.

Handmade silks from looms in the cottages of the peasants can still be purchased in Benares and they wear forever. Some are coarse, and some are fine, but they are all peculiar to this place and cannot be purchased elsewhere because the product is limited and merchants cannot buy them in sufficient quantity to make a profitable trade. The heavier qualities of silk are used chiefly for men's clothing. They wash like linen, they never wear out and are cool and comfortable. The brocades of Benares are equally famous, and are used chiefly for the ceremonial dresses of the rich and fashionable. Sometimes they are woven of threads of pure gold and weigh as much as an armor. These are of course very expensive, and are usually sold by weight. Very little account is taken of the labor expended upon them, although the designs and the workmanship are exquisite, because the weavers and embroiderers are paid only a few cents a day. Beside these heavy fabrics are costly tissues as fine as spiders' webs, also woven of silver and gold and silk and linen. They are used by the women as head dresses and scarfs and rich men use them for turbans. Sometimes an Indian noble will have seventy or eighty yards of this delicate gossamer wound about his head and the ends, beautifully embroidered, with long fringes of gold, hang gracefully down upon the shoulders.

It is almost impossible to go through the narrow streets of Benares in the middle of the day, because they are so crowded with men, women, children, priests, pilgrims, peddlers, beggars, mangy dogs, sacred cows, fat and lazy bulls dedicated to Siva, and other animate and inanimate obstructions. It seems to be the custom for people to live and work in the streets. A family dining will occupy half the roadway as they squat around their brass bowls and jars and cram the rice and millet and curry into their mouths with their fingers. The lower classes of Hindus never use tables, knives or forks. The entire family eats out of the same dish, while the dogs hang around waiting for morsels and a sacred cow is apt to poke its nose into the circle at any time. The street is often blocked up by a carpenter who is mending a cabinet or putting a new board into a floor.

A little farther along a barber may be engaged in shaving the face and head of some customer. Both of them are squatting face to face, as often in the middle of the road as elsewhere, and with bowls, razors, soap, bottles and other appurtenances of the trade spread out between them. Barbers rank next to priests in the religious aristocracy, and, as it is forbidden by the Brahmins for a man to shave himself, they are of much importance in the villages. Houses are usually set apart for them to live in just as we furnish parsonages for our ministers. The village barber has certain rights and exemptions that are not enjoyed by other people. He is not required to do military service in the native states; he does not have to pay taxes, and all members of his caste have a monopoly of their business, which the courts have sustained. The Brahmins also require that a man must be shaved fasting.

Another matter of great importance which the barbers have to do with is a little tuft of hair that is allowed to grow from the top of the head of a child when all the rest of the scalp is shaven. This is a commendable precaution, and is almost universally taken in the interest of children, the scalp lock being necessary to snatch the child away from the devil and other evil spirits when it is in danger from those sources. As the person grows older and capable of looking after himself this precaution is not so important, although many people wear the scalp lock or sacred topknot through life.

The sacred thread is even of greater importance in Hinduism, and the Brahmins require that each child shall be invested with it in his eighth year. Until that year also he must bear upon his forehead the sign of his caste, which Ryas, our bearer, calls "the god mark." The sacred thread is a fine silk cord, fastened over the left shoulder, hanging down under the right arm like a sash. None but the two highest castes have the right to wear it, although members of the lower castes are even more careful to do so. It is put on a child by the priest or the parent on its eighth birthday with ceremonies similar and corresponding to those of our baptism. After the child has been bathed and its head has been carefully shaved it is dressed in new garments, the richest that the family can afford. The priest or godfather ties on the sacred thread and teaches the child a brief Sanskrit text called a mantra, some maxim or proverb, or perhaps it may be only the name of a deity which is to be kept a profound secret and repeated 108 times daily throughout life. The deity selected serves the child through life as a patron saint and protector. Frequently the village barber acts in the place of a priest and puts on the sacred thread. A similar thread placed around the neck of a child, and often around its waist by the midwife immediately after birth, is intended as an amulet or charm to protect from disease and danger. It is usually a strand of silk which has been blessed by some holy man or sanctified by being placed around the neck of an idol of recognized sanctity.

The streets of the native quarters of Indian cities are filled with naked babies and children. It is unfashionable for the members of either sex to wear clothing until they are 8 or 10 years old. The only garment they wear is the sacred string, with usually a little silver charm or amulet suspended from it. Sometimes children wear bracelets and anklets of silver, which tinkle as they run about the streets. The little rascals are always fat and chubby, and their bright black eyes give them an appearance of unnatural intelligence. The children are never shielded from the sun, although its rays are supposed to be fatal to full grown and mature persons. Their heads being shaved, the brain is deprived of its natural protection, and they never wear hats or anything else, and play all day long under the fierce heat in the middle of the road without appearing any the worse for it, although

A HINDU BARBER

foreign doctors insist that this exposure is one of the chief causes of the enormous infant mortality in India. This may be true, because a few days after birth babies are strapped upon the back of some younger child or are carried about the streets astride the hips of their mothers, brothers or sisters without any protection from the sun.

All outdoors is an Indian barber-shop. The barbers have no regular places of business, but wander from house to house seeking and serving customers, or squat down on the roadside and intercept them as they pass. In the large cities you can see dozens of them squatting along the streets performing their sacred offices, shaving the heads and oiling the bodies of customers. Cocoanut oil is chiefly used and is supposed to add strength and suppleness to the body. It is administered with massage, thoroughly rubbed in and certainly cannot injure anybody. In the principal parks of Indian cities, at almost any time in the morning, you can see a dozen or twenty men being oiled and rubbed down by barbers or by friends, and a great deal of oil is used in the hair. After a man is grown he allows his hair to grow long and wears it in a knot at the back of his head. Some Hindus have an abundance of hair, of which they are very proud, and upon which they spend considerable care and labor.

The parks are not only used for dressing-rooms, but for bedrooms also. Thousands of people sleep in the open air day and night, stretched full length upon the ground. They wrap their robes around their heads and leave their legs and feet uncovered. This is the custom of the Indians of the Andes. No matter how cold or how hot it may be they invariably wrap the head and face up carefully before sleeping and leave the lower limbs exposed. A Hindu does not care where he sleeps. Night and day are the same to him. He will lie down on the sidewalk in the blazing sunshine anywhere, pull his robe up over his head and sleep the sleep of the just. You can seldom walk a block without seeing one of these human bundles all wrapped up in white cotton lying on the bare stone or earth in the most casual way, but they are very seldom disturbed.

You have to get up early in the morning to see the most interesting sights in Benares, which are the pilgrims engaged in washing their sins away in the sacred but filthy waters of the Ganges, and the outdoor cremation of the bodies of people who have died during the night and late in the afternoon of the preceding day. Hindus allow very little time between death and cremation. As soon as the heart ceases to beat the undertakers, as we would call the men who attend to these arrangements, are sent for and preparation for the funeral pyre is commenced immediately. Three or four hours only are necessary, and if death occurs later than 1 or 2 o'clock in the afternoon the ceremony must be postponed until morning. Hence all of the burning ghats along the river bank are busy from daylight until mid-day disposing of the bodies of those who have died during the previous eighteen or twenty hours.

The death rate in Benares is very high. Under ordinary circumstances it is higher than that of other cities of India because of its crowded and unsanitary condition, and because all forms of contagious diseases are brought by pilgrims who come here themselves to die. As I have already told you, it is the highest and holiest aspiration of a pious Hindu to end his days within an area encircled by what is known as the Panch-Kos Road, which is fifty miles in length and bounds the City of Benares. It starts at one end of the city at the river banks, and the other terminus is on the river at the other end. It describes a parabola. As the city is strung along the bank of the river several miles, it is nowhere distant from the river more than six or seven miles. All who die within this boundary, be they Hindu or Christian, Mohammedan or Buddhist, pagan, agnostic or infidel, or of any other faith or no faith, be they murderers, thieves, liars or violators of law, and every caste, whatever their race, nationality or previous condition, no matter whether they are saints or sinners, they cannot escape admission to Siva's heaven. This is the greatest possible inducement for people to hurry there as death approaches, and consequently the non-resident death rate is abnormally high.

We started out immediately after daylight and drove from the hotel to the river bank, where, at a landing place, were several boats awaiting other travelers as well as ourselves. They were ordinary Hindu sampans —rowboats with houses or cabins built upon them—and upon the decks of our cabin comfortable chairs were placed for our party. As soon as we were aboard the boatmen shoved off and we floated slowly down the stream, keeping as close to the shore as possible without jamming into the rickety piers of bamboo that stretched out into the water for the use of bathing pilgrims.

The bank of the river is one of the most picturesque and imposing panoramas you can imagine. It rises from the water at a steep grade, and is covered with a series of terraces upon which have been erected towers, temples, mosques, palaces, shrines, platforms and pavilions, bathing-houses, hospices for pilgrims, khans or lodging-houses, hospitals and other structures for the accommodation of the millions of people who come there from every part of India on religious pilgrimages and other missions. These structures represent an infinite variety of architecture, from the most severe simplicity to the fantastic and grotesque. They are surmounted by domes, pinnacles, minarets, spires, towers, cupolas and canopies; they are built of stone, marble, brick and wood; they are painted in every variety of color, sober and gay; the balconies and windows of many of them are decorated with banners, bunting in all shapes and colors, festoons of cotton and silk, garlands of flowers and various expressions of the taste and enthusiasm of the occupants or owners.

From the Sparrow Hills at Moscow one who has sufficient patience can count 555 gilded and painted domes; from the cupola of St. Peter's one may look down upon the roofs of palaces, cathedrals, columns, obelisks, arches and ruins such as can be seen in no other place; around the fire tower at Pera are spread the marvelous glories of Stamboul, the Golden Horn and other parts of Constantinople; from the citadel at Cairo you can have a bird's-eye view of one of the most typical cities of the East; from the Eiffel Tower all Paris and its suburbs may be surveyed, and there are many other striking panoramas of artificial scenery, but nothing on God's footstool resembles the picture of the holy Hindu city that may be seen from the deck of a boat on the Ganges. It has often been described in detail, but it is always new and always different, and it fascinates its witnesses. There is a repulsiveness about it which few people can overcome, but it is unique, and second only to the Taj Mahal of all the sights in India.

A bathing ghat is a pavilion, pier or platform of stone covered with awnings and roofs to protect the pilgrims from the sun. It reaches into the river, where the water is about two feet deep, and stone steps lead down to the bottom of the stream. Stretching out from these ghats, in order to accommodate a larger number of people, are wooden platforms, piers of slender bamboo, floats and all kinds of contrivances, secure and insecure, temporary and permanent, which every morning are thronged with pilgrims from every part of India in every variety of costumes, crowding in and out of the water, carrying down the sick and dying, all to seek salvation for the soul, relief for the mind and healing for the body which the Holy Mother Ganges is supposed to give.

The processions of pilgrims seem endless and are attended by many pitiful sights. Aged women, crippled men, lean and haggard invalids with just strength enough to reach the water's edge; poor, shivering, starving wretches who have spent their last farthing to reach this place, exhausted with fatigue, perishing from hunger or disease, struggle to reach the water before their breath shall fail. Here and there in the crowd appear all forms of affliction—hideous lepers and other victims of cancerous and ulcerous diseases, with the noses, lips, fingers and feet eaten away; paralytics in all stages of the disease, people whose limbs are twisted with rheumatism, men and women covered with all kinds of sores, fanatical ascetics with their hair matted with mud and their bodies smeared with ashes, ragged tramps, blind and deformed beggars, women leading children or carrying infants in their arms, handsome rajahs, important officials attended by their servants and chaplains, richly dressed women with their faces closely veiled, dignified and thoughtful Brahmins followed by their disciples, farmers, laborers bearing the signs of toil, and other classes of human society in every stage of poverty or prosperity. They crowd past each other up and down the banks, bathing in the water, drying themselves upon the piers or floats, filling bottles and brass jars from the sacred stream, kneeling to pray, listening to the preachers and absorbed with the single thought upon which their faith is based.

Such exhibitions of faith can be witnessed nowhere else. It is a daily repetition of the scene described in the New Testament when the afflicted thronged the healing pools.

After dipping themselves in the water again and again, combing their hair and drying it, removing their drenched robes—all in the open air—and putting on holiday garments, the pilgrims crowd around the priests who sit at the different shrines, and secure from them certificates showing that they have performed their duty to the gods. The Brahmins give each a text or a name of a god to remember and repeat daily during the rest of his or her life, and they pass on to the notaries who seal and stamp the bottles of sacred water, sell idols, amulets, maps of heaven, charts showing the true way of salvation, certificates of purification, remedies for various diseases, and charms to protect cattle and to make crops grow. Then they pass on to other Brahmins, who paint the sign of their god upon their forehead, the frontal mark which every pilgrim wears. Afterward they visit one temple after another until they complete the pilgrimage at the Golden Temple of Siva, where they make offerings of money, scatter barley upon the ground and drop handfuls of rice and grain into big stone receptacles from which the beggars who hang around the temples receive a daily allowance. Finally they go to the priests of the witness-bearing god, Ganasha, where the pilgrimage is attested and recorded. Then they buy a few more idols, images

BODIES READY FOR BURNING BENARES

of their favorite gods, and return to their homes with a tale that will be told around the fireside in some remote village during the rest of their lives.

But the most weird and impressive spectacle at Benares, and one which will never be forgotten, is the burning of the bodies of the dead. At intervals, between the temples along the river bank, are level places belonging to the several castes and leased to associations or individuals who have huge piles of wood in the background and attend to the business in a heartless, mercenary way. The cost of burning a body depends upon the amount and kind of fuel used. The lowest possible rate is three rupees or about one dollar in our money. When the family cannot afford that they simply throw the body into the sacred stream and let it float down until the fish devour it. When a person dies the manager of the burning ghat is notified. He sends to the house his assistants or employes, who bring the body down to the river bank, sometimes attended by members of the family, sometimes without witnesses. It is not inclosed in a coffin, but lies upon a bamboo litter, and under ordinary circumstances is covered with a sheet, but when the family is rich it is wrapped in the richest of silks and embroideries, and the coverlet is an expensive Cashmere shawl.

Arriving at the river an oblong pile of wood is built up and the body is placed upon it. If the family is poor the pile is low, short and narrow, and the limbs of the corpse have to be bent so that they will not extend over the edges, as they often do. When the body arrives it is taken down into the water and laid in a shallow place, where it can soak until the pyre is prepared. Usually the undertakers or friends remove the coverings from the face and splash it liberally from the sacred stream. When the pyre is ready they lift the body from the litter, adjust it carefully, pile on wood until it is entirely concealed, then thrust a few kindlings underneath and start the blaze. When the cremation is complete the charred sticks are picked up by the beggars and other poor people who are always hanging around and claim this waste as their perquisite. The ashes are then gathered up and thrown upon the stream and the current of the Ganges carries them away.

Certain contractors have the right to search the ground upon which the burning has taken place and the shallow river bed for valuables that escaped the flames. It is customary to adorn the dead with the favorite ornaments they wore when alive, and while the gold will melt and diamonds may turn to carbon, jewels often escape combustion, and these contractors are believed to do a good business.

All this burning takes place in public in the open air, and sometimes fifty, sixty or a hundred fires are blazing at the same moment. You can sit upon the deck of your boat with your kodak in your hand, take it all in and preserve the grewsome scene for future reminiscencing.

While the faith of many make them whole, while remarkable cures are occurring at Benares daily, while the sick and the afflicted have assured relief from every ill and trouble, mental, moral and physical, if they can only reach the water's edge, nevertheless scattered about among the temples, squatting behind pieces of bamboo matting or lacquered trays upon which rows of bottles stand, are native doctors who sell all sorts of nostrums and cure-alls that can possibly be needed by the human family, and each dose is accompanied by a guarantee that it will surely cure. These fellows are ignorant impostors and the municipal authorities are careful to see that their drugs are harmless, while they make no attempt to prevent them from swindling the people. It seems to be a profitable trade, notwithstanding the popular faith in the miraculous powers of the river.

Another class of prosperous humbugs is the fortune-tellers, who are found around every temple and in every public place, ready to forecast the fate of every enterprise that may be disclosed to them; ready to predict good fortune and evil fortune, and sometimes they display remarkable penetration and predict events with startling accuracy.

Benares is as sacred to the Buddhists as it is to the Brahmins, for it was here that Gautama, afterward called Buddha (a title which means "The Enlightened"), lived in the sixth century before Christ, and from here he sent out his missionaries to convert the world. Gautama was a prince of the Sakya tribe, and of the Rajput caste. He was born 620 B. C. and lived in great wealth and luxury. Driving in his pleasure grounds one day he met a man crippled with age; then a second man smitten with an incurable disease; then a corpse, and finally a fakir or ascetic, walking in a calm, dignified, serene manner. These spectacles set him thinking, and after long reflection he decided to surrender his wealth, to relinquish his happiness, and devote himself to the reformation of his people. He left his home, his wife, a child that had just been born to him, cut off his long hair, shaved his head, clothed himself with rags, and taking nothing with him but a brass bowl from which he could eat his food, and a cup from which he could drink, he became a pilgrim, an inquirer after Truth and Light. Having discovered that he could drink from the hollow of his hand, he gave away his cup and kept nothing but his bowl. That is the reason why every pilgrim and every fakir, every monk and priest in India carries a brass bowl, for although Buddhism is practically extinct in that country, the teachings and the example of Gautama had a perpetual influence over the Hindus.

After what is called the Great Renunciation, Gautama spent six years mortifying the body and gradually reduced his food to one grain of rice a day. But this brought him neither light nor peace of mind. He thereupon abandoned further penance and devoted six years to meditation, sitting under the now famous bo-tree, near the modern town of Gaya. In the year 588 B. C. he obtained Complete Enlightenment, and devoted the rest of his life to the instruction of his disciples. He taught that all suffering is caused by indulging the desires; that the only hope of relief lies in the suppression of desire, and impressed his principles upon more millions of believers than those of any other religion. It is the boast of the Buddhists that no life was ever sacrificed; that no blood was ever shed; that no suffering was ever caused by the propagation of that faith and the conversion of the world.

After he became "enlightened," Gautama assumed the name of Buddha and went to Benares, where he taught and preached, and had a monastery at the town called Sarnath, now extinct, in the suburbs. There, surrounded by heaps of ruins and rubbish, stand two great topes or towers, the larger of which marks the spot where Buddha preached his first sermon. It is supposed to have been built in the sixth century of the Chinese era, for Hiouen Thsang, a Chinese traveler who visited Sarnath in the seventh century, describes the tower and monastery which was situated near it. It is one of the most interesting as it is one of the most ancient monuments in India, but we do not quite understand the purpose for which it was erected. It is 110 feet high, 93 feet in diameter, and built of solid masonry with the exception of a small chamber in the center and a narrow shaft or chimney running up to the top. The lower half is composed of immense blocks of stone clamped together with iron, and at intervals the monument was encircled by bands of sculptured relief fifteen feet wide. The upper part was of brick, which is now in an advanced state of decay and covered with a heavy crop of grass and bushes. A large tree grows from the top.

There used to be an enormous monastery in the neighborhood, of which the ruins remain. The cells and chapels were arranged around a square court similar to the cloisters of modern monasteries. A half mile distant is another tower and the ruins of other monasteries, and every inch of earth in that part of the city is associated with the life and labor of the great apostle of peace and love, whose theology of sweetness and light and gentleness was in startling contrast with the atrocious doctrines taught by the Brahmins and the hideous rites practiced at the shrines of the Hindu gods. But these towers are not the oldest relics of Buddha. At Gaya, where he received the "enlightenment," the actual birthplace of Buddhism, is a temple built in the year 500 A. D., and it stands upon the site of one that was 700 or 800 years older.

Benares is distinctly the city of Siva, but several thousand other gods are worshiped there, including his several wives. Uma is his first wife, and she is the exact counterpart of her husband; Sati is his most devoted wife; Karali is his most horrible wife; Devi, another of his wives, is the goddess of death; Kali is the goddess of misfortune, and there are half a dozen other ladies of his household whose business seems to be to terrorize and distress their worshipers. But that is the ruling feature of the Hindu religion. There is no sweetness or light in its theology—it exists to make people unhappy and wretched, and to bring misery, suffering and crime into the world.

The Hindus fear their gods, but do not love them, with perhaps the exception of Vishnu, the second person in the Hindu trinity, while Brahma is the third. These three are the supreme deities in the pantheon, but Brahma is more of an abstract proposition than an actual god. For purposes of worship the Hindus may be divided into two classes—the followers of Siva and the followers of Vishnu. They can be distinguished by the "god marks" or painted signs upon their foreheads. Those who wear red are the adherents of Siva, and the followers of Vishnu wear white. Subordinate to these two great divinities are millions of other gods, and it would take a volume to describe their various functions and attributes.

Vishnu is a much more agreeable god than Siva, the destroyer; he has some human feeling, and his various incarnations are friendly heroes, who do kind acts and treat their worshipers tolerably well.

The "Well of Healing," one of the holiest places in Benares, is dedicated to Vishnu. He dug it himself, making a cavity in the rock. Then, in the absence of water, he filled it with perspiration from his own body. This remarkable assertion seems to be confirmed by the foul odor that arises from the water, which is three feet deep and about the consistency of soup. It looks and smells as if it might have been a sample brought from the Chicago River before the drainage canal was finished. It is fed by an invisible spring, and there is no overflow, because, after bathing in it to wash away their sins, the pilgrims drink several cups of the filthy liquid, which often nauseates them, and it is a miracle that any of them survive.

One of the most curious and picturesque of all the temples is that of the goddess Durga, a fine building usually called the Monkey Temple because of the number of those animals inhabiting the trees around it. They are very tame and cunning and can spot a tourist as far as they can see him. When they see a party of strangers approaching the temple they begin to chatter in the trees and then rush for the courtyard of the temple, where they expect to be fed. It is one of the perquisites of the priests to sell rice and other food for them at prices about ten times more than it is worth, but the tourist has the fun of tossing it to them and making them scramble for it. As Durga is the most terrific of all of Siva's wives, and delights in death, torture, bloodshed and every form of destruction, the Hindus are very much afraid of her and the peace offerings left at this temple are more liberal than at the others, a fact very much appreciated by the priests.

Another of the most notable gods worshiped at Benares is Ganesa, the first born of Siva and one of his horrible wives. He is the God of Prudence and Policy, has the head of an elephant, which is evidence of sagacity, and is attended by rats, an evidence of wisdom and foresight. He has eight hands, and from the number of appeals that are made to him he must keep them all busy. He is invoked by Hindus of all sects and castes before undertaking any business of importance. It is asserted that none of the million deities is so often addressed as the God of Wisdom and Prudence. If a man is undertaking any great enterprise, if he is starting in a new business, or signing a contract, or entering a partnership; if he is about to take a journey or buy a stock of goods or engage in a negotiation, he appeals to Ganesa to assist him, and leaves an offering at one of his temples as a sort of bribe. If a woman is going to make a dress, or a servant changes his employer, or if anyone begins any new thing, it is always safer to appeal in advance to Ganesa, because he is a sensitive god, and if he does not receive all the attention and worship he deserves is apt to be spiteful. Some people are so particular that they never begin a letter without saluting him in the first line.

Driving along the roads of this part of India one often sees stones piled up against the trunk of a tree and at the top a rude elephant's head, decorated with flowers or stained with oil or red paint, and there will always be a little heap of gravel before it. That elephant's head represents the god Ganesa, and each stone represents an offering by some one who has passed by, usually the poorest, who have not been able to visit the temple, and, having nothing else to offer, not even a flower, drop a stone before the rude shrine.

There are many sacred cows in Benares. You find them in temples and wandering around the streets. Some of them are horribly diseased and they are all lazy, fat and filthy. They have perfect freedom. They are allowed to wander about and do as they please. They feed from baskets of vegetables and salad that stand before the groceries and in the markets, and sometimes consume the entire stock of some poor huckster, who dare not drive them away or even rebuke them. If he should attempt to do so the gods would visit him with perpetual misfortunes. Children play around the beasts, but no one ever abuses them. Pilgrims buy food for them and stuff them with sweetmeats, and it is an act of piety and merit to hang garlands over their horns and braid ribbons in their tails. When they die they are buried with great ceremony, like the sacred bulls of Egypt.

Benares is the principal center of the idol trade, and a large part of the population are engaged in making images of the various gods in gold, silver, brass, copper, wood, stone, clay and other materials. Most of the work is done in the households. There are several small factories, but none employs more than ten or a dozen men, and the streets are lined with little shops, no bigger than an ordinary linen closet in an American house. Each opens entirely upon the street, there are no doors or windows, and when the proprietor wants to close he puts up heavy wooden shutters that fit into grooves in the threshold and the beam that sustains the roof. The shelves that hang from the three walls are covered with all kinds of images in all sizes and of all materials, and between sales the proprietor squats on the floor in the middle of his little establishment making more. The largest number are made of brass and clay. They are shaped in rude molds and afterward finished with the file and chisel. The large idols found in the temples are often works of art, but many of them and some of the most highly revered are of the rudest workmanship.

There is a funny story that has been floating about for many years that most of the idols worshiped in heathen lands are made in Christian countries and shipped over by the car load. This is certainly not true so far as India is concerned. There is no evidence upon the records of the custom-house to show that any idols are imported and it would be impossible for any manufacturer in the United States or Europe to compete with the native artisans of Benares or other cities.

XXVIII

AMERICAN MISSIONS IN INDIA

About 5,000 missionaries of various religions and cults are working among the people of India; two-thirds of them Protestants, and about 1,500 Americans, including preachers, teachers, doctors, nurses, editors and all concerned. Their names fill a large directory, and they represent all grades and shades of theology, philosophy, morality and other methods of making human beings better, and providing for the salvation of their souls. India is a fertile and favorite field for such work. The languid atmosphere of the country and the contemplative disposition of the native encourage it. The Aryan always was a good listener, and you must remember that India is a very big country—a continent, indeed, with a mixed multitude of 300,000,000 souls, some striving for the unattainable and others hopelessly submerged in bogs of vice, superstition and ignorance. There are several stages of civilization also. You can find entire tribes who still employ stone implements and weapons, and several provinces are governed by a feudal system like that of Europe in the middle ages. There are thousands who believe that marriage is forbidden by the laws of nature; there are millions of men with several wives, and many women with more than one husband. There are tribes in which women control all the power, hold all the offices, own all the property and keep the line of inheritance on their side. There are vast multitudes, on the other hand, in India who believe that women have no souls and no hereafter, and advocate the murder of girl babies as fast as they are born, saving just enough to do the cooking and mending and to keep the race alive. Communities that have reached an intellectual culture above that of any nation in Europe are surrounded by 250,000,000 human beings who cannot read or write. There are thinkers who have reasoned out the profoundest problems that have ever perplexed mankind, and framed systems of philosophy as wise as the world has ever known, and many of their wives and daughters have never been outside of the houses in which they were born; all of which indicates the size of the field of missionary labor and the variety of work to be done.

India contains some of the most sublime and beautiful of all the non-Christian religions, and perfect systems of morals devised by men who do not believe in a future life. More than 60,000,000 of the inhabitants accept Jesus Christ as an inspired teacher and worship the same God that we do under another name, and more than three times that number believe that the Ruler of All Things is a demon who delights in cruelty and slaughter and gives his favor only in exchange for suffering and torture. A tribe in northwest India believes that God lives on the top of a mountain in plain sight of them, and up in the northeast are the Nagas, who declare that after the Creator made men He put them into a cellar from which they escaped into the world because one day he forgot to put back the stone that covers a hole in the top. More fantastic theories about the origin and the destiny of man are to be found in India than in any other country, and those who have faith in them speak 167 different languages, as returned by the census. Some of these languages are spoken by millions of people; others by a few thousand only; some of them have a literature of poetry and philosophy that has survived the ages, while others are unwritten and only used for communication by wild and isolated tribes in the mountains or the jungles.

Christian missionaries have been at work in India for four hundred years. St. Francis Xavier was one of the pioneers. Protestants have been there for a little more than a century, and since 1804 have distributed 13,000,000 of Bibles. During the last ten years they have sold 5,000,000 copies of the Scriptures either complete or in part; for the Gospels in each of the great Indian languages, like two sparrows, can now be bought for a farthing. In 1898, 497,000 copies were issued; in 1902, more than 600,000; and thus the work increases. More than 140 colporteurs, or agents, mostly natives, are peddling the Bible for sale in different parts of India. They do nothing else. More than 400 native women are engaged in placing it in the secluded homes of the Hindus among women of the harems, and teaching them to read it. No commercial business is conducted with greater energy, eterprise and ability than the work of the Bible Society, in this empire, and while the missionaries have enormous and perplexing difficulties to overcome, they, too, are making remarkable headway.

You frequently hear thoughtless people, who know nothing of the facts, but consider it fashionable to sneer at the missionaries, declare that Hindus never are converted. The official census of the government of India, which is based upon inquiries made directly of the individuals themselves, by sworn agents, and is not compiled from the reports of the missionary societies, shows an increase in the number of professing Christians from 2,036,000 in 1891 to 2,664,000 in 1901, a gain of 625,000, or 30 per cent in ten years, and in some of the provinces it has been remarkable. In the Central Provinces and United Provinces the increase in the number of persons professing Christianity, according to the census, was more than 300 per cent. In Assam, which is in the northeastern extremity of India, and the Punjab, which occupies a similar position in the northwest, the increase was nearly 200 per cent. In Bengal, of which Calcutta is the chief city, the gain was nearly 50 per cent; in the province of Bombay it was nearly 40 per cent, and in Madras and Burmah it was 20 per cent.

The dean of the American missionary colony is Rev. R. A. Hume, of Ahmednagar, who belongs to the third, and his daughter to the fourth, generation of missionaries in the family. He was born in Bombay, where his father and his grandfather preached and taught for many years. Rev. Mr. Ballantine, the grandfather of Mrs. Hume, went over from southern Indiana in 1835 and settled at Ahmednagar, where the Protestants had begun work four years previous.

The first Christian mission ever undertaken by Americans in a foreign country was at Bombay in 1813, when Gordon Hall and Samuel Newall, fresh from Williams College, went to convert the heathen Hindus. The governor general and the officials of the East India Company ordered them away, for fear that they would stir up trouble among the natives and suffer martyrdom, but they would not go, and were finally allowed to remain under protest. A Baptist society in England had sent out three men—Messrs. Carey, Ward and Marshman—a few years before. They went to Calcutta, but the East India

Company would not permit them to preach or teach, so they removed to Gerampore, where they undertook evangelical work under the protection of the Dutch. But nowadays the British government cannot do enough to help the missionaries, particularly the Americans, who are treated in the same generous manner as those of the Established Church of England, and are given grants of money, land and every assistance that they officially could receive.

Speaking of the services of the missionaries during the recent famine, Lord Curzon said: "I have seen cases where the entire organization of a vast area and the lives of thousands of beings rested upon the shoulders of a single individual, laboring on in silence and in solitude, while his bodily strength was fast ebbing away. I have known of natives who, inspired by his example, have thrown themselves with equal ardor into the struggle, and have unmurmuringly laid down their lives for their countrymen. Particularly must I mention the noble efforts of missionary agencies of various Christian denominations. If there ever was an occasion in which it was open to them to vindicate the highest standards of their beneficent calling it was here, and strenuously and faithfully have they performed the task."

In 1901 the government of India recognized the labors and devotion of the American missionaries during the previous famine by bestowing upon Dr. Hume the Kaiser-I-Hind gold medal, which is never bestowed except for distinguished public services, and is not conferred every year. It is considered the highest honor that can be bestowed upon a civilian.

Sir Muncherjee Bharnajgree, a Parsee member of parliament, recently asserted that the American missionaries were doing more for the industrial development of the Indian Empire than the government itself. The government recognizes the importance of their work and has given liberal grants to the industrial schools of the American Board of Foreign Missions, which are considered the most successful and perhaps the most useful in India. It is significant to find that the most important of these schools was founded by Sir D. M. Petit, a wealthy Parsee merchant and manufacturer, at the city of Ahmednagar, where 400 bright boys are being trained for mechanics and artisans under the direction of James Smith, formerly of Toronto and Chicago. D. C. Churchill, formerly of Oberlin, Ohio, and a graduate of the Boston School of Technology, a mechanical engineer of remarkable genius, has another school in which hand weaving of fine fabrics is taught to forty or fifty boys who show remarkable skill. Mr. Churchill, who came out in 1901, soon detected the weakness of the native method of weaving, and has recently invented a hand loom which can turn out thirty yards of cloth a day, and will double, and in many cases treble, the productive capacity of the average worker. And he expects soon to erect a large building in which he can set up the new looms and accommodate a much larger number of pupils. J. B. Knight, a scientific agriculturist who also came out in 1901, has a class of forty boys, mostly orphans whose fathers and mothers died during the late famine. They are being trained in agricultural chemistry and kindred subjects in order to instruct the native farmers throughout that part of the country. Rev. R. Windsor, of Oberlin, is running another school founded by Sir D. M. Petit at Sirur, 125 miles east of Bombay, where forty boys are being educated as machinists and mechanics. At Ahmednagar,

Mrs. Wagentreiver has a school of 125 women and girls, mostly widows and orphans of the late famine, who are being taught the art of lacemaking, and most of her graduates are qualified to serve as instructors in other lace schools which are constantly being established in other parts of India. There is also a school for potters, and the Americans are sending to the School of Art at Bombay sixty boys to be designers, draughtsmen, illustrators and qualified in other of the industrial arts.

It is interesting to discover that the School of Industrial Arts founded by Sir D. M. Petit at Ahmednagar owes its origin to the Chicago Manual Training School, whose aims and methods were carefully studied and applied to Indian conditions with equally satisfactory results. The principal and founder of the school, James Smith, was sent out and is supported by the New England Congregational Church on the North Side, Chicago, and generous financial assistance has been received from Mr. Victor F. Lawson and other members of that church. It was started in 1891 with classes in woodwork and mechanical drawing, and has prospered until it has now outgrown in numbers and importance the high school with which it was originally connected.

This school is the most conspicuous example of combined English education and industry in western India, and has received the highest praise from government officers. Its grant from the government, too, is higher than that of any other school in the province. The government paid half of the cost of all the buildings and equipments, while a very large part of the other half was paid by people of this country, foremost among the donors being the late Sir D. M. Petit, Bart., who built and equipped the first building entirely at his own expense.

Mr. Churchill's workshops have also been very highly commended by the government inspectors, and his invention has attracted wide notice because it has placed within reach of the local weavers an apparatus which is an immense saving in labor and will secure its operators at least three times the results and compensations for the same expenditure of time and toil. It thus affords them means of earning a more comfortable living, and at the same time gives the people a supply of cheap cotton cloth which they require, and utilizes defective yarn which the steam power mills cannot use. The government inspectors publicly commend Mr. Churchill for declining to patent his invention and for leaving it free to be used by everybody without royalty of any kind.

It is exceedingly gratifying to hear from all sides these and other similar encomiums of the American missionaries, and it makes a Yankee proud to see the respect that is felt for and paid to them. Lord Curzon, the governors of the various provinces and other officials are hearty in their commendation of American men and women and American methods, and especially for the services our missionaries rendered during the recent famines and plagues. They testify that in all popular discontent and uprisings they have exerted a powerful influence for peace and order and for the support of the government. Lord Northcote, recently governor of Bombay, in a letter to President Roosevelt, said:

"In Ahmednagar I have seen for myself what practical results have been accomplished, and during the famine we owed much to the practical schemes of benevolence of the American missionaries."

On the first of January, 1904, the viceroy of India bestowed upon William I. Chamberlin of the American

Mission College at Madras the Kaiser-I-Hind gold medal for his services to the public. A similar medal was conferred upon Dr. Louis Klopsch of the Christian Herald, New York, who collected and forwarded $600,000 for direct famine relief and provided for the support of 5,000 famine orphans for five years. Other large sums were sent from the United States. The money was not given away. The American committee worked in co-operation with the agents of the government and other relief organizations, so as to avoid duplication. They provided clothing for the naked and work at reasonable wages for the starving. They bought seed for farmers and assisted them to hire help to put it in the ground. The rule of the committee in the disbursement of this money was not to pauperize the people, but to help those who helped themselves, and to require a return in some form for every penny that was given. Dr. Hume says: "The gift was charity, but the system was business." The American relief money directly and indirectly reached several millions of people and has provided for the maintenance and education of more than five thousand orphans, boys and girls, who were left homeless and helpless when their fathers and mothers died of starvation. More than 320 widows, entirely homeless, friendless and dependent, were placed in comfortable quarters, taught how to work, and are now self-supporting. Two homes for widows are maintained by the missionaries of the American Board, one in Bombay in charge of Miss Abbott and her sister, Mrs. Dean, with nearly 200 inmates, and the other at Ahmednagar, in charge of Mrs. Hume.

The medical and dispensary work of the American missions is also very extensive, and its importance to the peasant class and the blessings it confers upon the poor cannot be realized by those people who have never visited India and other countries of the East and seen the condition of women. As I told you in a previous chapter, ninety per cent of the Hindu population of India will not admit men physicians to their homes to see women patients, and the only relief that the wives, mothers and daughters and sisters in the zenanas can obtain when they are ill is from the old-fashioned herb doctors and charm mixers of the bazaars. Now American women physicians are scattered all over India healing the wounded and curing the sick. There are few from other countries, although the English, Scotch and German Lutherans have many missions.

XXIX

COTTON, TEA, AND OPIUM

Next to the United States, India is the largest cotton-producing country in the world, and, with the exception of Galveston and New Orleans, Bombay claims to be the largest cotton market. The shipments have never reached $50,000,000 a year, but have gone very near that point. Every large state in southern India produces cotton, but Bombay and Berar are the principal producers. The area for the whole of India in 1902-3 was 14,232,000 acres, but this has been often exceeded. In 1893-4 the area planted was nearly 15,500,000. The average is about 14,000,000 acres. Cotton is usually grown in conjunction with some other crop, and in certain portions of India two crops a year are produced on the same soil. The following table will show the number of bales produced during the years named:

	Bales of 400 lbs.		Bales of 400 lbs.
1892-3.........	1,924,000	1897-8.........	2,198,000
1893-4.........	2,180,000	1898-9.........	2,425,000
1894-5.........	1,957,000	1899-0.........	843,000
1895-6.........	2,364,000	1900-1.........	2,309,000
1896-7.........	1,929,000	1901-2.........	1,969,000

The failure of the crop in 1899-1900 was due to the drought which caused the great famine.

About one-half of the crop is used in the local mills.

The greater part of the remainder is shipped to Japan, which is the best customer. Germany comes next, and, curiously enough, Great Britain is one of the smallest purchasers. Indian cotton is exclusively of the short staple variety and not nearly so good as that produced in Egypt. Repeated attempts have been made to introduce Egptian cotton, but, while some of the experiments have been temporarily successful, it deteriorates the second year.

The cost of producing cotton is very much less than in the United States, because the land always yields a second crop of something else, which, under ordinary circumstances, ought to pay taxes and often fixed charges, as well as the wages of labor, which are amazingly low, leaving the entire proceeds of the cotton crop to be counted as clear gain. The men and women who work in the cotton fields of India are not paid more than two dollars a month. That is considered very good wages. All the shipping is done in the winter season; the cotton is brought in by railroad and lies in bags on the docks until it is transferred to the holds of ships. During the winter season the cotton docks are the busiest places around Bombay.

The manufacture of cotton is increasing rapidly. There are now eighty-four mills in Bombay alone, with a capital of more than $25,000,000, and all of them have been established since 1870, including some of the most modern, up-to-date plants in existence. The people of Bombay have about $36,000,000 invested in mills, most of it being owned by Parsees. There are mills scattered all over the country. The industry dates from 1851, and during the last twenty years the number of looms has increased 160 per cent and spindles 172 per cent. January 1, 1891, there were 127 mills, with 117,922 operatives, representing an investment of £7,844,000. On the 31st of March, 1904, according to the official records, there were 201 cotton mills in India, containing 43,676,000 looms and 5,164,360 spindles, with a combined capital of £12,175,000. This return, however, does not include thirteen mills which were not heard from, and they will probably increase the number of looms and spindles considerably and the total capital to more than $60,000,000.

The wages paid operatives in the cotton mills of India are almost incredibly low. I have before me an official statement from a mill at Cawnpore, which is said to give a fair average for the entire country. The mills of Bombay, Madras and Calcutta and other large cities pay about one-half more. At smaller places farther in the north the rates are much less. The wages are given in rupees and decimals of a rupee, which in round numbers is worth 33 cents in our money.

MONTHLY WAGES IN A COTTON MILL AT CAWNPORE FOR THE YEARS NAMED (IN RUPEES AND DECIMALS OF A RUPEE).

	1885.	1890.	1900.	1903.
Cardroom—				
Head mistry	17.00	24.80	34.90	33.00
Card cleaner	5.00	5.25	8.70	8.84
Spare hands	5.00	5.25	5.90	6.58
Muleroom—				
Head mistry	8.50	19.60	34.00	36.42
Minder	5.00	6.37	6.20	7.12
Spare hands	5.00	5.00	6.00	6.50
Weaving department—				
Mistry	13.50	18.00	18.80	17.81

Healder	5.00	5.50	7.60	7.09
Weaver	6.00	10.50	8.62	9.14
Finishing department—				
Washers and bleachers	6.00	18.00	18.70	21.25
Dyer	5.00	5.50	5.50	6.08
Finishing man	5.00	5.50	6.00	6.53
Engineering shop—				
Boiler mistry	6.00	9.00	9.30	10.16
Engine man	8.00	11.00	10.80	14.62
Oil man	6.00	6.00	6.20	6.64
Boiler man	6.00	6.00	6.90	7.31
Carpenter	10.00	10.00	11.10	11.67
Blacksmith	11.50	13.50	13.80	15.84
Fitter	....	10.00	11.00	13.98

These wages, however, correspond with those received by persons in other lines of employment. The postmen employed by the government, or letter carriers as we call them, receive a maximum of only 12.41 rupees a month, which is about $3.50, and a minimum of 9.25, which is equivalent to $3.08 in our money. Able-bodied and skilled mechanics—masons, carpenters and blacksmiths—get no more than $2.50 to $3.50 a month, and bookkeepers, clerks and others having indoor occupations, from $4.10 to $5.50 per month. Taking all of the wage-earners together in India, their compensation per month is just about as much as the same class receive per day in the United States.

The encouragement of manufacturing is one of the methods the government has adopted to prevent or mitigate famines, and its policy is gradually becoming felt by the increase of mechanical industries and the employment of the coolie class in lines other than agriculture.

At the same time, the problem is complicated by the fact that the greater part of the mechanical products of India have always been produced in the households. Each village has its own weavers, carpenters, brass workers, blacksmiths and potters, who are not able to compete with machine-made goods. Many of these local craftsmen have attained a high standard of artistic skill in making up silk, wool, linen, cotton, carpets, brass, iron, silver, wood, ivory and other materials. But their arts must necessarily decay or depreciate if the local markets are flooded with cheap products from factories, and there a question of serious consequence has arisen.

There is very active rivalry in the tea trade of late years. China formerly supplied the world. Thirty years ago very little was exported from any other country. Then Japan came in as an energetic competitor and sent its tea around everywhere, but the consumption increased as rapidly as the cultivation, so that China kept her share of the trade. About fifteen years ago India came into the market; and then Ceylon. The Ceylon export trade has been managed very skillfully. There has been an enormous increase in the acreage planted, and 92 per cent of the product has been sent to the United Kingdom, where it has gradually supplanted that of China and Japan. Australia has also become a large consumer of India tea, and the loyalty with which the two great colonies of Great Britain have stood together is commendable. In England alone the consumption of India tea has increased nearly 70 per cent within the last ten years. This is the result of careful and intelligent effort on the part of the government. While wild tea is found in Assam and in several of the states adjoining the Himalayas, tea growing is practically a new thing in India compared with China and Japan. It was not until 1830, when Lord William Benthinck was viceroy, that any considerable amount of tea was produced in India. He introduced the plant from China and brought men from that country at the expense of the East India Company to teach the Hindus how to cultivate it. For many years the results were doubtful and the efforts of the government were ridiculed. But for the great faith of two or three patriotic officials the scheme would have been abandoned. It was remarkably successful, however, until now the area under tea includes more than half a million acres, the number of persons employed in the industry exceeds 750,000, the capital invested in plantations is more than $100,000,000 and the approximate average yield is about 200,000,000 pounds. In 1903 159,000,000 pounds were exported to England alone, and the total exports were 182,594,000 pounds. The remainder is consumed in India, and more than a million pounds annually are purchased for the use of the army. Among other consumers the United States bought 1,080,000 and China 1,337,000 pounds. Russia, which is the largest consumer of tea of all the nations, bought 1,625,000 pounds, and this was a considerable increase, showing that India tea is becoming popular there.

The industry in India and Ceylon, however, is in a flourishing condition, the area under cultivation has expanded 85 per cent and the product has increased 167 per cent during the last fifteen years. The cultivation is limited to sections where there is a heavy rainfall and a humid climate, because tea requires water while it is growing as well as while it is being consumed. Where these conditions exist it is a profitable crop. In the valleys of Assam the yield often reaches 450 pounds to the acre. The quality of the tea depends upon the manner of cultivation, the character of the soil, the amount of moisture and sunshine and the age of the leaf at the time of picking. Young, tender leaves have the finest flavor, and bring the highest prices, but shrink enormously in curing, and many growers consider it more profitable to leave them until they are well matured. It requires about four pounds of fresh leaves to make one pound of dry leaves, and black tea and green tea are grown from the same bush. If the leaf is completely dried immediately after picking it retains its green color, but if it is allowed to stand and sweat for several hours a kind of fermentation takes place which turns it black.

There are now about 236,000 acres of coffee orchards in India, about 111,760 persons are employed upon them and the exports will average 27,000,000 pounds a year. The coffee growers of India complain that they cannot compete with Brazil and other Spanish-American countries where overproduction has forced down prices below the margin of profit, but the government is doing as much as it can to encourage and sustain the industry, and believes that they ought at least to grow enough to supply the home market. But comparatively little coffee is used in India. Nearly everybody drinks tea.

Three million acres of land is devoted to the cultivation of sugar, both cane and beet. During the Cuban revolution the industry secured quite an impetus, but since the restoration of peace and the adjustment of affairs, prices have gone down considerably, and the sugar of India finds itself in direct competition with the bounty-paid product of Germany, France, Belgium, Austria and other European countries. In order to protect its planters the government has imposed countervailing duties against

European sugar, but there has been no perceptible effect from this policy as yet.

The indigo trade has been very important, but is also in peril because of the manufacture of chemical dyes in Germany and France. Artificial indigo and other dyes can be produced in a laboratory much cheaper than they can be grown in the fields, and, naturally, people will buy the low-priced article. Twenty years ago India had practically a monopoly of the indigo trade, and 2,000,000 acres of land were planted to that product, while the value of the exports often reached $20,000,000. The area and the product have been gradually decreasing, until, in 1902, only a little more than 800,000 acres were planted and the exports were valued at less than $7,000,000.

The quinine industry is also in a deplorable state. About thirty years ago the Indian government sent botanists to South America to collect young cinchona trees. They were introduced into various parts of the empire, where they flourished abundantly until the export of bark ran nearly to 4,000,000 pounds a year, but since 1899 there has been a steady fall. Exports have declined, prices have been low, and the government plantations have not paid expenses. Rather than export the bark at a loss the government has manufactured sulphate at its own factories and has furnished it at cost price to the health authorities of the native states, the British provinces, the army and the hospitals and dispensaries.

One of the most interesting places about Calcutta is the Royal Botanical Gardens, where many important experiments have been made for the benefit of the agricultural industry of India. It is one of the most beautiful and extensive arboreums in the world, and at the same time its economic usefulness has been unsurpassed by any

GREAT BANYAN TREE — BOTANICAL GARDEN — CALCUTTA

similar institution. It was established nearly 150 years ago by Colonel Kyd, an ardent botanist, under the auspices of the East India Company, and from its foundation it was intended to be, as it has been, a source of botanical information, a place for botanical experiments, and a garden in which plants of economic value could be cultivated and issued to the public for the purpose of introducing new products into India. It has been of incalculable value in all these particulars, not only by introducing new plants, but by demonstrating which could be grown with profit.

The garden lies along the bank of the Ganges, about six miles south of the city, and is filled with trees and plants of the rarest varieties and the greatest beauty you can imagine. No other garden will equal it except perhaps that at Colombo. It is 272 acres in extent, has a large number of ponds and lakes, and many fine avenues of palms, mahogany, mangos, tamarinds, plantains and other trees, and its greatest glory is a banyan tree which is claimed to be the largest in the world.

A banyan, as you know, represents a miniature forest rather than a single tree, because it has branches which grow downward as well as upward, and take root in the ground and grow with great rapidity. This tree is about 135 years old. The circumference of its main trunk five and a half feet from the ground is 51 feet. Its topmost leaf is eighty-five feet from the ground. It has 464 aerial roots, as the branches which run down to the ground are called, and the entire tree is 938 feet in circumference. It is large enough to shelter an entire village under its foliage.

Several other remarkable trees are to be found in that garden. One of them is called "The Crazy Tree," because about thirty-five different varieties of trees have been grafted upon the same trunk, and, as a consequence, it bears that many different kinds of leaves. Its foliage suggests a crazy quilt.

Benares is the center of the opium traffic of India, which, next to the land tax, is the most productive source of revenue to the government. It is a monopoly inherited from the Moguls in the middle ages and passed down from them through the East India Company to the present government, and the regulations for the cultivation, manufacture and sale of the drug have been very little changed for several hundred years. There have been many movements, public, private, national, international, religious and parliamentary, for its suppression; there have been many official inquiries and investigations; volumes have been written setting forth all the moral questions involved, and it is safe to say that every fact and argument on both sides has been laid before the public; yet it is an astonishing fact that no official commission or legally constituted body, not a single Englishman who has been personally responsible for the well-being of the people of India or has even had an influential voice in the affairs of the empire or has ever had actual knowledge and practical experience concerning the effects of opium, has ever advocated prohibition either in the cultivation of the poppy or in the manufacture of the drug. Many have made suggestions and recommendations for the regulation and restriction of the traffic, and the existing laws are the result of the experience of centuries. But anti-opium movements have been entirely in the hands of missionaries, religious and moral agitators in England and elsewhere outside of India, and politicians who have denounced the policy of the government to obtain votes against the party that happened to be in power.

This is an extraordinary statement, but it is true. It goes without saying that the use of opium in any form is almost universally considered one of the most dangerous and destructive of vices, and it is not necessary in this connection to say anything on that side of the controversy. It is interesting, however, and important, to know the facts and arguments used by the Indian government to justify its toleration of the vice, which, generally speaking, is based upon three propositions:

1. That the use of opium in moderation is necessary to thousands of honest, hard-working Hindus, and that its habitual consumers are among the most useful, the most vigorous and the most loyal portion of the population. The Sikhs, who are the flower of the Indian army and the highest type of the native, are habitual opium smokers, and the Rajputs, who are considered the most manly, brave and progressive of the native population, use it almost universally.

2. That the government cannot afford to lose the revenue and much less afford to undertake the expense and assume the risk of rebellion and disturbances incurred by any attempt at prohibition.

3. That the export of opium to China and other countries is legitimate commerce.

The opium belt of India is about 600 miles long and 180 miles wide, lying just above a line drawn from Bombay to Calcutta. The total area cultivated with poppies will average 575,000 acres. The crop is grown in a few months in the summer, so that the land can produce another crop of corn or wheat during the rest of the year. About 1,475,000 people are engaged in the cultivation of the poppy and about 6,000 in the manufacture of the drug. The area is regulated by the government commissioners. The smallest was in 1892, when only 454,243 acres were planted, and the maximum was reached in 1900, when 627,311 acres were planted. In the latter year the government adopted 625,000 acres as the standard area, and 48,000 chests as the standard quantity to be produced in British India. Hereafter these figures will not be exceeded. The largest amount ever produced was in 1872, when the total quantity manufactured in British India was 61,536 chests of 140 pounds average weight. The lowest amount during the last thirty-five years was in 1894, when only 37,539 chests were produced. In addition to this from 20,000 to 30,000 chests are produced in the native states.

The annual average value of the crop for the last twenty years has been about $60,000,000 in American money, the annual revenue has been about $24,000,000, and the officials say that this is a moderate estimate of the sum which the reformers ask the government of India to sacrifice by suppressing the trade. In addition to this the growers receive about $5,500,000 for opium "trash," poppy seeds, oil and other by-products which are perfectly free from opium. The "trash" is made of stalks and leaves and is used at the factories for packing purposes; the seeds of the poppy are eaten raw and parched, are ground for a condiment in the preparation of food, and oil is produced from them for table, lubricating and illuminating purposes, and for making soaps, paints, pomades and other toilet articles. Oil cakes made from the fiber of the seeds after the oil has been expressed are excellent food for cattle, being rich in nitrogen, and the young seedlings, which are removed at the first weeding of the crop, are sold in the markets for salad and are very popular with the lower classes.

No person can cultivate poppies in India without a license from the government, and no person can sell his product to any other than government agents, who ship it to the official factories at Patna and Ghazipur, down the River Ganges a little below Benares. Any violation of the regulations concerning the cultivation of the poppy, the manufacture, transport, possession, import or export, sale or use of opium, is punished by heavy penalties, both fine and imprisonment. The government regulates the extent of cultivation according to the state of the market and the stock of opium on hand. It pays an average of $1 a pound for the raw opium, and wherever necessary the opium commissioners are authorized to advance small sums to cultivators to enable them to pay the expense of the crop. These advances are deducted from the amount due when the opium is delivered. The yield, taking the country together, will average about twelve and a half pounds, or about twelve dollars per acre, not including the by-products.

The raw opium arrives at the factory in big earthen jars in the form of a paste, each jar containing about 87½ pounds. It is carefully tested for quality and purity and attempts at adulteration are severely punished. The grower is paid cash by the government agents. The jars, having been emptied into large vats, are carefully scraped and then smashed so as to prevent scavengers from obtaining opium from them, and there is a mountain of potsherds on the river bank beside the factory.

Each vat contains about 20,000 pounds of opium, lying six or eight inches deep, and about the consistency of ordinary paste. Hundreds of coolies are employed to mix it by trampling it with their bare feet. The work is severe upon the muscles of the legs and the tramplers have to be relieved every half hour. Three gangs are generally kept at work, resting one hour and working half an hour. Ropes are stretched for them to take hold of. After the stuff is thoroughly mixed it is made up into cakes by men and women, who wrap it in what is known as opium "trash," pack it in boxes and seal them hermetically for export. Each cake weighs about ten pounds, is about the size of a croquet ball, and is worth from ten to fifteen dollars, according to its purity under assay.

The largest part of the product is shipped to China, but a certain number of chests are retained for sale to licensed dealers in different provinces by the excise department. In 1904 there were 8,730 licensed shops, generally distributed throughout the entire empire. But it is claimed by Lord Curzon that the average number of consumers is only about two in every thousand of the population.

The revenue from licenses is very large. No dealer is permitted to sell more than three tolas (about one and one-eighth ounces) to any person, and no opium can be consumed upon the premises of the dealer. Private smoking clubs and public opium dens were forbidden in 1891, but the strict enforcement of the law has been considered inexpedient for many reasons, chief of which is that less opium is consumed when it is smoked in these places than when it is used privately in the form of pills, which are more common in India than elsewhere. Frequent investigation has demonstrated that opium consumers are more apt to use it to excess when it is taken in private than when it is taken in company, and there are innumerable regulations for the government of smoking-rooms and clubs and for the restriction and discouragement of the habit. The amount consumed in India is about 871,820 pounds annually. The amount exported will average 9,800,000 pounds.

Opium intended for export is sold at auction at Calcutta at the beginning of every month, and, in order to prevent speculation, the number of chests to be sold each month during the year is announced in January. Considerable fluctuation in prices is caused by the demand and the supply on hand in China. The lowest price on record was obtained at the June sale in 1898, when all that was offered went for 929 rupees per chest of 140 pounds, while the highest price ever obtained was 1,450 rupees per chest. The exports of opium vary considerably. The maximum, 86,469 chests, was reached in 1891; the minimum, 59,632, in 1896.

The consumption in India during the last few years has apparently decreased. This is attributed to several reasons, including increased prices, restrictive measures for the suppression of the vice, the famine, changes in the habits of the people, and smuggling; but it is the conviction of all the officials concerned in handling opium that its use is not so general as formerly, and its abuse is very small. They claim that it is used chiefly by hard-working people and enables them to resist fatigue and sustain privation, and that the prevailing opinion that opium consumers are all degraded, depraved and miserable wretches, enfeebled in body and mind, is not true. It is asserted by the inspectors that the greater part of the opium sold in India is used by moderate people, who take their daily dose and are actually benefited rather than injured by it. At the same time it is admitted that the drug is abused by many, and that the habit is usually acquired by people suffering from painful diseases, who begin by taking a little for relief and gradually increase the dose until they cannot live without it.

In 1895 an unusually active agitation for the suppression of the trade resulted in the appointment of a parliamentary commission, of which Lord Brassey was chairman. They made a thorough investigation, spending several months in India, examining more than seven hundred witnesses, of which 466 were natives, and their conclusions were that it is the abuse and not the use of opium that is harmful, and "that its use among the people of India as a rule is a moderate use, that excess is exceptional and is condemned by public opinion; that the use of opium in moderation is not attended by injurious consequences, and that no extended physical or moral degradation is caused by the habit."

XXX

CALCUTTA, THE CAPITAL OF INDIA

Calcutta is a modern city compared with the rest of India. It has been built around old Fort William, which was the headquarters of the East India Company 200 years ago, and is situated upon the bank of the River Hoogly, one of the many mouths of the Ganges, about ninety miles from the Bay of Bengal. The current is so swift and the channel changes so frequently that the river cannot be navigated at night, nor without a pilot. The native pilots are remarkably skillful navigators, and seem to know by instinct how the shoals shift. For several miles below the city the banks of the river are lined with factories of all kinds, which have added great wealth to the empire. Old Fort William disappeared many years ago, and a new fort was erected a mile or two farther down the river, where it could command the approaches to the city, but that also is now old-fashioned, and could not do much execution if Calcutta were attacked. The fortifications near the mouth of the river are supposed to be quite formidable, but Calcutta is not a citadel, and in case of war must be defended by battle ships and other floating fortresses. It is one of the cities of India which shows a rapid growth of population, the gain during ten years having been 187,178, making the total population, by the census of 1901, 1,026,987.

The city takes its name from a village which stood in

the neighborhood at the time the East India Company located there. It was famous for a temple erected in honor of Kali, the fearful wife of the god Siva, the most cruel, vindictive and relentless of all the heathen deities. The temple still stands, being more than 400 years old, and "Kali, the Black One," still sits upon her altar, hideous in appearance, gorgon-headed, wearing a necklace of human skulls and dripping with fresh blood from the morning sacrifice of sheep and goats. She brings pestilence, famine, war and sorrows and suffering of all kinds, and can only be propitiated by the sacrifice of life. Formerly nothing but human blood would satisfy her, and thousands, some claim tens of thousands, of victims have been slain before her image in that ancient temple. Human offerings were forbidden by the English many years ago, but it is believed that they are occasionally made even now when famine and plague are afflicting the people. During the late famine it is suspected that an appeal for mercy was sealed with the sacrifice of infants. Residents of the neighborhood assert that human heads, dripping with blood and decorated with flowers, have been seen in the temple occasionally since 1870. It is the only notable temple in Calcutta, and is visited by tourists, but they are allowed to go only so far and no farther, for fear that Kali might be provoked by the intrusion. It is a ghastly, filthy, repulsive place, and was formerly the southern headquarters of that organized caste of religious assassins known as Thugs.

A little beyond the Temple of Kali is the burning ghat of Calcutta. Here the Hindus bring the bodies of their dead and burn them on funeral pyres. The cremations may be witnessed every morning by anyone who cares to take the trouble to drive out there. They take place in an open area surrounded by temples and shrines on one side, and large piles of firewood and the palm cottages of the attendants on the other. The river which flows by the burning ground is covered with all kinds of native craft, carrying on commerce between the city and the country, and the ashes of the dead are cast between them upon the sacred waters from a flight of stone steps which leads to the river's brink. There is no more objection to a stranger attending the burning ceremonies than would be offered to his presence at a funeral in the United States. Indeed, friends who frequently accompany the bodies of the dead feel flattered at the attention and often take bunches of flowers from the bier and present them to bystanders.

The Black Hole of Calcutta, of which you have read so much, no longer exists. Its former site is now partially built over, but Lord Curzon has had it marked, and that portion which is now uncovered he has had paved with marble, so that a visitor can see just how large an area was occupied by it. He has also reproduced after the original plan a monument that was erected to the dead by Governor J. Z. Howell, one of the sufferers. You will remember that the employes of the East India Company, with their families, were residing within the walls of Fort William when an uprising of the natives occurred June 20, 1756. The survivors, 156 in number, were made prisoners and pressed into an apartment eighteen feet long, eighteen feet wide and fourteen feet ten inches high, where they were kept over night. It was a sort of vault in the walls of the fortress, which had been used for storage purposes and at one time for a prison. The company consisted of men, women, children and even infants. Several of them were crushed to death and trampled during the efforts of the native soldiers to crowd them into this place, and all but thirty-three of the 156 died of suffocation. The next morning, when the leader of the mutiny ordered the living prisoners brought before him, the bodies of the dead were cast into a pit outside the walls and allowed to rot there. The monument to which I have alluded stands upon the site of the pit. To preserve history Lord Curzon has had a model of the old fort made in wood, and it will be placed in the museum.

Calcutta is a fine city. The government buildings, the courthouses, the business blocks and residences, the churches and clubs are nearly all of pretentious architecture and imposing appearance. Most of the buildings are up to date. The banks of the river are lined for a long distance with mammoth warehouses and the anchorage is crowded with steamers from all parts of the world. There is a regular line between Calcutta and New York, which, I was told, is doing a good business. Beyond the warehouses, the business section and the government buildings, along the bank of the river for several miles, is an open space or common, called the Maidan, the amusement and recreation ground of the public, who show their appreciation by putting it to good use. There are several thousand acres, including the military reservation, bisected with drives and ornamented with monuments and groves of trees. It belongs to the public, is intended for their benefit, and thousands of natives may be found enjoying this privilege night and day. An American circus has its tent pitched in the center opposite a group of hotels; a little further along is a roller skating rink, which seems to be popular, and scattered here and there, usually beside clumps of shade trees, are cottages erected for the accommodation of golf, tennis, croquet and cricket clubs. On Saturday afternoons and holidays these clubhouses are surrounded by gayly dressed people enjoying an outing, and at all times groups of natives may be seen scattered from one end of the Maidan to the other, sleeping, visiting, and usually resting in the full glare of the fierce sun. Late in the afternoon, when the heat has moderated, everybody who owns a carriage or a horse or can hire one, comes out for a drive, and along the river bank the roadway is crowded with all kinds of vehicles filled with all sorts of people dressed in every variety of costume worn by the many races that make up the Indian Empire, with a large sprinkling of Europeans.

The viceroy and Lady Curzon, with their two little girls, come in an old-fashioned barouche, drawn by handsome English hackneys, with coachman, footman and two postilions, clad in gorgeous red livery, gold sashes and girdles and turbans of white and red. Their carriage is followed by a squad of mounted Sikhs, bronzed faced, bearded giants in scarlet uniforms and big turbans, carrying long, old-fashioned spears. Lord Kitchener, the hero of Khartoum and the Boer war, appears in a landau driven by the only white coachman in Calcutta. Lord Kitchener is a bachelor, and his friends say that he has never even thought of love, although he is a handsome man, of many graces, and has contributed to the pleasure of society in both England and India. The diplomatic corps, as the consuls of foreign governments residing in India are called by courtesy—for all of India's relations with other countries must be conducted through the foreign department at London—are usually in evidence, riding in smart equipages, and they are very hospitable and agreeable people. The United States is represented by

General Robert F. Patterson, who went to the civil war from Iowa, but has since been a citizen of Memphis. Mrs. Patterson, who belongs to a distinguished southern family, is one of the recognized leaders of society, and is famous for her hospitality and her fine dinners.

The native princes and other rich Hindus who reside in Calcutta are quite apt in imitating foreign ways, but, fortunately, most of them adhere to their national costume, which is much more becoming and graceful than the awkward garments we wear. The women of their families are seldom seen. The men wear silks and brocades and jewels, and bring out their children to see the world, but always leave their wives at home.

There are several sets and castes in the social life—the official set, the military set, the professional people, the mercantile set, and so on—and it is not often that the lines that divide them are broken. During the winter season social life is very gay. The city is filled with visitors from all parts of India, and they spend their money freely, having a good time. Official cares rest lightly upon the members of the government, with a few exceptions, including Lord Curzon, who is always at work and never takes a holiday. Dinners, balls, garden parties, races, polo games, teas, picnics and excursions follow one another so rapidly that those who indulge in social pleasures have only time enough to keep a record of their engagements and to dress. The presence of a large military force is a great advantage, particularly as many of the officers are bachelors, and it is whispered that some of the lovely girls who come out from England to spend a winter in India hope to go home to arrange for a wedding. Occasionally matrimonial affairs are conducted with dispatch. A young woman who came out on the steamer with us, heart whole and fancy free, with the expectation of spending the entire winter in India, started back to London with a big engagement ring upon her finger within four weeks after she landed, and several other young women were quite as fortunate during the same winter, although not so sudden. India is regarded as the most favorable marriage market in the world.

Calcutta has frequently been called "the city of statues." I think Sir Edward Bulwer Lytton, the poet-viceroy, gave it that title, and it was well applied. Whichever way you look on the Maidan, bronze figures of former viceroys, statesmen and soldiers appear. Queen Victoria sits in the center, a perfect reproduction in bronze, and around her, with their faces turned toward the government house, are several of her ablest and most eminent servants. In the center of the Maidan rises a lofty column that looks like a lighthouse. Its awkwardness is in striking contrast to the graceful shafts which Hindu architects have erected in various parts of the empire. It is dedicated to David Ochterlony, a former citizen of Calcutta and for fifty years a soldier, and is a token of appreciation from the people of the empire. The latest monument is a bronze statue of Lord Roberts.

Facing the Maidan for a couple of miles is the Chowringhee, one of the famous streets of the world, once a row of palatial residences, but now given up almost entirely to hotels, clubs and shops. Upon this street lived Warren Hastings in a stone palace, and a little further along, in what is now the Bengal Club, was the home of Thomas Babbington Macaulay during his long residence in India.

The governor of the province of Bengal lives in a beautiful mansion in the center of a park called "Belvedere," just outside the city. There are few finer country homes in England, and associated with it are many historical events. Upon a grassy knoll shaded by stately trees occurred the historic duel between Warren Hastings, then governor general of India, and Mr. Francis, president of the council of state. They quarreled over an offensive remark which Mr. Francis entered in the minutes of the council. Hastings offered a challenge and wounded his antagonist, but the ball was extracted and the affair fortunately ended as a comedy rather than a tragedy.

There are many fine shops in Calcutta, for people throughout all eastern India go there to buy goods just as those in the northwestern part of the United States go to Chicago, and in the eastern states to Boston, Philadelphia or New York. Of course, the Calcutta shops are not so large and do not carry such extensive stocks as some dealers in our large cities, because they are almost entirely dependent upon the foreign population for patronage, and that is comparatively small. The natives patronize merchants of their own race, and do their buying in the bazaars, where the same articles are sold at prices much lower than those asked by the merchants in the foreign section of the city. This is perfectly natural, for the native dealer has comparatively little rent to pay, the wages of his employes are ridicuously small and it does not cost him very much to live. If a foreigner tries to trade in the native shops he has to pay big prices. Foreigners who live in Calcutta usually send their servants to make purchases, and, although it is customary for the servant to take a little commission or "squeeze" from the seller for himself, the price is much lower than would be paid for the same articles at one of the European shops.

Occasionally you see American goods, but not often. We sell India comparatively little merchandise except iron and steel, machinery, agricultural implements, sewing machines, typewriters, phonographs and other patented articles. One afternoon four naked Hindus went staggering along the main street in Calcutta carrying an organ made by the Farrand Company of Detroit, which has considerable trade there. American pianos are widely advertised by one of the music dealers. The beef packing houses of Chicago send considerable tinned meat to India, and it is quite popular and useful. Indeed, it would be difficult for the English to get along without it, because native beef is very scarce. It is only served at the hotels one or twice a week. That is due to the fact that cows are sacred and oxen are so valuable for draught purposes. Fresh beef comes all the way from Australia in refrigerator ships and is sold at the fancy markets.

The native bazaars are like those in other Indian cities, although not so interesting. Calcutta has comparatively a small native trade, although it has a million of population. The shops of Delhi, Lahore, Jeypore, Lucknow, Benares and other cities are much more attractive. In the European quarter are some curio dealers, who stop there for the winter and go to Delhi and Simla for the summer, selling brocades, embroideries, shawls, wood and ivory carvings and other native art work which are very tempting to tourists. Several dealers in jewels from Delhi and other cities spend the holidays in order to catch the native princes, who are the greatest purchasers of precious stones in the world. Several of them have collections more valuable and extensive than any of the imperial families of Europe. Prices of all curios, embroideries and objects of art are much higher in Calcutta than in the cities of northern India, and everybody told us it was the poorest place to buy such things.

The most imposing building upon the Chowringhee, the principal street, is the Imperial Museum, which was founded nearly a hundred years ago by the Asiatic Society, and was taken over by the government in 1866. It is a splendid structure around a central quadrangle 300 feet square with colonnades, fountains, plants and flowers. Little effort has been made to obtain contributions from other countries, but no other collection of Indian antiquities, ethnology, archæology, mineralogy and other natural sciences can compare with it. It is under the special patronage of the viceroy, who takes an active interest in extending its usefulness and increasing its treasures, while Lady Curzon is the patroness of the school of design connected with it. In this school about three hundred young men are studying the industrial arts. Comparatively little attention is given to the fine arts. There are a few native portrait painters, and I have seen some clever water colors from the brushes of natives. But in the industrial arts they excel, and this institute is maintained under government patronage for the purpose of training the eyes and the hands of designers and artisans. In the same group of buildings are the geological survey and other scientific bureaus of the government, which are quite as progressive and learned as our own. A little farther up the famous street are the headquarters of the Asiatic Society, one of the oldest and most enterprising learned societies in the world, whose journals and proceedings for the last century are a library in themselves and contain about all that anybody would ever want to know concerning the history, literature, antiquities, resources and people of India. Here also is a collection of nearly twenty thousand manuscripts in Sanskrit, Persian, Arabic, Hindustani and other oriental languages.

There is comparatively little poverty in Calcutta, considering the enormous population and the conditions in which they live. There are, however, several hundred thousand people who would starve to death upon their present incomes if they lived in the United States or in any of the European countries, but there it costs so little to sustain life and a penny goes so far that what an American working man would call abject destitution is an abundance. Give a Hindu a few farthings for food and a sheet of white cotton for clothing and he will be comfortable and contented.

The streets of Calcutta, except in a limited portion of the native section of the city, are wide, well paved, watered and swept. There is an electric tramway system with about twenty miles of track, reaching the principal suburbs, railway stations and business sections, and whether Moline (Ill.) got it from Calcutta or Calcutta borrowed the idea from Moline, both cities use the same method of laying the dust. The tramway company runs an electric tank car up and down its tracks several times a day, throwing water far enough to cover nearly the entire street. Other streets, where there are no tracks, are sprinkled by coolies, who carry upon their backs pig skins and goat skins filled with water and squirt it upon the ground through one of the legs with a twist of the wrist as ingenious and effective as the method used by Chinese laundrymen in sprinkling clothes. No white man can do either. The Hindu sprinkler is an artist in his line, and therefore to be admired, because everybody who excels is worthy of admiration, no matter what he is doing. The street sprinklers belong to the very lowest caste; the same caste as the garbage collectors and the coolies that mend the roads and sweep the sidewalks, but they are stalwart fellows, much superior to the higher class physically, and as they wear very little clothing everybody can see their perfect anatomy and shapely outlines.

Much of the road mending in India is done by women. They seem to be assigned to all the heavy and laborious jobs. They carry mortar, and bricks and stone where new buildings are being erected; they lay stone blocks in the pavements, hammer the concrete with heavy iron pestles, and you can frequently see them walking along the wayside with loads of lumber or timber carefully balanced on their heads that would be heavy for a mule or an ox. Frequently they carry babies at the same time; never in their arms, but swung over their backs or astride their hips. The infant population of India spend the first two or three years of their lives astride somebody's hips. It may be their mother's, or their sister's, or their brother's, but they are always carried that way, and abound so plentifully that there is no danger of race suicide in that empire.

Next to the Sikh soldier, the nattiest native in India is the postman, who is dressed in a blue uniform with a blue turban of cotton or silk cloth to match, and wears a nickel number over his forehead with the insignia of the postal service, and a girdle with a highly ornamental buckle. The deliveries and collections are much more frequent than with us. It is a mortification to every American who travels abroad to see the superiority of the postal service in other countries. That is about the only feature of civil administration in which the federal government of the United States is inferior, but, compared with India, as well as the European countries, our Postoffice Department is not up to date. You can mail a letter to any part of Calcutta in the morning and, if your correspondent takes the trouble, he can reach you with a reply before dinner. The rates of postage on local matter and on parcels are much lower than with us. I can send a package of books or merchandise or anything else weighing less than four pounds from Calcutta to Chicago for less than half the charge that would be required on a similar package from Evanston or Oak Park.

The best time for a stranger to visit Calcutta is during holiday week, for then the social season is inaugurated by a levee given by the viceroy, a "drawing-room" by the vice-queen and a grand state ball. The annual races are held that week, also, including the great sporting event of the year, which is a contest for a cup offered by the viceroy, and a military parade and review and various other ceremonies and festivities attract people from every part of the empire. The native princes naturally take this opportunity to visit the capital and pay their respects to the representative of imperial power, while every Englishman in the civil and military service, and those of social or sporting proclivities in private life have their vacations at that time and spend the Christmas and New Year's holidays with Calcutta friends. Moreover, the fact that all these people will be there attracts the tourists who happen to be in India at the time, for it gives them a chance to see the most notable and brilliant social features of Indian life. Hence we rushed across the empire with everybody else and assisted to increase the crowd and the enthusiasm. Every hotel, boarding-house and club was crowded. Every family had guests. Cots and beds were placed in offices and wherever else they could be accommodated. Tents were spread on the lawn of the Government House for the benefit of government officials coming in from the provinces, and on the parade grounds at the fort for military visitors. The grounds surrounding the club houses looked like military camps. Sixteen tents were placed upon the roof of the hotel where we were stopping to accommodate the overflow.

Good hotels are needed everywhere in India, as I have several times suggested, and nowhere so much as in Calcutta. The government, the people and all concerned ought to be ashamed of their lack of enterprise in this direction, and everybody admits it without argument. There is not a comfortable hotel in the city, and while it is of course possible for people to survive present conditions they are nevertheless a national disgrace. Calcutta is a city of more than a million inhabitants. Among its residents are many millionaires and other wealthy men. It is frequently called "the city of palaces," and many of the private residences in the foreign quarter are imposing and costly. Hence there is no excuse but indifference and lack of public spirit.

The Government House, which is the residence of the viceroy, is one of the finest palaces in the world, and in architectural beauty, extent and arrangement surpasses many of the royal residences of Europe. None of the many palaces in England and the other European capitals is better adapted for entertaining or has more stately audience chambers, reception rooms, banquet halls and ballrooms. It is truly an imperial residence and was erected more than a hundred years ago by Lord Wellesley, who had an exalted appreciation of the position he occupied, and transplanted to India the ceremonies, formalities and etiquette of the British court. The Government House stands in the center of a beautiful garden of seven acres and is now completely surrounded and almost hidden by groups of noble trees so that it cannot be photographed. It is an enlarged copy of Kedlestone Hall, Derbyshire, and consists of a central group of state apartments crowned with a dome and connected with four wings by long galleries.

The throne-room is a splendid apartment and the seat of the mighty is the ancient throne of Tipu, one of the southern maharajas, who, during the latter part of the eighteenth century, gave the British a great deal of trouble until he was deprived of power. The banquet hall, the council chamber, the ballrooms and a series of drawing rooms, nearly all of the same size, are decorated in white and gold, and each is larger than the east room in the White House at Washington. The ceilings are supported by rows of marble columns with gilded capitals, and are frescoed by famous artists. The floors are of polished teak wood; the walls are paneled with brocade and tapestries, and are hung with historical pictures, including full length portraits of the kings and queens of England, all the viceroys from the time of Warren Hastings, and many of the most famous native rulers of India. In one of the rooms is a collection of marble busts of the Cæsars. These, with a portrait of Louis XV. and several elaborate crystal chandeliers, were loot of the war of 1798, when they were captured from a ship which was carrying them as a present from the Emperor of France to the Nyzam of Hyderabad.

The palace cost $750,000 and the furniture $250,000, more than a hundred years ago, at a time when money would go three times as far as it does to-day. Lord Wellesley had lofty ideas, and when the merchants of the

East India Company expressed their disapproval of this expenditure he told them that India "should be governed from a palace and not from a counting-house, with the ideas of a prince and not those of a retail dealer in muslin and indigo."

Great stories are told of the receptions, levees and balls that were given in the days of the East India Company, but they could not have been more brilliant than those of to-day. The Government House has never been occupied by a viceroy more capable of assuming the dignities and performing the duties of that office than Lord Curzon, and no more beautiful, graceful or popular woman ever sat upon the vice-queen's throne than Mary Leiter Curzon. No period in Indian history has ever been more brilliant, more progressive or more prosperous than the present; no administration of the government has even given wider satisfaction from any point of view, and certainly the social functions presided over by Lord and Lady Curzon were never surpassed. They live in truly royal style, surrounded by the ceremonies and the pomp that pertain to kings, which is a part of the administrative policy, because the 300,000,000 people subject to the viceroy's authority are very impressionable, and measure power and sometimes justice and right by appearances. Lord and Lady Curzon never leave the palace without an escort of giant warriors from the Sikh tribe, who wear dazzling uniforms of red, turbans as big as bushel baskets, and sit on their horses like centaurs. They carry long spears and are otherwise armed with native weapons. Within the palace the same formality is preserved, except in the private apartments of the viceroy, where for certain hours of every day the doors are closed against official cares and responsibilities, and Lord and Lady Curzon can spend a few hours with their children, like ordinary people.

The palace is managed by a comptroller general, who has 150 servants under him, and a stable of forty horses, and relieves Lady Curzon from the cares of the household. Lord Curzon is attended by a staff of ministers, secretaries and aids, like a king, and Lady Curzon has her ladies-in-waiting, secretaries and aids, like a queen.

People who wish to be received at Government House will find three books open before them in the outer hall, in which they are expected to inscribe their names, instead of leaving cards. One of these books is for permanent residents of Calcutta, another for officials, and another for transient visitors, who record their names, their home addresses, their occupations, the time they expect to stay in Calcutta, and the place at which they may be stopping. From these books the invitation lists are made out by the proper officials, but in order to secure an invitation to Lady Curzon's "drawing-room" a stranger must be presented by some person of importance who is well known at court. At 9 o'clock those who have been so fortunate as to be invited are expected to arrive. They leave their wraps in cloakrooms in the basement, where the ladies are separated from the gentlemen who escort them, because the latter are not formally presented to the vice-queen, but they meet again an hour or so later in the banquet hall after the ceremony is over.

The ladies pass up two flights of stairs into waiting-rooms in the third story of the palace, pursuing a rather circuitous course over about half the building, guided by velvet barriers and railings, and at each corner stands an aide-de-camp or a gentleman-in-waiting, to answer inquiries and give directions to strangers. When the anteroom is at last reached, the ladies await their turns, being admitted to the audience chamber in groups of four. They are given a moment or two to adjust their plumage, and then pass slowly toward the throne, upon which Lady Curzon is seated. The viceroy, in the uniform and regalia of a Knight of the Garter, stands under the canopy by her side. There is no crowding and pushing, such as we see at presidential receptions at Washington and often at royal functions in Europe, but there is an interval of twenty-five or thirty feet between the guests. After entering the room each lady hands a card upon which her name is written to the gentleman-in-waiting, and, as she approaches the throne he pronounces it slowly and distinctly. She makes her courtesies to the viceroy and his lady, and then passes on. There is no confusion, no haste, no infringement of dignity, and each woman for the moment has the entire stage to herself.

On either side of the throne are gathered, standing, many native princes, the higher officers of the government and the army, the members of the diplomatic corps and other favored persons, with their wives and daughters, and their costumes furnish a brilliant background to the scene. The rest of the great audience chamber, blazing with electric lights, is entirely empty. The viceroy greets every lady with a graceful bow, and Lady Curzon gives her a smile of welcome. The government band is playing all this time in an adjoining room, so that the music can be only faintly heard, and does not interfere with the ceremony, as is so often the case elsewhere.

Having passed in review, the guests return to the other part of the palace by a different course than that through which they came, and find their escorts awaiting them in the banquet hall. When the last lady has been presented,

THE PRINCES OF PEARLS

the viceroy and Lady Curzon lead the way to the banquet hall, where a sumptuous supper is spread, and the gentlemen are allowed to share the festivities. The formalities are relaxed, and the hosts chat informally with the guests.

It is a very brilliant scene, quite different from any that may be witnessed elsewhere, particularly because of the gorgeous costumes and the profusion of jewels worn by the native princes. At none of the capitals of Europe can so magnificent a show of jewels be witnessed, but the medals of honor and decorations which adorn the breasts of the bronzed soldiers are more highly prized and usually excite greater admiration, for many of the heroes of the South African war were serving tours of duty in India when we were in Calcutta.

The viceroy's levee is exclusively for gentlemen. No ladies are expected, and a similar ceremony is carried out. It is intended to offer an annual opportunity for the native princes, and officials of the government, officers of the army, the Indian nobility and private citizens of prominence to pay their respects and offer their congratulations to their ruler and the representative of their king, and at 9 o'clock on the evening appointed, two days later than Lady Curzon's reception, every man of distinction in that part of the world appears at the palace and makes his bow to the viceroy as the latter stands under the canopy beside the throne. It might be a somber and stupid proceeding but for the presence of many natives in their dazzling jewels, picturesque turbans and golden brocades, and the large contingent of army officers, with their breasts covered with medals and decorations.

This reception is followed a few days later by a state ball, which is considered the most brilliant function of the year in India. Invitations are limited to persons of certain rank who have been formally presented at Government House, but Lady Curzon is always on the lookout for her fellow countrymen, and if she learns of their presence in Calcutta invitations are sure to reach them one way or another. She is a woman of many responsibilities, and her time and mind are always occupied, but few Americans ever visit Calcutta without having some delightful evidence of her loyalty and thoughtfulness.

There were many other festivities for celebrating the New Year. All the English and native troops in the vicinity of Calcutta passed in review before the viceroy and Lord Kitchener, who is the commander-in-chief of the forces in India.

In one of the parks in the city was a native fair and display of art industries, and at the zoological gardens the various societies of the Roman Catholic church in Calcutta held a bazaar and raffled off many valuable and worthless articles, sold barrels of tea and tons of cake, and sweetmeats to enormous crowds of natives, who attended in their holiday attire. There was a pyramid of gold coins amounting to a thousand dollars, an automobile, a silver service valued at $1,000, a grand piano, a carriage and span of ponies, and various other prizes offered in the lotteries, together with dolls and gingercake, pipes and cigar cases, slippers, neckties, pincushions and other offerings to the god of chance. Fashionable society was attracted to the fair grounds by a horse and dog show, and various other functions absorbed public attention.

The great sporting event of the year in India is a race for a big silver cup presented by the viceroy and a purse of 20,000 rupees to the winner. We took an interest in the race because Mr. Apgar, an Armenian opium merchant, who nominated Great Scott, an Austrian thoroughbred, has a breeding farm and stable of 200 horses, and everything about his place comes from the United States. He uses nothing but American harness and other accoutrements, and as a natural and unavoidable consequence Great Scott won the cup and the purse very easily, and his fleetness was doubtless due to the fact that he was shod with American shoes. The programme showed that about half the entries were by natives. His Royal Highness Aga Khan, the Nawab of Samillolahs; Aga Shah; our old friend of the Chicago exposition, the Sultan of Johore, and His Highness Kour Sahib of Patiala, all had horses in the big race. Some of these princes have breeding stables. Others import English, Irish, Australian, American and Arabian thoroughbreds. There was no American horse entered for the viceroy's cup this year, but Kentucky running stock is usually represented.

There are two race tracks at Calcutta, one for regular running, the other for steeple chasing, and, as in England and Ireland, the horses run on the turf, and most of the riders are gentlemen. A few professional jockeys represent the stables of breeders who are too old or too fat or too lazy to ride themselves, but it is considered the proper thing for every true sportsman to ride his own horse as long as he is under weight. The tracks are surrounded by lovely landscapes, an easy driving distance from Calcutta, and everybody in town was there. The grand stand and the terraces that surround it were crowded with beautifully dressed women, many of them Parsees, in their lovely costumes, and within the course were more than 50,000 natives, wearing every conceivable color, red and yellow predominating, so that when one looked down upon the inclosure from a distance it resembled a vast flower bed, a field of poppies and roses. The natives take great interest in the races, and, as they are admitted free, every man, woman and child who could leave home was there, and the most of them walked the entire distance from the city.

The viceroy and vice-queen appear in the official old-fashioned barouche, drawn by four horses, with outriders, and escorted by a bodyguard of Sikhs in brilliant scarlet uniforms and big turbans of navy blue, with gold trimmings. The viceroy's box is lined and carpeted with scarlet, and easy chairs were placed for his comfort. Distinguished people came up to pay their respects to him and Lady Curzon, and between visits he wandered about the field, shaking hands with acquaintances in a democratic fashion and smiling as if he were having the time of his life. It is not often that the present viceroy takes a holiday. He is the most industrious man in India, and very few of his subjects work as hard as he, but he takes his recreation in the same fashion. He is always full of enthusiasm, and never does anything in a half-hearted way. Lord Kitchener came also, but was compelled to remain in his carriage because of his broken leg. The police found him a good place and he enjoyed it.

On the lawn behind the grand stand, under the shade of groups of palm trees, tables and chairs were placed, and tea was served between the events. Ladies whose husbands are members of the Jockey Club can engage tables in advance, as most of them do, and issue their invitations in advance also, so that Viceroy's day is usually a continuous tea party and a reunion of old friends, for everybody within traveling distance comes to the capital that day. Every woman wore a new gown made expressly for the occasion. Most of them were of white or of dainty colors, but they did not compare in beauty or elegance with the brocades and embroidered silks worn by bare-legged natives. Half the Hindu gentlemen present had priceless camel's hair and Cashmere shawls thrown over their shoulders—most of them heirlooms, for, according to the popular impression, modern shawls do not compare in quality with the old ones. Under the shawls they wear long coats, reaching to their heels like ulsters, of lovely figured silk or brocade of brilliant colors. Some of them are finished with exquisite embroidery. No Hindu women were present, only Parsees. They never appear in public, and allow their husbands to wear all of the fine fabrics and jewels. With shawls wrapped around them like Roman togas, the Hindus are the most dignified and stately human spectacles you can imagine, but when they put on European garments or a mixture of native and foreign dress they are positively ridiculous, and do violence to every rule of art and law of taste. Usually when an oriental—for it is equally true of China, Japan and Turkey—adopts European dress he selects the same colors he would wear in his own, and he looks like a freak, as you can imagine, in a pair of green trousers, a crimson waistcoat, a purple tie, a blue negligee shirt and a plaid jacket.

If you want to see a display of fine raiment and precious stones you must attend an official function in India, a reception by Lord or Lady Curzon, for in the number, size and value of their jewels the Indian princes surpass the sovereigns of Europe. One of the rajahs has the finest collection of rubies in the world, purchased from time to time by his ancestors for several generations, most of them in Burma, where the most valuable rubies have been found. Another has a collection of pearls, accumulated in the same way. They represent an investment of millions of dollars, and include the largest and finest examples in the world. When he wears them all, as he sometimes does, on great occasions, his front from his neck to his waist is covered with pearls netted like a chain armor. His turban is a cataract of pearls on all sides, and upon his left shoulder is a knot as large as your two hands, from which depends a braided rope of four strands, reaching to his knee, and every pearl is as large as a grape. You can appreciate the size and value of his collection when I tell you that all of the pearls owned by the ex-Empress Eugenie are worn in his turban, and do not represent ten per cent of the collection.

Other rajahs are famous for diamonds, or emeralds, or other jewels. There seems to be a good deal of rivalry among them as to which shall make the greatest display. But from what people tell me I should say that the Nizam of Haidarabad could furnish the largest stock if these estimable gentlemen were ever compelled to go into the jewelry business. We were particularly interested in him because he outranks all the other native princes, and is the most important as well as the most gorgeous in the array. His dominions, which he has inherited from a long line of ancestors—I believe he traces his ancestry back to the gods—include the ancient City of Golconda, whose name for centuries was a synonym for riches and splendors. In ancient times it was the greatest diamond market in the world. It was the capital of the large and powerful kingdom of the Deccan, and embraced all of southern India, but is now in ruins. Its grandeur began to decay when the kingdom was conquered by the Moguls in 1587 and annexed to their empire, and to-day the crumbling walls and abandoned palaces are almost entirely deserted. Even the tombs of the ancient kings, a row of vast and splendid mausoleums, which cost millions upon millions of dollars, and for architecture and decoration and costliness have been surpassed only by those of the Moguls, are being allowed to decay while the ruling descendant of the men who sleep there spends his income for diamonds.

The magnificence and extravagance of these princes are the theme of poems and legends. There is a large book in Persian filled with elaborate and graphic descriptions of the functions and ceremonies that attend the reception of an envoy from Shah Abbas, King of Persia, who visited the court of Golconda in 1503. Among other gifts brought by him from his royal master was a crown of rubies which still remains in the family, although many people think the original stones have been removed and imitations substituted in order that the nizam may enjoy the glory of wearing them. When his ambassador went back to Persia he was accompanied by a large military escort guarding a caravan of 2,400 camels laden with gifts from the nizam to his royal master.

The present capital of the province, the city of Haidarabad, was founded in 1589 by a gentleman named Kutab Shah Mohammed Kuli, who afterward removed his household there on account of a lack of water and a malarial atmosphere at Golconda. He called the city in honor of his favorite concubine. The name means "the city of Haidar." The province includes about 80,000 square miles of territory, and has a population of 11,141,946, of whom only 10 per cent are Moslems, although the ruling family have always professed that faith.

The present nizam is Mir Mahbub Ali, who was born

in 1866, was partially educated in England and is very popular with all classes of people—particularly with those who profit by his extravagance. The revenues of the state are about $20,000,000 a year, and the people are very much overtaxed. The nizam's taste for splendor and his desire to outdo all the other native princes in display have caused the government of India considerable anxiety, and the British resident at his capital, whose duty is to keep him straight, enjoys no sinecure.

Haidarabad is one of the oldest cities in India, with a population of 355,000, inclosed by a strong wall six miles in circumference. The city stands in the midst of wild and rocky scenery and is one of the most interesting places in India, because the nizam is fond of motion and music and color, and has surrounded himself with a large retinue of congenial spirits, who live at his expense and pay their board by amusing him. As the most important Moslem potentate except the Sultan of Turkey, he has attracted to his service Mohammedans from every part of the earth, who go about wearing their distinctive national costumes and armed with quaint weapons—Turks, Arabs, Moors, Afghans, Persians, Rajputs, Sikhs, Marathas, Pathans and representatives of all the other races that confess Islam. His palaces are enormous and are filled with these retainers, said to number 7,000 of all ranks and races, and the courtyards are full of elephants, camels, horses, mounted escorts and liveried servants. It reminds one of the ancient East, a gorgeous page out of the Arabian Nights.

INDEX